What Christian Leaders Are Saying About This Book

"This is the one I recommend. *Personal Disciplemaking* is the most workable method for making disciples I have ever seen."

Jay Carty, Church Consultant
YES Ministries

"This is the most comprehensive, practical approach I've seen to date. If the reader will faithfully apply the principles contained in this book, he or she will become effective at disciplemaking."

Howard Hendricks
Chairman, Center for Christian Leadership
Dallas Theological Seminary

"Finally! A resource for the serious disciplemaker is now available. Thoroughly biblical and user-friendly, this book deserves a place on the shelf of every pastor and Christian worker."

Mark McCloskey
Director of Training, Campus Ministry
Campus Crusade for Christ

"Finally, we can get serious about disciplemaking!"

Ross Gunn III, Youth Pastor
Freemont Community Church
Freemont, CA

"Many times Christians sense the need to disciple others, but they encounter two major problems. They do not know *how* to help another person grow in his relationship with Christ, and they feel spiritually inadequate themselves. *Personal Disciplemaking* goes a long way toward solving both problems."

Dick Katz
National Director, Prison Ministry
Campus Crusade for Christ

"As I read *Personal Disciplemaking,* I found myself asking, 'In almost 2000 years, why hasn't someone developed this system long before now?' I highly recommend this work."

Heather Goodenough, President
Cannon Beach Conference Center

"Christopher Adsit's humorous style of writing draws you into each page. A very helpful and enjoyable work."

Jay Wheeler, Phoenix Metro Director
Christian Businessmen's Committee

"Christopher B. Adsit has encouraged Lay Witnesses for Christ like few people could ever do. Now God has led him to supply us with the most thorough tool for discipling people around the world."

Sam Mings, Founder and President
Lay Witnesses for Christ

"A thorough, easy-to-use discipleship process that provides complete flexibility for successful one-on-one discipleship. I'm not aware of any more effective system."

John Klein, Associate National Director
Athletes in Action

"The most practical and best-organized approach to disciplemaking available! Not only is the material a pleasure to read, but I've personally used this system with good results."

Herb Evans, Teaching Pastor
Grace Community Fellowship
Eugene, OR

"Biblical, clear, practical, proven! If this vision is grasped and the principles applied, men and women worldwide will be raised up who will have tremendous opportunity to walk closely with Christ and be equipped for the ministry."

Tinker Melonuk
Navigator Representative, UCLA

"A treasurehouse of help for disciplers! Pastors and other Christian workers are indebted to Christopher Adsit for this book."

Jeff Wells, Senior Pastor
Redeemer's Bible Fellowship
Roseburg, OR

"One of the most practical and comprehensive works ever published on the discipling process."

Alan Heller, Director of Training
Neues Leben International

"Who says discipleship has to be dull? In a fresh, readable, and sometimes humorous style, Adsit has designed a bibically-based plan for discipleship that goes beyond theory. A thorough, practical tool."

Jonathan B. Edwards, Senior Pastor
Pulpit Rock Church
Colorado Springs, CO

"By following these principles, you will have the framework in which effective discipleship becomes a reality."

Don Richardson,
Associate Pastor of Evangelism and Discipleship
Calvary Church of Santa Ana, CA

Personal

DISCIPLE-MAKING

*A Step-by-step Guide
for Leading a Christian From
New Birth to Maturity*

Christopher B. Adsit

Published by
Campus Crusade for Christ
Integrated Resources
100 Sunport Lane
Orlando, FL 32809

Library of Congress Cataloging-in-Publication Data
Adsit, Christopher B.
    Personal disciplemaking: A step-by-step guide for leading a Christian from new birth to maturity.
    1. Witness bearing (Christianity).
    2. Christian life—1960-   I. Title
  BV4520.A33 1988   88-2783
ISBN 0-89840-213-1 (pbk.)

Originally published by Here's Life Publishers, © 1988.
Subsequently published by Thomas Nelson Publishers, © 1993.

Unless otherwise indicated, Scripture quotations are from *The New American Standard Bible,* © The Lockman Foundation, 1960, 1962, 1963, 1968, 1971, 1972, 1975, 1977.

For More Information, Write:

L.I.F.E. — P.O. Box A399, Sydney South 2000, Australia
Campus Crusade for Christ of Canada — Box 300, Vancouver, B.C., V6C 2X3, Canada
Campus Crusade for Christ — Pearl Assurance House, 4 Temple Row, Birmingham, B2 5HG, England
Lay Institute for Evangelism — P.O. Box 8786, Auckland 3, New Zealand
Campus Crusade for Christ — P.O. Box 240, Colombo Court Post Office, Singapore 9117
Great Commission Movement of Nigeria — P.O. Box 500, Jos, Plateau State Nigeria, West Africa

To my indescribable jewel of a wife,
Rahnella,
without whom life would be
a tremendous bore
and hardly worth mentioning.
I love you!

And to the three men who patiently discipled me
back in the good ol' days:
Dick Kreider
Wayne Feigal
Jay Wheeler
Each could see the harvest in a plowed field. Thanks!

CONTENTS

# FOREWORD

"DISCIPLESHIP" – a greatly misunderstood word in the Christian vocabulary of our day, but Chris Adsit has cleared away the fog of confusing terms and weak applications. This is an excellent manual on the whole subject of making disciples. It tells you about levels of growth in the life of the believer and it shows you what is needed at each level. Many resources, insights and ideas are presented that help the serious-minded disciplemaker to know when and why his goals of discipleship are being accomplished.

Never in the twentieth-century history of discipleship has such a comprehensive and organized manual been developed and it comes out of practical experience. The material has been tested in a multitude of ways. Chris has consulted with many Christian leaders, and it is obvious that he has put much time and effort into this outstanding volume.

You can use this book right away. Churches, missions, parachurch agencies, etc., will all find this manual to be the answer to a longstanding problem: How do we make disciples of all nations? And how will we know when the task has been completed?

I highly recommend this volume to every disciplemaker who is serious about getting the job done. I also recommend that every believer in Jesus Christ take a close look at the book and ask, "Have I ever been discipled?" After examining the material carefully, I am certain that every believer can profit greatly from following the chart and the material presented.

To Chris Adsit, our special thanks from disciplemakers everywhere, and from believers desperately in need of discipleship. You have done us all a tremendous favor. Your book is a blessing; all your effort and time was well-spent! Thanks for caring and for sharing your work!

David Hocking
Speaker, The Biola Hour
Pastor, Calvary Church of Santa Ana

ACKNOWLEDGMENTS

If it hadn't been for the incredible faithfulness, consistency and generosity of our Support Team, I would never have had the freedom to research and write this book. These people are the greatest bunch of encouragers this side of the moon. Thanks, big Team! We're in this together!

Many thanks also to four men who took time out of their already-too-busy schedules to read this Behemoth and give me extremely valuable and insightful feedback: Herb Evans; Dick Katz; John Klein; Mark McCloskey.

I praise God for David Hocking, pastor of my home church — Calvary Church of Santa Ana, California — for his strategic ministry to me over the years and for the crucial role he played in urging me to make the concepts in this book available to the body. He helped me greatly in the early conceptualization of the Disciplemaker's Growth Grid, gave valuable suggestions regarding the general structure of this book, and steered me around many of the land mines that first-time authors encounter. You mean a lot to me, brother!

Thanks, too, to Jean Bryant, who did a tremendous job of editing this tome and putting it in its final form. Editors seldom get the credit they so richly deserve for the very difficult service they perform, but I'm here to see that she does! (Do NOT edit this out, Jean!)

I must also extend my gratitude to Leroy Eims for first introducing me to the concept of disciplemaking through the use of training objectives in his classic book, *The Lost Art of Disciplemaking.*

One hundred and seventy-one disciplemakers from all over the world took the time to respond to a very extensive questionnaire on disciplemaking I sent out, and a great many of their insights are found in this volume. I wish I could name each one here, because most of them were quite diligent in their responses, so great is their commitment to disciplemaking.

Finally, and with eternal gratitude, I must thank and praise the Lord Jesus Christ for His faithfulness to me and to my family — especially during the years it took to put this book together. It wasn't enough that He delivered me from the domain of darkness and transfered me into His kingdom, granting me eternal life, the privilege of sonship and the joy of His unending presence — He also has made it obvious that His grace, mercy and supernatural aid extends to the here and now on planet Earth . . . even when you're writing a book.

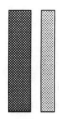

INTRODUCTION

Disciplemaking? It's not that difficult. Here are a few practical tips.

First, become omniscient. By being "all-knowing," you can easily identify where a Christian is on his journey toward spiritual maturity.

Next, master predestination so you can map out an efficient path for him. Of course, his own "free moral agency" might give you trouble, but if he'll devote himself to you body, soul and spirit, your difficulties should be few.

Then, become omnipresent. If you're with him every moment of every day, you can help him sort through his various experiences. In fact, the best plan would be to beam him directly to heaven, into an environment perfectly suited for spiritual growth.

Oh, and don't forget to lay in an infinite supply of love, patience, time and energy.

You do realize, however, that these attributes are hard to attain — anywhere outside the Trinity. And for those of us who lack them, helping another person grow spiritually can be a bit complicated. Many of us see the needs of Christians around us and we want to lend them a helping hand toward spiritual maturity. But when it comes time to actually launch out, we're stumped. Trying to identify specific needs of a young Christian, figuring out how to help meet those needs, allowing for variety of personalities and commitment levels, determining exactly what to say and do (that will turn him on, not off), figuring out what materials to use and how much of it is my job and how much is the Holy Spirit's . . . it's no wonder we hesitate.

Most of us can think up a few general strategies — like: "Bring him to church"; "Get him into the Bible"; "Teach him about praying." But how do we break it down to specifics? What should I actually do when we get together next Tuesday at 11:45? And after he's going to church, reading the Bible and praying, what else am I supposed to do? Can I motivate him to deepen and broaden his relationship with God, to go on with Him for the long haul?

Questions like those are what this book seeks to answer. You'll discover the first twelve things to do with a brand new Christian. Instead of relying on a "materials-oriented" approach, you'll learn how to assess a person's spiritual profile and tailor-make a program to suit his makeup and needs. You'll see what the Bible has to say about the long-term process of spiritual growth, and how you can fit into it. You'll learn what the all-important roles of the Holy Spirit and the body of Christ are in the disciplemaking process. You'll gain practical insight from disciplemakers all over the world. And we'll have a little fun along the way.

Before we get started, I'd like to shoot up a few flares to get your attention and to brighten your way.

First, this book is not a "skimmer." I've tried to keep it interesting and light, but it's not recreational reading. It's more of a survival manual. You read it once to get the big picture, while you're at home in your easy chair, then you go back and read pertinent parts again when you're lost in the woods. You'll also find step-by-step instructions on how to use the tools you have available.

Second, I'll be referring to the person you are trying to help as "your disciple," but you must realize right from the start that he's not really *your* disciple. Our objective is to help a person become a disciple of Jesus Christ, not of you or me. What a stagnant muddle this world would be in if we made only duplicates of ourselves! This planet does not need another me, but it sure could stand a few people who are more like Jesus, and that's what we aim to produce.

Even that statement is incorrect. We don't produce anything. In 1 Corinthians 3:7 we see: "So then neither the one who plants nor the one who waters is anything, but [it is] God who causes the growth." God is running the show. We are tools in His hands — nothing more, nothing less. Some would-be disciplemakers have missed that point and have tried to set themselves up as gurus, expecting the commitment and the obedience that is reserved for the Lord Jesus Christ. Beware of that trap — we serve a jealous God.

Third, whenever I write of the disciple in this book, I use the masculine gender. You can see that this book is already long enough without adding further volume by constantly writing "he or she" when referring to the disciple by personal pronoun. Please understand that I am using the generic "he," and translate accordingly.

As useful as they would be, omniscience and omnipresence are tools we'll never use in disciplemaking. But don't let that hold you back. God has supplied His church with "everything pertaining to life and godliness,"[1] so that each of us might be effectively involved in the "equipping of the saints for the work of service, to the building up of the body of Christ; until we all attain to the unity of the faith and of the knowledge of the Son of God, to a mature man, to the measure of the stature which belongs to the fullness of Christ."[2] Since God wants it done, He'll enable us to do it.

My prayer is that this book will be a useful tool in His hands as He equips you to equip others.

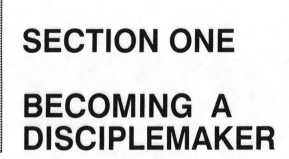

SECTION ONE

BECOMING A DISCIPLEMAKER

1
THE PRIORITY

As I stood staring at the tombstone in that dusty Wyoming graveyard, Jerry's words haunted me.

"God, the Word of God, and the souls of men . . . "

Jerry White — then an instructor at the Air Force Academy, now the president of the Navigators — had spoken slowly, deliberately. "According to the Bible, these are the only things that will last eternally. To the extent that you are involved in these three things, you are involved in eternity."

I'd first heard Jerry say that a few weeks earlier while attending a Navigator meeting at Colorado State University, but it hadn't sunk in. I had been a Christian for only a month, and such lofty thoughts had not yet found a place in my me-centered world. Yet Jerry's words apparently had dropped a seed as they flew through my mind. That seed had fallen onto fertile soil, and was now beginning to grow.

"God, the Word of God, and the souls of men . . . " I turned the words over and over in my mind, pondering their significance. "Eternity . . . reaching through to this side of death . . . in only three forms . . . "

Such cosmic notions would never have occurred to me in the hustle, bustle, froth and fury in the spring of 1970 on my college campus. With all the racket of war protests, a Stones concert, parties, the giddy freedom of a college freshman . . . who could hear a still, small voice?

So the Lord arranged to have me shipped off to the oil fields around Gillette, Wyoming, for a summer of roustabout work. There, life was whittled down to the basics. How do I tighten this pipe? How will I eat until my first paycheck comes? How do I cope with this terrible loneliness? Where is my life going?

When you're in these sink-or-swim situations your values and convictions rapidly crystallize. God's close oversight of the process at this crucial stage was particularly evident that day I started thinking about eternity.

I had parked my old Ford on the prairie a few miles outside of town, and was living in it. That particular morning I had awakened with the worst sore throat in history. The doctor I went to contributed to my misery with a shot to the behind, and he told me to go back home and go to bed. Lacking both home and bed, I decided to go out to the city's old graveyard where I could rest in peace (so to speak). I searched for a good-sized tumbleweed shadow to stretch out in, and came across the tombstone, which read:

Cyrus Calderson

Born: March 3, 1883

Died: April 8, 1925

I knew nothing about old Cyrus—who he was, what he had done in his life, how he had died—but a little arithmetic with his dates generated a disturbing chain of thoughts.

Cyrus Calderson has been dead longer than he was alive.

That may not seem an earth-shaking observation to you, but it unnerved me. It occurred to me that of all the activities Cyrus had ever been involved in during his entire existence—working, playing, learning, courting, marrying, parenting, talking, eating, sleeping—he had now spent more time just decomposing than everything else put together. And he would continue to do so for a long, long time. For the first time I was struck with the brevity of life and the enormous finality of death. My next thought was, *Someday, that will be true of me, too.*

A hailstorm of thoughts and questions began pelting me. *Wait! Cyrus isn't really here in this grave—it's just his corpse. The real Cyrus is . . . where? Heaven? Hell? If he hasn't been lying here beneath this soil, what has he been doing all these years? Did he know where he was going? Forty-two years on the*

*living side of the grave, and now forty-five on the other . . .
with thousands—no, millions—of years still ahead of him!
This side was nothing in comparison! A tick of the clock. An
eye-blink. What did he do to get ready? What can I do? What
can anybody do? Does what we do on this side of death have
any connection with what happens on the other side? What does
this stupid, oil-field job of mine have to do with eternity?*

That's when Jerry White's words began to bear fruit in my
mind. *God, the Word of God, the souls of men . . .*

Slowly, the darkness started to fade. Not only did I begin to
see the daybreak of God's eternal priorities, but they began to
illuminate everything else as well, just as dawn makes the surrounding landscape visible after a moonless night. The more I
thought about it, the more clearly I could see. In a moment of
time, God had reordered my life's priorities. For the first time
I understood that I could do something of *eternal significance,*
something that would give real meaning to my short life here
on earth.

I wasn't sure right then how to go about the "souls of men"
part, but I had a few ideas about the other two things. I knew
I needed a stronger relationship with Jesus Christ, so the rest
of the summer saw me getting up early each day to spend time
in prayer and Bible reading before heading out to the "crude
patch." I began memorizing Scripture. Life threw up one barrier after another, and I watched in wonder as the Lord blasted
each to smithereens, bolstering my growing faith. My relationship with Christ grew far beyond the intellectual "nodding acquaintance" I'd experienced up until then, and flamed into a
dynamic love affair. For me, that summer in the oil fields
punched eternal life into high gear.

Through the next several years my "graveyard commitments" deepened and broadened. Many factors facilitated that
process, but none so extensively as the faithful input of three
men—Dick, Wayne and Jay—who agreed to disciple me. These
men took significant time away from their studies or their
families—sometimes both—in order to "explain to me the way
of God more accurately," and they planted eternal values in my
life. Working in concert with the Holy Spirit, they built a sense

of purpose into my soul that made each day an adventure. Under their guidance, I saw God begin to use this cracked and leaky vessel in potent ways to further His kingdom.

Before long I recognized that the most strategic use of my few "eye-blinks" on earth would be to reproduce in others what the Holy Spirit — through the efforts of these three men — were producing in my life. I began to figure out the "souls of men" part of Jerry White's three-pronged observation. I wanted to become an integral part of God's grand design of bringing to spiritual maturity a people who would glorify Him and be at the forefront of His reconquest of planet Earth. I committed myself to disciplemaking.

One of the first guys I worked with was a fellow track athlete, Bob Parry. A hot-shot quarter-miler out of Maryland, he was one of the best in the country during his senior year of high school. The track coach knew I was a Christian, and he had heard Bob was too, so he asked me to try to persuade Bob to come to CSU. I was interested in seeing him join the team, too, but for reasons different from the coach's.

I called Bob and told him that we had a decent track team, a great Christian fellowship, and — oh, yeah, the school was OK too! I told him he could do well athletically at any school he picked, but in time, the sports accolades would fade, and he'd have little to show for the time he invested. But if he came to CSU, he would get long-term, in-depth training in the three subjects that have eternal significance — God, the Word of God, and the souls of men. And I could guarantee it, because I'd do it personally. If Bob had known at the time how meager my knowledge and experience were in that last area, he would have signed on with UCLA.

After praying about it, though, Bob headed for the Rockies. I was so excited! I was going to disciple somebody! He was to arrive in the fall — I had three months to get ready. But how? I could vaguely remember how Dick, Wayne and Jay had discipled me, but where should I start with this guy? I knew almost nothing about him. Though I didn't divulge it to anyone, I was scared spitless about it. This turned out to be to my benefit, because it drove me to desperate prayer.

Bob had been a Christian for a few years, and in high school he had been involved with Young Life. His relationship with the Lord was important to him, but I could tell he hadn't had much practical training in spiritual matters. In my prayers for Bob, I asked the Lord specifically what Bob needed to learn, and to guide me in how to help him. We began to study the Bible together. We prayed together. I taught him how to share his faith. We went witnessing together. I taught him how to lead Bible studies. Our camaraderie grew as we agonized, sweated, ached, lived and died together during track workouts. We grilled each other on Scripture memory. As time passed I saw that, far beyond a discipler/disciplee relationship, we were becoming best friends.

We began rooming together in the dorm and our little cubicle became Grand Central Station for much of CSU's track and Christian populations. We organized nightly prayer meetings there, sometimes cramming twenty-five people into our 14' by 14' room. We led Bible studies. We worked out strategies for winning the track team to Christ. We climbed into each others' lives, moaned together over girlfriend woes, cracked the whip over each other regarding homework. When our bodies had been destroyed in workouts and rigor mortis was setting in, together we cursed the day we chose track over baseball, but our shouts of exultation were loud and strong when one of us won a race. We built each other up when we needed building, we blasted each other when we needed blasting. Eventually, Bob became the best man at my wedding and a bottomless reservoir of challenge and encouragement to me.

In time, my friend began to multiply the life of Christ into the lives of others. One of his disciples ended up a computer wiz at NASA, carrying on a ministry in Houston with members of the space shuttle program. One went from being a star player on CSU's basketball team to influencing upper-level management for Christ within an international corporation. Another became an influential lobbyist for a Christian organization based in Washington, D.C. Another is a policeman in a Denver suburb and effectively represents Christ there.

Bob invested a great deal of time in Chuck Kovac, the

fullback on CSU's football team. They grew to be best friends and they married sorority roommates who were also best friends. The four of them ministered to each other a great deal, and together they ministered to others as well. When Chuck graduated, he went to work with a major commercial operation in Denver, and began to influence many people for Christ. Through his church he started several home Bible studies and a Navigator "Colossians 2:7" study. A few years later, he took a job as an engineer with an electric company and opened a new office in San Diego.

In that fast-paced, people-choked environment, Chuck met Brian Roble, a cynical, agnostic businessman who was struggling with drug and alcohol addiction. Brian had just checked into a chemical dependency program, and for the first time in his life knew he needed the help of a "higher power." Chuck and Brian began to study the Bible together and pray together, and eventually Chuck was able to lead Brian to a personal relationship with Jesus Christ. They and their wives became fast friends, and spent many happy hours building each other up in the faith. Brian is clean now, is teaching catechism to children in his church, and is a facilitator in a twelve-step alcoholic recovery program, passing on to dozens of others what he now knows to be true about the "higher power." They in turn are passing those truths on to still others.

The apostle John wrote in 3 John 4: "I have no greater joy than this, to hear of my children walking in the truth." I'm beginning to understand what John was talking about. Back in Gillette, staring at Cyrus's tombstone, my heart cried out for a life of significance. In the years that have passed since then, I've had a glimpse of what it means to become a link in the eternal chain of spiritual multiplication. This chain, that began with Jesus, added links through Dick, Wayne and Jay, through me, through Bob, through Chuck, and through Brian, and it continues to add links through others. As I look back at the fruit that is remaining, my heart wants to burst with His eternal joy!

ON-GOING MOTIVATION

As time marched on, I learned five facts which confirmed

my initial commitment to disciplemaking. If you're not already sold out to spiritual multiplication through this process, I hope these five observations will launch you in that direction.

1. Disciplemaking is the logical and caring thing to do with new Christians.

How do you treat babies? Would you bring one home from the hospital and say, "OK, Ralph. Welcome to the group. Your bedroom is upstairs and to the left. Extra blankets are on the chair if you get cold. The pantry is just off the kitchen and the can opener is on the counter. Diapers are in your closet. No loud music or crying after 10 P.M. If you have any questions, there are lots of people around here who would love to help you out—just ask them!"

Ridiculous.

Little Ralphie would not survive. You would show a great deal more care than that for any newborn.

Why should spiritual babies be treated with any less concern? When a person becomes a Christian, he has in fact been born as an infant into the spiritual realm, and is as unfamiliar with that environment as a physical baby is with a delivery room. A spiritual baby needs someone to take an interest in him—someone to love him, to protect and affirm him during the early days of his spiritual life.

"Why, that's the Holy Spirit's job," someone might say. "Don't you have any confidence in the sovereignty of God?"

Of course I do, but that doesn't mean I would allow my naked infant to play in the snow, trusting in the sovereignty of God to keep her from pneumonia. My poor child would reap what I sowed.

We think nothing of devoting eighteen years of our lives to making sure that our natural children grow and get educated. It's only right that we render the needed care and nurture to spiritual children as well—probably not as much as eighteen years, but enough time and energy to assure their spiritual maturity. I know multitudes of Christians who are far older in the Lord than eighteen years, but because they have had no one to oversee and encourage their growth, they function as spiritual infants.

2. Humans require accountability and discipline to achieve important goals.

When I ran track in college, I specialized in the 400-meter hurdles. One day during my sophomore year, coach Del Hessel called me to his office and asked me what my athletic goals were.

A pretty gung-ho sort of guy in those days, I replied, "Coach Hessel, I don't believe in doing anything half-heartedly—let's go to the Olympics!"

You can't imagine how my coach responded to that. Rather than patting me on the back and saying, "What a nice idea—have fun," that man began to *hurt* me! Frequently!

He made me go on long runs up in the mountains, and it made my lungs burn. He made me run stadium stairs until my legs fell off. He made my muscles cramp from lifting weights. He made me jump over hurdles, and sometimes I would trip over them and my knees would turn into cinder soufflé.

The monster! When I was tired and wanted to rest, do you think he would let me? Not on your life! Why, it was as if he didn't even care that I was suffering. Here I shared such a pleasant thought with him about the Olympics, and in response he clamped a bunch of obnoxious disciplines on my life and began to inflict pain on a daily basis.

But it was exactly what I needed—and wanted. On my own, I never would have worked hard enough to become a great athlete—or even an average one. Yet, even under my coach's mentoring, I still was tempted constantly to look for the short-cut, the easiest way through a workout. But because I was willing to submit to his guidance, and because he was willing to take the time and energy necessary to hold me accountable and oversee my development, by my senior year I was an All-American, placing fifth at the NCAA Division One National Championships. I didn't quite make the Olympics, but I did reach my fullest potential—of that I'm sure. And I look back at Del Hessel as one of the most valuable men in my life. He got behind me and pushed me toward my goals.

The point? It's our nature to follow the path of least resistance. In almost every area of life, if we are serious about attaining a certain goal, we must seek out some person or system that will hold us accountable, keep us on track, and keep us going when the going gets tough.

Our tendency is the same when it comes to our spiritual life. Our ultimate goal is to be conformed to the image of Jesus Christ. Isn't it logical that we should take advantage of every resource available — including the guidance and accountability provided by a brother or sister who is more mature in the Lord?

And as we grow spiritually, shouldn't we desire to be that "helper" to others also? The Scriptures say: "Iron sharpens iron, so one man sharpens another" (Proverbs 27:17). We need to learn how to be the "one man," skilled at sharpening other growing Christians. We need more Del Hessels in the spiritual realm — men and women about whom mature Christians will one day say, "I'm where I am today in large part because that person got behind me and pushed."

3. Disciplemaking gives meaning and purpose to life.

There are two large lakes in Israel: the Sea Of Galilee and the Dead Sea. The Sea of Galilee has a number of rivers flowing into it, and to the south, the Jordan river flows out of it. It's a beautiful, healthy lake, full of aquatic life. The Jordan rolls southward for about sixty miles, and then into the Dead Sea. Several other rivers flow into the Dead Sea as well, but it is a rare body of water in that no river flows out of it. Because of this, the mineral content of the water is extremely high, choking out all possibility of life. They don't call it the Dead Sea for nothing.

Many Christians — like the Dead Sea — always take, never give. They have sat in churches, prayed, and studied the Scriptures for years. They could pass on so much that would feed life to new Christians, but nothing flows out of them.

We gain wisdom, knowledge and experience, not only that

we can benefit, but also that *others* can benefit when we pass it on (2 Corinthians 1:3,4).

When you're actively involved in helping another Christian grow, cooperating with the Holy Spirit to reproduce the life-giving characteristics of Christ that have been produced in you, you're fitting in with the eternal, magnificent plan of God. Are you interested in meaning and purpose? There are none higher!

4. It's the only strategy that will get the job done.

"So you want to work for me, eh?" said the rich-but-stupid land baron. "What should I pay you for tilling my ground?"

"Oh, I wouldn't require much," replied the young-but-smart plowman. "Do you like to play chess?"

"Well, of course! What intelligent man doesn't? But what does that have to do with your wages?"

The young man pulled out a chess board from his luggage. "If you will put a penny on the first white square, that will be my first month's wage. Then, at the end of my second month, double it—put two pennies on the second white square. Then, double it again each month, until you have filled each of the thirty-two white squares. After that, I'll work the rest of my life for you for free."

This offer the land baron could not pass up. He figured out that he would have to pay this man a salary for only a little less than three years, and then he could count on the plowman's labor for decades to come—at no cost! And besides, a penny for a month's work? Exceptional value! At the end of a year, that would only be $20.48 total! He felt a little twinge of guilt about taking advantage of this foolish youth—but not much.

"Done!" cried the land baron. They entered into a contract and the young plowman went to work.

Things were a little tight for the plowman that first year. You can't buy many hamburgers for $20.48. But an interesting thing began to happen. The wages that the land baron had to put on the thirteenth square came to $40.96. The fifteenth square required $163.84. The twentieth square took $5,242.88

and the thirtieth, $5,368,709.12. The thirty-second and final square required a whopping $21,474,836.48. The young plowman could afford to work for free after that, since the land baron had paid him a total of $42,949,672.95 for less than three years' work, and was now bankrupt anyway.

Can you see the awesome potential of the principle of multiplication? Let's apply that principle to the spread of the gospel, and compare two ministry strategies. Plan A involves cranking up the "Win-the-World-for-Christ Evangelistic Association," which, by hook or by crook, is going to see one thousand people gain a saving knowledge of Christ every day. Plan B involves just you, winning one person to the Lord each year, and training that person to live a victorious, reproductive Christian life — then the two of you doing the same with two more people the next year. Continuing in this activity, and applying the principle of multiplication, your numbers would double each year thereafter.

How long should the association lease office space to coordinate the activities of Plan A? Go for the loooong-term lease, because at a thousand souls a day, it will take the Evangelists 13,698.6 years to win the world's five billion inhabitants to the Lord. But when you take into account the current world population growth rate (births minus deaths), more than 217,000 per *day,* you realize they're fighting a losing battle.

On the other hand, you and the people you discipled under Plan B will see five billion people come to a vital, thoroughly-grounded knowledge of the Lord about midway through the twenty-eighth year. And even if the population is up to ten billion by then, you'll hit *that* the next year.

Obviously, if the chain breaks at a weak link, you'll miss your goal. But you can see the mathematical possibility of winning the entire world to Christ through multiplication.

5. Disciplemaking is the core of the Great Commission.

A person's last utterances are often taken as the most significant he ever speaks. Through them he seeks to leave a legacy to the people who are important to him. He tries in those final few breaths to communicate to his loved ones the thing closest to his heart.

Among the last things Jesus had to say to His disciples just before He was taken up to glory was the following:

> All authority has been given to Me in heaven and on earth. Go therefore and make disciples of all the nations, baptizing them in the name of the Father and the Son and the Holy Spirit, teaching them to observe all that I commanded you; and lo, I am with you always, even to the end of the age (Matthew 28:18-20).

Making disciples was the pursuit that weighed so heavily on the heart of Jesus. It's what He asked us to do, just before He left. He didn't say, "Go therefore and make church buildings"; or, "Go therefore and develop bus programs"; or, "Go therefore and get converts." All of those activities are terrific, in proper context. But when they become the focus of our ministry—when the means to the end becomes the end itself—we are no longer conforming to the final wishes of Jesus Christ.

You are in love with your Lord, right? If He were suddenly to appear before you today and ask you to do something for Him, I'll bet you'd do it. Immediately, diligently, selflessly—because of your love for Him. In a way, He *has* appeared before you today, in the Spirit of His Word which you just read two paragraphs ago. He's asked you to make disciples. Surely you wouldn't deny Him His heart's greatest desire?

BUT WHO AM I?

God sent Moses to three schools: one at his mother's knee, one in Pharaoh's court, and one in the wilderness. When he had received his third diploma, God appeared to him and said, "Moses, I've got a little job for you. I'm going to rescue My people from Egypt, and I'd like you to be My representative to Pharaoh. Your education is complete; pack your bags."

Moses was flabbergasted. His first response to God was, "Who am I, that I should go to Pharaoh, and that I should bring the sons of Israel out of Egypt?" (Exodus 3:11).

Would you say this demonstrated a lack of faith on Moses' behalf? Perhaps, but it also demonstrated (unfortunately) a realistic self-image. For half of his life he had been nothing but a caretaker of animals. He had tried being a hero once before, forty years earlier, and had failed miserably. He had no credentials, no credibility, and no confidence whatsoever in his ability to pull off such an astounding feat.

As you contemplate a ministry of disciplemaking, you may come up with a personal inventory that looks a lot like Moses'. You may see yourself as shy, slow of speech, uneducated, unintelligent, undisciplined, unknowledgeable about the things of God, whatever. Would you like to hear some good news? *None of that matters.* Because God says to you the same thing He said to Moses in the next verse, "Certainly, I will be with you!" He says to you the same thing He said to the eleven disciples, "Lo, I am with you always" (Matthew 28:20).

God isn't hunting for highly trained, extremely capable, hard-driving big-shots who can formulate magnificent plans to win the world for Christ. He's looking for faithful men and women who are willing to carry out *His* plans in *His* magnificent ways. In any ministry you're involved in, never, never get the idea that you're running the show, or that it all depends on you. Your pride will guarantee your failure (1 Peter 5:5). The Holy Spirit is in charge, and all we need to do is echo Paul's words to the risen Christ, "What shall I do, Lord?" He'll take it from there. What you now see as deficits in your life, God can turn into assets—if you'll cooperate with Him in the process.

GETTING OFF ON THE RIGHT FOOT

The journey toward becoming a proficient disciplemaker starts with a single step—the same step I took in that Gillette graveyard. If you'll take that first step, the next ten thousand will be a whole lot easier. Decide to dedicate your life to the priorities of God; ignore the side paths and rabbit trails that your human nature begs you to explore; point your life toward "the other side"—and God *will* use you to make disciples.

2
THE PRODUCT

Rich? Even for a Texan, he was well off. People would scoff at his land holdings — a mere forty acres — until they found out it was downtown Dallas. He didn't want to wear his glasses while driving, so he had all of his Rolls Royces fitted with prescription windshields!

One day, this rich old boy decided to go into the manufacturing business. He spared no cost in constructing the most magnificent plant ever built. He had the best assembly lines, the best sales force, the best executives, the best buildings, the best corporate planes, yachts and helicopters, the best of *everything.*

The plant was finally completed and it was time to begin production. All the workers were in their places. The equipment was clean, lubricated and in perfect working order. The media showed up in force, eager to report on the opening of this tremendous operation.

The owner placed that crucial phone call to the plant manager, "OK, Billy Bob, go ahead and fire 'er up!"

There was a moment of silence at Billy Bob's end of the phone. Finally, he spoke. "Boss, I'm afraid we've got a little problem here."

"What could possibly be the matter?" the owner exploded. "I supplied you with the best of everything! The media is here, waiting for some action! What in the world is the hold-up?"

"Well, Boss," the manager stammered, "you haven't told us yet what we're supposed to manufacture."

A little far-fetched? "Form follows function," any architect worth his drafting pen will tell you. The best way to produce a product is to determine first what the product is going to be, and *then* build the appropriate manufacturing plant.

Why do so many Christians make the same blunder the Texan made when it comes to the process of disciplemaking? They have all the resources imaginable to be effective. They have direct access to the Holy Spirit. They have the drive and the desire. There are plenty of people available who could become disciples — somewhere in the neighborhood of five billion. The problem is, most potential disciplemakers aren't sure what the finished product is to be. How they expect to set about "making disciples" — or how they'll know when the process is "complete" — is beyond me.

To keep you from making that mistake, we will look in this chapter at what we're trying to produce in this venture known as disciplemaking.

"DISCIPLE" DEFINED

When you are searching for the exact meaning of a word used in the Bible, you must take two important steps: (1) Go back to the Greek, Aramaic or Hebrew to find its literal definition; and (2) look at how the word is used in context. When you apply these two principles to the word *disciple,* step one will make it clear that a biblical disciple owns a certain *attitude,* and step two will demonstrate that this attitude manifests itself in certain *actions.* First, let's look at the definition — and the "attitude." Biblical Greek for the English "disciple" is *mathetes,* which comes from the word *manthano* which means simply "learn."[1]

So, a *mathetes* is "a learner, i.e., pupil."[2] But what kind of "learning" are we talking about? Book-learning? Head knowledge? The kind of learning where you listen to a teacher, take notes, cram for the final, regurgitate the course content onto a piece of paper and then forget it?

J. H. Thayer makes it clear in his treatment of the word *manthano* (learn) that a *mathetes* is a special kind of learner — one who learns "by use and practice."[3] Ah-HA! So we're talking about a person who not only thinks, but who also *does.* He puts shoe leather to his convictions. Arndt and Gingrich explain in their *Greek-English Lexicon of the New Testament* that the learning he does is not by any means confined to an academic classroom. Under their treatment of *manthano* you'll find:

> to learn, appropriate to oneself, less through instruction than through experience or practice (Hebrews 5:8; 1 Timothy 5:4,13; Titus 3:14).[4]

But what effect should this learning have? Harold K. Moulton spells it out for us: "to learn by practice or experience, *acquire a custom or habit*"[5] (emphasis mine). Get it? The focus is not on the mere acquisition of new knowledge, though that is involved, but on the acquisition of a new "custom or habit" — a changed life! This kind of learning is taken in, practiced, and incorporated into a transformed lifestyle. This concept of spotlighting "thought accompanied by endeavor" (as one expositor puts it[6]) as opposed to the simple gaining of knowledge is talked about throughout the Bible:

> *God* (through Moses): "And it [the Word] shall be with him, and he shall read it all the days of his life, that he may learn to fear the Lord his God, by carefully observing all the words of this law and these statutes" (Deuteronomy 17:19).
>
> *Ezra:* "For Ezra had prepared his heart to seek the law of the Lord, and to do it . . . " (Ezra 7:10).
>
> *David:* "Thy word I have treasured in my heart, that I may not sin against Thee" (Psalm 119:11).
>
> *John:* "The one who says, 'I have come to know Him,' and does not keep His commandments, is a liar, and the truth is not in him" (1 John 2:4).
>
> *James:* "But prove yourselves doers of the word, and not merely hearers who delude themselves" (James 1:22).
>
> *Paul:* "For not the hearers of the Law are just before God, but the doers of the Law will be justified" (Romans 2:13).
>
> *Jesus:* "Everyone who comes to Me, and hears My words, and acts upon them, I will show you whom he is like: [the man who built his house on the rock, instead of the sand]" (Luke 6:47-49).
>
> "My mother and My brothers are these who hear the word of God and do it" (Luke 8:21).
>
> "On the contrary, blessed are those who hear the word of God, and observe it" (Luke 11:28).

We could go on and on. We are keeping our eyes peeled for an attitude of being a "learner" — someone who *takes in and applies* new information that comes from God.

How can we tell if that is happening? We'll tell by our disciple's *actions*. Jesus said, "So then, you will know them by their fruits" (Matthew 7:20). God made it clear to the prophet Samuel that "man looks at the outward appearance, but the Lord looks at the heart" (1 Samuel 16:7). Oh, how we wish we could see the heart as God sees it, and get a 100 percent accurate picture of a man! Unfortunately, all we can see are externals. However, Jesus told us the outward appearances — or a man's actions — ultimately reflect the man's heart (Mark 7:20-23). True, these outward appearances can be cloaked, and *not* accurately portray what's on the inside, but they are, nevertheless, all we human beings have to go on. And with the helpful insight of the Holy Spirit, we'll eventually be able to figure out if the changed lifestyle is coming from a truly changed heart.

So what kinds of actions are we looking for? Let's follow step two and check out how the word is used in the context of the Scriptures.

"DISCIPLE" IN CONTEXT

As we examine New Testament usage of the word *disciple,* we'll find some confusing facts. On the one hand, we read about Jesus placing some pretty high standards on people who want to be called His disciples — things like: taking up your cross, following Him, and taking all the criticism and persecution He endured (Matthew 10:24-38); giving up all of your possessions (Luke 14:33); being so much in love with Him that your relationship with your family looks like *hatred* in comparison (Luke 14:26); and being willing to die for Him (Matthew 10:39).

On the other hand, sometimes people who are called disciples in the Bible behave in very "un-disciple-ish" ways. They appear to be: spiritually dull (Matthew 13:36; 16:6-11; John 14:5-10; 16:16-20); spiritually impotent and faithless (Matthew 17:15-20); used as patsies by Satan (Matthew 16:21-23; 26:14-16); full of spiritual pride (Mark 10:35-45; John 13:36-38); uncommitted (John 6:66); lacking in compassion for others (Mark 10:13,14); violent and wrathful (Luke 9:54,55; John

18:10,11); secretive about their devotion to Jesus (John 19:38); opposing Jesus' intentions (John 13:5-11); deserting Jesus in his greatest hour of need (Matthew 26:69-75; Mark 14:43-46, 50).

So what is a disciple? Spiritual superman or spiritual dud? The answer is: both. A disciple is a person in *process*. The process begins when a person receives Christ and becomes a learner, and will continue as long as the person keeps learning. He starts out as a baby, not in any way meeting the criteria of a *mature* disciple, nor is he expected to. Just like the disciples who traveled with Jesus, he'll make awkward mistakes from time to time. But as long as he's learning, and he's making progress, we don't get nervous.

From time to time in this process, Jesus will up the ante for His learners. We see this in John 6 when He urged a large band of His disciples to trust Him for deeper, more significant parts of their lives. But many of these "learners" were offended, decided to stop learning, and didn't walk with Him anymore (verse 66). They could no longer call themselves His disciples. They stopped growing. Then He turned to the twelve, and asked them a very pointed question: "You do not want to go away also, do you?" Their insightful answer was, "Lord, to whom shall we go? You have the words of eternal life" (verses 67,68). They agreed to the increased demands. They wanted to keep maturing.

To the growing disciple today He'll say, "You've been doing well; you have been demonstrating that you are a learner. But now it's time to graduate to the next class. More will be expected now. Are you willing to accept this new challenge?" If the disciple says yes, he continues to learn, he continues to grow, he continues to be used in the work of the kingdom—he continues to be a disciple. But if he is not willing to go on, Jesus says, "Then you cannot be My disciple. Your eternal destiny is by no means in jeopardy, and you can repent at any time and we'll resume class. But as long as you maintain that stance, you are not My learner."

This being the case, you will find that most brand-new Christians are disciples, because they have such an intense drive to learn more about their relationship with God and they haven't had much opportunity to bail out yet.

On the other hand, you may find a fellow who has been pastoring a church for twenty-five years, has a seminary doctorate, has memorized half of the Bible, has led hundreds of people to the Lord, and yet is *not* a disciple, because there came a time when he said, "No. I'm not willing to go any further. I will not make that sacrifice. I'm not interested in any more learning."

To him, Jesus has said, "You cannot be my disciple."

The Biblical, Contextual Definition of a Disciple

So just what is a disciple?

A disciple is a person-in-process who is eager to learn and apply the truths that Jesus Christ teaches him, which will result in ever-deepening commitments to a Christ-like lifestyle.

The concept of disciple does not portray a stage of growth or level of expertise that we hope to achieve some day. I've seen some definitions of a disciple that list character qualities and disciplines even the twelve apostles couldn't live up to until many years after Christ's ascension — if then! Yet despite their shortcomings, they are unhesitatingly called "the disciples" throughout the Gospels. Two hundred and thirty-eight times, to be exact.

Instead, the concept of disciple represents an *attitude of commitment.* If the learning attitude is there, the character qualities and disciplines will eventually show up; but not all at once, and not in any highly predictable sequence or at any prescribed rate. There are too many variables involved. All we can say with certainty is that they *will* show up.

A Christian learner will demonstrate continual dynamism, flux, change and growth. He'll never "arrive," because the Lord will continue to expose areas where He wants to bring about deeper commitments and more profound changes. C. S. Lewis captured this concept well, writing during World War II:

> In all of us God "still" holds only a part. D-Day is only a week ago. The bite so far taken out of Normandy shows small on the map of Europe. The resistance is strong, the casualties

heavy, and the event uncertain. There is, we have to admit, a line of demarcation between God's part in us and the enemy's region. But it is, we hope, a fighting line; not a frontier fixed by agreement.[7]

WHEN ARE WE DONE?

If the disciple never arrives, will we ever *have* a "finished product" as we talked about in the opening paragraphs of this chapter? Jesus' prime directive was: "Make learners." How far do we take that? A few pages back we saw that a brand-new Christian would qualify as a learner, so if we're sure a person is a Christian with a learning attitude, is it OK to say "adios" to him and go make *another* disciple?

To answer those questions, it's a good idea to think in terms of two analogies: a corn stalk and a child.

Suppose someone told us to go make corn. To do this we must first break up the soil, plow in some fertilizer, and get our irrigation system in place. Next, we push a corn seed into the ground and get it wet. We chase the birds away, water it every few days, and wait. In time, a shoot appears. At this point we could rightfully say, "There's your corn!" A scientific analysis of its various features would prove our assertion to be true. But we wouldn't end our work there, would we? Within that three-inch-high shoot resides the capability, in time, to grow, mature and produce fruit. But we know our work isn't finished until we see ears of corn on the dinner table.

It's the same way with a disciple. Within a brand-new Christian is the capability to grow, mature and bear fruit. He is indeed a learner. But our job isn't done until the disciple reaches that point, becomes stable, and begins reproducing spiritual fruit.

How long will this process take? How much time and energy should I plan on pouring into this "cornstalk" before it's finally mature and fruit-bearing? Here's where we leave the cornstalk analogy and jump over to the child analogy.

It takes a long time to turn kids into adults, but the intensity of our work and their need for supervision diminishes as they mature. During their first few years, we do almost *every-*

thing for them. As they grow, they can handle more of life's complexities on their own, requiring less direction and regulation from us. When they hit the indistinct age of "adulthood," we give them the boot — our job is done. It's time for them to stand on their own. But even then, our input doesn't cease — it just changes its clothes. Before, it wore the trappings of parental training, now it looks more like the good advice of a close friend.

The point is that while the discipling relationship is a long-term one, the time and energy you must commit to that relationship lessens as the disciple matures. But it should never stop completely. Paul bumped into Timothy around A.D. 53, at which time he began discipling him. Fourteen years later his good advice was still gaining admission to Timothy's heart (2 Timothy). I'm not in daily communication with my first three disciplers. But when I'm dealing with a toughie, their on-going counsel and encouragement over the years has been a tremendous asset to me.

A DISCIPLE'S DESCRIPTION

"Can't we get into a little detail yet?" you may be asking. "After all you've said, I still don't have a clear picture of what the finished product is supposed to look like. Can't you give me a description, a list of characteristics, a photo, something?"

To produce *that* photo would require a very complicated camera indeed, because a mature disciple is a very complicated creature. It's like asking for a photo of a snowflake. One flake would look like that, but no other one would. Because of the various gifts, abilities, skills, backgrounds, education, capacities, likes and dislikes each of us were blessed with, mature disciples are as unique as snowflakes.

One may have tremendous strengths in the area of preaching the Word; another may be a mighty prayer warrior; another may be a witnessing machine. Yet each may be a mature disciple. That's the essence of being different members of the same Body.

There are some characteristics which are meant to be held by all who walk with Christ, and by the end of this book my hope is that you'll have a good understanding of what those are and how to be part of the process that will incorporate them into your disciple's life. But you'll also need to be aware of the *special* qualities, convictions, and habits that characterize your disciple in unique ways—and you'll need to know how to help him develop them. We have seen the long-shot, panoramic picture in this chapter: He learns from Jesus and applies what he learns. The detail will come into better focus as we move along.

THE DISCIPLEMAKER'S ROLE

Where do you—the disciplemaker—fit in? You become the primary human agency through which God works to bring the disciple to maturity. Your main responsibility is to provide an environment which will enhance the growth process. You are helping him to put on and adjust Jesus' yoke, so he can learn from *Him* (Matthew 11:29). You must not imagine that it's up to you to cause growth in your disciple. That's God's job. Nor should you think you are the only one needed to set up an agreeable environment for him. Your relationship with the disciple is a lot like the farmer's relationship to the seed. The farmer can plant it, water it, cultivate it, call in the fertilizing crew, call in the crop dusters and call in the harvesters, but it's God who causes the seed to grow. If the farmer does a good job of carrying out his responsibilities, the seed will grow rapidly and produce much fruit. If we are responsible about our disciplemaking, the men and women we are working with will likewise grow and reproduce.

If you want to be a responsible, fruitful farmer, you'd better find out about the process of plant growth. If you want to be a responsible, fruitful disciplemaker, familiarize yourself with the process of spiritual growth. When all is said and done, we see that our finished product is really a person-in-process, always growing, never totally finished.

So we must know the process, in order to recognize the product. God has made it quite clear in His Word that certain conditions and procedures will aid the process of spiritual growth. We need to discover those conditions and procedures before we crank up the "Disciplemaking Factory." The next two chapters will give you some practical insight in that regard.

3
THE PROCESS

From time to time while I was in college, a bunch of us would fan out and knock on doors in our building, just to see if we could find anyone interested in talking about the gospel. In my early days as a witnessing Christian, I was a wee bit off in both my motivation and approach. I was definitely interested in seeing people come to know Christ, but I was equally interested in the chase, the debate, the intellectual give-and-take; seeing the foe weakened as he had to relinquish a point; myself emerging the victor after a titanic battle, the walls around us bloody with rhetoric, philosophies, quotes and logic.

The zenith of my misplaced zeal was my (now embarrassing) practice of making up Scripture. If a fellow's argument backed me into a corner, I'd simply invent a statement (complete with chapter and verse) that facilitated my escape. It's too bad no one ever asked me to show it to them in the Bible — it would have ended that folly in a hurry!

My problem in those days was that I didn't have a clear idea of how I fit into the process of witnessing. I thought it was up to me to argue people into the kingdom — that the better I became at debate, the more fruit I'd see. I didn't understand the Holy Spirit's role in evangelism — that it was *His* job to convict the non-Christian of sin, righteousness and judgment, not mine. I didn't understand that my Bible fabrication — using a lie to tell the truth — had the effect of totally nullifying the supernatural power of my witness. I just figured that it was my job to "convert" people any way I could so that, like Paul said, "I may by all means save some" (1 Corinthians 9:22).

As time passed I learned what really went on during a witnessing session. I learned to identify the Holy Spirit's role, my

39

role, Satan's role, the key issues, what the non-believer was up against, and the proper place and use of apologetics. In short, I figured out *how I fit into God's process* of calling people out of the kingdom of darkness into the kingdom of His Son. This knowledge made me considerably more useful to Him in witnessing.

Now, if you hope to prove useful to God as a disciple*maker,* you'll need to figure out how you fit into His process of disciple*making.* Several entities are involved, and you'll want to make sure you're playing your role and not trying to play theirs. You'll want a clear understanding of why *you're* involved in the process and what your responsibilities are.

THE PROCESS DEFINED

In order to get a better grasp of it, let's try to capsulize the process of disciplemaking.

> *Disciplemaking is seeking to fulfill the imperative of the Great Commission by making a conscientious effort to help people move toward spiritual maturity—drawing on the power and direction of the Holy Spirit, utilizing the resources of the local church, and fully employing the gifts, talents and skills acquired over the years.*

The four key components in this description are:

1. The fulfillment of
   the Great Commission   ) The overall purpose

2. The Holy Spirit   )

3. The local church   ) The primary agencies involved

4. The disciplemaker   )

To be sure that we have a firm grasp on the "why" of disciplemaking, we'll be concentrating in this chapter on the significance of Christ's Great Commission. In chapter 4 we'll take a closer look at the respective roles of the three primary agencies involved in the process.

THE GREAT COMMISSION: DIVINE IMPERATIVE

When Jesus gave us the Great Commission in Matthew 28:19,20, exactly what was He telling us to do?

In the *New American Standard Bible* the passage reads:

> Go therefore and make disciples of all the nations, baptiz-
> ing them in the name of the Father and the Son and the Holy
> Spirit, teaching them to observe all that I commanded you; and
> lo, I am with you always, even to the end of the age.

Though it may not look like it in English, if you know Greek
you'll see right away that there are three adverbial participles
in this long sentence ("go," "baptizing," and "teaching"), all
modifying the imperative "make disciples." Remember your
high-school grammar? Here's a little refresher course: An adverbial participle is a word that looks like a verb, but acts as an
adverb. Here's an example: "He burst into the room shouting
'Fire!'" "Shouting" is the participle, telling us what he was
doing as he "burst" (verb) into the room. What we have in the
Matthew passage are three verbish-looking words all modifying the main verb of the sentence "make disciples," (one word
in Greek) which happens to be an "imperative" or command.
"Go" would more accurately be translated "going," so it isn't
actually a command.

At first glance, "going," "baptizing," and "teaching" all look
like verbs, and we think, "Oh, I get it — Jesus told us to go, baptize and teach!" Close, but not quite right. Those are nice things
to do, but Jesus actually and grammatically commanded us to
"make disciples." The "going, baptizing, teaching" tell us *how
we do it. Making disciples* is the end, the focus, the command.
Going, baptizing and *teaching* are the means, the method, the
activity.

You can picture a good parallel by imagining how Paul
Revere's boss might have instructed him just before his famous
ride. The three participles are italicized, and the main verb is
bold-faced:

> As you are *riding* through towns, **shout**, "The British
> are coming!" — *waking* up anyone who's asleep and *stop-
> ping* at each tavern where patriots might congregate.

The main thing Paul's boss wanted him to do was to shout.
But he was to do it in the context of *riding, waking* people up
and *stopping* in taverns. If he did those three things without
shouting about the advance of the British, he not only would

have disobeyed orders, his whole ride would have been in vain. Conversely, if he shouted about the British only while standing in his barn, and didn't bother to ride through towns, wake up sleepers and stop at taverns, the residents of his barn would have been well prepared for the invasion, but the rest of us might be eating a lot more fish and chips these days.

It's the same with Jesus' instructions. If all the church does is to go, baptize and teach, with no concerted movement toward making disciples, she's not following His orders. On the other side of the coin, if she tries to make disciples outside the divinely mandated process of going, baptizing and teaching, she's still setting herself up for failure.

So how do going, baptizing and teaching combine forces to make disciples? Let's have a look at them one-by-one.

Going

Taking into account the location of this word in the construction of the original Greek sentence, an even more precise translation would be, "As you are going . . . " It presupposes that the hearers are already going. It relates to disciplemaking in two ways:

First, it corresponds to the concept of *evangelism*. It's pretty tough to make disciples out of non-Christians, so the first step in moving people toward spiritual maturity is to move them toward being born-again into the spiritual realm. Jesus is saying, "Make disciples by winning people to the kingdom."

Second, it directs us to take the *initiative*. The job won't get done if we are staying, only if we are going. In both our witnessing and in our discipling, we need to step out, make a move, shun pacifism and become activists. This may mean going across the ocean to a foreign continent, or it may mean going across the street to a neighbor. Here Jesus is saying, Make disciples by taking the initiative! Don't wait for them to come to you—go to them first!

Baptizing

The Greek participle *baptizontes* used here comes from *baptizo* which means "dip, immerse, submerge."[1]

The idea is that one is introducing an object into a new environment, which will affect the object in some way. If you baptize a dirty cup into a clean-flowing river, you introduce it into the new environment of clean water, and that new environment will have the effect of cleaning it. When a repentant sinner is baptized by the Holy Spirit upon conversion, he is introduced into the new environment of the spiritual realm, which will have eternal effects on him. The type of baptism talked about in the Great Commission passage refers to water baptism which the disciplemakers are directed to perform on those who believe. It relates to the disciplemaking process in two ways:

First, when a person undergoes water baptism, he is openly identifying with the *kingdom* of God. He is unashamedly proclaiming to the world that he is a follower of Jesus Christ. As he is introduced to the environment of the baptismal water, submerged, and brought back up again, he is identifying with the death, burial and resurrection of His Lord. He is telling the world that he has now been introduced into the new environment of the Spirit.

In the early days of the church, this act could spawn anything from cat-calls to murder from the believer's unsaved family and friends—and in many parts of the world this goes on even today. Public water baptism was a high price to pay just so one could say, "I am a disciple of Jesus Christ." This open identification with Christ and His kingdom is one of the first and most crucial conditions Jesus places on a person's right to continue calling himself a disciple (Luke 9:26; Romans 10:9,10). So in this part of His mandate, Jesus is saying, "Make disciples by helping people become openly identified as Mine."

Second, when a person undergoes public water baptism, he is also openly identifying with the *people* of God. He is saying to the world, "I'm throwing in my lot with these people. If push comes to shove, I'm on their side now." And this commitment must run two ways. After water baptism, the newly-identified believer needs the church members to do a lot more than just shake his hand, slap him on the back and say, "Live long and prosper," and then leave him to fend for himself. They now have the responsibility of incorporating him into their local body for the purposes of protection, instruction, and ministry.

So here Jesus is also saying, "Make disciples by helping people become integrated into My body."

Teaching

If a disciple is defined as a "learner," one would logically suppose there is something he should be "taught." We know from our discussion in chapter 2 that the teaching should not end up in storage as mere "head knowledge." Head knowledge alone is "dead knowledge." Rather, it should be *applied* in order to bring about a *changed life.*

I hope you'll notice some very crucial wording in this part of Christ's directive. He didn't say, "Teaching them to *know* all that I commanded you." He made it very clear that it's "teaching them to *observe* all that I commanded you." Our job isn't done when our disciples simply know His commands, regardless of how vast their knowledge might be. We've done what He asked when our disciples are doing His commands.

David Dawson, founder and director of "Equipping the Saints" and a veteran of some thirty years with the Navigators, has summarized this thought in what some of us like to call "Dawson's Law":

> Biblical principle requires application, which results in methodology, which allows for production in the life and reproduction in others. But biblical principle not applied results in activity without productivity, which precludes both production in the life and reproduction in others.

Learning the principles that Jesus taught without setting about to apply them may produce a lot of heat and smoke, but no light. How do you teach someone to observe something? It's primarily a three-stage process.

1. Learn it. First comes the simple transference of information, or what I would call *head knowledge* – but in the good sense. This is the primary use of the Greek word for "teaching" – *didaskontes* (lexical form: *didasko*) which Jesus used in His Great Commission. It has to do with the *intellect.* But it's not just a "here, read this" type of teaching; it's conscientious, accountable, "teach-it-till-it's-learned" type of teaching. According to Dr. Klaus Wegenast, commenting on *didasko,* "What is taught may be knowledge, opinions or facts, but also artistic and technical skills, all of which are to be *systematically* and *thoroughly* acquired by the learner as a result of the *repeated activity* of both teacher and pupil"[2] (emphasis mine). The disciple must come to learn it.

2. Love it. Unfortunately, most teachers stop at stage one — if they even get that far. We must progress to the second stage, which is the gaining of conviction, or what I would call *heart knowledge.* It has to do with the emotion. The teacher has to help the learner come to the point where he personally owns the information he has acquired. The eighteen-or-so inches from head to heart is in fact a looooong way, and if the teacher doesn't do his best to see that the information taught makes that journey, the disciple will never be an observer of the commands of Jesus. The disciple must come to the point of saying, "This isn't just a bunch of theory; this is reality! This is truth! This is life! This is for ME!" The disciple must come to love it.

3. Live it. If true conviction has been developed, it won't stop at loving it. It will move on to the third stage, which is the application to life, or what I would call the *hand knowledge.* It has to do with the volition or will. The trip is a little longer from heart to hand, but if it's truly in the heart, it will eventually get to the hand. The discipler's main job is to help the disciple in the practical out-working of the conviction in the form of actions. The disciple must come to live it.

Through the course of this book, I purpose to give you practical ways to help your disciple come to "learn it, love it and live it." It may seem misty and theoretical to you at this point, but as we press on together, the picture will clear up.

THERE'S THE SCRIPT; WHERE'S THE CAST?

So, in a nutshell, what did Jesus tell us to do with our lives? He said we should make disciples by *going* (taking the initiative to win people to Christ and follow them up), *baptizing* (helping them to be publicly identified with Christ, His kingdom and His people through incorporation into a local church) and *teaching* (helping them learn, love and live His commandments).

That should be enough to keep us busy for the rest of our

lives! But am I the Lone Ranger in this process? Can I sit down in a room with a brand new Christian, follow the above recipe and end up with a mature disciple? Is this a one-man show?

Not on your life! There are other players in this drama too, and it is imperative that you get to know them and what their roles are so you can keep from bumping into each other during the performance. Now that you are familiar with the "Divine Imperative," you'll become acquainted with the other "DI's" — the "Divine Influence," the "Divine Incubator" and the "Divine Instrument" in the next chapter. Onward!

**RECOMMENDED RESOURCES
FOR EVANGELISM TRAINING**

WITNESSING WITHOUT FEAR by Bill Bright. A reader-friendly, step-by-step guide that will help your disciples learn to share their faith with confidence. This helpful book was awarded the Evangelical Christian Publishers Association's "Gold Medallion" as 1988's best book in evangelism and missions. It is suited for both individual and group use, and is endorsed by national Christian leaders including Billy Graham and James Kennedy.

TELL IT OFTEN, TELL IT WELL by Mark McCloskey. A well-reasoned, biblically based, and philosophically sound case for initiative evangelism. The author is Campus Crusade's director of training for the Campus Ministry, and his book has become the text for evangelism and outreach classes in several seminaries.

Both books are available at Christian bookstores,
or from Here's Life Publishers.
(Call 1-800-854-5659; in California call 714-886-7981.)

4
THE PRINCIPAL PLAYERS

You know you're in trouble as an actor when during the intermission you receive a note from the show's producer that says, "I'm in the back row. Wish you were here."

I wonder if God might sometimes have that same sentiment about my contribution to *His* production. I louse up my lines, forget proper characterization, try to upstage everyone else, speak too loudly or too softly, sometimes take liberties with the script . . . it must aggravate Him.

God has it in His mind that the story should unfold in a certain way. I can decide to do it my way and end up sitting in the back row, or I can do it His way and fit gracefully into the whole, enhancing the performance and glorifying the Author. I don't know about you, but I've taken the first option too many times. Fortunately, He always has been gracious enough to give me another chance. And another. But wouldn't it be more productive if I determined to fit into *His* script, rather than trying to alter it to fit my tastes?

If we are convinced that God is directing this show, we would do well to find out how each player fits into the overall production, and then practice our own roles diligently. Let's take a look at the other members of the cast.

THE HOLY SPIRIT:
DIVINE INFLUENCE

Mark Twain once made a statement about the weather that applies to a lot of things, including disciplemaking: "Thunder is good; thunder is impressive; but it is lightning that does the work."[1]

Too often would-be disciplemakers get overly impressed by

47

the wrong things. We see big churches, extensive programs, silver-tongued orators, large congregations, all kinds of hubbub and heat and smoke, and we exclaim, "Surely the Lord is in this place!" There is nothing wrong with any of those things, but we must realize that big ideas have about as much effect on the world as thunder, unless they are energized by the lightning of the Holy Spirit.

The apostle Paul put it this way: "So then, neither the one who plants nor the one who waters is anything, but God who causes the growth" (1 Corinthians 3:7). We may be pretty impressive ministers of the gospel, at least in our own eyes. We may be tenth-generation Christians, Bible college graduates, seminary wiz-kids, and fully trained in all ministry skills by a variety of organizations, but we are of little use for the furtherance of the kingdom of God if we are not plugged into the power and the program of the Holy Spirit. As Stephen Bly, a pastor, author and conference speaker, says, "No matter how self-sufficient we think we have become, only God can bring growth, maturity, and harvest."[2] Dr. Ron Jenson, former president of the International School of Theology, put it well when he said, "We need to be convinced that we are no more able to cause growth than we are able to cause conversion."[3]

Jesus was not exaggerating when He said in John 15:5, "Without Me you can do NOTHING" (emphasis mine, but probably His too!). Oh, we may *try* to do it without Him. We put together our great plans and well-thought-out objectives, recruit the workers, raise the money, build the project, crank out the publicity, call the media, and then pray, "Lord, please bless our efforts, Amen," and can't figure out why in the world the whole operation slides right into the outhouse. We forget that this is *His* operation. *He's* the Master, *we're the workers.* This is *His* world that needs saving, not ours. Let God be God, and you be you!

E. M. Bounds, the great man of prayer from the last century, laments the false ministries of the unanointed:

> Truth unquickened by God's Spirit deadens as much as, or more than, error. It may be the truth without admixture; but without the Spirit its shade and touch are deadly, its truth error, its light darkness . . . The preacher may feel from the

kindling of his own sparks, be eloquent over his own exegesis, earnest in delivering the product of his own brain; the professor may usurp the place and imitate the fire of the apostle; brains and nerves may serve the place and feign the works of God's Spirit, and by these forces the letter may glow and sparkle like an illumined text, but the glow and sparkle will be as barren of life as the field sown with pearls.[4]

It's easy to see the hopelessness of ministry without the energizing of the Holy Spirit by taking a quick look at the lives of the first disciples:

> Never forget the absolute necessity of the Holy Spirit's power. After years of being discipled personally by Jesus, most of the disciples deserted Him at the cross and one betrayed Him. It was Pentecost that made the ultimate difference! Filled with the Holy Spirit, these disciples went out to change the world![5]

As you begin to disciple someone, you may find yourself thinking things like, *What should I do to help this person shape up? He obviously needs me to start this maturation process for him. Now that I'm on the scene, he's really going to start growing! Let's see, the first thing I think I'll do is such-and-such. Then I'll . . . And then I'll . . .*

Meanwhile the Holy Spirit is saying, "Hold on there, friend! You're the new kid on the block! I have been working in this fellow's life since before he was born! I know him inside-out and I've got plans for him! Don't you think you ought to consult with *Me* before you start monkeying around with *My* program?"

We can fly into the Holy Spirit's plans like a sparrow into a jet engine—and get fried in the process—or we can cooperate with Him in the perfect plan He has in mind. God's Spirit says to us, "I'd love to have you on the team I'm putting together to help this child of Mine grow, but I'll not tolerate the pride of a grandstander."

It is vital that when we think about this process of disciplemaking, we see ourselves as a tool in the hand of God. He is far more concerned about and active in the disciple's growth than we can ever imagine. The apostle Paul, one of the greatest disciplemakers of all time, knew precisely who was in charge of the process:

- *1 Corinthians 3:5,6* – What then is Apollos? And what is Paul? Servants through whom you believed, even as the *Lord* gave opportunity to each one. I planted, Apollos watered, but *God* was causing the growth.

- *2 Corinthians 3:18* – But we all, with unveiled face beholding as in a mirror the glory of the Lord, are being transformed into the same image from glory to glory, just as from *the Lord, the Spirit.*

- *Galatians 3:2,3* – This is the only thing I want to find out from you: Did you receive the Spirit by the works of the Law, or by hearing with faith? Are you so foolish? Having begun by the *Spirit,* are you now being perfected by the flesh?

- *Philippians 1:6* – For I am confident of this very thing, that *He* who began a good work in you will perfect it until the day of Christ Jesus.

- *Philippians 2:13* – For it is *God* who is at work in you, both to will and to work for *His* good pleasure.

- *1 Thessalonians 5:23,24* – Now may the *God* of peace *Himself* sanctify you entirely . . . Faithful is *He* who calls you, and *He* also will bring it to pass.

(All emphases above are mine.)

Besides allowing the Holy Spirit to run His show, we would do well to look to His leadership in discipling. It's the *smart* thing to do. Think about the relationship Jesus and Peter had. Being a professional fisherman, Peter probably taught Jesus a lot about fishing.[6] But one day Jesus said to Peter (Luke 5), "Go fish over there."

Peter might have said something like, "Look, Jesus. You're a carpenter. You don't know beans about fishing. This isn't the right time of day for it, and that isn't the right spot for it. Now, sit down and let me handle the fishing around here."

But Peter understood the authority of Jesus, so he let down his net in the spot Jesus directed him to, and hauled in enough fish to repopulate Sea World. Nothing makes it easier to catch your limit than a buddy who can tell the fish where to go!

By the same token, it's easier to be an effective evangelist if you're walking with the one who can tell *people* where to go. It's easier to be an effective disciplemaker if you're walking with the inventor and director of life and growth. All our programs, dedication, zeal and sacrifice aren't worth a truck-load of bait if we aren't in vital union with the one who is in charge.

THE LOCAL CHURCH: DIVINE INCUBATOR

The Bible likens the church to a physical body, and with good reason. Just as each individual cell in our bodies needs a variety of other cells nearby in order to function properly, so each Christian needs a variety of other Christians around him in order to grow and perform all of the functions God has in mind for him. The cells in our bodies know beyond a shadow of a doubt that they desperately need each other, and would never be able to exist without a little help from their friends. It's the same within the body of Christ. Never get the idea that you are the only "blood vessel" that your disciple needs. Who ever heard of a cell having contact with only one other cell? The only time we see *that* condition is when we are looking at a lower form of life, and your disciple certainly does not qualify as that.

It pains me to point it out, but the truth must be known: We all have weaknesses and blind spots. We over-emphasize some things and under-emphasize other things. We are imma-ture in several areas. So let's ask ourselves a question: Do we want to transfer those same deficiencies to our disciples?

That is exactly what will happen if we try to be his one and only "blood vessel." Carbon copies of myself I definitely do not want! Ralph Waldo Emerson said, "Never attempt to make anyone to become like yourself. God knows and you know that one of you is enough."[7]

This is one of the primary reasons Jesus Christ instituted the church. Paul said in Ephesians 4:11-13:

> And He gave some as apostles, and some as prophets, and some as evangelists, and some as pastors and teachers . . .

For what purpose?

> . . . for the equipping of the saints . . .

Equip them to do what?

> . . . for [their] work of service, to [their] building up of the

body of Christ . . .

With what goal in mind?

> . . . until we all attain to the unity of the faith, and of the knowledge of the Son of God, to a mature man, to the measure of the stature which belongs to the fullness of Christ.

The most ideal environment in which disciplemaking can take place is within the context of a local church. There your disciple can have contact with a wide variety of people — including some who have strengths to counteract your weaknesses, gifts where you are giftless, talents where you are a dud, and skills where you are all thumbs. As a disciplemaker, you are responsible to oversee and guide the development of this growing disciple while depending on the Holy Spirit, but when you find yourself skating on thin ice, in the church context you can always yell for someone who knows where the thick ice is.

About now someone might be saying, "But you don't know my church. It's a nice enough place, but the people there don't have the foggiest notion about disciplemaking. Our church is more like a spiritual day-care center than an outfitter for the army of God." I know what you mean. It's a sad state of affairs, but it seems that the great majority of churches in the United States are more concerned about keeping the saints "sitting on the premises" than "standing on the promises." Churches today, by and large, have become great places for Christian education, but not so hot for Christian training. Multnomah School of the Bible president Joe Aldrich points out that most Christians have been educated far beyond their willingness to obey. Many churches today will teach you *what* Jesus commanded, but you're not likely to be taught to *observe* what He commanded. And we can't lay the blame completely on the pastors' doorsteps, either, because more often than not they are dishing out only as much as their congregation is willing to swallow.

So you've got two options: Go to a different church where you will feel confident about steering your disciple to others for effective cross-training, or become a catalyst in your own church to get people tuned in to disciplemaking. That second option is easier said than done, I know, but with the Lord's help it *can* be done if you are willing to go for it.

A word to those of you working within para-church organizations — especially those involved with high school and college students: Many of you have a tendency to plug your disciples into your ministry on campus and exclude the local church. You've got a lot going on — people are witnessing, leading students to the Lord, discipling, growing, fellowshipping, praying, reading the Word. Who needs an institution? But if you neglect to teach your disciples how they can be integrated effectively into a local church ministry, you're making a big mistake.

Through the years I have observed many people who came to a saving faith in Jesus at college, got plugged into a campus movement, had a truly effective ministry, graduated, moved away and bombed out. Why? Because the only context in which they were taught how to prosper spiritually was that of a campus-oriented para-church ministry. They never learned how to minister (or be ministered to) in the context of a local church body — which is more than likely what they would have been involved with the rest of their lives. For this reason, perhaps more than any other, you *must* do your utmost to get these disciples into the ministry of a local church.

THE DISCIPLEMAKER: DIVINE INSTRUMENT

OK! So the Holy Spirit is calling the shots in this process, and the local church is providing an environment conducive to growth. Where do we disciplemakers fit in?

As alluded to earlier, we need to see ourselves primarily as the "earthly instruments" God uses to facilitate the maturing process in His children. There are several different analogies we could use to describe our role, but the best is that of the servant-shepherd overseeing the flock for the owner. While it carries with it the concept of the sheep (the disciple) belonging to someone else, it makes it clear that the shepherd is carrying *some* responsibility as well, and he needs to apply himself conscientiously to the protection and development of his charges. Scripture makes it quite clear that while the Holy Spirit is the disciple's primary influencer, He does it in partnership with the disciplemaker:

- *Acts 20:28* – Be on guard for yourselves and for all the flock, among which the Holy Spirit has made you overseers, to shepherd the church of God which He purchased with His own blood. [God owns the flock, but we oversee it.]

- *1 Corinthians 4:1,2* – Let a man regard us in this manner, as servants of Christ, and stewards of the mysteries of God. In this case, moreover, it is required of stewards that one be found trustworthy. [We are the stewards of great mysteries, but we are answerable to Christ.]

- *Galatians 4:19* – My children, with whom I am again in labor until Christ is formed in you . . . [We labor, but Christ is being formed.]

- *Colossians 1:28,29* – And we proclaim Him, admonishing every man and teaching every man with all wisdom, that we may present every man complete in Christ. And for this purpose also I labor, striving according to His power, which mightily works within me. [We proclaim, admonish, labor and strive, but we do it energized by His power working within us.]

- *2 Timothy 2:1,2* – You therefore, my son, be strong in the grace that is in Christ Jesus. And the things which you have heard from me in the presence of many witnesses, these entrust to faithful men, who will be able to teach others also. [Our desire is that our disciples would follow our examples, but that they do it in the strength of the grace of the Lord.]

This same sentiment is evident even in our classic Great Commission passage, Matthew 28:18-20: "All authority has been given to *Me*, therefore, *you* make disciples . . . and *I'll* be with *you*" (my paraphrase).

The *disciple* also needs a proper perspective of the partnership between his discipler and the Holy Spirit. There is a dual commitment needed on his part, which is seen frequently in those whom Paul discipled:

- *2 Corinthians 8:5* – And this, not as we had expected, but they first gave themselves to the Lord and to us by the will of God.

- *Galatians 4:14* – . . . but you received me as an angel of God, as Christ Jesus Himself.

- *1 Thessalonians 1:6* – You also became imitators of us and of the Lord, having received the word in much tribulation with the joy of the Holy Spirit.

The Three Pillars of Disciplemaking

A three-legged structure is stable. As long as all three legs are functional, it won't easily wobble or tip. When you're trying to get an idea of your role as a disciplemaker, think of it in terms of the Three Pillars of Disciplemaking: *Prayer, Relationship* and *Content.* If you are trying to carry out your shepherding responsibilities while lacking one of these pillars, you're in for a tumble.

Prayer. Ask yourself a simple question: Do you think Jesus was telling the truth when He said what He said in John 15:5, ". . . Without Me you can do nothing"? If you do, this conviction had better be demonstrating itself in your actions. If you are truly interested in seeing that disciple grow, and if you truly believe that it's God who causes the growth, you'll be on your knees often and long interceding for that disciple.

I once led a fellow to Christ who was a real wild man. At the time of his conversion he was living with a girl, and I was at a loss to know how to handle that situation. So many areas of his life needed to change that I was afraid he might alienate himself from me and not go on with the Lord if I confronted him with this issue right off the bat. So I didn't say yay or nay about it; I just began praying that God would work it out.

A few weeks later, the fellow strolled up to me and said, "Hey, Chris! Sue and I went to Las Vegas last weekend!"

Oh great. Now he's into gambling. What in the world is the Lord doing?

"Yeah, we got to thinking that God probably didn't like us living together, so we got married!"

Praise God! Prayer works! The "wild man" continued to grow in Christ and eventually became a youth pastor.

Relationship. There's a saying disciplemakers like to kick around a lot that goes, "Most things of importance are better *caught* than *taught.*" The idea here is that if our disciples aren't observing it in our lives, it's not likely they'll ever absorb what we are trying to teach them. Brian Arensen, a missionary with Africa Inland Mission in Tanzania, further illumined that point when he said, "Christianity is to be lived out, not programmed in."

Too often, a disciplemaker's actions will not match his

words, and his poor, exasperated disciple finally explodes, "I can't hear what you're saying! Your life is talking too loud!" To instruct, "Do as I say, not as I do," simply doesn't cut it.

The growing disciple needs a role model—and my friend, God has elected *you*! I'm not saying we should transgress Emerson's admonition to not make people in our own image. But the disciple needs to be able to see that what you're telling him remains true even when it takes to the shoe leather. Does this make you nervous? I can understand if it does—but it really shouldn't. If we are abiding in Christ and walking in the power of the Holy Spirit, we need never fear that our lives will be a disappointment to our disciples. It's not that we need to set impossible standards for ourselves, thinking we must be living sinless lives before we can become disciplemakers. More than likely, we will blow it from time to time, and it's good for our disciples to see that, too. It lets them know that we put our pants on one leg at a time just like they do, and it teaches them by example how we deal with spiritual defeat.

But we must take our responsibility as role models seriously. Paul did. He didn't hesitate to exhort his disciples to follow his example—not because he was so proud of himself, but because all the while he was conscientiously following the Lord's example.

- *1 Corinthians 11:1*—Be imitators of me, just as I also am of Christ.

- *Philippians 3:17*—Brethren, join in following my example, and observe those who walk according to the pattern you have in us.

- *Philippians 4:9*—The things you have learned and received and heard and seen in me, practice these things; and the God of peace shall be with you.

- *2 Thessalonians 3:9*—Not because we do not have the right to this, but in order to offer ourselves as a model for you, that you might follow our example.

Jesus also recognized the powerful influence relationship-building would have on His disciples. The Scriptures tell us that Jesus chose twelve men to be "with Him" (Mark 3:14). For several years, those twelve were Jesus' constant companions, observing His life in a wide variety of contexts.

If you are interested in providing your disciple with the maximum amount of aid, then you need to relate to him along a wide front. Paul's training of Timothy didn't involve merely book-learning. In 2 Timothy 3:10,11 Paul said that Timothy also followed his "conduct, purpose, faith, patience, love, perseverance, persecutions, sufferings . . . " Talk about a broad spectrum of experiences!

Develop a friend-to-friend *relationship*. Teaching will be involved in the discipling process — a lot of it — but don't let your relationship stop at the teacher-pupil level. Do fun things together, work together, goof off together, travel together, minister together, laugh together, cry together. Let him into your life, your home, your family. Discipling requires that you have a relationship with the total person, not just with his "religious cubbyhole."

Content. But don't stop there. Relationship without *content* is practically worthless. I can hang around a guy from now until doomsday, and he may observe my life inside and out. But unless I say, "I do these things for these reasons . . . and this is the effect they have . . . and here's how you can get started . . . " thereby injecting some *content* into the program, I won't have much effect on that person's life.

It may be true that some things are better caught than taught, but other things must be taught before they can be caught. When Jesus told us we should be "teaching them to observe all that I commanded," He was speaking in educational terms. People need to be educated. Can you imagine a jet pilot saying to a friend, "You've seen me fly this bird plenty of times. Why don't you take 'er up this time?" It may *look* easy — seems like all you have to do is hold the stick, put your feet on the pedals and wiggle them around a little, adjust the thrust, and you're flying! The friend could have caught all that, but there is a lot more to flying that he needs to be taught.

I recently had a conversation with Dr. Earl Radmacher, president of Western Theological Seminary, in which he shared a surprising, yet valid viewpoint. He said, "People say, 'Enough *information* — let's have *application*!' I beg to differ. I think we don't *have* the information. Application can only be as good as

the information. I could administer the American Accredita-
tion of Bible Colleges Test to the members of every church in
this country, and the average score of *any* church would be far
worse than failing." What a sad testimony.

Dr. David P. Bertch, professor of Pastoral Ministries at Tyndale Theological Seminary in Amsterdam, Holland, capsulizes
in a practical way the content that needs to be passed on to our
disciples. He puts it into three vital and inter-linked components:

1. The What To's. These deal with the "Right Things" —
knowledge, understanding, principles, norms, standards, laws,
absolutes. A person can find the what to's in the Scriptures.
They are the non-negotiables of the Christian life, the godly
characteristics and lifestyle that need to be built into God's
children. They answer the question: What does God want me
to do or be?

2. The Why To's. These deal with the "Right Reasons" for
doing the right things — motives, values, presuppositions. Also
found in the Bible, these need to permeate the entire disciplemaking process. They answer the questions: Why should
I do this? What will this accomplish? A growing disciple should
never be expected to do something until he knows why. Skirt-
ing this component is a prime ingredient of cults — don't follow
in their footsteps!

3. The How To's. These deal with the "Right Ways" of doing
the right things for the right reasons — techniques, methods,
procedures, steps. These are not necessarily found in the Bible,
but they must not violate clear biblical teaching. They recognize that "there's more than one way to skin a cat." They are
relative concepts and are often tied to culture, to time constraints, or to the gifts and ministry style of the disciple or the
disciplemaker. They answer the question: How do I do it?

It is crucial that all three of these components be involved
in the disciplemaking process. As Dr. Bertch puts it, "If a person does the right thing in what he thinks is the right way, but
for the wrong reasons, he will eventually end up doing the
wrong thing in the wrong way!"

An example of a *what to* would be: Christians ought to witness. Its corresponding *why to* would be: so that others might be saved. When it comes around to the *how to,* you can take your pick—there is no one-and-only way. You might teach your disciple to utilize the "Bridge Illustration" or you might go for the "Four Spiritual Laws" booklet. Someone else might prefer the "Roman Road," or the "Bridge to Life" tract. The *whats* and *whys* are non-negotiables, while the *hows* are flexible— within reason. (It just wouldn't do to go out witnessing with a shotgun.)

The *what to's* should become the focus of our disciplemak- ing endeavors; that is, our job is complete when the *what to's* are in the life. But the naked actions of a person are worth- less—whether right or wrong—if they are done with the wrong motives. The *why to's* form the motivational basis. We'd rather focus our attentions on these, but since we can't see or measure them, we focus on the *what to's* while continually expressing, modeling, checking and encouraging our disciples in the *why to's.*

The *how to's* form the means to the end. You may actually spend a great deal of time on *how to's* in your disciple's life, so you must be careful not to allow them to become the end rather than the means because that generates problems. This was the main difficulty with the Pharisees in Jesus' day: They had the *hows* nailed, but Jesus called them whitewashed tombs because they were unconcerned about the *whats* and the *whys.*

FITTING THE PLAYERS INTO THE PLAY

In previous chapters we've talked about the right *priority* with regard to disciplemaking, the desired *product,* and the *process,* and in this chapter you have met the *principal players.* Now it's time to get down to the nitty gritty of the *pattern* for growth. The next chapter will help you identify the different stages of growth your disciple will go through and how your role will change. You'll be able to anticipate his needs at each phase, and adjust your approach and your role appropriately.

5
THE PATTERN

I have an astounding daughter named Jessica. She amazes me! She has mastered the art of going to the bathroom all by herself, she speaks in complete sentences, she walks without falling (usually), she brushes her teeth by herself, she executes a pretty decent cartwheel. In fact, she can even read some simple books. Pretty good for a twenty-two-year-old, don't you think?

Hold on a minute. Why am I so excited about an adult being able to perform such childish tasks? You probably think that either Jessica is severely retarded, in which case those really are great accomplishments, or else I'm pretty easy to please.

The dilemma is easily resolved when I tell you I was just kidding—she's only five, and she really can do all those things. We're all breathing a little easier now, aren't we? We expect those kinds of activities from a five-year-old, but if we're talking about a twenty-two-year-old, we're worried.

Why is that? Most of us gauge the growth of our children according to "behavioral evaluation charts" constructed by child development experts. For instance, by six weeks, a baby should be able to hold his head up at a 45-degree angle while lying on his stomach. By six months, he should be able to bear some weight on his legs. By about one, he should be trying to walk. By about two, he should have a pretty good vocabulary, and be able to construct simple sentences. If we aren't seeing our children pass those mileposts, we get nervous.

Those charts are not absolute, but they're helpful. They clue us in to possible problems, enabling us to take measures that we hope will correct them. Plus, they make it easier for us to know how to help our children develop.

Throughout the Bible, parallels are frequently made between physical growth and spiritual growth. In John 3, Jesus said that each person needs to be born both physically and spiritually. Paul called believers who had not grown spiritually "babies" (1 Corinthians 3:1). Peter said new believers should desire God's Word like a new baby desires milk (1 Peter 2:2). John addressed believers according to several categories (1 John 2:12-14). Just as experts have put together behavioral evaluation systems for physical development, so the Bible has given us similar criteria for spiritual development.

By knowing what should characterize a disciple at each level of growth, we get a better idea of how we can help that disciple in his pilgrimage toward maturity. Growth, whether physical or spiritual, is dynamic. Physical needs change, and the needs of a developing Christian change as well as he matures spiritually. Our role as his spiritual parent must therefore change. Our objectives will need to change. Our methods will need to change.

Paul recognized that growing Christians reside on different levels of maturity, and that certain strategies would be appropriate for some levels but not for others:

- *1 Corinthians 3:1-3a* — And I, brethren, could not speak to you as to spiritual men, but as to men of flesh, as to babes in Christ. I gave you milk to drink, not solid food; for you were not yet able to receive it. Indeed, even now you are not yet able, for you are still fleshly.

- *Hebrews 5:12-14* — For though by this time you ought to be teachers, you have need again for some one to teach you the elementary principles of the oracles of God, and you have come to need milk and not solid food. For every one who partakes only of milk is not accustomed to the word of righteousness, for he is a babe. But solid food is for the mature, who because of practice have their senses trained to discern good and evil.

When your two-year-old came howling into the kitchen with a scraped knee, you probably scooped him up in your arms, covered him with kisses, and said things like, "Ooooo, poor baby! Mommy's big boy get an owie? Want mommy kiss it all better?" And it worked great! Try that same therapy when he reaches sixteen, and he'll be mortally insulted.

Likewise, we disciplemakers will need to adjust our tactics, our expectations and the themes of our relationship with our disciple as he grows.

LEVELS OF GROWTH

I mentioned earlier that the apostle John categorized growing Christians into different levels of growth. When you read most of the English translations of 1 John 2:12-14, you'll only see three categories, but the Greek makes a clear distinction between the children of verse 12 (*teknia* or "infants") and the children of verse 13 (*paidia* or "child with respect to age"), giving us four levels. Let's see what we can learn about each.

Baby

I am writing to you, little children [infants], because your sins are forgiven you for His name's sake (1 John 2:12).

The New Testament translates three Greek words into the English "baby": *teknia*[1], *brephos*[2], and *nepios*[3]. As you study the places where these three words appear in Scripture, you can learn a lot about the characteristics of babies — both physical and spiritual — and how we are to relate to them. Several are listed below. They should give you some good ideas about how to relate better to a brand new Christian.

- They are helpless, and need much care and protection (Luke 2:12,16; Acts 7:19).
- They crave nourishment (1 Peter 2:2).
- But they are not yet able to handle meat and solid food (1 Corinthians 3:1-3; Hebrews 5:11-14).
- Their speaking, thinking and reasoning processes are inadequate and must be transformed (1 Corinthians 13:11).
- They are easily deceived (Ephesians 4:14).
- They should receive proper nourishment, both physical (Acts 7:20) and intellectual (Acts 7:21)[4].
- They should be gently cherished[5] by their parents (1 Thessalonians 2:7).
- Even at this age, they should be getting scriptural input

(Timothy did! See 2 Timothy 3:15).

- Their parents are anxious that Christ be formed in them (Galatians 4:19).

- They should be committed to Jesus by their parents (Luke 18:15).

- They have no authority, but are under guardians and managers until they mature (Galatians 4:1,2).

- God reveals special things to them rather than to the (supposedly) wise and intelligent (Matthew 11:25).

- They are innocent with regard to evil (1 Corinthians 14:20).

- Their sins have been forgiven (1 John 2:12).

- God in them is greater than he that is in the world (1 John 4:4).

Child

I have written to you, children, because you know the Father
(1 John 2:13b).

The New Testament translates four Greek words into the English word "child," but only three of them relate to this study: *teknon,*[6] *pais,*[7] and *paidion*[8].

Three facts about the word *pais* should interest you.

First, in addition to "child," this word also can denote "young servant" or "slave,"[9] identifying the spiritual child's role as a servant rather than someone thrust into a position of leadership or authority. After Samuel anointed young David, God assigned the boy to the position of servant. David didn't immediately become some spotlighted evangelical as happens so often these days with great athletes or media stars who become Christians.

Second, *paideuo*, which comes from the same root word as *pias,* is the Greek word for "chasten" or "discipline." As you who have kids know, chastening is a big part of how we relate with our children. They need it! Solomon recommended it highly several times in Proverbs. In the same spirit, we should not feel bad about having to "chasten" those we are discipling who are at the child level. It's tough to do, I know, but the Bible characterizes the spiritual child as helpless, inexperienced and foolish,[10] and Solomon says that the "rod of discipline will remove [foolishness] far from him" (Proverbs 22:15). If we love our spiritual children, we'll let them know in no uncertain terms when they're traveling down the wrong road. They can handle it. As Solomon said, "He will not die" (Proverbs 23:13).

Third, *paideia* (there's that same root again) is the Greek word for "training" or "instruction."[11] Just like our twentieth-century children, the kids in Bible days spent much of their time being trained. This should also characterize the major pursuit of the spiritual child. During this phase, he needs to be "at school," learning the fundamentals of walking with the Lord. He may be accumulating a lot of head knowledge that doesn't seem to be seeping down to the heart and hand, but it will in time. We saw the same phenomenon in ourselves as we grew up, didn't we?

As a fifth grader, I had no respect whatsoever for the rules of good literary style or grammar. I didn't care how important it was to not split infinitives, that we should avoid clichés like the plague, that exaggeration is a billion times worse than just stating the facts, that parenthetical remarks (no matter how relevant) are unnecessary, and that one should never, never, *never* generalize.[12] But nowadays, all those rules are my bread and butter! I've mastered them completely, you can see, and they are thoroughly ingrained in my heart and hand. But it took time to get them there. *Pais*-hood is predominantly a time of learning. The loving and living come along in full force as the person matures.

Here are a few more things the Bible says characterize (or should characterize) the physical child and the relationship between him and his parents. See what parallels you can come up with for the *spiritual* child.

- He is still relatively helpless and in need of his parents' protection (Matthew 2:13-16) and provision (2 Corinthians 12:14).

- They should grow mentally, physically, socially and spiritually (Luke 2:52).

- Jesus used a child to demonstrate the kind of spiritual humility necessary to inherit the kingdom of God (Matthew 18:1-4).

- Children were eager to come to Jesus, who had a soft spot for them as well (Mark 10:13-16).

- A child should obey his parents (Ephesians 6:1).

- He should respect his father and the discipline he dishes out (Hebrews 12:9,10).

- Servanthood is a prime quality he should own[13] (Philippians 2:22).

- He can recognize the majesty of the Lord—openly and unashamedly glorifying Him (Matthew 21:15; 1 John 2:13).

- The child is capable of learning and should be allowed to sit with the adults in heavy teaching sessions (Acts 20:7-12).

- He is sometimes capable of making strategic contributions (John 6:9).

- Yet he is seen as still deficient in spiritual understanding (2 Corinthians 14:20).

- God doesn't take kindly to those who would cause a child to stumble (Matthew 18:6).

Adolescent

*I have written to you, young men, because you are strong,
and the word of God abides in you,
and you have overcome the evil one* (1 John 2:14).

The New Testament uses several words to designate an adolescent, all of which come from the same root word *neos* which means "new, not previously existent, just now appearing, in short: new, young."[14] *Neos* is " . . . most commonly used, chiefly in the comparative, to designate the age-range of youths from twenty to thirty years old . . . but also now and again as a noun to denote an inexperienced person, a novice."[15]

One of the primary characteristics of an adolescent is that he is beginning to take on responsibilities. Adolescents start to take their places as movers and shakers in society—some with good results, and some with not-so-good results. *Neos,* or one of its forms, is used to describe the following people:

- The rich young man who came to Jesus asking how to find eternal life (Matthew 19:16-22);

- The young Saul, before whom Stephen's murderers laid their coats (Acts 7:58);

- The young Gospel-writer Mark (most Bible scholars assume it was Mark), who fled naked during the ruckus when Jesus was betrayed (Mark 14:51,52);

- The young men who carried out Ananias and Sapphira after they had lied to the Holy Spirit (Acts 5:6-10);

- The prodigal son, who demanded his share of his father's estate, and then squandered it in loose living (Luke 15:11-24);

- Paul's nephew, who overheard the plot on Paul's life and persuaded the centurion commander to take special measures to protect Paul (Acts 23:16-22);

- Poor, sleepy Eutychus, who fell out of the rafters while listening to a long exposition by the apostle Paul (Acts 20:9-12);

- Timothy, whom Paul urged to set a good example for his flock despite his youth (1 Tim. 4:12);

- Younger women, whom older women were to teach to love their husbands and children and to be godly wives (Titus 2:4).

In each case, the Scriptures speak of youths who were starting to take on adult roles. In the same sense, we need to help our adolescent-level disciples begin to assume responsibility and authority. Not too much yet, but enough to try out their wings a bit. If we don't start sliding some responsibilities their way, they will not only cease to develop, but they'll probably get frustrated and upset—just as our real-life adolescents have conniption fits whenever they're "treated like a child."

Here are a few other qualities that will be seen in adolescents and some guidance recommended for them:

- They continue to manifest a servant's heart, not above doing "the dirty work" (Luke 22:26; Acts 5:6-10).

- They are urged to maintain humility and proper respect for their elders (1 Peter 5:5,6).

- They are urged to keep their lusts and passions in check (2 Timothy 2:22, Titus 2:4-6).

- They are gaining strength and experiencing spiritual victory (1 John 2:14).

- They are making more decisions on their own (John 21:18).

Adult

I have written to you, fathers, because you know Him who has been from the beginning (1 John 2:14).

There are several clues in the Bible as to what the characteristics of an adult should be.[16] Adulthood is our ultimate goal—not only for our disciples, but also for ourselves. But just like real-life adulthood, when one reaches this level it doesn't mean he stops maturing. It only means he is now qualified to take on certain responsibilities and privileges, many of which will enhance or accelerate his continued growth. Can you imagine a person who says when he reaches the age of twenty-one, "There! I made it! I have hit the pinnacle of maturity, so let me sit here in this rocking chair, and let the world come to me and plumb the depths of my vast wisdom and experience." We'd probably inform that young whippersnapper that, though he is an adult, he still has a lot of learning and growing to do.

There are three reasons to be well-informed about what should characterize an adult Christian. First, if we know what an adult looks like, we'll recognize when our disciple reaches that level, and will be able to relate with him appropriately. Second, we'll be better able to see what our maturing disciple is lacking, and be much more efficient in helping him grow. Third, if we're ignorant of how an adult is supposed to act, it will be virtually impossible for us to act like one, thus splintering our hopes of effectively modeling the Christian life for our disciple's benefit. Let's look at a number of "adult" characteristics:

Grower. A spiritual adult has made his relationship with God his top priority, which results in his own continuing growth. As John described the fathers as knowing "Him who has been from the beginning." Paul also sees an ultimate goal of growth: "Until we all attain to the unity of the faith, and the knowledge of the Son of God, to a mature man, to the measure of the stature which belongs to the fullness of Christ . . . to grow up in all aspects into Him, who is the head, even Christ (Ephesians 4:13,16).

Nurturer and cherisher. A spiritual adult takes care of spiritual babies. One expositor observes that *pater* (father) is "from a root signifying a nourisher, protector, upholder."[17] The very things spiritual babies need the most! What a coincidence! See Isaiah 49:15a; 66:12,13; 1 Thessalonians 2:7,8.

Protector and provider. The Bible shows adults often involved in the business of protecting and providing for children. Adults should perform this role, of course, because the young, to varying degrees, are unable to protect and provide for themselves. Watch a robin for a while. Or a cow. Or a lion. Or even an ant. If those beings assume their roles as protectors and providers so readily, how much more willingly should spiritual adults perform those roles for growing Christians? I'm not talking about carrying this on indefinitely, because all growing things eventually need to protect and provide for themselves. But when they're young, they need us. See Matthew 2:13-16; 2 Corinthians 12:14.

Interceder. Parents in the Bible went to great lengths when it came to interceding for their children (2 Kings 4:18-37; Mark 5:21-23; 9:24; John 4:49). As spiritual adults, we can intercede for our "children" in two ways: in prayer, and in the world. It's already been said how great a priority we should place on praying for our disciples, but in certain situations we also can intercede physically for them. It's all part of getting involved in every area of their lives. If your disciple has expressed anxiety about going to the county courthouse to pay a traffic fine, what a great opportunity to go along. Or if she's been abandoned by her husband, has a nursing child, and is having difficulty getting relief from welfare — go with her and help her figure it out.

Teacher. A spiritual adult teaches younger Christians what they need to know to enjoy a viable relationship with God. This clearly was one of the major jobs of parents in Old Testament times. In those days, the spiritual input for a child was the responsibility of the parents, not the Sunday school teacher, and that holds true for us spiritual parents today. Paul blasted the Christians in Hebrews 5:12 with this indictment: "By now you should be teachers; instead, you're babies! You should be giving, but you're still taking."

Here, the opposite of a baby is a teacher. The opposite of input is output. Input is fine for babies; output is the goal for adults. See also Deuteronomy 4:9; 6:6-9,20-25; 11:18-21; 32:45-47; 1 Chronicles 28:9; Proverbs 4:1-5.

Trainer. A spiritual adult goes beyond mere education of younger Christians. He takes as much interest in his spiritual offspring as a real parent would his children. Paul said, "I do not write these things to shame you, but to admonish you as my beloved children. For if you were to have countless tutors [*paidagogos* = instructors] in Christ, yet you would not have many fathers; for in Christ Jesus I became your father through the gospel" (1 Corinthians 4:14,15). A father's training is deeper and much more from the heart than a tutor's could ever be. See also Ephesians 6:4; 1 Thessalonians 2:10-12; Philemon 10.

Discipline-er. But an adult, just like our earthly fathers and mothers, doesn't hesitate to add some teeth to the training. The Christian church in America today is so full of spiritual "wimps" mainly because it is led by so many wimpy spiritual "parents"—leaders who are unwilling to hold growing Christians accountable, to rebuke them when they sin, to say what needs to be said despite the negative feedback. Spiritual adults discipline their "children" because they love them, not because they're on some kind of demented power trip. See Proverbs 3:12; 13:24; 23:13,14; Hebrews 12:4-13.

Sympathizer. On the other hand, a godly parent, physical or spiritual, isn't a tyrant in his disciplining. He knows the difference between the firm, loving hand of a father, and that of an oppressor or tormentor. Just as God said in 2 Samuel 7:14-16 that He would do with Solomon, both physical and spiritual fathers need to find the balance of love and discipline. See also Psalm 103:13,14; Proverbs 12:18; Luke 15:20; Galatians 4:19; Ephesians 6:4.

Encourager. It seems that with some parents, both physical and spiritual, the only reason they open their mouths is to yell about yet another error their child has committed. Growing Christians need a lot of encouragement. The spiritual adult encourages them *to* do better and encourages them *when* they do better. We all need to be "Home on the Range" disciplemakers—you know, "where seldom is heard a discouraging word." See Deuteronomy 3:28; Proverbs 12:18; 2 Corinthians 1:3-7; 7:4; Ephesians 4:29; 1 Thessalonians 2:11,12; 2 Timothy 2:1; Hebrews 10:25.

Responsible worker. When a person becomes an adult, he takes on a wide variety of adult roles and responsibilities. Though specialists are important in the field of medicine, "spiritual specialists" aren't nearly as useful. The broader our scope of skills and experiences, and the more responsible we are with them, the more valuable we will be to our spiritual family. See Genesis 2:24; Isaiah 22:20-24; Hebrews 5:12a,14.

Manager. Paul said that the spiritual elder "must be one who manages his own household well, keeping his children under control with all dignity (but if a man does not know how to manage his own household, how will he take care of the church of God?)" (1 Timothy 3:4,5). He also must be able to manage himself (Ephesians 5:16). One of the primary factors in your success or failure in disciplemaking will be your ability to *manage your time.* I recently surveyed 160 disciplemakers from all over the world—pastors, missionaries, para-church staffers, educators, laymen and lay women, asking them what the biggest hindrance to their effectiveness was. By far, their number-one answer was: inadequate time management. Take heed!

Advisor. In Genesis 45:8, Joseph, revealing himself to his long-lost brothers, said, "God has made me a father to Pharaoh . . . " By that he meant that he had become one to whom Pharaoh looked for counsel and advice—someone with wisdom. A father is seen as a person of knowledge and authority—the guy with the answers. See also Judges 17:10; 18:19.

Need meeter. One of the primary reasons God created parents was that kids had lots of needs. They had to have someone who loved them enough to want to meet those needs. How many times have you seen a plaque saying, "God couldn't be everywhere at once, so He invented mothers"? Though the theology is off, the sentiment is well-taken. God put within parents a strong desire to look for and provide continually for the needs of their children. The same is true with spiritual adults — they see a ministry of "meeting other people's needs" as the primary reason for their existence. See Matthew 7:9-11; Mark 10:45; 3 John 4.

Server. "Wait a minute! I thought it was the child and the adolescent who had to work on that servant's heart business. When does a person get to be the servee?"

Never.

Jesus made it quite clear that if we want to be the "greatest" (*mizon,* translated "elder" in Romans 9:12), we must be the servant of all (Matthew 20:25-28). Just look around you, and you'll find this to be true. Whenever I am with people who have met personally some of our great Christian leaders such as Billy Graham, Bill and Vonette Bright, Dawson Trotman, Lorne Sanny, Jerry White, or Ralph Winter, inevitably those I am with start swapping stories. It's interesting that, almost without fail, they do not talk about the physical stature, the bearing, the eloquence, the intelligence, or even the holiness in these leaders. Even though they may have spent no more than sixty seconds with the person, it's the humility and servant's heart in the leader that makes the strongest impression. If there is one thing God loves and rewards, it's humility (James 4:6,10; 1 Peter 5:5,6).

Apron-string cutter. A good parent is one who has trained his child to be independent. A selfish parent is one who attempts to keep the child forever bound in the proverbial apron strings. Natural growth involves our child eventually leaving the nest. Knowing that, it would be the kindest thing for us to prepare him for that separation, and even urge them toward it when the time is right.

In the same way, we need to keep our disciple's independence as a long-term objective. Train him to feed himself, dig his own well, make his own decisions. Jesus said His disciples would be greatly rewarded if they left father and mother for His sake. Father and mother can make that decision easy or hard for their child. See also Genesis 2:24; Matthew 10:29; Luke 15:12 (the prodigal son's father knew that his son wasn't ready for independence, but he also knew there was no stopping him; he therefore willingly sent him off to study at the School of Hard Knocks).

CHANGING GROWTH RELATIONSHIPS

In a spiritual sense, we have a tendency to think that the greatest thing we Christians can do is beget babies. Consequently, what we have here in America today is the largest spiritual nursery in history. "Easy-believism" has given people the idea that all God asks of them is to include Jesus in their portfolio, then they can go about their business as if nothing had happened. People gladly accept the eternal life Jesus offers, but they often tell Him to peddle His lifestyle elsewhere.

God wants His children to grow. He's pleased when they do and is not pleased when they don't. He has a time line and plans for each of us. I'm not going to debate how specific those plans are, but He does say, "I plan for you to *grow up!* I want you out of the nursery and into the foxhole! I need soldiers, not bed-wetters. I need finishers, not starters. I need people who can plow straight furrows, and if you're going to keep looking back, you're not fit for My kingdom" (Luke 9:57-62).

Our job, as disciplemakers, is to help spiritual babies grow up. This is not an overnight process and it is not easy. If something is growing, it's changing, and that requires us to change our tactics, too. As Shakespeare said, "Everything that grows holds in perfection but a little moment."[18]

As your disciple grows, your relationship with him will change throughout the process. You will need to adjust the theme of your relationship accordingly. Following are some insights into those adjustments.

THE DISCIPLE'S MAIN NEED

As a BABY: protection, love, basic knowledge. A brand new Christian needs protection from Satan, discouragement, bewilderment, doubts, cults, etc. He also needs to know that he is loved and that he belongs to more than just another social club — he belongs to a genuine *family.* Finally, he needs to get some basic idea as to what this new life with Christ is all about.

As a CHILD: consistent, strong guidance. Now he "goes to school"; more is required of him and a stronger hand is applied. Discipline and accountability are introduced into his life. He needs someone to pay a lot of attention to him, help him along almost every step of the way, and be an example for him. In this context, he begins to get educated — he begins to learn what it means to be a citizen of the kingdom of God (Isaiah 28:9).

As an ADOLESCENT: strength, experience, responsibility. At this stage, he needs a little more breathing room, a little more chance to try, to fail, and then to bounce back on his own. The load needs to be increased to develop his strength; otherwise he'll remain a spiritual Casper Milquetoast the rest of his life. He needs more responsibility in order to gain experience and wisdom and to feel the fulfillment of a job accomplished.

As an ADULT: leadership ability, consistent self-discipline. Now the main thing he needs to do is launch out toward a lifetime of responsibility and reproduction. Most adults jump at this in the physical realm, but in the spiritual realm, many Christians drop back at this level and become professional pew-sitters. The adult disciple needs someone to continue shouting, "Don't stop now! Keep going!" He needs to develop an intense desire for a closer walk with the Lord, ever-deepening commitments to Him, and greater fruit-production. His strongest line of dependence must be upon the Lord rather than on men, yet he must sustain the proper interdependence necessary for effective Christian fellowship.

THE DISCIPLE'S KEY MOTIVATOR

For the BABY: his spiritual vacuum. Babies spend almost every waking minute trying to satisfy what appears to be an insatiable appetite. Similarly, the baby Christian has an almost unquenchable thirst for knowledge about his new relationship with God. He'll read his Bible for hours, go to church every time the doors open, and unabashedly share his new-found faith with his friends. There's a "God-shaped vacuum," as Pascal said, that is finally starting to feel some content. And it feels real good! Help him fill it!

For the CHILD: his discipler. But almost inevitably, there comes a time when the new Christian starts to slow down. As improbable as it sounds, he gets accustomed to life as an eternal being indwelt by the almighty God of the universe, and loses some of his fire. That's why the disciplemaker has to become the key motivator for a while. Just like a schoolboy may do most of his homework "because the teacher said I had to," so the spiritual child may frequently complete his Bible study for no other reason than that he knows you're going to check up on him. But that's all right for now. God's Word doesn't return void (Isaiah 55:10-12).

For the ADOLESCENT: himself. As time goes on, however, and as the disciple maintains the disciplines of the Christian life, a change will begin to take place. The adolescent begins to knuckle down, not because the teacher or the discipler says to, but because he wants to. He's been to the firing line a few times and he did miserably. He doesn't want to go through such failure again, so he prepares for his own sake. He's beginning to experience what a long-term, deep-rooted relationship with Jesus is like, and he wants more of it.

For the ADULT: God and the ministry. As the disciple's relationship with the Lord becomes increasingly dear to him, he finds that his drive to continue growing comes directly from his desire to please his Father, and to hear Him eventually say, "Well done, thou good and faithful servant!" The strange force that causes him to stay up past midnight preparing a Sunday school lesson or praying for one of his spiritual children, is due to a deep sense of responsibility he feels toward the ministry God has entrusted to him and because he loves God.

DISCIPLEMAKER'S ROLE

With the BABY: mother to nourish and cherish. The best thing I can do is spoon-feed my disciple and let him know that

I think he is somebody special, worthy of my rapt attention. Here he needs big doses of love, unconditional acceptance and protection. I also need to help him begin to understand the basic fundamentals of surviving and growing as an exalted creature in a fallen world.

With the CHILD: teacher to equip for service. During this stage, it's necessary to become less lovey-dovey and a little more like a teacher. Just as the schoolteacher needs to get across to his students that there are certain desirable behaviors and certain undesirable behaviors, so the child-discipler needs to start introducing an environment of accountability. I need to help him get a good grasp of the basics of Christian life, a foundation on which he can build his lifetime of fruitful service for our Master.

With the ADOLESCENT: coach to help him develop strength and responsibility. By this time, he's had an abundance of book-learnin', and it's time to let him begin proving himself. I need to make the load a little heavier so he'll be strengthened by it, and I need to give him a little more responsibility. It's time for me to move to the sidelines, and yell, "You know what to do, now get in there and DO IT!" As a good coach, I'll continue to make things a little rough on him, but we both know it's for good reasons — no pain, no gain. I'll take him out of the game if things get too rough, patch up his wounds, show him where he went wrong, and then send him back in again.

With the ADULT: peer to motivate for the long haul. At this level, it's him and me, side by side, facing the foe together. I need to *work* at keeping him going. Paul said in Hebrews 10:24: "And let us consider and give attentive, continuous care to watching over one another, studying how we may stir up (stimulate and incite) to love and helpful deeds and noble activities."[19] There aren't a lot of passive verbs in that verse. This is not the time to relax and let the disciple slip into the Pearly Gate Glide. This is the time to encourage him to shoot it into overdrive and make full use of all he has received!

STAND BY FOR MORE DETAIL

Any "scope and sequence chart" worth its horizontal axis would provide a lot more detail than I've given you here. Do not dismay; that comes later. What I've tried to do in this chapter is give you the big picture of the pattern. After going over the first twelve things one should do with a brand new baby Christian in Section Two, we'll get down to the nuts and bolts of what a growing Christian should look like in each area of his life, at each level of growth. For now, let's keep it general for one more chapter, and look into some of the practical *do's* and *don'ts* of disciplemaking.

6
THE PRECEPTS

Whenever someone we greatly admire gives us a list of *do's* and *don'ts,* we consider it a treasure. I've been involved in disciplemaking for nearly twenty years, but I know there is still much I need to learn. So I went after advice from others who also have been involved in making disciples.

I sent out questionnaires to a large number of disciplemakers all over the world, including laymen and laywomen, denominational missionaries, para-church missionaries, pastors, Christian administrators, Christian educators in both secular and sacred schools — as broad a sampling as I could put together. I asked them seventeen key questions about disciplemaking, and, to my astonishment (and to their credit) 161 people responded. Some took as long as *five hours* to complete their response, demonstrating the depth of their commitment to sharing the wisdom the Lord had entrusted to them.

Three of the questions I asked were:

1. What would you say is the single, most important character quality a disciplemaker can possess?

2. Can you list a few other "high priority" character qualities for a disciplemaker?

3. Could you share one or two important *do's* or *don't's* regarding disciplemaking that you've learned through the years?

The responses I received were pure gold! It would take another book to contain the twenty-eight primary character qualities, the seventy-seven high priority character qualities (some overlap), and the sixty-one *do's* and the twenty-eight *don'ts,* along with the many insightful comments the disciplemakers added. In this chapter we will look at twenty precepts, the *do's* and *don'ts* most frequently mentioned in their responses, integrating the character qualities.

Along with those disciplemakers' comments, I've thrown in a few insights and stories of my own — since I'm the writer and am allowed to. So let's take the rest of this chapter to examine these precepts, to, as Marcus Aurelius advises, "consider the wise, what they shun and what they cleave to."[1]

Precept 1. Develop a Heart for God

One of the most important pursuits of the disciplemaker has nothing to do with his disciple. It has to do with his own inner life — developing a heart to know and love God. Jesus put it this way in Matthew 22:37,38: "You shall love the Lord your God with all your heart, and with all your soul, and with all your mind. This is the great and foremost commandment." Of the total of 161 survey responses, this was mentioned forty-seven times as one of the most crucial character qualities for the disciplemaker to develop. Casey Bartels, staff member with the Athletes in Action wrestling team, noted: "A growing love relationship with the living God is vital. When all of our self-effort and external obedience grinds to a halt, the thing that keeps us going is a personal relationship with God."

No matter what kind of ministry you want to get involved in, it should be the result not of over*work*, but of over*flow* — the overflowing life, vigor and power of Christ dwelling within us. As Steve Mousetis, an associate staff member with the Athletes in Action track team, wrote: "Spend a lot of time with the Lord. Our hearts need to beat with His, and our burdens should be His. When that's true of us, our disciples are more likely to 'catch fire,' because *we'll* be aflame." Jesus instructed us in John 15:5-7 to "abide in Me." The Greek word for abide is *meno* which means "to be in close and settled union."[2] I like to think of it as "to remain constant and consistent in relationship." Jesus gave us a picture of what it means to abide in Him when He said He was the vine and we were the branches. If we branches stay connected to the vine, we'll produce fruit — and fruit is what disciplemaking is all about, right?

Whenever the flow is interrupted between a tree and one of

its branches, the first thing the branch stops producing is fruit. Next to go is any new growth. Then it loses its already-existing leaves, and finally the branch itself withers and dies. Can you think of the human, spiritual parallels of each of those stages of death? If you determine to produce fruit, and stay out of the burn pile, you will take *whatever* steps are necessary to keep a constant and consistent relationship with God. Your relationship with Him must be your number-one priority (Matthew 6:33). Without Him, *you can do NOTHING!*

Precept 2. Develop a Heart for Your Disciple

After Jesus related the greatest commandment (Matthew 22:37,38), He moved on to the next greatest commandment: "And the second is like it, 'You shall love your neighbor as yourself' " (verse 39). Not surprisingly, the disciplemakers I surveyed agreed with the emphasis Jesus placed on love, mentioning this character quality far more than any other. That's fairly significant, wouldn't you say? There's a big difference between looking at your disciple as a project or a ministry and loving him for the beloved child of God he is. Take a look at some of these comments:

Geoff Gorsuch (of The Navigators in Strasbourg, France): "Psychiatrists across the board seem to agree that the best results happen when the psychiatrist himself 'takes a risk' with the patient. That is, when he steps down from his aloof, cool professionalism, and becomes involved! Genuine love is a risk. Can we love freely? On whose terms? For what ends? Agape love is unconditional. One gives! Period!"

Yayoi Ikeda (Campus Crusade for Christ, Tokyo): "A new believer grows in the atmosphere of love. He may forget all the facts he learns, but he will never forget the memories in which he was loved by his discipler."

Ed Lee (Child Evangelism Fellowship, Southern California Director): "Love sees beyond present behavior and circumstances and overlooks wrongs. It is patient and longsuffering. It breaks down barriers. It provides stimulation and encouragement. It does not give up."

Steve Morgan (Regional Coordinator, Athletes in Action):

"Everything else I do as a discipler should be a result of my love, compassion and concern for the disciple. If I love, I'll be faithful and encouraging and exhortative and corrective. I'll be obedient to God's Word and loyal to my disciple."

John Newland (Maintenance Supervisor, Navigators Headquarters): "Love causes a man to give of himself to another (John 15:13). Without love the gifts of the Spirit are nothing (1 Corinthians 13:1-3). By love I see a man's potential (2 Corinthians 5:14-16)."

Lloyd Peckham (Wycliffe Linguist in Irian Jaya): "Love is the mark of a disciple (John 13:34,35). Boiling 1 Corinthians 13 down into one main character quality, the result would probably be 'consistent attention to another's interests' (Philippians 2:4,20)."

Richard Ruhl (Evangelical Presbyterian Church Assistant Pastor, Colorado Springs): "Compassion is the embodiment of the saving gospel and the Christian life response all rolled into one!"

Beryl Stannard (Navigators Women's Staff Counselor and Trainer, England): "Love will find a way to get through, to stick with another, to build another up (1 Corinthians 8:1), to help another succeed. Love is 'caught' and therefore will be passed on."

Bob Vidano (The Navigators, Cyprus): "As I love God and people, I will seek *their* best at *my* expense (John 12:24)."

The kind of love you will need for your disciple is the kind that is talked about in 1 Corinthians 13—*agape* love. Lorne Sanny, while he was president of the Navigators, shared this definition of *agape* love: "an unselfish concern for another that freely accepts another and seeks his good." You'll notice it's totally "other-centered." The only way to exhibit this kind of love for another is through the power of the Holy Spirit. You can't conjure this up or grit your teeth and squeeze it out. It's part of the fruit of the Spirit (Galatians 5:22). So as you hit your knees each day to pray for your disciple, be sure to spend some time praying for yourself, asking God to help you love your disciple with pure *agape* love, the way Jesus does.

Many disciplemakers also pointed out that it's not enough merely to *have* love for your disciple, you must also *communicate* and *demonstrate* that love. Psychiatrists tell us that one of the greatest needs people have is to be loved. Let your disciple *know* that he is loved — through your words and your actions.

Precept 3. Live a Godly Life

This would be the natural outflow of Precept 1 listed a few pages back, "Develop a heart for God." Jesus said that if we love Him, we will obey Him (John 14:15,21,23). But don't get the idea that just being a Christian is evidence that you love Jesus and that you therefore will automatically be obedient to Him in every respect. Obedience *starts* with a mindset, by it comes down to *actions* in the end. Obedience is saying yes to God and no to the world, the flesh and the devil. Obedience is making right choices even when they're tough.

This precept is important for several reasons — let's look closely at two:

First, *disobedience short-circuits the plan and power of God,* both of which we need desperately as disciplemakers. I don't think most of us have even begun to understand how big a factor personal purity is in the fruitfulness of our ministries. Recall the passage in Joshua 7 where God had just given Joshua and the army of Israel a tremendous victory in the conquest of Jericho, and clearly instructed them to take no spoil whatsoever. A man named Achan said, "Well, just a little bit of disobedience won't hurt," and he snuck out of Jericho with a coat, some coins and a wedge of gold. Because of this, God saw to it that Joshua's entire operation — the *main thing* he was doing on earth — ground to a screeching halt. He'll have the same attitude toward our disobedience.

In 1 Samuel 15, Saul, the king of Israel, was instructed to go out and "utterly destroy" the Amalekites and to not spare even the livestock. After the battle, he came sauntering up to the prophet Samuel with, "Praise the Lord, Brother! I've done everything God told me to!"

Samuel cocked his head to the side and listened. "Funny

thing, Saul. I seem to hear sheep and oxen. What do you make of it?"

Saul answered, "Well, we did spare a *few* of them . . . but only the best ones—for sacrifices!"

Samuel replied, proclaiming the judgment of God, "To *obey* is better than sacrifice . . . Because you have rejected the instruction of the Lord, He has rejected you from being king."

Why should God have a different attitude toward us? If we want to work for God, we must abide by the terms of our contract. He is a God of love, but He is also a God of justice.

Remember Samson in Judges 14-16? He was a man mighty in every way you can imagine, one of the most Spirit-filled people of his time. But he had one weakness in his armor: women. Satan worked on that weakness until even the mighty Samson was finally destroyed. He's looking for our weakness, too. But he'll look in vain if we remain obedient to the Lord.

We can cite instance after instance, in both the Bible and the here-and-now, where disobedience deprived a man or a woman of the plan and power of God. We here in the twentieth century have a terrifically warped sense of sin. Often, the main criteria we use to decide whether we will sin is, "How likely is it that I'll be discovered?" We tend to classify sins into two categories: big and little. Of course, we would never think of sinning the big sins like murder, armed robbery, or rape. After all, we're Christians. But most have little hesitancy sinning the little sins like lust, envy, materialism, gossiping and the like.

Let me clue you in to something: Little sins grieve God, quench the Spirit, hamper your ministry and interrupt your life-line to Him just as readily as big ones do. On top of that, little sins are like lion cubs—they don't stay little and cute for long. You can make pets of them, but they eventually grow up, turn on you, and devour you. Solomon said, "Dead flies will cause even a bottle of perfume to stink! Yes, a small mistake can outweigh much wisdom and honor" (Ecclesiastes 10:1, Living Bible). Get rid of the flies—they'll spoil *everything*.

A second reason we should live godly lives is, *it is vital that we set a good example for our disciples.* As Dave Hannah, founder and director of Athletes in Action, wrote: "You simply cannot take people beyond where you are spiritually. We must walk with God in order to model and impart His truths."

Mary Ann Lurvey, former Navigator associate and Child Evangelism Fellowship staffer adds: "How can we truly impart to another a way of life unless we are following in that way ourselves? Christ came not only to teach us about the Father, but also to show us the Father."

Paul had no hesitation in instructing the Philippians: "The things you have learned and received and heard and seen in me, practice these things; and the God of peace will be with you" (Philippians 4:9). How could he set himself up as an example to people? Easy — he simply walked his talk. There was no element of pride in his statement. He followed Christ, and as he followed Christ, he knew that his disciples were in no danger when they followed him.

It's important to realize that teaching by example was central to Christ's strategy of disciplemaking. As Eddie Broussard, a Navigator representative in Memphis, wrote: "He chose twelve to be *with Him*. He wanted to impact their lives by example, and not by formal teaching only. He taught them to obey by showing them. He built faith in them by the way He lived while they looked on. Faith is more 'caught' than taught! It cannot be caught without the kind of interaction that life-on-life exposure provides."

But so many people will say, "Well, now, I don't want people following my example; I'd rather they follow Christ's example." I'd prefer that, too. The problem is, your disciples won't. At least, not in their early stages. The concept of "following Christ" is too abstract for them. They are interested in how a real flesh-and-blood Christian looks, acts and reacts, and as their spiritual parent, you're elected. As American Baptist chaplain Mark Bartel wrote: "They want to hear how my spiritual life functions, what I do, what works for me, my fears and hopes. That fleshes it out for them and encourages them that it can be done, or that they aren't the only ones who struggle."

Ross Gunn, youth pastor at Freemont (California) Community Church adds: "If they don't see it in my life, they won't believe it's really possible to live it."

Just as a real-life child looks up to and imitates his parents, so your disciple will copy you. He'll accept a great deal of what you accept and he'll leave out much of what you leave out. The question is not whether you should be an example to him — it's whether you will be a good example or a bad one. You'll be making a significant impression on your disciple either way.

In His "high-priestly prayer," Jesus gave us a tremendous amount of leading on this issue when He said, "And for their sakes [His disciples] I sanctify Myself, that they themselves also may be sanctified in truth" (John 17:19).

Live a sanctified life for the sake of your disciples! Set your standards higher than you might normally set them — for their sakes. For instance, you may feel that there is no problem with drinking wine, and for decades you have easily controlled your alcoholic intake. But one day your disciple may see you raising a glass, and from that he concludes that drinking is totally acceptable. After all, if such a spiritual person as you drinks, it must be OK. So he goes to the cocktail parties, keggers, and bars drinking with no thought of the consequences, and before long finds himself controlled by it, heading for alcoholism. Apparently he couldn't control it as easily as you. It would be better — for his sake — if you sanctified yourself, set yourself apart as holy. Instead of using your freedom in Christ as an opportunity for your own gratification, use it to help your disciple (Galatians 5:13). Instead of seeing how close you can get to the line, why not see how far you can get from it?

You'll never be able to say to your disciple, "Do as I say, not as I do." The Pharisees played that game, and Jesus publicly and soundly condemned them: "The scribes and the Pharisees have seated themselves in the chair of Moses; therefore all that they tell you, do and observe, but do not do according to their deeds; for they say things, and do not do them" (Matthew 23:2,3). As Ron Magnus, area supervisor for the Navigators Military Ministry so lithely put it: "Your walk talks and your talk talks, but your walk talks louder than your talk talks."

Precept 4. Be a Friend

This would be the natural outflow of Precept 2 above, "Develop a heart for your disciple." This and Precept 5 tied as the most frequently mentioned *do* among the responding disciplemakers. I like how college pastor Mark Bartel went so far as to define disciplemaking in terms of this precept: "Disciplemaking is basically friendship with a vision."

At the core of this precept is an admonishment to take the old "teacher/pupil, master/slave, guru/guree" relationship and give it the boot. People need friends, not babysitters. Have fun with each other! Brian Arensen, a pastor trainer with Africa Inland Mission in Tanzania observed: "Who wants to follow the example of a dill-pickled saint?" Cultivate a genuine relationship, not a "professional" one. As mentioned before, your disciple isn't a project, he's a person!

Don't get stuck in the same old grind of meeting each Tuesday at 7 A.M. for breakfast and Bible study. What a rut! A rut, by the way, has been defined as a grave with the ends kicked out. If you want to keep your discipling relationship lively, do a wide variety of things together: attend some sporting events together; go fishing together; take vacations together; fix a car together; minister together; plant a garden together; eat together; laugh together; cry together. Disciplemaking entails developing the total person, not just passing on Bible knowledge. So we must get involved in all aspects of our disciple's life. It's one thing to model Christlikeness when sitting across the dinner table from a guy and you've had two hours to prepare and you're filled with the Spirit. It's quite a different matter when you're out in the woods together; your truck is stuck in the mud up to its axles; it's getting cold and dark and you can hear wolves howling in the distance! You couldn't build a better spiritual incubator!

Remember that a real relationship is two-way. Your disciple is going to learn a lot from you, but you can learn a lot from him as well. Let him know that! Tell him you need someone like him to keep you in line, to pray for you, to encourage you, to teach you.

Denny Repko, a Navigator representative in Pasadena, California, exhorts us: "Make sure it is *not one way!* You must be willing to learn from your disciple and to communicate that your feet are clay also." By doing this, we not only become true friends with our disciples, but we also help our disciples eventually get the idea that they need to shift their focus from us to Jesus. Not accomplishing this, Repko goes on to say, "could be the most serious mistake disciplemakers have made through the years."

Precept 5. Meet Your Disciple's Needs Individually

See each disciple as unique. Disciplemaking is no assembly-line process where mature Christians are cranked out like cars. As Navigator mid-east director Bob Vidano wrote: "Just because God has used you to help disciple a person one way one time, don't necessarily think you will do it with another the same way." Each time God is done making a person, He breaks the mold, and then strictly admonishes us not to try jamming any of His creations back into any other molds (see Romans 12:2, Phillips translation[3]). There are two molds that disciplemakers inadvertently (or advertently) try to make their disciples squeeze into from time to time: themselves or a "program."

Kenneth Watters was instrumental in the early development of two of the most influential and vital ministries of this century: The Navigators and Wycliffe Bible Translators. The number-one *don't* that he listed on his survey was simply: "Don't make a clone." There is no way we will be able to prevent our disciples from imitating us in a lot of ways (and because of that we need to be good examples) but there is only one "image" that they should be fashioned after, and that's God. We do not want our disciples singing that old Frank Sinatra song to us with a little twist, "I Gotta Be You!"

Sam Talbert, associate pastor at Calvary Church of Santa Ana, California, agrees: "Don't assume that your disciple will be like you when he is finished. He is an individual who must grow into what God wants him to be. When he is like me, he may only be half done!"

Don't think a person gets discipled by simply running him

through a set program, either. Programs can be helpful, but if you think the program can do it all, you're in for a big disappointment. Omaha Navigator representative Charlie Johnston wrote: "Stick with the regimented program and you'll develop graduates of a program. Meet the felt needs with scriptural truth in the context of a genuine relationship and you'll develop a friend and colaborer in the gospel for life."

Precept 6. Realize That God Is in Charge

The disciple is not "your baby." He's not even "your disciple," as I mentioned in the Introduction. He is a disciple of Jesus Christ. You are merely the tool Jesus uses to facilitate growth. You and I are not great reservoirs of spiritual knowledge, truth and ability. God is! We are the conduits through which He may flow. It's true that we control the volume of God's life-giving waters flowing through us (take a good, long look at 2 Timothy 2:19-21), but in the final analysis, we are only responsible to be leakless conduits.

This should be good news to a lot of people! It's not up to you! You are not responsible for the disciple's growth! In 1 Corinthians 3:7 we see that we are responsible to plant and to water, but God causes the growth! Jim Watters, a Wycliffe linguist in Mexico, mentioned the importance of "a mindset that is focused on God as the most important 'other' in his life. Without this focus, the 'successes' in disciplemaking can lead to pride and the 'failures' to overwhelming discouragement."

Your attitude should be, "Lord, I'm Your channel . . . I'm Your tool . . . I'm your slave. You are far more intelligent, far more concerned, far more involved in this disciple's growth than I could ever imagine. What do You want to do in his life?" When we try to "play God," the critics will boo every time.

Pastor Loren Fischer of the Milwaukie (Oregon) First Baptist Church wrote: "Don't eliminate or concoct divine struggle. Just *be there* for the disciple!"

God is doing incredible, magnificent things in the disciple's life. Be there. Plug into His plans. The Holy Spirit is setting the pace of this race, and the perceptive disciplemaker will have plenty to concentrate on just to keep up!

Precept 7. Pray for Your Disciple

In his contribution to the *do's* and *don'ts*, Southern California Navigator representative Fred Wevodau wrote only three *do's*: "Pray, pray, pray!" If you truly believe Precept 6 above, if you truly believe that "God causes the growth," if you truly believe that "without Me you can do nothing," then you'll be in prayer for your disciple early, often, long and late. Write his name on the flyleaf of your Bible. Write it on the wall right in front of where you pray every day. Tape it to the mirror in your bathroom. Better yet, tape it to the inside of your eyeglasses.

E. M. Bounds has a classic quote on this subject:

> What the Church needs today is not more machinery or better, not new organizations or more and novel methods, but men whom the Holy Ghost can use—men of prayer, men mighty in prayer. The Holy Ghost does not flow through methods, but through men. He does not come on machinery, but on men. He does not anoint plans, but men—men of prayer.[4]

As Hudson Taylor wrote during the years he was preparing to answer God's call to go to China: "How important to learn, before leaving England, to move man, through God, by prayer alone."[5]

Precept 8. Be Patient

It takes time to produce quality. God can whip out a squash in two months, but He takes about a thousand years to produce a decent sequoia. He'll also take His time producing a mature disciple. Cooperate with Him in this. Don't get uptight if your disciple isn't growing as fast as you'd like. Can you imagine a farmer planting wheat, and getting upset a day later because his crop wasn't ready?

Reverend Harvey Cutting, pastor of the Congregational Church of the Valley in Sun Lakes, Arizona, wrote: "Be patient! People being what they are—fragile, vacillating, carnal, lazy, lustful, greedy, and proud—they'll often disappoint you, even break your heart! Patience will recognize the work is God's, and He's just not through with the individual yet!"

William Pencille, professor and pastor with South American Mission adds: "There is just no way to 'instant maturity.' Real maturity will be built by God in His way and time, not by my program."

Precept 9. Be Persistent

Being patient doesn't mean you sit back and do nothing, however. You need to take the initiative continually with the disciple, acting as a catalyst for his faith and commitment. Especially in the early days of a new Christian's life, there's a war going on for his heart. Satan throws everything he can at him (and you) to keep that baby Christian from committing himself too deeply to Christ, while the Holy Spirit fights to seal his switch from Satan's side to ours. You need to be on God's side — actively, tirelessly, tenaciously.

When I became a Christian, I was a freshman in college, and wasn't real interested in getting involved with what I figured were "religious fanatics." I liked Jesus, but wasn't too sure about the Christians. Fortunately, Dick Krieder, the guy who led me to faith in Christ, wouldn't leave me alone; he was constantly inviting me to Christian functions.

The night I finally caved in was a classic in discipling tenacity! He came down to the dorm cafeteria and invited me to go with him and a few of the guys to see a Billy Graham movie in the next town. I said I didn't think I could make it because I had to finish dinner. He said he'd wait. I said I had a bunch of homework to do. He asked what it was precisely that I had to do that night. I told him, and he sat down and reworked my week's schedule, totally clearing out that evening. I told him that the track coach wanted us in bed by 10 P.M. He expressed amazement as to why I had never held to that curfew before. I told him I didn't have any money. He plopped a five-dollar bill down on the table.

I was licked. But it was sweet surrender, because that night turned out to be a major turning point in my life regarding my commitment to Christ.

Precept 10. Don't Push Too Hard

This is the other side of the coin for Precept 9. Dick pushed me pretty hard, but it worked in this case because he was also standing right on top of Precepts 6 and 7. God was leading him to keep the heat turned up on me.

Sometimes, though, when we're not listening too closely to the Spirit, we'll push beyond where we should, and problems are sure to result. Ken Watters from Wycliffe: "The discipler is not to push but to help steer." You've got to remain flexible with your disciple. Be willing to back off sometimes if he's not responding.

How hard can we push? That depends on the disciple's level of commitment. It's vitally important that you have a clear understanding with your disciple as to what your relationship is. If he expects you to hold him accountable, and there has been clear communication between you about it, push away! But if there is confusion about your relationship, and you start pushing when he's not ready, your friendship could be knocked for a loop.

Precept 11. Involve Your Disciple in All Three Group Dynamics

Those would be (1) *one-to-one*, (2) *small-group* and (3) *large-group*. There really isn't a single "best" environment that will take in the whole of disciplemaking. Certain dynamics will meet certain needs better than others, so we must be sure to include them all. Jesus provides the best example for this. Take a look at Matthew 14 to see Him discipling in the context of the large group (verses 13-21), the small group (verses 22-27), and individually (verses 28-33).

The *one-to-one* dynamic will provide intimacy, where the disciple and I can get eyeball to eyeball on the individualized, personal, nitty-gritty issues that affect his life. As mentioned in chapter 4, there's nothing like the one-to-one tutoring/mentoring/apprenticing relationship to bring about accelerated growth rates.

The *small-group* dynamic provides camaraderie, where the disciple can get into some give and take with people besides you. He gets to see that you aren't the only one who thinks as you do. Cross-training occurs. He gets to be a "giver" instead of primarily a "taker." He rubs elbows with peers, encouraging and being encouraged.

The *large-group* dynamic provides vision and momentum. He sees himself as part of an exciting, concerted movement. There's something about large group enthusiasm that's contagious. Often in these contexts our disciple's vision is lifted far beyond his little hamlet to the fields of the world, and a deep, lifetime commitment is made.

Precept 12. Excel in Observation, Discernment, Critique

If one of the primary roles of a disciplemaker is to be a need-meeter, he'd better be able to discern what the needs are. Navigator mid-east director Bob Vidano: "To disciple a person, you must *know* him. To know him you must be observant."

One of the first steps toward doing this is to become a *listener*. Deanna Suder, wives coordinator for the Athletes in Action wrestling team wrote: "Sometimes we're so anxious to get through *our* agenda that we miss the real needs of those we're working with."

Precept 13. Be a Humble Servant to Your Disciple

Bob Sparks, with Church Discipleship Ministries in Nairobi, Kenya, made a thought-provoking observation: "Humility is most important because the very title 'disciplemaker' seems to lead many to feel that somehow they are a special brand of 'Green Beret' Christian, indispensable to the rest of the body. It is so easy for subtle pride and arrogance to slip in and this is so offensive to the Lord. As Thomas à Kempis said, 'What good does it do to speak learnedly about the Trinity if, lacking humility, you displease the Trinity?' "

The reason you are involved in disciplemaking in the first place is that you want to be used by God to further His kingdom, right? Jesus made it clear that if you want to be great or greatly used by God, you must become a servant (Matthew 20:25-28).

Your disciple wasn't put on this earth to enhance *your* ministry; rather, *you* were put here to enhance *his!* That's what disciplemaking is all about. As Vangie Hedstrom, Navigator Women's representative in Richmond, Virginia, wrote: "In servanthood we see love, humility and sensitivity. These are what comprise genuine caring for another individual."

Precept 14. Be Open and Honest

It's hard to find men and women of complete integrity these days. But if you'll commit yourself to it, you can expect significant help from God and you'll have a profound effect on your disciple. Don't put on a phoney front. Be honest, vulnerable and real. Share your hurts, defeats, limitations and fears with your disciple. Christianity isn't a crutch — it's a whole hospital! We all need some patching up, and if you try to act like you don't, it will prove to be a real enigma and frustration to your disciple when he sees himself getting shot up all the time. Let him know that you bleed too. Let him see how you deal with failure. Help him understand that we don't live in Disneyland, and that sometimes things get pretty tough, even for disciplemakers. But we learn to pick up the pieces, dust ourselves off and carry on.

Steve Highfill, pastor of the Cypress (California) Evangelical Free Church wrote: "My people will grow more by watching my response to my own mistakes and shortcomings than they will by a charade that suggests I never fail and they shouldn't either."

However, you can take this too far. Michael Shaffer, night manager of the Marriott Orlando World Center, calls for "reasonable transparency." You don't have to phone your disciple every time you sin to give him the blow-by-blow description. You want to share your trials, but you don't want to focus on them.

Make it clear from the outset that you can't perform magic. The fact that you are meeting with him doesn't guarantee he is now on the fast track to sinless perfection. You can help him, and God will enable him, but it ultimately comes down to his desire to grow, his desire to hang in there, his desire to obey God, his desire to make the right choices. His failure to pan out will not be on your shoulders!

Precept 15. Hold Your Disciple Accountable

People will do what you *inspect*, not necessarily what you

expect. As mentioned in chapter 1, humans require account-ability and discipline to achieve important goals. If an athlete didn't have a coach holding him accountable, he'd never do the work required to make him a champion. If you and your disciple agree that you are both going to memorize two verses of Scripture a week, follow through with it! Check up on him every week. If you require members of your Bible study group to have their study done before the meeting, don't allow those who haven't completed it to participate in the discussion. It's part and parcel of living a disciplined Christian life. Frequently disciplemaker-control is the kick-starter to self-control, a fruit of the Spirit.

When you see sin in your disciple's life, as tough as it is to do, you must confront it. As Navigator representative Richard Taylor of Cockeysville, Maryland, wrote, "Be a confronter. While there is cost or pain with it, there is more cost or pain without it. Pay now or pay later."

You do a person a tremendous disservice if you refrain from pointing out an embarrassing stain on his shirt when the stain is caused by a slit artery. Solomon said:

> He who says to the wicked, "You are righteous,"
> Peoples will curse him, nations will abhor him;
> But to those who rebuke the wicked will be delight,
> And a good blessing will come upon them.
>
> (Proverbs 24:24,25)

I don't know about you, but I've got enough problems without nations abhorring me on top of it all, so I'll let my disciple know when he's off. If we reprove a wise man (and we'll assume our disciples are wise), he'll love us for it (Proverbs 9:8).

But a word of caution: Do it because you love, not because you like to cut. Proverbs 12:18 says: "There is one who speaks rashly like the thrusts of a sword, but the tongue of the wise brings healing." What is your motive, cutting or healing? Decapitation or surgery? We've been called to love, not to judge. If you can't tell the difference between a loving rebuke and judgmental jab, better not do either for now.

Precept 16. Be Encouraging

Confrontation should be only an occasional island on a sea of encouragement. Affirm your disciple's personal worth whenever you get the chance. Catch him doing something right. Help him win at what he's doing. As Dale Harlan of Sudan Interior Mission in Ethiopia wrote: "Communicate a high estimation of what your disciple is able to become. The 'Pygmalion Principle' is that people will rise to our expectations. If people think they are able to do something, then they are apt to be successful in achieving the goal." So don't focus on your disciple's weaknesses—be sure you're building up his strengths as well.

Precept 17. Don't Try to "Back-stroke" Disciplemaking

Many people treat disciplemaking as if it were a hobby—something they can pick up every now and then if they feel like it. It's one of the few tasks around that will have eternal results, and yet we think, "Oh, no! I'll leave that for the theologians. I could never be good at that! Where would I find the time anyway?" So people either avoid it completely, or they dabble at disciplemaking to ease their consciences.

I do not hesitate to say that being a disciplemaker requires commitment.

- *Acts 20:31:* Therefore be on the alert, remembering that night and day for a period of three years I did not cease to admonish each one with tears.

- *Colossians 1:28,29:* And we proclaim Him, admonishing every man and teaching every man with all wisdom, that we may present every man complete in Christ. And for this purpose also I labor, striving according to His power, which mightily works within me.

Frankly, the most formidable hurdle to overcome is the time problem. Deep down we all really want to become good disciplemakers, but we don't know where to find the time for it. As mentioned in chapter 5, an overwhelming number of the disciplemakers responding to the survey acknowledged inadequate time management as the biggest hindrance to their disciplemaking ministries. So part and parcel of following this precept will be: Learn to manage your time effectively!

Precept 18. Don't Waste Your Time With the Uncommitted

When you're working with a baby Christian (before he's decided whether he will commit his life whole-heartedly to Christ), you need to be patient and persevering regardless of the commitment level. But there comes a time when, as church analyst Jay Carty says, "You've got to say, 'Be wheat or be chaff. Either paint or get off the ladder; cook or get out of the kitchen. Get serious or get out of my life.' "

This may sound harsh, but it has to be done. The chaff will do nothing but drain you physically, emotionally and spiritually. You only have so many hours in the day, and so many days in your life; invest them wisely. Paul admonished Timothy to commit his life "to faithful men, who will be able to teach others also" (2 Timothy 2:2).

As Yutaka Ikeda, associate pastor of Suita Bible Gospel Church in Tokyo, Japan, observed: "Be careful whom you select to be your disciple. Christ never chased after his disciples — they followed Him."

Precept 19. Do Your Paperwork!

It may seem like a small thing to you, but if you don't keep good records, it's hard to keep track of where your disciple has been, what you're doing with him and where he's going. And if you're working with more than one disciple at a time, it's quite difficult to keep them separated in your mind! Paperwork adds direction and accountability to your discipling relationship. Set up a notebook with a section for each person you're working with. In each section have a *Bio* sheet with pertinent, personal information, an *Objectives* sheet for the training objectives and prayer requests you and the Holy Spirit work out for this disciple, and a *Diary,* for recording (1) what you plan to cover at each meeting, and (2) what you actually cover. As you read back over your entries, you will be amazed at how easy it is to see progress — or the lack of it.

Precept 20. Be Willing to Be Made Usable

Never stop being a disciple yourself; never stop learning; never stop looking for deeper commitments you can make to

Christ. Paul told his spiritual son Timothy that if he would separate himself from worldliness, he would be made a "vessel for honor, sanctified, useful to the Master, prepared for every good work" (2 Timothy 2:20,21). We all want to be usable, but getting there is no picnic. The product is highly desirable, but we'd just as soon avoid the process.

In the vast plains of the Serengeti in southeast Africa, about the only thing that grows are gnarly old acacia bushes. These don't provide very straight arrow shafts for the little bushmen that inhabit the plains, so they've formulated an ingenious process to keep their quivers full. First they go out and find a suitable branch; it doesn't matter if it's got a 30-degree angle in it, just so it's the proper thickness and length. Next they'll build a fire, and right beside the fire they'll drive two rows of pegs into the ground, about six to eight inches apart. Then they'll put the branch into the fire to get its juices flowing, making it pliable. When it's hot enough, they'll fish it out of the fire and jam it between the two rows of pegs and let it cool. It's a little straighter, but still looks more like a boomerang than an arrow. So it's back to the fire, move the pegs a little closer together, jam the shaft between the rows and let it cool again. It's getting straighter. Back to the fire, back to the pegs, back to the fire, back to the pegs . . . until finally the pegs are right next to each other, with only an arrow's width between them. When the bushman pulls it out this last time, he's got a perfectly straight arrow that's useful to its maker.

We like the part about "useful to the maker," but it's that fire and that bending we'd just as soon avoid. If you want to be made useful, though, you've got to take the tough with the easy. We learn from the account of Shadrach, Meshach and Abednego in Daniel 3 that God doesn't always take His children around the fire—sometimes He meets them in the middle of the furnace.

7
THE PANORAMA

"The pilot and co-pilot are both dead!" cried the stewardess as she burst from the cockpit to the cabin of the Boeing 727. "Does anybody know how to fly a plane?"

"We-e-e-ell, shoot, Horace," said an old hillbilly to his neighbor. "I reckon I can drive just about anythin' that rolls. Think I'll give this buggy a shot."

"Do tell, Josh," said his traveling companion. "I'll be yore co-pilot."

So the two old fellows tottered up to the cockpit, strapped themselves in and took over the controls. After about ten minutes they spotted the landing strip, decreased altitude, and prepared to land.

"Say, Josh? Don't that runway look awful short to you?"

"It sure do. I think we're comin' in too fast fer it. Better give me full flaps and throw them engines in reverse the second we touch ground!"

"Check!"

They hit the runway with a terrible jolt and Josh shouted, "We're goin' way too fast! Gimme full reverse thrust, stand on the brakes and start prayin'!"

"Dad-burnit, Josh! We ain't never gonna stop in time!"

The tires screamed, the engines roared in reverse, and Josh and Horace each sweated five pounds of bullets, but somehow the nose wheel stopped six inches before the end of the runway. The two men slumped exhausted in their seats.

"Ho-o-o-whee! That was close!" said Horace, catching his breath. "I declare—that had to be 'bout the *shortest* runway I ever did see!"

"You ain't kiddin'! You know the funny thing about it, though," Josh said as he looked to his right and left, "It appears to be 'bout two miles wide . . . "

What those hillbillies missed was the panoramic view. They got one little glimpse of runway from 5,000 feet and headed straight for it. Never mind that they were approaching it sideways; all they wanted was to get that plane *down* — any way they could! If they'd had a broader perspective of their landing area instead of focusing on one little slot of it, they'd have sweated considerably fewer bullets.

As a disciplemaker, you need to have the panoramic view, too. That's the purpose of this chapter. When you've got the big picture as to what you're hoping to accomplish with a brand-new Christian, it'll be a lot easier to head the right direction on the runway.

PUNCTURING A PRESUMPTION

Let's start off by dispelling a prevalent, erroneous presumption that a disciplemaker often makes as he sets out to help another Christian grow in his faith. It says, "If I can get my disciple to complete this material, he'll be discipled."

Wrong, wrong, wrong! Do I sound dogmatic about that? It's one of the few strong stands I'll take on a secondary issue. The reason is that it is simply an absurd position.

Back in 1977, when I was competing for the Athletes In Action track team, we were one of the few post-college teams with enough finances to provide transportation and equipment for our athletes. For this reason, many athletes wanted to join us — both Christians and non-Christians. But since our purpose as a team was to introduce others to Christ through our witness, we felt strongly about maintaining a high degree of spiritual integrity among our athletes. So we decided to require all prospective team members to complete a series of Bible study booklets before we would officially accept them.

I tell you, we were excited about all these national- and international-caliber athletes completing the studies and joining the team! National champions, Olympic gold medalists, world record holders . . . we were getting quite proud of the impact we were having on the track world, "discipling" all these in-fluential athletes!

There was only one problem: They were going through the material, but the material was also going through most of them — like water through a sieve. For a while, we allowed these athletes to join our team and represent Jesus Christ to the ath-letic world simply on the basis of some completed material and a personal interview. But we quickly changed our ways when we learned that many of these so-called ambassadors were living lives that were in no way pleasing to Christ.

Just because someone reads an article, looks up some Bible verses, and writes answers to some questions, that doesn't necessarily mean he's gaining any spiritual maturity. As men-tioned in chapter 3, the growing process involves the disciple "learning it" (gaining the information), "loving it" (gaining the conviction), and "living it" (manifesting the information and the conviction in his lifestyle). As disciplemakers, we have to pursue *that* process, not the material-completion process.

It would have been relatively easy for me to take the sub-jects the Bible says are important for growing Christians to learn about, and make a nice Bible study series that you could hand to your disciple and let it go at that. But there are two reasons I didn't: (1) There are mountains of wonderful Bible studies already available; and (2) I want to help you become a disciplemaker, not a Bible-study-distributor. There is a big dif-ference between the two. To become a disciplemaker requires that you discern the unique needs of your growing disciple and construct a program to meet those needs. It requires that you be able to flex with the variables of your disciple's life. It re-quires that you be there to answer the questions that aren't in the books, to bind up the wounds he suffers, to challenge him to go beyond where he would normally go. The Bible-study-dis-tributor knows nothing of these things, and his disciples turn out to be plastic, shallow clones.

DISCIPLE-ORIENTED APPROACH

If we aren't going to learn a materials-oriented way of dis-cipling, what else is there? Well, how about if we learn to "teach others also," using the same methods we use in other avenues of education? No matter what kind of training system you examine (i.e., secular or Christian academic education, vocational training, specialized instruction, etc.), the normal sequence goes something like this:

1. Identify long-term goals
2. Set up intermediate training objectives
3. Determine curriculum
4. Choose materials designed to help the student achieve the training objectives (based on the student's previous education and present capacities)
5. Construct evaluation procedures to help assess when the student has reached the objectives and, ultimately, the long-term goals.

So, in contrast to the materials orientation, we will take the disciple-sensitive, training-objective-oriented approach. Let's walk through these five steps and see how the program fits in with each of them.

Step 1. Identify Long-Term Goals

If we utilize our definition of a disciple found in chapter 2, and add a little more behavioral detail to it, we could use the following as a *long-term goal* for disciplemaking:

> To work in concert with the Holy Spirit to produce a person-in-process eager to learn and apply the truths that Jesus Christ teaches him, resulting in ever-deepening commitments to a Christlike lifestyle manifested in the areas of prayer, Bible study, fellowship, witnessing, personal growth, ministry, and family life.

As I mentioned before, it will be tough to know when we've hit that goal, because it's a perpetually moving target. A true disciple is in constant flux: always learning, growing, changing. As Paul wrote in 2 Corinthians 3:18: "And all of us . . . are constantly being transfigured into His very own image in ever increasing splendor and from one degree of glory to another . . ." (Amplified Bible). Something that is constantly growing is never "grown up," never finished. Even when one is mature, he must continue to grow. Does a sequoia ever stop growing? If it does, it's dead. Will we ever have "perfect" faith on this earth? Will we ever be perfectly generous? Perfectly loving? Will we ever develop our gifts and talents perfectly?

Our long-term goal may not be as clear-cut as we might like, but it still gives us a visible "pillar of fire" we can head for.

Step 2. Set Up Intermediate Training Objectives

At this point we get the chance to start putting some flow and detail into our program. These *training objectives* form the stepping stones toward maturity for our disciples. They are the building blocks of discipleship. In his excellent book, *The Lost Art of Disciple Making,* Leroy Eims emphasizes the importance of using training objectives to help our disciples progress toward Christlikeness:

> This progress cannot be accomplished haphazardly. It has to begin somewhere and then go somewhere, like the educational process from kindergarten to graduation from high school. The student has to master many lessons, assimilate many facts, and learn to do many things. But the way must be planned and organized. A person doesn't learn calculus while playing in the sandbox.
>
> In helping a young Christian grow, you must have a step-by-step building program in mind; you must have certain objectives you want him to attain before he undertakes others. You want to see him go from taking in spiritual milk to partaking of spiritual meat.[1]

So our first task is to develop training objectives for a brand new Christian. When a person receives the Lord, what are the first few things that we disciplemakers should help him establish in his life? That's what Section Two — all twelve chapters — is about.

Everyone is different. The immediate needs of newborn Christians vary. The amount of time that will need to be spent on each training objective will differ according to the new Christian's background and ability to assimilate and apply information. Because of this, I am offering the following training objectives only as suggestions. The subjects covered were arrived at after many years of study and experience, but they are not canonical. I want to encourage you to listen closely to the direction of the Holy Spirit and re-shape these training objectives however He may lead you.

NEWBORN CARE

THE FIRST 12 TRAINING OBJECTIVES
FOR A BRAND NEW CHRISTIAN

1. *Assurance of salvation* — The disciple is sure that if he has honestly asked Christ to enter his life:

   a. Christ has indeed come into his life;

   b. He has been reborn as a whole new creation;

   c. His sins — past, present and future — have been forgiven;

   d. A new relationship has been established between him and God;

   e. He will never again be separated from God.

2. *Scope and significance of salvation* — The disciple understands in greater detail the scope and significance of what occurred when he invited Christ into his life, which produces a deeper commitment and greater motivation to go on with Christ.

3. *Filling of the Holy Spirit* — The disciple has a basic understanding of and avails himself of the ministry of the Holy Spirit.

4. *Identity in Christ* — The disciple has a basic understanding of his new identity in Christ and the struggle that exists between his old nature and his new.

5. *Basic growth principles* — The disciple has a basic understanding of spiritual growth principles and is aware of the beneficial influences of time, adversity and the sovereignty of God.

6. *Fellowship* — The disciple has a basic understanding of the importance of Christian fellowship and is beginning to attend Christian functions.

7. *The Word* — The disciple has a basic understanding of

the importance of biblical input, is familiar with the physical layout of the Bible, and has begun to read the Bible on his own.

8. *Prayer* — The disciple has a basic understanding of the importance of prayer, knows the fundamentals of prayer, and is beginning to pray on his own.

9. *Witnessing* — The disciple has a basic understanding of the importance of witnessing, knows the primary elements of the gospel and can tell another person how to become a Christian.

10. *Spiritual warfare* — The disciple has a basic understanding of fundamental facts concerning adversity, Satan, temptation and sin.

11. *Time management* — The disciple has a basic understanding of the principles of time management and has begun a strategy to utilize his time better.

12. *Vision* — The disciple understands how significant he is to the advance of the kingdom of God, has a clear picture of some of the broad plans God has in mind for him, and is motivated to actively pursue his spiritual development and his relationship with God.

Now, some education buffs might be saying, "But wait. Many of those training objectives are not specific enough. Where is the time frame? Where are the specific measurables that will indicate a completed objective?" Various distinctives will exist in any discipler/disciple relationship, and the time frame will vary from person to person, depending to a large degree on the disciple. The target behavior will vary depending on what the disciplemaker (with his unique ministry background) feels is desirable. However, as I develop each of those training objectives in the coming chapters, I'll share some helpful suggestions.

Others may say, "I see a rather large void in these twelve training objectives. Shouldn't there be something in there about the nature of God or the person of Christ?" An excellent observation. Gaining an accurate concept of God is probably the most vital and far-reaching study you or your disciple will ever engage in. A. W. Tozer put it so aptly, "What comes to our minds when we think about God is the most important thing about us."[2] But since God is infinite, it will take us more than an everlasting lifetime to explore the depths of His vastness. That's what eternal life is all about—getting to know God (John 17:3). Paul's lifetime objective was "that I may know Him . . . " (Philippians 3:10), and he counted all other pursuits as rubbish compared to "the surpassing value of knowing Christ Jesus my Lord" (verse 8). At the core of disciplemaking is helping our disciple cultivate his relationship with God—to "know" Him.

Therefore, a primary function of every training objective listed above is to equip our disciples for a lifetime of getting to know God. He will begin a study of God, Christ and the Holy Spirit soon after the completion of these twelve training objectives. And I'm assuming you'll be passing on a significant amount of basic theology in an informal way as you progress through the objectives; it would be almost impossible not to. But what we want to accomplish in this newborn care phase is to help the disciple get all his new machinery in place and functioning so he can get on with the business of growing. In-depth, long-term study of the nature of God will come shortly.

Step 3. Determine Curriculum

What specific steps will you take to help your disciple achieve each training objective? You may have a broad idea of what needs to be done, but what *exactly* are you going to do at your scheduled meeting next Tuesday at 3 P.M.? And how will it fit the panoramic view of this growth process?

I have some tested and proven strategies I'd like to share with you. They form the bulk of chapters 9 through 12. Each chapter is a resource you can use in order to tailor-make a program for your disciple. With the help of the Holy Spirit, you'll learn what will work with your disciple and what will bomb. You'll figure out if he'll respond more readily to an organized, regimented, high-accountability approach or a more laid-back, relationship-oriented approach. You'll find out how much input he's already had in certain areas and will adjust your input accordingly, so as to minimize duplication and subsequent boredom.

Each of the twelve chapters in Section Two will be organized according to the following format:

1. *Objective.* A restatement of the training objective.

2. *Biblical basis for this objective.* This section is for you more than for your disciple. It's meant to give you a more biblical handle on each training objective, and to show you why that particular objective is scriptural and therefore important. In this section you will find lists of verses pertaining to the subject. You should look them up on your own and write a brief summary of each. I suggest you start a notebook in which to write these summaries, so you can quickly refer back to them. Checking each verse will immerse you in the subject and keep you a step or two ahead of your disciple.

3. *Applicable definitions.* If there are any words relating to the training objective that might be open to question, we will define them.

4. *Pep talk for the disciplemaker.* If you were my disciple, and you were trying to get the hang of discipling someone else, these are the things I would say to you. This section of each chapter is designed to get you excited about the training objective, give you a little extra insight, warn you about pitfalls to avoid, explain certain aspects in more detail, and share some of my personal experiences.

5. *Broaching the subject.* In this section I'll give you some specific ways to get into the objective at hand. Some subjects are a little touchy, and you might like a few ideas on how to open the topic and stimulate interest and motivation in your disciple.

6. *Suggestions for growth.* This will always be the largest section of each chapter and will include such things as verses to share, general suggestions, illustrations, personal experiences of mine and others, printed materials and quotes, along with some activities you and your disciple can get together on. Sometimes I'll be specific

about what you ought to share, because the nature of the training objective will be pretty cut and dried. At other times I'll pass on a broad spectrum of ideas you can choose from. In some cases, as you read through what I've presented, the Holy Spirit will give you completely different ideas that would be more productive in your situation. He may jog your mind about something you heard or saw in the past, or He may remind you how that concept was established in your life. *By no means* am I presuming to say that you must choose from the ideas I have presented, or that I have collected the only viable ways of helping a disciple achieve the training objective. As the title of this section represents, these are merely *suggestions* for growth.

Many of these suggestions revolve around the importance of getting into the Word with your disciple. When he's a little older in the Lord, he'll have ample opportunities to dig in there on his own, but for a while he needs to see how you use the shovel. For instance, I may make a suggestion such as, "Ask your disciple, 'What do you think are some of the broad, general plans God has for your life?' Let him share his ideas with you and then look up the following verses with him: Psalm 16:11; John 8:12; John 15:16; 2 Corinthians 9:8."

I'll usually give you a list of verses about a mile and a half long, so you'll need to go through it first and pick out the ones you like the best (again, you'll find it helpful to write summaries of the verses in a notebook). Don't choose too many or your session together will go too long. Then, find the first reference with your disciple, have him read it aloud and discuss it with him. Taking Psalm 16:11, your conversation might go something like this:

YOU: Let's see what the Bible says God's got in store for us. Why don't you read this verse out loud, Ringo.

DISCIPLE: OK. It says, "Thou wilt make known to me the path of life; in Thy presence is fullness of joy; in Thy right hand there are pleasures forever."

YOU: King David wrote this. You know, the guy who killed Goliath, and later became the king of Israel?

What do you think he was trying to get across here? What plans did he say God has in store for us?

DISCIPLE: Well, that He'll show us the path of life, that we'll have joy, and pleasures. Hey, I kinda like those ideas!

YOU: Who wouldn't? What do you think he meant by "path of life"?

DISCIPLE: I guess he meant the opposite of the path of death. Probably the way to heaven or something.

YOU: I think so, too. Do you think that "path" will be some kind of rose-strewn, pink-tinted journey filled with sunshine and bluebirds?

DISCIPLE: Uh, I'm not sure. Will it?

YOU: Well, how much do you remember about David's life?

DISCIPLE: Not much.

YOU: His life wouldn't be characterized as a life of ease by any means. He had to fight wars; the previous king was always trying to murder him; he fell into sin; his favorite son led a rebellion against him; another son died in infancy; one of his wives turned on him. Once even God Himself unleashed a terrible plague on Israel because of something David did. So what does this tell you about David's path of life?

DISCIPLE: I guess it's not always fun 'n' games.

YOU: Right. But in the end, where does the path lead?

DISCIPLE: I'd say heaven.

YOU: I'd say so, too. God will help us in real ways to experience the abundant life throughout our time here on earth—even in the midst of tremendous adversity. But when it's all said and done, and they lay us in our graves, our lives are really just beginning!

DISCIPLE: I never thought of that before!

YOU: Notice something else here. It says that we will experience "fullness of joy." Where does it say we'll experience it?

DISCIPLE: In His presence.

YOU: What do you think is happening when we are not experiencing fullness of joy?

When I say, "Look up the following verses with your disciple," it's so you and your disciple can delve into the Word together, giving him a chance to think it through under your guidance, and giving the Holy Spirit an opportunity to illuminate the Scriptures for the both of you as you discuss them. Without even knowing it, he'll be learning some important principles of hermeneutics (Bible interpretation) and how to extract practical, applicable truth from the Scriptures.

From time to time, your disciple may have some really off-the-wall observations. It's inevitable. When it happens, avoid reactions such as, "*WHAT?! Have you gone MAD?* Of all the hair-brained, knuckle-headed . . . " Instead, focus on the positive. Say something like, "Well, that's an interesting point of view"; or, "Interesting . . . what makes you think that?" or, "Maybe. What do you think of this idea . . . ?" or, "I hadn't thought of it that way before. Here's how someone once explained it to me . . . "

Sometimes your disciple will ask you a question you don't know the answer to. At those times, don't try to fake it. Just say, "I don't know. I'll find out for you this coming week and get back to you on it." Then write down the question (so you won't forget it), and be ready to report back to him next time.

7. *Further resources.* This is a list of Bible studies or booklets you can refer to when you want some additional information on the subject.

8. *P.S. For the disciplemaker.* Occasionally, after I have finished all of the suggestions for growth, there might still be a thing or two I'd like to pass on to you before closing the subject. Those comments will be in this section. It'll have the same function as the pep talk, but it's at the end instead of the beginning.

9. *Ending the session.* This section will contain some ideas on how you might tie together all the loose ends

on the subject and close with a bang. It might include some practical application, a way of summarizing the subject, or a way of helping the disciple set his sights on the next week's topic by integrating what we just covered with what we're about to cover.

10. *Assignment for next time.* Assuming you cover the training objectives in the order listed, this section will suggest assignments you can give your disciple that will get him thinking about next week's training objective.

11. *Evaluation.* This section includes ideas that will help you discern when your disciple has met each training objective.

Step 4. Choose Materials

I stated earlier that we should not follow a materials-oriented disciplemaking program; I didn't say we shouldn't use prepared materials. The trick is using the right materials at the right time. The prevalent programs these days employ the shotgun approach: *Fire away — if we leave a big enough crater, we're bound to have hit the target.*

Instead, I advocate the sharpshooter approach: *Take a good look at the target and then aim at the bulls eye.* In most prepared Bible study series, we may be doing a bang-up job teaching our disciple about, say, the importance of Christian stewardship (because it's on the schedule), but the next, most crucial step of growth in the disciple's life (and the area in which the Holy Spirit is working) might be in the area of lust. It would be much more desirable to cooperate with God in *His* program, figure out the disciple's area of *need*, and *then* haul out the materials designed to meet it.

One could argue, "Hey, a new Christian needs everything! What difference does it make if you start him with prayer or with witnessing?" In the early stages of growth, it may not make much difference . . . then again, it may make a lot of difference. It depends on the person, his background, and what God wants done. That's why it's important that we, at all times, show deference to the Holy Spirit's right to decide how a person should be trained. On the other hand, since we know that the needs of older Christians are going to be operating on various time schedules, it's a good idea to get accustomed to addressing even the new Christian's needs on an individual basis.

As for the materials you draw from, you may want to use the ideas in the "Suggestions for Growth" sections, or you may prefer to use prepared fill-in-the-blank type studies. Or you may want to combine the two. The prepared materials will give the disciple the opportunity to study the Bible privately (which we want to heartily encourage) and then the two of you can go over his completed studies together. An excellent strategy! In each training objective chapter I have included a section called "Further Resources," listing several studies that apply to the objective at hand.

I am most familiar with the materials found in Campus Crusade for Christ's "Ten Basic Steps Toward Christian Maturity"[3] Bible study series (ten booklets, six to eight lessons per booklet, plus Leader's Guide) and The Navigators' *Design for Discipleship*[4] Bible study series (seven booklets, four or five lessons per booklet, plus Leader's Guide), and Campus Crusade's "The Discipleship Series."[5] They are all excellent, and comparable in their handling of the subjects studied. I will usually list several lessons. I wouldn't suggest going over them all — pick one, two or (at the most) three studies. Almost every prepared lesson from all three series are integrated into the twelve Newborn Care Training Objectives, but I've taken them out of their original sequence.

I'll also mention another series of Bible studies with a little different twist. It is Campus Crusade for Christ's "Transferable Concepts,"[6] written by Bill Bright. This is a series of nine small, tract-sized booklets (also available in combined single-volume) that cover several key concepts that a growing Christian must grasp. They each contain an article on the topic (such as "How To Be Sure You Are A Christian," "How To Be Filled With The Spirit," "How To Pray," etc.), a study guide (ideas for personal application of the material covered), an amplified outline (for review), thought questions (great to use to stimulate some discussion), and a short fill-in-the-blank Bible study. These are excellent materials to send home with your disciple to read in preparation for the training objectives.

Since in some cases I have listed five or six prepared lessons applicable to a particular training objective, you might be tempted to go over all of them, thinking, *How can I leave any of these out? There is so much good stuff here.* You need to remember that during this Newborn Care phase, we are just hitting the high points on each of these subjects. You can go into more depth later. Give your disciple a first-grade education in all subjects first, then go back later for the second-, third-, and fourth-grade treatment.

Step 5. Construct Evaluation Procedures

In this process we're working toward our disciple's fulfilling each training objective. How will you know when he has? The wording for some of the training objectives is a little short in terms of measurable behavior, so at the end of each objective are a number of questions you can ask yourself, plus some you can ask your disciple if you feel you need more feedback from him about the objective at hand. You'll often be able to conclude that your disciple has fulfilled a training objective by observing his life, listening to his thoughts on a subject and discussing the objective with him. At other times you'll need to ask some direct questions. In those circumstances, read though the "Evaluation" section at the end of each training objective and decide which questions to ask. (Write them down so you won't forget them.) Remember, the basis for evaluation is not just the *how to's* (the means, the mechanics), but also the *what to's* (the scriptural injunctions) and the *why to's* (the motivation).

PROCEEDING FROM PANORAMA TO PERSONAL APPROACH

Now that you have a bird's-eye view of disciplemaking, it's time to move into the specifics of how to deal with the uniquenesses that reside in the person God has entrusted to your care. The next chapter will start you down the road to tailor-making a program especially suited for your disciple.

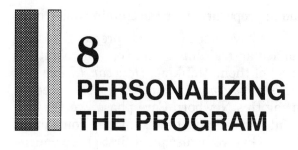

8
PERSONALIZING
THE PROGRAM

We can't even begin to imagine the complex creativity of our creator! He'll see to it that even something as mundane as a snowflake will have no duplicates. Multiply that creativity by three trillion — roughly the number of cells in our bodies — and you get something of an idea of how unique we human beings are!

Any disciplemaking program that does not take into account the extraordinary singularity we each possess is doomed to failure. In this chapter we'll learn how to challenge a Christian to begin a discipling relationship, how to assess his current spiritual status, and how to begin mapping out a strategy personalized for him.

TWO DIFFERENT STRATEGIES

Some of you need input on how to begin discipling a person you have just led to the Lord. Others need to know how to disciple a Christian who has been saved for a while, but just hasn't had much training yet. You'll want to approach each case differently.

If you have just led someone to Christ, it's relatively simple: Start at Training Objective #1: "Assurance of Salvation" (chapter 9). Actually, you may have already covered much of training objective #1, because it is primarily material you want to share with a person immediately after he has received Christ. For future reference, read training objective #1 carefully and write whatever notes you feel would be helpful on the flyleaf of your Bible. Then you will always be prepared to move immediately into assurance of salvation when you lead a person to Christ. If you finished training objective #1, go on to #2. The vast majority of disciplemakers in the survey agreed that assurance should be the first topic covered with a new Christian, and both Training Objective #1 and Training Objective #2 relate to that subject. After that, feel free to alter the sequence of training objectives.

If you anticipate discipling someone who has been a Christian for a while, but you know for certain he has had virtually no input about Christian things, treat him just like a brand new Christian.

However, if you are about to begin discipling someone who has had some previous spiritual training, or has been going to church for a year or two, you need to take a different path. Instead of subjecting that disciple to repeated onslaughts of material he's been over time and time again, you'll need to determine where he is spiritually and find out what roads he's already traveled, so you can start where he left off.

How do you find out what he's had and what he needs? In educational terms, you'd give him a diagnostic test. The foreboding sound of that instrument has struck fear in the hearts of many a student, so instead let's call it a "self-evaluation questionnaire." Following are a number of questions that pertain to each of the first twelve training objectives. There may be more than one question for each. Either type these questions out, or duplicate the appropriate pages in this book and have your disciple evaluate himself. Then, the two of you should spend from thirty to forty-five minutes discussing his answers. This isn't meant to be any kind of scientific survey, just an aid to communication. You'll be amazed at how much you'll learn about the spiritual background of your disciple in this short time.

CHRISTIAN FUNDAMENTALS
SELF-EVALUATION QUESTIONNAIRE

Directions: Answer each question by circling the most appropriate answer. Don't be tempted to respond untruthfully in order to put yourself in a more positive light, or to say what you think people want to hear—answer honestly. If it seems that none of the options presented are quite right, choose the one that most closely describes you, and put a question mark in the margin next to it.

1. I am [not sure, fairly sure, positive] that if I were to die today, I would go immediately to heaven.

2. I am [not sure, fairly sure, positive] that, before I met Christ and invited Him into my life, I was a sinner, headed for hell.

3. I have [minimal, average, thorough] knowledge of what the Bible is talking about when it says I am a "new creation."

4. I am [not sure, fairly sure, positive] that all my sins have been forgiven.

5. I am [not sure, fairly sure, positive] that my salvation is permanent, and that I will never again be separated from God.

6. I have [minimal, average, thorough] knowledge about the many important changes that took place in me after I asked Christ into my life.

7. I have a [minimal, average, thorough] understanding of how to be filled with the Holy Spirit.

8. I have [minimal, average, thorough] knowledge of the tension that exists between my new nature and my old nature and why I still struggle with temptation even though I am a "new creation."

9. I have [minimal, average, thorough] knowledge of the activities I can undertake that will help me to grow spiritually in a balanced, steady fashion.

10. I have a [minimal, average, thorough] understanding of why it is important for me to be involved actively in fellowship with other Christians.

11. I attend church [never, rarely, sometimes, weekly, twice a week].

12. I read the Bible [never, rarely, sometimes, frequently].

13. I [don't understand, have some idea, know very

well] what people mean when they call the Bible the "Word of God."

14. I know that prayer is simply talking to God, and I don't have any real difficulty doing it [agree, disagree].

15. On the average, I have a period of personal, concentrated prayer _____ days a week, each session lasting about _____ minutes.

16. Right now, I could do a [poor, fair, good, great] job of telling another person how to become a Christian if the opportunity presented itself.

17. I feel [petrified, hesitant, willing, strongly motivated] to tell others about how they might come to a saving knowledge of Christ.

18. I am [not sure, fairly sure, positive] that adversity is a normal part of the Christian life; when I experience trials, I [never, rarely, sometimes, often] get mad at God and [never, rarely sometimes, often] go to Him for help.

19. I know that Satan is real [yes, no], that he seeks my downfall [yes, no], and I have [no, some, extensive] knowledge about how to resist him.

20. I have a [minimal, average, thorough] knowledge of what to do when I sin, in order to restore fellowship between God and myself.

21. I am [terrible, fair, pretty good, very good] at managing my time, goals and priorities in life.

22. I have [no, a vague, a fairly clear, a very clear] idea about what I want to accomplish in life.

23. I have a workable program in place that helps me to set and reach personal goals successfully and manage my day-to-day activities effectively [agree, disagree, "sort of"].

24. I see myself as having the potential of being [minimally, somewhat, very, extremely] signi-

ficant to the advance of the kingdom of God.

25. I would say that at this point I am [minimally, somewhat, very, extremely] motivated to pursue my spiritual development and my relationship with God actively.

When he's done with the questionnaire, go over it with him, question by question. Encourage him to expand on his answers. For instance, perhaps he answered question 2 with, *I am [positive] that, before I met Christ and invited Him into my life, I was a sinner, headed for hell.* You might ask him, "Why are you so positive about that?"

Perhaps he'd answer, "Because the Bible says in Isaiah 53:6, 'All we like sheep have gone astray' and Romans 3:23 says 'All have sinned and fall short of the glory of God.' "

It wouldn't be stretching it to assume he needs no more input on that question. But if he were to answer, "Well, because I took drugs once about five years ago, and that's what made me a sinner," you know that he's got a flawed view of sin and the nature of man, and will need to learn more.

On question 3 he might have answered, *I have an [average] knowledge of what the Bible is talking about when it says I am a "new creation."* You might say to him, "I notice you circled average here. What *do* you know about what it means to be a new creation?"

Or on question 11 about church attendance, you could ask a series of questions such as, "Where do you attend? How often do you go? Do you like it there? How long have you been going? What's the pastor like? Do they get into the Bible much there? What made you decide to go there? What do you like best about it?"

I'm not talking about giving him the third degree, but those are the kinds of questions that might come up in any normal conversation when two people talk about their churches.

After your discussion—as *soon* as possible—spend some time alone with God asking for discernment as you evaluate your disciple's current spiritual status. Look at each of the Newborn Care Training Objectives listed in chapter 7, read over the disciple's self-evaluation questionnaire answers and any notes you made during your discussion, and determine what training objectives are already operating in his life. Then decide which one you should cover together first.

I can't stress enough how important it is that you be yielded to the Spirit during this exercise, trusting Him to guide your thinking. If we rely solely on our own crooked powers of discernment, we're bound to be off-kilter in our evaluations. On the other hand, the Spirit is vitally concerned that this new babe in Christ be followed up well, and He'll put His hand into the process as much as you'll let Him.

THE DISCIPLEMAKER'S NOTEBOOK

To do the best job of discipling, you will need to put together a notebook. It will be invaluable in planning, tracking and evaluating your disciple's growth.

Get a regular three-ring notebook, some dividers and some lined notebook paper. Use one divider per disciple. Behind each divider, you should have three components: A biographical data sheet, a training objectives sheet, and a wad of blank sheets for your one-to-one diary.

Biographical Data Sheet

This is where you keep your disciple's personal information — the things you don't want to forget. Here are some you might want to include:

Name
Address
Home phone
Office phone
Date began discipling
Employment
Birthday (physical)
Birthday (spiritual)
Spouse's name
Kids' names
Anniversary
Church
Educational background

Religious background
Family background
Previous training
Previous ministries
Current ministries
Hobbies, sports, recreation
Spiritual gifts
Natural talents
Acquired skills
Personal goals
    Intermediate
    Life's mission

I do not suggest giving him an application form to fill out, or running down the list like a jail's booking officer. You can find out most of these things just in the natural context of your relationship.

Training Objectives Sheet

On this sheet, type or write out each of the twelve training objectives. Not only will this sheet help you keep the panoramic view in mind, but it will also give you a great focal point when you pray for your disciple. Leave space to the right of the training objectives for notations such as *Has head knowledge of this, but not in life*; or, *Doing this, but examine motives*; or, *High priority!*

Also leave space for a nice, big check mark when you feel he's attained the objective. Hold it! Is our objective merely to check off training objectives? *No!* Our objective is to help our disciple grow in Christlikeness. These notes and checks simply help us organize our thinking as we guide our disciple toward spiritual maturity. Don't ever let yourself get confused about that.

One-to-One Diary

Draw a vertical line right down the middle of a sheet of your lined notebook paper. Title the left side *Planned*, and the other side *Did*. This will become invaluable to you in tracking where you've gone with your disciple, how he has responded, and how he (and *you*) have progressed. On the *Planned* side, enter a date and exactly what you plan to do during your next meeting. Write down subjects you want to cover, questions you want to ask, verses, illustrations, quotes you want to share, anything you think is relevant. After your meeting, enter on the *Did* side what you actually covered, any impressions you got while you were together, questions your disciple asked, problems he's had, victories he's experienced, prayer requests, etc. Then draw a line all the way across the page under the two entries for that date.

What you planned and what you did often will not match. You may have prepared one thing, and your disciple may have had a heavy-duty question on a different subject that took the whole session to handle. That's OK. If possible, stick with your plan, so you make progress toward your goal; but always be open to allowing the Holy Spirit to change your plans. You're there to meet your disciple's needs; he's not there to get squeezed into your agenda.

CHALLENGING YOUR DISCIPLE TO MEET

At the end of Training Objective #1 (Assurance of Salvation) I have listed some ideas for getting the new Christian back together with you for further training. They're in the section titled "Ending the Session."

But if we're talking about someone who has been a Christian for a while, again, you'll need a little different approach. Here are some strategy components for your consideration:

1. Begin praying that the Lord will place on your potential disciple's heart a hunger to grow spiritually and an affinity for you. Also pray that He will give you a pure, selfless, *agape*-type love for him.

2. Get together with him informally, sporadically, always asking the Lord to keep you spiritually discerning and challenging. Pray some of the prayers of Paul for him.

3. Begin discipling him covertly, that is, discipling him on a short-term basis without him knowing it. There's really nothing cloak-and-dagger about it. Covert disciplemaking is simply good, committed fellowship with no formal discipler/disciple relationship having been established. Ask the Lord to give you insight regarding a crucial area of need in his life, and then keep your eyes peeled for an opportunity to help meet it.

4. Try to steer him to the Word whenever you have the opportunity. The more he reads the Word, the more hunger for spiritual things will be produced. So:

   • Share insights you've been receiving from the Word

   • Take him to church, Bible studies, Christian concerts, fellowships

   • Help him resolve a conflict by taking him to the Scriptures

- Whet his appetite by pursuing his area of interest in the Bible (i.e., politics, science, psychology, etc.)

- Loan him Christian teaching and music tapes

- Talk about the Bible with other Christians while he's around

5. Ask him challenging questions like these when you have a natural opportunity:

- What do you want your life (or ministry, or walk with the Lord) to be like a year from now? Five years? Twenty years? Have you worked at some plans to reach those goals?

- Are you doing anything right now to enhance your growth toward spiritual maturity? Do you wish you were doing more?

- There are only three things that will last for eternity: God, God's Word, and people. To what extent would you say you're currently involved with those three things? Would you like to be more involved?

- What do you think would happen in your life if you spent more time reading the Bible (or praying, or witnessing, etc.)?

- [Referring to the Parable of the Four Soils in Matthew 13, ask him,] Looking at your life these days, which kind of soil do you think is most characteristic of you? [If he says the good soil, ask him,] Do you think you're 30-, 60- or 100-fold soil?

6. Help him see his strengths and how they could be used to help others and to further the kingdom of God.

7. Get him involved in some sort of ministry activity with you.

8. If you are in some position of authority at church or with your ministry team, ask him to share his testimony at a meeting of some sort. This will motivate him to sharpen up his ministry skills.

9. Share your weaknesses and woes with him and ask him to pray for you.

10. Let him see your joy and enthusiasm—it's contagious!

11. Communicate and demonstrate love and trust to him. Be creative.

One last very important component of the strategy: *Ask him!* You might say something like, "Barney, I've been watching you, and I see that you've really got a heart for the Lord. It's exciting to see you (think of something exciting ministry-wise that he does . . . there must be something!). I've been receiving some training in the area of disciplemaking and have been praying that the Lord would give me an opportunity to use what I've been learning to help someone else grow in their faith. I know we've been relating to each other in several ministry contexts up to now, but I was wondering if you would be interested in getting some more in-depth, personalized spiritual training—more-or-less formalizing our relationship into a discipling one. What do you think?"

One of his first questions will probably be, "How much time will it take?" It's a fair question. If he's like just about everyone else living in the twentieth century, he doesn't have a lot of it to spare. I would say something like this: "My plan is to cover twelve subjects that are vital to growth for any Christian. The actual time-table is flexible, depending on the training you've already received, how consistent we can be in getting together, and how deeply you want to get into each subject. But on the average, we'd be looking at a ninety-minute meeting once a week for around five months. You might spend another hour or two a week in personal Bible study or reading. At the end of the twelve subjects, you'd have the opportunity to evaluate how our time went and decide if you wanted to go on from there."

At this stage, it's important for the disciple to see some parameters on this undertaking—even if they are a little vague. This way, he knows that if he ends up not liking it, he'll be able to bail out gracefully after a few months.

WHERE DO YOU MEET?

A lot of people like to do their discipling over a meal at a restaurant, meeting for lunch, breakfast or coffee. I don't. When you've set aside ninety minutes to meet with a person, and you are eating during that time, you blow a good thirty to forty-five minutes on the meal. Besides that, you can't really spread out to study the Word on a restaurant table. It's tough to concentrate, it's nearly impossible to do any significant praying, you spill coffee on your Bible, and if you or your disciple wants to discuss something personal, there is some hesitancy to do so in a public place. The best bet is to meet in a home, an office where the secretary has been instructed to hold all calls, a park, a church, an abandoned ice house — anyplace quiet and private, with a minimum of distractions.

If the only time you or your disciple can meet is during lunch, agree to meet somewhere with sack lunches. Eat fast, and get down to business!

When you are just starting out, sharing a meal together is a nice, unthreatening way to get your relationship off the dime, but once you've met for a couple of weeks, make arrangements to meet elsewhere if at all possible.

GO FOR IT!

OK! You've got all the raw materials, you've got the big picture, you've got the Holy Spirit as the architect and general contractor. It's time to go build a disciple! For your own education, I suggest that you read through the next twelve chapters even if you don't actually have someone to disciple right now. This way, you'll be well prepared in advance and familiar with every step of the process, and you'll feel much more confident when you do start to disciple someone. Have fun!

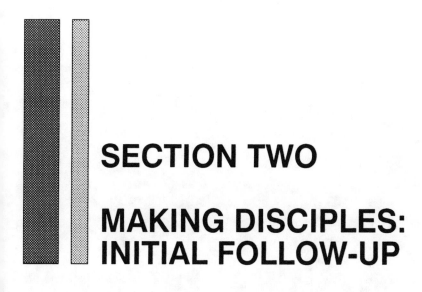

SECTION TWO

MAKING DISCIPLES: INITIAL FOLLOW-UP

9 TRAINING OBJECTIVE #1

ASSURANCE
OF SALVATION

■ OBJECTIVE

The disciple is sure that if he has honestly asked Christ to enter his life:

a. Christ has indeed come into his life;

b. he has been reborn as a whole new creation;

c. all his sins — past, present and future — have been forgiven;

d. a new relationship has been established between him and God;

e. he will never again be separated from God.

■ BIBLICAL BASIS FOR THIS OBJECTIVE

It is clear from Scripture that God would have us *know* we are saved. There is no need to doubt, and with the question resolved once and for all in the new convert's mind, he can go about the business of growing up in Christ and becoming an effective ambassador of God.

Time for Bible study — you get to do some digging for yourself!

John 3:16-18	Acts 10:43	Colossians 1:12-14
John 5:24	Acts 16:31	Colossians 2:13,14
John 6:37	Romans 8:1-3	Hebrews 7:24,25
John 6:51	Romans 8:31-39	Hebrews 13:5
John 10:27-29	Romans 10:13	1 Peter 1:23
John 11:25,26	Ephesians 1:4-7	1 John 2:12
John 17:1-3	Ephesians 1:13,14	1 John 4:15-17

Each of the passages at the bottom of the preceding page deals with the salvation Jesus Christ has bought for us; each gives us insight into why or how we can *know* we are saved. In your notebook, jot down a brief summary for each verse or passage. It will make a memorable study and it will be easier to locate passages you want to refer to later.

■ APPLICABLE DEFINITIONS

Assurance of Salvation: The conviction that, though he was previously lost and separated from God, he is now redeemed by Christ's sacrificial death on the cross and saved for all eternity. He may or may not have had a dramatic experience upon conversion, and he may or may not feel any different, but he has the settled confidence that Christ *has* entered his life, has saved him, has re-created him, and will never leave him or forsake him.

■ PEP TALK FOR THE DISCIPLEMAKER

You've just led someone to Christ! This is absolutely *the* most fantastic event that will ever occur in that person's life! A soul has just been redeemed from the hand of the enemy! Snatched from the jaws of death! He has been translated instantly from the kingdom of darkness into the kingdom of the Son of God! Reborn! Handed the most precious gift in the universe: eternal life! Adopted by the Almighty God of the universe and named as a co-heir with Jesus Christ . . .

And yet, as the newly born Christian lifts his expectant eyes from the "sinners prayer," I've seen soul-winners respond to this unbelievably triumphant event with, "Well, Joe, uh, great. You're a Christian now. Uh, that wasn't so bad, was it? Now, let's finish reading through this tract here . . . "

Does the term "anticlimactic" apply? It's not like the guy just signed his name to an insurance policy. He just stepped into eternity! Show a little spunk! A little excitement! Rejoice with the person! Give him at least some sense of the magnitude of the decision he just made! If he understands right from the outset that what he did in asking Christ into his life was a lot more than just joining a social club, when the doubts and adversities come (and they *will* come), he'll be much more likely to endure them, rather than to say, "Who needs to go through all this hassle for the sake of one insignificant decision?"

Now about those doubts and adversities. Up to this point, your disciple has been enjoying the relative calm of Satan's harbor. There has been no need for him to experience the rough seas and shipwrecks that the devil can whip up when he wants to. That's not to say that non-Christians don't experience difficulties; they do. And they endure them without the benefit of the indwelling God of the universe, which is a pretty hopeless circumstance. But now, on top of the normal, everyday bummers and disasters of life, this new Christian has just engaged the prince of darkness as his sworn enemy.

The brand new Christian is in a terribly vulnerable state. Satan's main objective at this point is to convince him that "praying that prayer" was insignificant. If Satan can do this, he has killed the seed before it has sprouted. He will have successfully inoculated the new Christian against catching the "real disease." The next time this guy is approached with the gospel he'll say, "Oh, I tried that once and it didn't work. It's OK for you, but it's just not for me . . . "

You may ask, "Was that person saved?" No one but God can say for sure. Many scenarios exist:

- He may have "prayed the prayer," but not with sincerity, in which case he never was saved.

- He may have prayed the prayer and truly believed, but then rejected the lifestyle and ministry God had in store for him — in which case he himself is saved, but he will amass a lifetime's worth of wood, hay and stubble that will burn to a crisp at the judgment seat of Christ (1 Corinthians 3:11-15).

- It could be that he was saved, has rejected God's lifestyle and ministry, will go through a period of great defeat and adversity but will later come to his senses, finishing out his life in victory and fruitfulness (cf. the prodigal son: Luke 15:11-32).

But that's not a question you need to ask regarding the new "babe in Christ" sitting across from you. Your job is to do whatever you can to prevent *any* of the above from happening!

Throughout this second section on follow-up, as I mentioned in the last chapter, my plan is to give you more ideas and material than you are ever likely to use. Your job will be to become familiar with each chapter and pick the tools you feel you'll be able to use with ease and skill. If you don't care to use the format given here, no problem! My goal is to stimulate your thinking so you can formulate your own unique presentation.

What are most brand new Christians expecting? Just about the only input most of them have had regarding the spiritual or supernatural has come out of Hollywood, so they're looking for "The Force" to turn them into Jedi Knights. They expect God to take on the form of George Burns and walk up to them and introduce Himself. Earthquakes! Signs and wonders in the heavens! The Hallelujah Chorus in full stereophonic Dolby sound! Angels ricocheting off the walls!

Instead, they pray a prayer . . . and . . . nothing. Now, some *do* experience a great sense of relief, or joyfulness, or a deep satisfaction that what they did was "right." One fellow who received Christ with me said, "It feels like a big hole in my chest just got filled up!" I know of many conversion experiences that are pretty dramatic; in most cases, however, there is no physical or emotional experience at all.

Now Satan steps in: "It didn't 'take' with you, my friend. And it never will, because it's a sham. Where's the change? How are you any different now from before you prayed that silly prayer?"

Because of this, the first thing you need to do is *defuse the "experience bomb."* The new Christian simply needs to know he does not have to sense any dramatic changes immediately upon conversion. It may burst his bubble of spiritual misconceptions, but his feet will thereby gain solid ground. Assure him that change has indeed taken place, but it's not the type one can necessarily feel.

Next, he needs to *grasp the truth of what just happened.* If you can get across to him the five concepts listed in the objective, he'll have enough to deflect the fiery darts of Satan.

The assurance-of-salvation objective is so important that you should make it your goal to cover it as thoroughly as you can immediately after the new Christian's conversion. Don't put it off till the next meeting—there may not be one! If you simply don't have time, then be sure to make plans to get together again as soon as possible, even that same day. If you have met "like two ships passing in the night" (like on an airplane, while vacationing, or during a volcanic eruption), be absolutely sure to get his address and sit down *that very night* and write him a long letter on the subject of assurance.

Let me emphasize something I barely touched on above. A person isn't saved by "praying a prayer." The "sinner's prayer" isn't some kind of a magical incantation that, when uttered, automatically ushers one into the kingdom of God. It's meant to be a true expression of an attitude of the heart. You may have just taken a person through a phenomenal presentation of the gospel, and he may have said some words about Christ coming into his life, but if the words didn't come from his heart, that's all they were: *words*. Ephesians 2:8,9 says that we are saved by grace through *faith*. Romans 10:10 tells us it is with the *heart* that you believe and are justified. If you want to do an interesting little study sometime, compare John 8:31 and 8:44. Jesus described "the Jews who had believed Him" (verse 31) as belonging to "your father the devil" (verse 44). And James 2:19 says, "You believe that there is one God. Good! Even the demons believe that—and shudder." It's one thing to "believe" in Jesus, but it's quite another thing to have "faith" in Jesus. Belief is merely intellectual assent. Faith involves volition and commitment. Faith saves; belief doesn't.

The person who "prayed," then, may or may not have actually become a Christian. What can you do to determine which was true in his case? Nothing at all. Only God knows what's truly in a person's heart. Then how should you proceed? Take the new Christian at his word! Assume that he meant it from his heart, and relate to him as a bona fide, brand new Christian from then on. If he did merely mumble some words that weren't really from his heart, it's because he wasn't ready to commit his life to Christ yet—there was still something in his way. But there is a very good chance that, as you treat him like a Christian and go over the follow-up material, that barrier might be removed and sometime during the process he'll take a genuine step of faith.

■ BROACHING THE SUBJECT

Immediately upon the completion of his prayer (or as soon as you hear from him that he has asked Christ into his life), you might say something like, "Joe, I want to be the first to welcome you to God's Forever Family! What you just did, if you really meant it, will be the most significant and far-reaching decision of your life! You're about ten seconds down the road of an adventure that's going to last *billions* of years! You may not feel any different right now, but I'd like to take a couple of minutes to give you just a small inkling of the incredible things that the Bible says just happened in your life."

Or, after expressing your excitement about his decision, you may ask him, "What thoughts are going through your mind right now?" or, "What do you feel like right now?"

If he says, "I just saw heaven rolling back like a scroll!" or something to that effect, rejoice with him! But he'll need to know soon that he can't base his faith on an emotional experience.

If he says, "I really don't feel any different," you can share with him that it's OK—even expected—not to feel different, that the Christian life is not based on emotions or feelings, but on the *facts* that are laid down in the Bible.

■ SUGGESTIONS FOR GROWTH

Some new Christians are going to need extensive input on this subject, while others will do fine on an abbreviated version. It depends on their backgrounds and on how much excess philosophical baggage they've got on board. It will be up to you, with the help of the Holy Spirit, to determine how deeply you'll need to dive into this important area.

I. Defuse the "experience bomb."

In Campus Crusade for Christ's evangelistic tract (available from Here's Life Publishers) "Have You Heard of the Four Spiritual Laws?"[1] there is an excellent illustration to this end.

On page 12 they show a train engine labeled "Fact" pulling a coal car labeled "Faith" and a caboose labeled "Feeling." Either use the tract and read him the text that's written there, or draw and explain your own diagram.

Here's how they draw it in the book:

Explain that the engine, "Fact," represents what we know to be true on the basis of the Word of God.

The coal car, "Faith," represents our beliefs, our confidence in certain truths, which leads to opinions and actions. When we say we have faith in something, we are saying we believe it to be absolutely true, and we are willing to take action based on that belief. If I say I have faith that a certain chair will hold me up, I won't hesitate to sit down on it.

The caboose, "Feelings," represents our subjective, emotional sensitivities and impressions. The train will run with or without the caboose, but it goes nowhere without the engine. Also, the train moves only if you shovel coal from the coal car into the engine. In the same way, our Christian lives will move only if we place our *faith* in the *facts* of God's Word.

Now, as the engineer, you could hop up into the caboose and start hollering, "OK! Let's get this train moving! Start shoveling that coal back into here! Fire up this caboose and we'll get rolling! C'mon, everybody, SHOVEL!" Just as the caboose has no ability to power a train, so your feelings have no ability to empower or direct your life as a Christian. It doesn't matter how much faith you put in your feelings, they won't get you anywhere. The facts will. Jesus said in John 8:32, "Then you shall know the *truth,* and the truth will set you free." David said in Psalm 119:105, "Your word is a lamp to my feet and a light for my path," not my hunches, intuition or feelings.

II. Help him to understand the truth
of what just happened.

As mentioned in the stated training objective for "Assurance of Salvation," there are five key points that the new Christian needs to grasp:

A. Christ has indeed come into his life.

Revelation 3:20 says: "Here I am! I stand at the door and knock. If anyone hears my voice and opens the door, I will come in and eat with him, and he with me." Ask the new Christian, "What do you think the 'door' in this verse represents?" (The door of his life — his heart; his will.) "Did you open that door? What does it say He'll do if you open the door?" (Come in.) "So where would you say Jesus is right now?" (Inside of me!)

I know some people are hesitant to use Revelation 3:20 to prove that Christ will come into the lives of those who ask Him to — they feel it is being used out of context. It's true that the verse is contained in a message the Lord sent specifically to the church of Laodicea, and that its most strict interpretation should be considered in that context, but the idea that is communicated can be found throughout Scripture. It's just that it is most eloquently and simply expressed here. We know that God is taking the initiative with the unbeliever; He's knocking on the unbeliever's "door" (Romans 5:8; 2 Corinthians 5:18-20; 1 Peter 3:18). We know that the unbeliever must hear (John 5:24; Romans 10:17) and respond (John 3:16; Acts 16:30,31), and when he does, Christ will come into his life (John 1:12; 14:16,17,23; Colossians 1:27). You might prefer to share all of those verses, or simply share Revelation 3:20 with him and explain about the context later.

B. He has been reborn as a whole new creation.

Share 2 Corinthians 5:17 with your disciple: "Therefore if any man is in Christ, he is a new creature; the old things passed away; behold, new things have come." Ask him what he thinks the verse is talking about when it says he has become a "new creature." After he's taken a good stab at it, take him over to John 3 and have him read verses 1-8 about the conversation between Jesus and Nicodemus. Explain to him that every person living today has been born into the physical realm—but that one birth wasn't enough. Since God exists in the spiritual realm, it is necessary that we be born into that realm as well in order to have fellowship with Him. That occurred when we invited Christ into our life. We didn't have much choice about our first birth, but we have total control of our decision about our second birth.

You might want to talk about the three-dimensional man. We were all born into this world as two-dimensional, with a body and a mind. We were physical and mental, but when we asked the Spirit of Christ to enter our life, we gained a third dimension, the spiritual. Until that time, it had been impossible for us to relate with God or to experience His presence, because He existed on a plane we had no access to. When we were born into the spiritual realm, we then received the supernatural equipment that makes relating with God possible.

One of the primary ramifications of this fact, and one that we must help the new Christian grasp, is that, since he is now a spiritual being, there is power available to him in the form of the indwelling Spirit of God, which wasn't there before. He is now different down to the very core of his being. Help him to understand that these differences may not be apparent immediately, but as he matures in Christ, they will become more and more evident. Here are a few other verses you might want to consider sharing with him on this subject:

Psalm 51:10	2 Corinthians 3:18	Galatians 6:15
Ezekiel 36:26,27	2 Corinthians 4:6,7	Ephesians 2:4-6,10
Acts 1:8	Galatians 2:20	2 Timothy 1:7

C. All his sins—past, present and future— have been forgiven.

Look up each of the passages at the top of the following page and jot a summary of it in your notebook. Share one or two of them that really speak to you on this subject. Don't overwhelm the poor guy with seven or eight verses, just make your point and move on.

Psalm 32:5	Jeremiah 33:8	Colossians 2:13,14
Psalm 103:3	Matthew 26:28	Hebrews 8:12
Psalm 103:12	Acts 10:43	Hebrews 10:16,17
Isaiah 1:18	Acts 26:17,18	1 John 1:9
Isaiah 38:17	Ephesians 1:6,7	1 John 2:12
Isaiah 43:25	Ephesians 4:32	Revelation 1:5

You (and he) may be wondering about the "future" part of the objective: His sins, past, present and *future,* have been forgiven. This question is resolved with simple logic: It's not logical that God would forgive only the sins we have committed up to the point of conversion, and then impute all subsequent sins to our account. None of us would make it, if that were the case. His forgiveness is timeless (Hebrews 10:12). He sees the entire scope of our sin with one look, and lays *all* of our iniquities on Christ (Isaiah 53:6; 1 Peter 3:18). If He hadn't died for all of our sin — past, present and future — He could never "bring us to God." (There is probably no need to go into all of this with the new convert. I share it mainly for your benefit, and just in case he asks.)

D. A new relationship has been established between him and God.

This objective really covers two bases:

- He needs to know that he really was lost before conversion.

- He needs to know that the reasons behind his lostness are gone now, and things are totally different between him and God.

He probably has a pretty good grasp of the first point, or he would not have felt a need to be saved. But it's good to feel him out on that subject as you talk — he may see his commitment to Jesus Christ as a nice idea, but not essential for salvation.

The second point will probably be a new concept for him. He needs to understand that, far from being an enemy of God and utterly separated from Him, he is now looked upon by God with incredible favor. The Lord has loved him all along, but now, at long last, He can express that love directly! He now sees the new Christian as a friend, an heir, a genuine, legitimate son! Check these verses and share one or two with the new convert:

John 1:12	2 Corinthians 5:17
Romans 5:6-8	Ephesians 2:1-7
Romans 8:15-17	

E. He will never again be separated from God.

This is where I am going to get into trouble with those of you who do not believe in the eternal security of the believer. I know that there are a few verses in the Bible that, if you look at them a certain way, seem to indicate that it is possible for one to lose his salvation. But as I have studied the Word, it seems that the overwhelming weight of proof is in favor of eternal security — that once you are saved, you are saved for good. Jesus told us that He would give those who believed in Him *eternal* life (Matthew 19:29; John 3:16,36; 5:24; 6:40,47; 10:28; 17:2,3; etc.). The only word that Jesus ever used to describe the kind of life that He would impart to those who belonged to Him was *aionios,* which means "indeterminate as to duration, eternal, everlasting, forever."[2] Some try to say it refers not to the quantity (or duration) of life God gives, but to the quality. In fact, it refers to *both.* J. Guhrt asserts in Brown's *Dictionary of New Testament Theology:*

> The word *eternal* here indicates a definite quality: It is a different life from the old existence typified by hate, lack of love, sin, pain and death. Eternal life does not therefore just begin in the future, it is already the possession of those who have entered upon fellowship with Christ. Thus John 3:15 speaks of having eternal life in the present. But there is also a temporal sense, so that eternal (*aionios*) indicates the quantity of this life: Because it belongs to Christ, who himself is the Life, it has no end.[3]

Further, we know that *aionios* must refer to "never-ending" life for four reasons. First, because of how it is contrasted in 2 Corinthians 4:18 with *proskairos,* which means "for a season." Second, because of how it is used to describe things we know for sure are everlasting in time, such as God (Romans 16:26), His power (1 Timothy 6:16), His glory (1 Peter 5:10), the Holy

Spirit (Hebrews 9:14), etc. Third, because of the many other Greek words that Jesus could have used if He had meant anything other than "endless." Finally, because Jesus used *aionios* in Matthew 25:46 to describe both the punishment of the wicked and the life of the righteous. If eternal life is not endless, then neither is eternal punishment—a revelation which ought to lift Satan's spirits considerably.

One more shot. Let's assume, for a moment, that one *can* lose his salvation. Old Joe Jones (fictitious name) became a Christian on June 10, 1978, at which time he received "eternal life." But then came that fateful day, October 12, 1985, when Joe did whatever it is that one does to lose his salvation, and he lost his. A few months later, Joe died. About a millenia after that comes the Great White Throne Judgment, and Joe stands before God.

The books are opened, and God says, "Joe Jones, I see here that you had everlasting life at one time, but it only lasted for 7 years, 4 months and 2 days. Tough luck, friend. If only you'd died a little sooner, you would have had eternal life eternally."

Is it possible to say that a person had eternal life for only 7 years, 4 months and 2 days? No. Whatever else you might say about his life, you couldn't say it was ever eternal, or he'd still have it. The most you could say is that it was "temporarily eternal," which is not eternal at all.

Jesus said that He would never leave or forsake us (Hebrews 13:5), that He would never drive away those who come to Him (John 6:37), and that nothing is able to snatch His sheep away (John 10:27,28). In those three verses Jesus says we can't run away, He won't throw us away, and we can't be taken away. Was He mistaken in old Joe Jones's case?

If, after all that, you still think it's possible for a person to lose salvation, you need not proceed any further with this objective. It will seem silly to you! Your theology doesn't allow for "assurance of salvation," so move on to the next training objective. But for the rest of you, look up these three verses and jot down a summary next to them in your notebook:

Hebrews 13:5*b*   John 6:37   John 10:27,28

Share these verses with the new Christian and follow them with the statement I made above: "That means that Jesus has said we can't run away, He won't throw us away, and we can't be taken away. Once you're in, you're IN!"

Additional illustrations to share with your disciple:

1. The persistent request. There once was a young boy who made the decision to ask Christ into his heart, but wasn't sure that He had really come in. So every evening around the dinner table as the family would pray together, the boy would once again ask Jesus to come into his life. After a week of this, his father got an idea. Later that evening . . . "Johnny? Would you come into the living room, please?"

Johnny came bounding in. "Sure, Dad, what's up?"

But his dad called out again, "Johnny! I'm talking to you! Please come in to the living room!"

"Dad, I'm right here in front of you!"

"Johnny! I really need you in here — NOW!"

"I AM here, Dad!"

"Jooooohnnyyyy!"

"What's wrong with you, Dad? I've been standing right in front of you since the first time you called me!"

"I know you have been, son. Seemed a little crazy for me to keep calling you to come in here, didn't it?"

"Sure did!"

"Well, let me ask you something, Son. How do you think Jesus feels about you when you keep asking Him to come into your life?"

2. The father-son relationship. You will always be the son (or daughter) of your father. Even if it were legally possible for your earthly father to declare that you were no longer his child, or if it were possible for you to have your father's name deleted from all of your birth records, the undeniable, bottom-line fact of the matter is that he IS your father, genes, chromosomes, Roman nose, cleft chin and all. He was the one who gave you life, and nothing will ever change that. It's an unalterable fact of history.

It's the same way with your heavenly Father. When you were born again, the life that you were given came from God (John 1:12,13; 3:5,6). In John's first epistle, he calls Christians "born of God" (1 John 3:9; 4:7; 5:4,18), meaning that they were given life uniquely from God—He "bore" them. We're not merely adopted sons, though some biblical writers use that concept to demonstrate certain aspects of our son-ship. In the spiritual realm we are literal sons and daughters of God, because He gave birth to us. That, too, is an unalterable fact of history. Second Timothy 2:13 says, "If we are faithless, he will remain faithful, for he cannot disown himself."

3. *Noah and the ark.* When Noah and his family entered the ark, it was God who saw to it that the door was securely shut and sealed behind them (Genesis 7:16). It's the same way with us. Once we have entered Christ, God shuts the door behind us and seals it with His Holy Spirit (Ephesians 1:13,14).

4. *Double protection.* You are safe and surrounded by Jesus Christ ("in Christ"—2 Corinthians 5:17), and He, in turn, is surrounded by God (Colossians 3:1-3). That means that anything that gets to you must first make its way through both the Father and the Son (John 10:28-30).

5. *The Certificate of Debt.* Read Colossians 2:13,14:

> When you were dead in your sins and in the uncircumcision of your sinful nature, God made you alive with Christ. He forgave us all our sins, having canceled the written code, with its regulations, that was against us and that stood opposed to us; he took it away, nailing it to the cross.

Stories have come to us down through the ages that in Jesus' day, when a criminal was tried and convicted, he was put in prison and a "Certificate of Debt" was posted outside his cell, listing all of his crimes against particular people and/or against society. Often, when capital punishment by crucifixion was ordered, this Certificate of Debt was nailed on the condemned man's cross, so that all who passed by would know what he was being executed for.

Each of us has been tried and found guilty before God. This verse tells us that, upon salvation, God took away the Certificate of Debt that had been nailed to the wall outside our prison doors. Since there is no longer any certificate around describing our crimes, we are no longer compelled to remain in custody—we're free to go. But as we travel to Golgotha and take a close look at Jesus and the cross that is killing Him, we see our certificates fluttering in the wind, nailed just above His bloody head.

■ FURTHER RESOURCES

"How To Be Sure You're A Christian," Transferable Concept #1 by Bill Bright, available from Here's Life Publishers. It's an excellent booklet to send home with a new believer. It covers the concept that becoming a Christian involves a three-fold commitment: intellectual, emotional and volitional. It hits several reasons people hesitate to make those commitments, and gives good counsel as to why we should make them. It ends with some clear thoughts on how a person can know for sure that he is saved.

More Than a Carpenter by Josh McDowell (Tyndale House Publishers) would be great for someone who is still not too sure about the historicity of Christianity, or about the validity of Jesus' claim to be God. Or, if the person you are following up is from a culture that has little contact with Christianity or Jesus Christ, this would be an excellent book for getting him acquainted. The book primarily covers the "Liar, Lunatic or Lord Trilemma" first expressed by C. S. Lewis in *Mere Christianity.*

"The Uniqueness of Jesus," which is the introductory booklet to Campus Crusade for Christ's Bible study series, "Ten Basic Steps Toward Christian Maturity." It's an evangelistic Bible study but it also contains a raft of helpful information for someone who wants a firmer grasp of what he did when he invited Christ into his life. It has nineteen pages of tract-like text about the unique character Jesus was in history, about His claims and about His redemptive work. This section is followed by six short Bible studies (fill-in-the-blank type) covering sixteen pages.

"The Christian Adventure," Step 1 in the "Ten Basic Steps" series, would be another great booklet to send home with the new Christian. Lesson 1, "The Christian's Certainty," is right up our alley regarding assurance of salvation. Lesson 2 is titled "The Person of Jesus Christ," and will give the new convert a more extensive grasp of who Jesus Christ is. The rest of this "Step" would be for a little later.

"The Discipleship Series"[4] is another Campus Crusade for Christ publication. This series is designed primarily for use in a group study, but is easily adaptable for one-to-one. Book 1 of this series is entitled "Discovery Group," and lesson 1 will provide some good insight for the new Christian regarding assurance of salvation.

"Your Life In Christ," which is Book 1 in the Navigator's *Design for Discipleship* series, would give your new disciple a good, broad knowledge of some of the most important concepts regarding God, salvation and assurance of salvation. The four fill-in-the-blank studies are just right for a new Christian.

■ ENDING THE SESSION

Whatever you do, be sure to get his name and phone number, and give him yours. It's so important that you keep in contact with him now, which you can't do if you don't know how to get hold of him. You may agree to meet somewhere for a follow-up appointment, but get his name and phone number anyway. If your wires get crossed, or if one of you can't make it for some reason, you'll need to notify each other of changed plans.

Be sensitive toward the new Christian's time constraints. Remember, there's a good chance he didn't schedule time to be born again that day, so if it appears he's running late for an appointment or a class, don't try to monopolize his time. Spend as much time as you can with him, but don't take advantage of his hospitality.

Make an appointment with him as a follow-up to his decision. By making that appointment, you will be telling the new Christian:

- You're important to me; I care about you.

- What you have been doing is extremely significant and far-reaching; there is much more you need to know, and I'm eager to teach you.

- What you've done will probably raise further questions in your mind; I want to be there to help you find answers.

- You are beginning an incredible journey; you are a high enough priority to me that I am willing to make room in my life to get you started on the right path.

So before you part company, agree on a time and place to get together again. How soon? The sooner the better! Tomorrow wouldn't be too soon; anything over three days could be dangerous.

Here's an idea on how you might be able to slide gracefully into setting up an appointment. At the end of your time together, share 2 Corinthians 5:17 with him: "Therefore, if anyone is in Christ, he is a new creation; the old has gone, the new has come!" Then share something like this: "Bill, it says here that when you asked Christ to come into your life, God made you into a whole new creation. It says that the old has gone and the new has come. Do you have any idea what it's talking about? [He'll probably say no.] Well, I've spent quite a bit of time looking into that, and have discovered some pretty amazing things. We don't have a lot of time here today, so what would you think about getting together again Wednesday after work for about 45 minutes? I think what I have to share will really help you grow in your new relationship with God."

If you prefer, rather than 2 Corinthians 5:17, you might use 1 Corinthians 2:6-10a or verse 12 as a good take-off passage.

What if he says no?

It's not very likely, but if it happens, your best move is back off—for now. Many people don't want to be pushed. They've got salesmen pushing them, bosses pushing them, teachers pushing them, peers pushing them, parents pushing them, a spouse pushing them, and this new Christian may just be "pushed out." Tell him you understand, and that you want him to know that, if he has any questions, you're available any time, day or night. Leave him with some sort of follow-up material, your name and phone number, a Bible if he doesn't have one, and a lot of warmth and good-will. Then go to your knees (well, wait till you're out of his sight). You'll need to give the Holy Spirit a chance to work in his life for a while to develop in him a thirst for living water. Your faithful prayers for this new Christian will greatly enhance that process.

After a few days, get back in touch with him and invite him over to the house for dinner, a ball game, a movie — something non-threatening and on neutral ground. You be the judge, but inviting him to church or to a Bible study might not be the best thing to do yet. He may fear falling into the hands of a bunch of fanatic reformers. Remember, he may be pretty amazed at the courage and commitment you showed by witnessing to him, and he may be hesitant to throw in with you for fear that you'll expect him to do the same thing tomorrow. He needs to know you're a regular human being just like he is, and there's nothing to fear in Christians or the Christian life. This insight can best be gained as he observes you in your natural habitat.

On the other hand, you may sense that he is now hungry for Christian fellowship. A lot of lonely people are just dying to find a group to plug into. So plug him in! Like I've said before, everyone's different, so you need to be flexible to accommodate those differences. For more on this, see Training Objective #6.

In the course of your time together, you might casually ask him how things have been going since he's become a Christian. Has he noticed any changes yet? Has he had a chance to read any of the material you left with him? Any questions? Hopefully, he'll have something to say that will give you the chance for a little input. Don't get too preachy, though. You still want to help him feel relaxed around you and other Christians. A sermon now could be counter-productive.

If it seems right to you, ask him again if he'd like to get together with you in a few days to learn more about his new relationship with God. Or, you may want to hold off, and just keep working on becoming his friend for a while. You and the Holy Spirit will have to decide on timing.

■ ASSIGNMENT FOR NEXT TIME

Be sure to give him something to take home to read. If you shared the "Four Spiritual Laws" booklet with him, ask him to take it home and read it over again. If you drew out the Navigator bridge illustration, encourage him to take your art work home and review it. Maybe you could show him how to look up the verses you wrote down.

Another good idea is always to have some kind of prepared follow-up study tucked away in your Bible, purse, glove box, bowling bag, etc. You can purchase one or more of the materials I mentioned in the Further Resources section above, or develop your own. You might even want to photocopy portions of books, Bible studies or magazine articles that build on your unique style of witnessing and the content you usually share.

If you are caught off-guard and simply don't have anything with you, be sure to at least suggest he read a certain portion of Scripture. I like to suggest a new convert begin reading the Gospel of John. It's pretty easy to find, most people have heard of it before, and it very clearly presents Jesus as the Son of God, a concept he needs to grasp early.

■ EVALUATION

Following are some questions to ask the new convert, after you've had some input, in order to determine if he does indeed have assurance of his salvation. Don't ask all of them, just one or two that you feel are best:

1. If you were to die tonight and stand before God, and He were to say, "Why should I let you into My heaven?" what would you say?

2. If someone were to ask you, "How can I be sure I'm a Christian?" what would you say?

3. What are some things you can do to make yourself worthy of God's love? (Trick question. "Nothing" is the right answer.)

4. Do you really think that you're good enough for God to save you? (Another trick question. "No" is the right answer. We'll never be good enough to deserve salvation. We are saved only on the basis of God's grace (Ephesians 2:8,9; Titus 3:5). Well, how good must you be? (We're not saved on the basis of our goodness; it's on the basis of God's grace. This must be firmly grasped by the new Christian, so keep emphasizing it!)

5. Draw a line with 0% at one end and 100% at the other end, like this:

0%_____100%

Ask him to put an X on the line where it would indicate how certain he is that if he were to die tonight, he would go to heaven.

If you determine that he still isn't sure of his salvation, try to learn what is hindering that conviction and help him over that specific barrier. Following are a few common reasons people lack this assurance:

1. They misunderstand the basis of salvation: grace; undeserved merit. Jesus paid the penalty for our sins and God forgave us. There is nothing we can do to earn it or to lose it.

2. They never actually have received Christ personally (or are not sure).

3. They are looking for an emotional experience.

4. They rely on day-to-day feelings.

5. They lack the knowledge that it is God who keeps us.

RECOMMENDED RESOURCE FOR FOLLOW-UP

THE FIRST YEAR OF YOUR CHRISTIAN LIFE by Steve Pogue. A friendly, basic guide for the new believer that helps him understand his new commitment to Christ and get started in successful prayer, Bible study, fellowship, and witnessing. It's especially ideal for those new Christians you are unable to follow up personally; or, you can give this book to your disciple as supplementary reading. Churches are using it successfully in their New Converts classes.

Available March 1989 at Christian bookstores,
or from Here's Life Publishers.
(Call 1-800-854-5659; in California call 714-886-7981.)

10 TRAINING OBJECTIVE #2

SCOPE AND SIGNIFICANCE OF SALVATION

■ OBJECTIVE:

The disciple understands in greater detail the scope and significance of what occurred when he invited Christ into his life, which produces a deeper commitment and a greater motivation to go on with Christ.

■ BIBLICAL BASIS FOR THIS OBJECTIVE

- 1 John 5:11-13; Romans 8:15-17: God desires that we know for certain that we are saved.

- 2 Corinthians 11:3; Ephesians 2:8,9; Acts 16:30,31: The simplicity of salvation by grace through faith cannot be denied, yet the significance and scope of salvation is vast and many-faceted. It involves issues that the prophets of old, the apostles and even the angels have longed for eons to investigate and understand (1 Peter 1:10-12; Ephesians 3:8-10).

- Hebrews 1:1,2; 2 Peter 1:16-21: The mysteries of salvation have now been made clear to us through God's written Word.

- 2 Peter 1:10-12; Hebrews 6:11,12,19,20: It follows that the more a person knows about the magnitude of his decision to follow Christ, the more committed he will be to that decision.

- Ephesians 6:13-17: This increased knowledge will help him begin to "take up the full armor of God" so that he will be able to "stand firm."

Albert Barnes, the great theologian of the mid-1800s, commented on verse 17 ("take the helmet of salvation"):

The idea here is that a well-founded hope of salvation will preserve us in the day of spiritual conflict and will guard us from the blows which an enemy would strike. The helmet defended the head—a vital part—and so the hope of salvation will defend the soul, and keep it from the blows of the enemy. A soldier would not fight well without a hope of victory. A Christian could not contend with his foes, without the hope of final salvation; but, sustained by this, what has he to dread?[1]

■ PEP TALK FOR THE DISCIPLEMAKER

Assuming this is your first follow-up meeting with the new Christian, you actually have two objectives for this session. First, to further establish a good, friendly rapport with him, and second, to help him get a clearer picture of what happened to him when he asked Christ into his life. We'll talk about the first point later under "Broaching the Subject," but let's chat about the second point right now.

There is no way (short of the supernatural intervention of God) that a five-minute-old Christian can grasp all the things you shared with him about his salvation the last time you were together. He has needed some time to evaluate his decision and let it sink in a little. By now his mind may be full of questions regarding what happened when he "prayed that prayer." He has agreed to meet with you; he has demonstrated his commitment by showing up; and he is hungry for some answers!

For new Christians who have little or no follow-up, it's usually months before they finally grasp the significance of their decision. When I invited Christ into my life, I didn't tell anybody for several weeks, and therefore had no immediate follow-up. As a result, I spent considerable time bewildered about my so-called "new life in Christ." I was looking for something dramatic to happen, and it wasn't happening. *I must not be doing this right,* I thought. I suppose I asked Christ to come into my life fifty times during that period, expecting that, just like with an old lawn mower, if I gave it just the right amount of oomph and body English, I could get 'er started. As I look back on that period, and remember the despair I felt, the sin I engaged in, and the pull that the world exerted on me, I can see that it really *was* only by the grace of God that I made it through!

But your friend doesn't need to go through all that, does he? By getting—with your help—a clear picture of what happened he'll see that he is part of an incredible, eternal movement of God, and that he has been re-created and abundantly supplied to be a significant part of that movement.

■ BROACHING THE SUBJECT

Don't dive into the lesson right away. Spend some time getting to know each other. Show some personal interest in him. Help him see that you're a friend, not a college instructor or a guru. Here are a few ideas regarding what to cover early in this first, all-important meeting. You probably won't want to hit *all* these things, just a few that you feel comfortable with.

1. What's his family background? Brothers? Sisters? Married? Kids?

2. Where is he from originally, and what brought him here?

3. Where does he live? (You're not necessarily looking for an address to write down—you're just interested in what part of town. You might be neighbors.)

4. What does he like to do with his free time? Hobbies? Sports?

5. Where did (or does) he go to high school or college? Major? Sports?

6. Does he have a job? What does he do? How long has he done it?

7. What has been his religious background up to this point?

Don't fire these off in rapid succession as if he's going through a job interview. These are just things that might come up in any casual conversation. You'll want to share about your life, too, but keep it brief. It's not that you want to be secretive about your background, but you're trying to put him at ease, and people generally love to talk about themselves.

Now slide on into more spiritual subjects by asking him something like, "How have things been going since last Tuesday? Have you noticed any changes or come up with any questions?"

Don't forget to listen! Don't be so intent on galloping on to
your prepared lesson plan that you gallop right over the guy's
fragile, developing spirit! He might have some heavy-duty
questions that have been plaguing him for the past several days
(or years!) that he's dying to ask you. At this stage of his growth,
he's like a newborn baby, and if you don't meet his immediate,
felt needs first, he'll not hold still for anything else. Have you
ever tried to get a photograph of a smiling, contented infant
when that infant is in dire need of a diaper change? You might
as well try to hug water. If you don't change that diaper first,
you'll never get your photo. The same principle holds true with
the new Christian. Meet the felt needs first, then move on to
the other important subjects.

You might start by saying something like, "Well, Bill, last
time we were together you took the most significant step of
your life. Do you remember that verse I shared with you about
becoming a 'new creation' (2 Corinthians 5:17)? I'd like to show
you what the Bible says is included in 'The New You.' These
passages all talk about what happened to you when you asked
Christ to come into your life."

All told, I'm listing seventeen points to cover in this training objective. I know that's a lot, but remember, you don't have
to wade through a doctoral dissertation on each one of them.
Just hit the high points, helping him get the big picture about
the incredible things that have happened to him.

■ SUGGESTIONS FOR GROWTH

In order to give the new Christian a well-rounded view of
his new position, I like to divide the session up into two parts:
his condition *before* Christ entered his life, and his condition
afterward.

FIRST, THE BAD GOOD NEWS –
Your condition before Christ.

Some may think this is a negative way to start, but I've
found it helpful for a new Christian to see exactly what he's
come out of. It should help him appreciate the salvation he has
received just that much more.

With each point, I'll include a comment or two that I might make to somebody I was following up. Don't feel you must do it the same way I do, or even use the same examples, parables or verses. Develop the ones that will best fit your personality and style of ministry. And as I mentioned before, it's best to look up the Scripture with your disciple, let him read the verse, and ask him what he thinks it is saying.

1. A condemned sinner—Romans 3:23

"This means that you, along with all the rest of us, had missed the mark of God's perfect righteousness. Did you know that the word *sin* was originally a Greek archery term? They would shoot their arrows at a target and then measure the distance between where the arrow hit and the bullseye. That distance was called the 'sin' of the arrow. With us, the bullseye is complete and total righteousness, doing everything God wants us to do and not doing anything God doesn't want us to do. Even though most of us were aiming at that bullseye, we all missed."

2. Separated from God—Isaiah 59:2

"Even though God loved you, your sins had set up a great gulf between you and Him. Like it says here, He wouldn't even listen to you while you were in that condition. Before you asked Christ into your life, did God seem silent and far away? Well, this is why."

3. Headed for hell—Revelation 20:11-15

"When you invited Christ into your life, your name was written in the 'book of life' talked about here. If you had died before accepting Christ's forgiveness, this passage would have been talking about you."

If you think that passage might be a little too heavy for him, use Matthew 25:31-46 instead and develop it like this:

"When you invited Christ into your life, you were changed from a goat to a sheep. Quite a metamorphosis, eh? If you had died before accepting Christ's forgiveness, this passage says that your destiny would have been 'eternal fire' and 'eternal punishment.' By the way, did you ever wonder how, if God is such a loving God, He could send people to hell? This passage tells us that God doesn't send anybody to hell. They go there of their own free will. It says here that hell was originally created to be a place of eternal judgment only for the devil and his followers, not for humans. But many humans have decided to quit following God and follow Satan instead, either not realizing—or not *wanting* to realize—that his final destination is hell. God's total concern right now is to snatch people *off* that road to eternal judgment, not put them on it."

4. Unable to please God—Isaiah 64:6

"Were there times, before you were a Christian, that you looked at your life, compared yourself with others who were more sinful than you, and thought, *I'm not such a bad guy. My good far outweighs my bad. I ought to make it to heaven*? I know I used to think that way. And relative to some other people here on earth, you and I probably were pretty good people. But God says that, compared to His righteousness, the kind of righteousness it takes to get into heaven, the best we could be was like filthy rags. We were fooling ourselves, Bill. We thought that God's standards for right and wrong were relative, but in reality, they were absolute—and the absolute standard was His own perfection. Now, I'm not trying to lay a guilt trip on you here. I'm just trying to show you what we've been saved from, the hopelessness of our previous circumstances, and the incredible magnitude of the salvation God has given us."

It's good to reassure the new Christian that you're not trying to put him down or describe him as some dirty, rotten sinner who isn't worth the mud it took to put him together. He just needs to know that his life before Christ was not acceptable to God. Nothing personal—we were all in that boat once.

NEXT, THE GOOD GOOD NEWS—
Your condition after Christ.

1. You were declared righteous
in the eyes of God—Hebrews 10:12-14

"When you asked Jesus Christ to come into your life the other day, what you did, in essence, was ask God to transfer the penalty for your sins over to Christ's account. He died on the cross almost 2000 years ago, but it wasn't until the other day that His sacrifice was finally applied to you.

"It's like this: Say you and I were a couple of burglars, and we were caught red-handed robbing a home for disabled orphans. They haul us off to court. We are tried, found guilty and, because of the nature of our crime, the judge pronounces a very harsh penalty. His sentence: We must bestow all of our earthly goods to the disabled orphans home.

"I say to the judge, 'I know we are guilty, but my friend here has a family to care for. I don't want to see them suffer. I'd like to pay his fine for him.'

" 'That's very noble,' says the judge, 'But you're going to be a little short after paying your own fine. You'll have nothing left with which to pay his! Request denied!'

"But at that moment, the judge's son, who has been watching the proceedings, steps up to the bench. He's an old friend of yours, but you never realized how great a friend he was until that moment. He says, 'Dad, I'll pay both their fines. You can take all that I have to satisfy their sentences, only let them each go free.'

"That's what happened when you were saved. Jesus approached the bench of His Father and said, 'I'll take his penalty.' Because He had never sinned, and had no sentence of His own to serve, He was able to take yours. Your sins were transferred to His 'record,' and now, whenever the Father looks at your record, He sees that it's clean. There's not a mark on it."

2. Your sins were forgiven and forgotten — Hebrews 10:15-17

"This is how it was possible for you to be declared righteous in God's eyes: Something had to be done about your sins. Your sins had separated you from God and were pulling you to hell. There could be no association between a holy God and sinful man, or God would be sanctioning and endorsing sin. God told us what was right and wrong, and also told us what the consequences of our disobedience would be, yet every one of us has refused to obey Him. A holy, righteous God can't just say, 'Oh, well, boys will be boys!' and let it slide. When those sins were removed from your record, though, God no longer had any reason to keep His distance. When He looks at you now, all He can see is the sinless righteousness of Jesus Christ!

"Notice one more fact about this passage: It says He won't even remember our sins any more. As far as He knows, we have never sinned. When we were justified before God, from then on it was 'just-as-if-I'd never sinned'! He won't hold our sinful past against us, because in His eyes, we have no sinful past!"

3. The Holy Spirit entered your life—Romans 8:11

"Where does this passage say the Holy Spirit is now? ["In me."] Right! From now on, God is as close to you as your heart and lungs! When you asked Christ to come into your life, He entered your life in the form of His Holy Spirit. You will continue to have problems in your life, but you can take courage, because you are now indwelt by the Supreme Problem Solver of the Universe!"

4. You have been born again—John 3:1-8

"I know the term 'born again' has become a rather trite and meaningless expression, referring to anyone who experiences a profound change in his lifestyle. But the way it was originally used by Jesus has nothing to do with a lifestyle—except coincidentally. It had to do with an actual birth. Everybody who is alive today has been born into the physical realm. But the kingdom of God is a completely different dimension: the spiritual realm. In order for one to be able to enter God's kingdom, he must be born a second time, this time into the realm of the Spirit. This is what happened to you when you gave your life to Christ. Before, you were only a body and a soul. Now you are three-dimensional: body, soul and spirit. You've been born twice: physically and spiritually."

5. You were given eternal life—1 John 5:11,12

Take a book, slip a dollar bill into it, and hand it to your disciple.

"Here's a book. If I offer you the book, and you take it, what have you got, just a book? ["No, I've got a book with a dollar bill in it."] Right. This book represents Jesus Christ and the dollar bill represents eternal life. If you receive this book, you also get the dollar bill. When you received Jesus, you also received eternal life, because eternal life is found 'in Jesus.' Where is Jesus Christ right now in relation to you? ["Inside of me."] If you have Jesus, then what else do you automatically have? ["Eternal life."] Right! Like this verse says, if you have the Son, you have the life!"

6. You were made into a new creation – 2 Corinthians 5:17

"Physically, we can't see any difference in ourselves as a result of being born again. But spiritually, in ways we can't see, we are a totally new creature! We have been outfitted with spiritual equipment that, if we could only see it, would blow our minds. The 'New You' is as different from the 'Old You' as a cornstalk is from a corn seed, and it's going to take us a lifetime to familiarize ourselves with all this new potential we've been given."

7. You were reconciled to God – 2 Corinthians 5:18

"What do you think the term *reconciled* means? [Let him answer.] You hear the term in divorce courts a lot, but in a little different form: 'irreconcilable differences.' Usually this means that one or both of the marriage partners decide they don't like the other, and no longer want to have anything to do with that person. That is somewhat the way it was between us and God, except that while we didn't want Him, He did want us. The Father has been working a long time to draw you back to Himself, and through Christ's death on the cross and the work of the Holy Spirit, He finally accomplished that just the other day. You're together again – the divorce is off . . . permanently!"

8. You are no longer at war with God – Romans 5:1

"Even though God has been deeply in love with us our whole lives, He has had to look upon us as enemies, because we had joined Satan's rebellion against Him.

"We'll talk more about this later, but let me give you a quick overview.[2] It all started centuries ago, long before man had been created. The Bible says that God created thousands of angels, and the number one angel, Lucifer, the most beautiful and intelligent of them all, decided he wanted to take over God's position as God. The essence of his rebellion was that he didn't want anyone, not even the God of love and light, to rule over him. One-third of the angels joined Lucifer in this uprising, and there followed a war that would make World War III look like a game of checkers. Some Bible scholars think that the entire physical universe was left in shambles at the end of this battle.

"The forces of God won, and Lucifer (also known as Satan) and his followers (now called demons) were thrown out of God's kingdom. But Satan has never changed his mind. He still wants to be top dog, and he is still determined to be 'God' to people. When the first humans were created, he even convinced them to join his rebellion, and as a result, every one of their offspring have had a natural tendency to rebel against God's authority.

"There came a time in our lives when you and I made the decision to become traitors to God's forces and follow Satan. It wasn't at all obvious to us at the time — Satan's recruiting methods are far too clever. If we had known we were following in the footsteps of the originator of evil, we might have high-tailed it back the other direction. We thought we were just 'doing our own thing' or being the 'captain of our own soul' or whatever noble-sounding phrase seemed good at the time. The bottom line was that we didn't want God telling us what to do.

"Because of this stubborn self-will of ours, we actually joined Satan's rebellion, and became enemies of God. But God loves His enemies, and His battle strategy is not to kill us but to win us with love and to bring about our defection from Satan's loyalists. You and I were His enemies, but now He's made us His friends. We're at peace with Him."

9. Redeemed from the hand of the enemy — Colossians 1:13,14

"Do you know what *redeemed* or *redemption* means? [Let him answer.] The actual Greek meaning of the word is 'to buy back or out from,' as in buying a slave out from a slave market with a view to setting him free. That's what Christ did when He died on the cross. By shedding His blood, He redeemed or bought us back from Satan's slave market. He paid for us with His own death.

"It reminds me of a story I heard a long time ago. There was once a little boy who loved boats. If it was nautical, he was into it. When he was old enough to do it well, he decided to make a model sail boat. He labored for weeks on it, meticulously working out every detail of the vessel. Finally his boat was ready to go on its maiden voyage. The boy took it to a big lake, and cast it off. He was in seventh heaven watching his little boat plying the waters at the end of the string he held tightly in his hand. Suddenly, a gust of wind gave the little boat a jerk, and the string came loose from the boat. Sadly he watched as the boat sailed slowly out to the middle of the lake, and out of his sight.

"A few days later he happened to go with his parents to the town on the other side of the lake. As he walked past the toy store, his eyes almost popped out of his head — in the window he saw his boat! He ran into the store to tell the owner the boat was his, but the man wouldn't believe him. 'How do I know you're telling the truth? Who says this is your boat? If you want it, you'll have to pay for it just like anybody else.'

"For the next several weeks, the boy worked hard until he had finally earned enough money to buy the boat back. He got his parents to drive him back to the store, slapped the money down on the counter, looked the store owner square in the eye and said, 'NOW! GIVE ME MY BOAT!' The owner took the money, walked over to the window, picked up the boat and handed it to the boy.

"As the boy left the store, he could be heard talking gently to his precious boat, 'Now you're mine twice: once because I made you, and once because I bought you.' "

10. Brought into the kingdom of God — Colossians 1:13,14

"Another thing you see in this passage is that God has brought us into the kingdom of His Son. As I mentioned earlier, before Christ came into our lives we belonged to Satan's kingdom; we were part of his army, aiding his rebellion. But when the love of God kidnapped us from his domain, we didn't just become refugees with no place to hang our hats. We were escorted into the glorious kingdom of God!

"I know that's pretty hard for you to grasp. After we talked the other day, you probably went home to the same old house, ate dinner at the same old table, watched the same old TV, went to sleep in the same old bed, got up the next morning and went to the same old job, and you probably had not even a fleeting glance at anything that looked like a glorious kingdom. Well, a major component of the Christian life is believing in things you can't see.

"St. Augustine once said, 'Faith is to believe, on the Word of God, what we cannot see, and its reward is to see and enjoy what we believed.' It's true that we can't see any physical difference in the kingdom that we live in, but the Bible says that, in some unseen, spiritual dimension, we have been snatched out of the kingdom of darkness and deposited right smack in the middle of the kingdom of God. Satan is no longer our king, and we owe Him no more loyalty. We now swear our devotion to Jesus Christ who is our sovereign. The more time we log in this new kingdom, the more clearly we will be able to see it — in our attitudes, our actions, our allegiances, our priorities and the circumstances that surround us daily."

11. You became an adopted child of God, with all of the accompanying rights and privileges — Romans 8:15-17

"A lot of people talk about 'the fatherhood of God and the brotherhood of man' and apply it to all human beings. It's a nice thought, and I sure hope that someday everyone in the world will function like one big, happy family, but the Bible says that God was not our Father until the day we invited Christ into our lives. He was our creator, but we did not begin to enjoy the benefits of His fatherhood until we were born again.

"It's not like He merely said, 'OK, now you can be on My team'; or, 'Now you can come live in My kingdom.' He said, 'I want to make you My *son*. I want to give you a place in My household. I want to make you an heir to My kingdom. I want to make all of My resources available to you. I want to nurture you, care for you, be there for you. I want you to call me Daddy (which is what *Abba* means in the passage listed above).'

"It would take a long time to go over all of the things we have acquired as co-heirs with Christ. Winning the grand prize on 'Wheel of Fortune' wouldn't hold a candle to it!

"But notice the last sentence of this passage, the one about sharing in His sufferings. What do you think that means? [Give him a chance to answer.] I get the idea from this that walking with Christ is not going to be like an afternoon at Disneyland. While Jesus was on earth, He went through some pretty tough times. Even the Son of God experienced adversity! This verse tells us that being a son of God, a brother of Jesus Christ, does not guarantee we will not endure hardship while here on earth.

"But look at what else it says: If we share in His sufferings, we will also share in His glory. We may have some rough times here as Christians, but in the end, it will be worth it all! Some people like to scoff at Christianity and say, 'I'm not interested in some pie-in-the-sky-by-and-by religion.' And the Christians get embarrassed by that. But the fact of the matter is, for the child of God, there *is* pie-in-the-sky! Sure, God helps us out while we're here on earth — we have advantages that non-Christians never dream about. However, it will not be just a bowl of cherries — you may get some of the pits! But this verse tells us that eventually we will partake of the glory of Jesus Christ, and our 'light, momentary distress' (as the apostle Paul calls our time here on earth in 2 Corinthians 4:17), will seem like nothing at all in comparison!"

12. A wall of supernatural protection was set up around you — Psalm 34:7

"As a kid, you probably heard about a 'Guardian Angel.' Well, here he is! Anything that gets to you has to first get through him, and the Bible describes these beings as very powerful.

"Again, this is not to say that, now that you belong to God, nothing negative will ever happen to you. It only says that you have a source of supernatural protection that wasn't there before, and any outside influence you encounter must receive the approval of 'the angel of the Lord' first. He will sometimes allow adversity and physical suffering to get through to you, because he is in direct communication with the Father at all times, and God knows that some trials and tribulations will ultimately be good for you. And He also knows exactly how much you can handle. God will never give you more than you can bear (1 Corinthians 10:13)."

13. All the angels in heaven know you and are rejoicing over you – Luke 15:10

"What rejoicing there was in heaven the day you invited Christ into your life! Several verses in the Bible indicate the angels' keen awareness and interest in every detail of what's going on here on earth (Psalm 91:11; 1 Corinthians 11:10; Hebrews 12:1; 1 Peter 1:12). By watching your life, Bill, they will learn about the effects of the grace of God. They learn more and more about God by watching how He takes care of you, and how you respond back to Him. You can be sure that you will never be alone, no matter how isolated you may feel."

■ FURTHER RESOURCES

For good fill-in-the-blank type studies about the scope and significance of what happened at salvation, take a look at the following Bible study series. You could use them as resource material for your own learning, or send one home with the new Christian to study on his own, provided, of course, he knows his way around a Bible.

"Ten Basic Steps Toward Christian Maturity,"[3] a Bible study series developed by Campus Crusade for Christ:

- Step Introduction: "The Uniqueness of Jesus" [All lessons apply.]

- Step 1, Lesson 1: "The Christian's Certainty"
  Lesson 2: "The Person of Christ"

"The Discipleship Series"[4] by Campus Crusade for Christ:

- Book 1, Lesson 1: "How to Be Sure You're a Christian

Design for Discipleship,[5] a Bible study series by The Navigators:

- Book 1, Chapter 1: "God Cares for You"
  Chapter 2: "The Person of Jesus Christ"
  Chapter 3: "The Work of Christ"

- Book 5, Chapter 1: "Who Is God?"

■ P.S. TO THE DISCIPLEMAKER

Does that seem like a lot to cover in one 45-minute to an hour session? It does to me, too! But I wanted to give you *more* material than you can use so that you could choose one of the following options:

1. Spend longer than an hour.

2. Choose only a few of the points I listed above.

3. Spend two or three sessions covering these concepts.

4. Go over all of the points, but comment only briefly on each one.

5. Talk real fast.

As you share these verses with the new Christian, be sure to write out the reference to each one — the whole name, not just an abbreviation — and let him take the paper home with him. Suggest that he look those verses up again later. Does he have a Bible? Does he know how to use the table of contents?

How will you remember all of these verses to share with him? I've got three suggestions:

1. You could jot the references on a note card, and look at it for each verse (don't worry about him seeing the card — he'll probably be impressed and flattered at the effort you put into your preparation on his behalf). Give him the card when you're done.

2. You could type out the points on a couple of pieces of paper that you would use as a focal point during your discussion with him. When you're done, let him take the sheets home so he can look up the verses on his own again later. Leave enough space between points so that you (or he) can jot down notes or draw diagrams. Make copies of your sheet (before you doodle on it) — you might be able to use it over and over with subsequent converts.

3. You could write a chain reference in your Bible. In the front of your Bible, write the verse for the first point on your list. Turn to that verse, and in the margin next to it, write the reference for the second point. Turn to

it, and do the same with the third, etc. You might even want to jot a thought or two that you want to remember about that verse in the margin. This way, you can flip from one verse to the next, not having to take the time to refer back to notes or a list each time. But if you use this option, be sure to write down the verse references for him, to give him something to take home and study later.

■ ENDING THE SESSION

Summarize; whet his appetite; set the next appointment. Before you part company, be sure to set up another appointment with him. You might set it for the same time next week, but it would be better if you could get together again within the next three or four days. You might say something like:

"Well, Bill, what do you think of the points we went over today? [Hopefully, he found them interesting and stimulating and is motivated to learn more.] I hope that one thing you got out of today's session was that there is a whole lot more to being a Christian than sitting on hard, wooden pews and paying attention to a lot of do's and don'ts. The Christian life is a *relationship* with a real person. Just before Jesus was crucified, He told His disciples that He had to go away, but that He would send the Holy Spirit in His place to be our 'paraclete' or helper. As we saw today, when you became a Christian, the Holy Spirit entered your life. One of the most important concepts you need to understand is who the Holy Spirit is and how you can fully appropriate the power He has made available to you.

"If you've got some time next Friday [or next week], I'd love to get together with you again and show you what the Bible tells us about that. What do you say?"

He'll say, "You bet, buddy! Let's go for it!"

But if he doesn't, if he seems hesitant to set a time to get together again, better back off. "Bill, I don't want to be pushy with this. You think about it and let me know if you're interested in learning more. I just want you to know I'm available, and I'm praying for you!"

Then follow the suggestions under the "Ending the Session"

section of Training Objective #1 in the part titled: "What if he says no?"

End with prayer. "You mean even in a public place?" Maybe. You need to be the judge of that. There are pros and cons. It may embarrass him right under the table, and he could dread meeting with you the next time, anticipating the repeated humiliation. On the other hand, it might be good for him to get his first taste of being openly identified with Christ. It could increase his commitment to both God and his relationship with you. You'll have to weigh the options and decide.

If you are meeting in a private place, like his home, a park, an abandoned mine shaft, I highly recommend a short prayer. Again, the decision is up to you. For the first few times you get together, it would probably be best if you did all the praying, without putting him on the spot. By listening to you, he'll more easily understand the simplicity of prayer.

■ ASSIGNMENT FOR NEXT TIME

The next subject you should cover with your disciple is the filling of the Holy Spirit. It would be a good idea for you to give him something to read on that subject in order to whet his appetite for your next time together. It's never too soon for him to begin to understand this all-important ministry. It could mean the difference between him standing or falling during the early days of his walk with Christ, not to mention his later days.

Dr. Bill Bright, founder and president of Campus Crusade for Christ, has said on many occasions that if he were sitting in a chair, and had a non-Christian on his right and a Christian who didn't understand the ministry of the Holy Spirit on his left, and he only had ten minutes and absolutely *had* to make a choice as to which one he would spend that ten minutes talking with, he would choose the Christian. That's how vital he feels an understanding of the Holy Spirit's ministry is.

A Christian who doesn't have a handle on the ministry of the Holy Spirit is destined for a life of defeat, despair and fruitlessness, while a Christian controlled and empowered by the Spirit can potentially win, build and send hundreds of other Christians in his lifetime. For this reason, we've got to be sure the new Christian comprehends this concept.

Leave with him one of the following:

"Have You Made the Wonderful Discovery of the Spirit-Filled Life?" Developed by Campus Crusade for Christ and available from Here's Life Publishers, this sixteen-page tract describes three kinds of people—natural, spiritual and carnal (1 Corinthians 2:14—3:3)—and how to appropriate the power of the Holy Spirit to become a spiritual man. It also goes into spiritual breathing—what a person should do when he sins. Confession is described as exhaling, and re-surrendering one's life to Christ is termed inhaling.

"How to Experience God's Love and Forgiveness," Transferable Concept #2 by Bill Bright, also available from Here's Life Publishers. An expansion of the tract mentioned above, it includes a short Bible study at the end.

If it might be a while before you see the new Christian again (like two weeks), you may want to give him Transferable Concept #3 as well, titled "How to Be Filled With the Spirit." It goes into more detail concerning who the Holy Spirit is, why He came, what it means to be controlled and empowered by the Holy Spirit, and how one can live consistently under His guidance.

■ EVALUATION

If he had trouble answering some of the questions from Training Objective #1's evaluation section, now would be a good time to bring them up. After this session, no doubt should remain as to his eternal destiny. He should be able to answer those questions properly with no hesitation whatsoever.

Formulate additional questions to see if he grasped the seventeen points talked about in this training objective. Here are a few examples, a question or two for each of the points covered:

1. Is it enough to just be trying hard to be a good person? Can that person be considered a Christian?

2. Why do you think God seemed silent to you before you became a Christian?

3. Does God send people to hell, or do people send themselves there?

4. Can we make it to heaven if "our good outweighs our bad"?

5. What needed to be taken care of in order for you to be saved? [My sin.]

6. What happened to your sin?

7. Where is the Holy Spirit now in relation to you?

8. What do you think the term *born again* means?

9. Having received Jesus Christ, what did you receive at the same time, according to 1 John 5:11,12?

10. What's the difference between the "New You" and the "Old You"?

11. What do you think it means when we say we have been reconciled to God? In what ways were we at odds with God?

12. What do you know about Satan's rebellion against God? How were we cooperating with Satan in this rebellion before we became Christians?

13. What do you think it means to be redeemed?

14. What differences do you notice about yourself or your surroundings now that you dwell in the kingdom of God rather than the kingdom of the devil?

15. What do you think about the phrase: "the Fatherhood of God and the brotherhood of man"? How does it apply to you? In what ways is God your Father?

16. What additional protection do you have now as a child of God?

17. What do the angels have to do with your salvation?

Don't feel you need to ask all of the above questions, or grill him mercilessly on these matters. Use just a few of them, or similar ones you formulate, to dig a little deeper in areas you might be especially concerned about. You could ask them during a discipling session, when you're done and walking out to your car or in a casual conversation later in the week. Employ them in a variety of contexts. Be flexible and spontaneous, and sensitive to the leading of the Holy Spirit!

11 TRAINING OBJECTIVE #3

FILLING
OF THE HOLY SPIRIT

■ OBJECTIVE

The disciple has a basic understanding and avails himself of the ministry of the Holy Spirit.

■ BIBLICAL BASIS FOR THIS OBJECTIVE

Following are a number of verses that address the subject of the filling of the Holy Spirit. Look up each reference and jot down a brief summary in your disciplemaker's notebook. In each case, I've included a thought or two about why I think the verse is important to the concept of the filling of the Holy Spirit.

- Acts 1:8: The Holy Spirit is the source of power in the Christian's life; we must be able to draw on His power in order to live an abundant and fruitful life.

- Romans 8:5,6: We have the option of setting our minds on either our old sinful nature or the things the Spirit desires. Each option carries its own unique consequences. Also, it is possible for the Spirit to control our minds.

- 1 Corinthians 2:14,15: The man controlled by the Spirit is able to discern spiritual truth.

- Ephesians 4:30: It is possible for us to act in a way contrary to the desires of the Holy Spirit, causing Him to grieve.

- Ephesians 5:16: The man controlled by the Holy Spirit is able to live a pure, righteous life.

- Ephesians 5:18: We are commanded to be filled with the Spirit, literally: "be being filled." We must have the option of being filled since a command can be either obeyed or ignored.

164

- Ephesians 5:25: This is an exhortation; therefore, it is possible for us to choose not to live in line with the designs and intentions of the Spirit.

- 1 Thessalonians 5:19: It is possible for us to hamper the work of the Holy Spirit in our lives.

■ APPLICABLE DEFINITIONS

The indwelling of the Holy Spirit: the entering of the Holy Spirit into the life of a repentant sinner as he is saved; the fact that the Holy Spirit permanently lives within those who are born again. This occurs in the life of every believer at the moment of salvation (John 14:16-18; John 16:7; Romans 8:9-11; 1 Corinthians 6:19). This is also known as the "baptism of the Holy Spirit." In Greek, to *baptize* means "to dip," and carries with it the idea of "being immersed into a new environment." When we were "baptized in the Holy Spirit," we were brought into the environment or sphere of influence of the Spirit (1 Corinthians 12:13).

The filling of the Holy Spirit: the directing, controlling and empowering influence of the Holy Spirit in the life of a believer who has submitted his will to the will of God. Filling may occur frequently, even daily and hourly, in a believer's life. Filling depends upon the initiative and obedience of the believer.

■ PEP TALK FOR THE DISCIPLEMAKER

As mentioned in the previous chapter, understanding the ministry of the Holy Spirit could well be one of the most important concepts your new-believer friend will ever learn.

Billy Graham recently said that 90 percent of the Christians in the United States are carnal Christians, people who are living lives of defeat and impotence because they either will not or don't know how to allow the Holy Spirit to control and empower their lives. A Gallup poll taken in the early '80s told us that well over half the people in the United States consider themselves born-again Christians. So where are they hiding? Where is their influence? Where are their voices in our legislatures, our universities, our media, our businesses, our streets? In most cases, they have quietly disconnected from the source of their power: the Holy Spirit. For whatever reasons, they have decided to set their minds on what their sinful natures desire, rather than on what the Spirit desires (Romans 8:5,6). As a result, it is increasingly difficult for the Holy Spirit to find open conduits through which He can influence the world.

Unless we give the Holy Spirit free reign in our lives, He'll never enjoy free reign in our country (at least, not before the coming of Christ). Your disciple needs to learn early that the Holy Spirit wants to direct and empower him to do the will of God.

When it comes to wanting to do the will of God, most new Christians can put us veterans to shame. They are usually so fresh, eager and committed to doing anything God wants them to do that you have no problem motivating them. The only thing they lack is knowledge concerning how to go about it effectively.

By the way, how about you, my disciplemaking friend? Have you given the Holy Spirit free reign in your life? Or are there still areas to which you will not allow God access? Has He prompted you to do something you have dragged your feet about? Is your life characterized by a lack of power or a lack of fruit? If so, maybe you'd better turn that stethoscope on yourself, doc. Remember, you will be able to take your disciple only as far as where you are in your own spiritual growth.

The controversy.

There is a controversy regarding the extent of the role of the Holy Spirit in maturing us. Some say that Christian maturity comes only as a direct result of the Holy Spirit's work in our lives. If you aren't growing, or spending time in prayer and in the Word, or witnessing for the Lord, it's because, somewhere along the line, you took control of your life away from the Holy Spirit and are trying to run it yourself. These people hold that if you simply take a minute and re-enthrone Him through prayer, you will again experience His power in your life, and things will fall back into place.

The other side says maturity will come about only as a result of a faithful, obedient walk with the Lord. The Holy Spirit is always there, but He empowers your life and makes you grow gradually through "renewing your mind" as you discipline yourself in Bible study, prayer, etc. The more time you log in His Word, for instance, the more you'll see His power and direction in your life.

Then there is a third side (which I throw my lot in with) that supports a combination of those two concepts, holding that elements of both contribute to power and growth in the Christian life. If we think only about the Holy Spirit, not bothering to obey God in such things as Bible study, prayer, fellowship, witnessing, etc., we might be emotionally tied to God, but we would be of little use due to a lack of depth in our lives. Conversely, if we are intensely disciplined in carrying out the mechanics of the Christian life to the exclusion of developing a genuine relationship with God through the Holy Spirit, we might be well-informed and impressive, but still be of little use because God has not been allowed to steer that knowledge toward where He wants it. Both components — depending on the supernatural empowering of the Spirit, and developing personal obedience and discipline — are required.

It's cyclical: We look to Him for power, direction and motivation — He gives it, and then looks to us to respond in obedience, commitment and discipline. As we do that, we are moved to a greater love and dependence on Him, and we draw more deeply on His power. He gives more, enabling us to pursue greater depths of obedience and commitment. The wheels go round and round . . .

Our goal is to produce balanced disciples. So much success in the Christian life is found in the balance between *discipline* and *relationship*; the teeth-gritting decision to say no to our old nature, and yet to run emotionally to the arms of our "Daddy" for protection. We need good old-fashioned will power to haul us out of bed at 6 in the morning to have a quiet time (discipline), which results in the beauty of the give and take of communion with the Lover of our souls (relationship). Sometimes grim determination is required to memorize Scripture, yet there is unbounded delight when our Father takes that Word, breathes life into it and says, "This is what I want to say to YOU!"

It is a cycle, but we can short-circuit it at any point. We must never tell our disciples that, if they will just say the magic words, they'll turn into "Super-Christian!" By the same token, they must know that pure discipline is no ticket to maturity either, or the Pharisees would have been the spiritual giants of Jesus' day.

■ BROACHING THE SUBJECT

Your disciple probably has had some ups and downs since your last meeting, and no doubt has some questions. Let him talk. Ask questions of your own. Draw him out. Ask him about what he shared during your last meeting. For instance, suppose he had told you he made an offer on a new house. Ask him if it went through. Or maybe he was a little anxious about a test coming up at school. Ask him how it went. If you have begun to keep a one-to-one diary of your meetings with him, you probably have written down this kind of information after each meeting. Not only does this provide information for your own times of prayer, but it also will mean a lot to your disciple when he sees you care enough to listen and remember what he shares with you. On the other hand, your silence on issues that are important to him will be deafening.

You can make the transition into the subject of the filling of the Holy Spirit by saying something like this, "Remember the last time we were together, and I shared with you that when you invited Christ into your life, the Holy Spirit took residence in your heart? I was wondering . . . have you noticed any changes since He entered your life? [He may say yes, and share some with you, or he may say no. It doesn't really matter which.] You know, Bill, the more mature you get in your new life with Christ, the more obvious the influence of the Holy Spirit will become.

"It's sad, though, that the great majority of Christians in this country don't see the Holy Spirit working in their lives. Either they don't want to allow Him to, or they don't *know how* to allow Him to. Why don't we spend a little time on the subject of how to experience the benefits of the Holy Spirit?"

Another way to open the subject would be, "What did you think of the little booklet I gave you last time? Did you get a chance to read it? Did it make sense to you?"

Or, you might share this illustration with him. Pour an inch or two of water into a glass, and then ask your disciple, "Would you say this glass has water in it? ["Yes."] Would you say it's filled with water? ["No, it's only about half full."] That's the way it is with most Christians and the Holy Spirit. All Christians are automatically indwelt by the Holy Spirit, just like this glass is 'indwelt' by the water, but not all are 'filled' with the Holy Spirit. There is an important difference."

Now, fill the glass to the brim with the water. "Is the glass filled now? ["Yes."] Right. It takes a special set of circumstances for us to call this glass full. It's the same way with being filled with the Holy Spirit; it doesn't happen automatically. But when our lives are filled with the Holy Spirit, that means we have asked Him to direct, control and empower us to do His will. It's not the same as the 'emptying of one's self' as many Eastern mystical religions teach, where total obliteration of self is the supreme goal, so that the gods are everything and we are nothing. Instead, it's simply coming to a decision that you want to do the things God wants you to do, and that you're giving Him permission to empower you to carry out that decision. In a way, you are asking Christ to live out *His* life through you."

Bump the glass and let a little of it spill out onto the table or floor. "But it's not always smooth sailing in the Christian life. Our lives get a little upset at times; we get frustrated with how things are going, or we don't like the way God is directing our lives, and we take back the control. That's what sin is. Before we came to Christ, we basically said, 'God, I'll not have You rule over me!' just as Satan said. Yet when we became Christians, we asked God to be our King, and we became His loyal subjects. When we sin, we're going back to our old attitude and saying to God, 'Get off that throne! I don't like the plans You cooked up. I want to take over again.' We rejoin Satan's rebellion. When this happens, it's just like spilling out some of this water. The glass is still indwelt by water, but it is no longer full. Our lives are still indwelt by the Holy Spirit, but we are no longer filled. He is not directing, controlling or empowering us. But that doesn't have to be a permanent condition. Just as I can refill this glass [fill the glass to the brim again], so you can be refilled by the Holy Spirit. Today let's look at what the Bible says about all this."

■ SUGGESTIONS FOR GROWTH

As I mentioned in chapter 7, Campus Crusade for Christ has developed some excellent materials that provide a useful foundation as you pursue these initial follow-up training objectives ("Newborn Care"). Especially pertinent to the objective at hand is their tract, "Have You Made the Wonderful Discovery of the Spirit-Filled Life?" and a series of three Transferable Concepts:

T.C. #2, "How to Experience God's Love and Forgiveness"
T.C. #3, "How to Be Filled With the Spirit"
T.C. #4, "How to Walk in the Spirit"

Following are some ways you can use these materials to help your disciple accomplish this all-important objective.

1. If he has read Campus Crusade for Christ's tract, "Have You Made the Wonderful Discovery of the Spirit-Filled Life?" . . .

Go over the booklet with him again, page by page, asking additional questions. With most people, it would be an insult to their intelligence for you just to read the tract over to them again, after they've already done so once, so be prepared to expand upon the information that is there.

Here are some questions you might ask, but think of some on your own, too.

Pages 2 & 3:

1. Do you understand these three circle diagrams?

2. Which one was represented by the glass that I filled and then bumped?

3. This verse, 1 Corinthians 2:14, says that the things of the Spirit of God are foolishness to the natural man. What examples of that can you think of that were in your life before you knew Christ, or are in the lives of others you know right now?

4. What do you see as the primary difference between the

natural man here and the spiritual man? How about between the spiritual man and the carnal man?

5. If you were to look at the behavior of a natural man, and compare it with the behavior of a carnal man, do you think you'd be able to tell any difference?

6. Is the carnal man saved?

Pages 4 & 5:

1. What do you think Jesus meant here in John 10:10 when He said we could have an "abundant life"? Do you think that means we'd have no more problems?

2. In this second verse, John 15:5, what do you think Jesus meant when He said, "He who *abides* in me"? What does it mean to abide? [It means to remain constant in relationship with.] In what ways would you say our relationship with God is like the relationship of a vine to its branches? [If he can't think of any ways, give him some of your ideas.]

3. In this third verse, doesn't it look like they used bad grammar here? They use the singular term *fruit,* but then they go on and list a plurality of fruits: love, joy, peace, etc. Do you think this was a mistake, or do you think God might be trying to tell us something? [This one will probably be over his head, so you could just share with him how, when the Spirit begins to produce fruit in a Christian's life, He produces *all* of these things. Love, joy, peace, etc., are all components of the singular fruit of the Spirit. If only *some* of these things are being produced in a person's life, then something is not right; something is hindering the Spirit's work, and it's time for self-examination.]

4. Look at all of these character traits listed on page 5. Would you say that each of these is in your life right now? [He'll probably say no.] Why not? You have the Spirit living inside of you, don't you? It says right here that He'll produce this kind of fruit in your life. ["Uh, well . . . uh . . . "] Mind if I share with you what I think? Like it says right here under the diagram,

"One who is only beginning to understand the ministry of the Holy Spirit should not be discouraged if he is
not as fruitful as more mature Christians who have
known and experienced this truth for a longer period."
A newly planted apple seedling doesn't start producing
apples the next morning, neither will the Holy Spirit
make you a really fruitful Christian right away. It takes
time. Don't stop looking for the fruit, but you'll need
to be a little patient at first.

I hope that gives you some ideas about how to ask questions
as you go through the booklet.

Another thing you might do is write down some cross-
referenced verses for some of the points ahead of time, and then
look them up with your disciple. For instance, you might look
up a few of the verses about the carnal man which are listed on
pages 5 and 6, and discuss them.

When you get to page 12 of the booklet, be sure to ask him
(assuming he read the booklet before your meeting) if he has
prayed that God would fill him with the Spirit yet. If he says
he has, rejoice with him! Ask him if he is convinced he is *still*
filled with the Spirit. If he says yes again, say terrific, and go
on with the study. If he says no, you might ask him why not,
and ask him if he'd like to stop right now and ask to be filled
again with the Spirit. If he says no, don't press him. He's
probably just shy about doing it in public or in front of you.
Just urge him to do it as soon as possible.

2. **If he hasn't read Campus Crusade's "Have You
    Made the Wonderful Discovery of the Spirit-Filled
    Life?" and you'd like to use that booklet . . .**

It's very simple: Just read through the booklet with him. I
would suggest stopping occasionally to ask him questions, get
some feed-back, amplify or personalize a point, make sure he's
awake, etc. This will avoid the "canned" approach, and keep
the session much more interesting to him.

Start off with a statement like: "About the easiest and
clearest way I know of to explain the ministry of the Holy Spirit
is through the use of this little booklet. It may seem pretty
simplistic to you, but the truths that are contained in it are

among the most profound and life-changing I've ever come across. What I'd like to do is just read through it with you, and as we go along, if there's anything you don't understand or want to ask about, just stop me and we'll talk about it."

3. If he has already gone over Campus Crusade for Christ's "How To Experience God's Love and Forgiveness" (Transferable Concept #2) . . .

Option #1. Go over the "Thought Questions" in the back of the booklet with him. They do a great job of expanding upon the material in the booklet. You might want to reiterate the questions, or put them in other terms if he doesn't grasp them as they are. Whenever a Bible verse is mentioned in the question, look it up with him. You want to get your disciple used to going to God's Word for answers. When a question refers back to certain pages in the booklet, turn back to them so he can refamiliarize himself with the subject.

Be sure you've looked at those thought questions yourself before you meet with your disciple. Some of them are toughies! Think about them on your own, and be prepared to give intelligent insight into each question's answer. Perhaps you can even think of supplementary illustrations or personal experiences that will shed additional light on the questions.

Option #2. Go over the "Bible Study" at the end of the booklet. While the thought questions amplify and build on material in the booklet, the Bible study tends to cover new ground, providing additional facts about the ministry of the Holy Spirit.

Option #3. If you have the time, go over *both* the thought questions and the Bible study.

Option #4. Since Transferable Concepts #2, #3 and #4 all deal with the ministry of the Holy Spirit, you may want to spend three meetings in a row on this subject. Send your disciple home after each session with a new Transferable Concept to read in preparation for your next time together. Transferable Concept #2 all by itself isn't really adequate to cover the whole subject, since it ends at "exhaling" (confession) and doesn't explain the concept of "inhaling" (filling). A person could spiritually asphyxiate! So after giving him #2, you also should give him #3 and follow that up with #4. You might even assign him the Bible study questions to answer each week on his own, depending on his motivation level and his personal time constraints. This would delay his moving on to other areas he needs to cover under "Newborn Care," but he would become firmly grounded in the work of the Spirit, which would be healthy. You decide.

Let me remind you again that this is one of the primary distinctives of this discipling program: "You decide." My function is only to give you ideas, stimulate your thinking, and present options. But the areas you cover and the pace at which you cover them are entirely up to you, based on your background, your evaluation of your disciple's status, and the input you receive from the Holy Spirit.

Option #5. An alternative to actually using the Campus Crusade for Christ materials on the ministry of the Holy Spirit in your follow-up sessions is for you to get the materials and formulate from them your own presentation of His ministry. I don't know of any more succinct collection of doctrine and helpful insight on this subject than those little booklets. They do a great job of covering the following areas:

- Who the Holy Spirit is
- What His function is
- Why Christians still sin
- One of the Christian's primary problems: the lack of the Holy Spirit's control in his life
- Three types of people: natural, spiritual, carnal
- The basis on which one can be filled with the Spirit
- How to go about being filled with the Spirit
  - confession of sin
  - reappropriation of the fullness of the Spirit
- Spiritual conflict
- Living a life of faith

■ FURTHER RESOURCES

If you'd like to use some good, fill-in-the-blank type Bible studies about the Holy Spirit, here are a few to choose from:

"Ten Basic Steps Toward Christian Maturity" Bible Study Series by Campus Crusade for Christ:

- Step 1, Lesson 3: "The Christ-Controlled Life"
- Step 2, Lesson 4: "The Abiding Life"
  Lesson 5: "The Cleansed Life"
- Step 3, "The Christian and The Holy Spirit" (The introduction and all 6 Lessons)
- Step 7, Lesson 6: "Witnessing and the Holy Spirit"

"The Discipleship Series,"[1] by Campus Crusade for Christ:

- Book 1, Lesson 2: "How to Experience God's Love and Forgiveness"
  Lesson 3: "How to Be Filled With the Holy Spirit"
  Lesson 4: "How to Walk in the Spirit"
- Book 2, Lesson 5: "Putting Practical Faith Into Action"
- Book 3, Lesson 8: "Obeying God's Direction"

Design For Discipleship Bible Study Series by The Navigators:

- Book 1, Chapter 4: "The Spirit Within You"
- Book 5, Chapter 3: "The Holy Spirit"

■ EXTRA ILLUSTRATIONS

1. *The Bird-Blotch.* This is a good one for new Christians who wonder, "What if I can't think of all my sins? What if I forget to confess some? Will they still be held against me?" It has to do with 1 John 1:9: "If we confess our sins, He is faithful and righteous to forgive us our sins and to cleanse us from all unrighteousness."

You're driving down the road in your car. All of a sudden, right there on the windshield—SPLAT! A dive-bombing starling has found his mark. It's right in your field of vision. As you drive along, you're constantly aware of it, and after a while, it bothers you so much you head for the car wash. You pay your money, enter the car wash, emerge from the other side and—sure enough—that bothersome bird-blotch is gone. But as you look at your car, you notice something else: The whole car is clean. No more mud on the tires, the splash-marks that were on the running boards are gone, the roof no longer has a layer of dust on it, the chrome is sparkling, all of the windows are crystal clear and the bird-blotch you didn't even know about on your trunk is gone too!

In a way, that's what happens to us when we confess our known sins. If God were to bring all our sins to our attention all the time, we probably would be overwhelmed with our sinfulness. In His wisdom, He makes us aware of only a few at a time, in quantities we can handle. Then an amazing thing happens: As we obediently confess those He has brought to mind, He runs us through His "Holy Car Wash" and, as it says in the verse, "purifies us from all unrighteousness."[2]

2. *The Drunk*. When a person drinks too much, he relinquishes control of his body to the effects of the alcohol and ends up doing things he wouldn't naturally do. When drunk, meek people sometimes become boisterous, the timid become combative, the shy become performers, the off-key become singers. Ordinarily they'd never act like that! But the alcohol takes over.

The apostle Paul in Ephesians 5:18 warns us not to let alcohol control our lives. Instead, we are to allow the Holy Spirit to control us. In the same way that alcohol prompts us to do extraordinary things when it takes over, so the Spirit—when He's in control—prompts us to act in ways we might not ordinarily act. He causes us to love the unlovely, and He makes us joyful in times of sorrow, peaceful when our world is blowing up, patient with those who deserve to be flogged, kind to jerks, good to creeps and gentle to brutes. Now *that's* unnatural.

3. *The Hot-Rodder*. I go to visit a friend. When he answers the door, he is grinning from ear to ear, and I soon discover why. He has just bought a brand new Spitz Beardog XK 2000 Turbo Maxi Road Cruiser! He is so proud of it!

"Take a look under the hood! It's got 16 cylinders and 128 valves, overhead *and* underhead cams, a 20-barrel carburetor, computerized fuel injection, high-compression radiator bolts and a nuclear-powered overdrive for when I need a little extra kick! What do you think?"

"It's fanTAStic!" I enthusiastically reply. "Let's take 'er out for a spin. Would you mind if I drove it?"

"Not at all. Hop in!"

So I jump in behind the wheel, but instead of my friend getting into the passenger seat, he goes around behind the Spitz, bends over, firmly places his shoulder against the beautiful chrome-plated bumpers, digs his heels into the ground and starts pushing.

"What on earth are you doing?" I cry.

"Why, I'm taking you for a ride. What do you think?"

"For a ri . . . Why don't you just put the key in, start up the engine and drive down the street?"

"Key? Engine? What do you mean, 'Start up'? Isn't this the way it works?"

Unfortunately, many Christians are just like my fictitious friend. When they invited Christ into their life, they gained access to the most effectual power on earth, that of the loving Spirit of God. Yet so many are completely unaware of the help available to them, and are trying to live the Christian life in their own power. Instead of sitting and driving, they're out back pushing.

4. *The Bulldozer.* Once I volunteered to work at my church. It was built right up against a hill, and there was barely enough room to fit a sidewalk between the back corner of the church and the hill. But we wanted to put a driveway through that slit, so we could have access to additional parking space in the rear. Well, I showed up at 8:00 one Saturday morning, shovel in hand, expecting dozens of others to be there as well. Three others showed. Nevertheless, we started digging. We dug for four hours, and it didn't seem like we made a dent in the side of that hill. My hands were blistered; my back was sore; I was sunburned. It was a miserable experience.

When we broke for lunch, I noticed that half a block down the street, several men were excavating with a bulldozer. As we ate, we saw the bulldozer unexpectedly lumber up the driveway of our church. It stopped right in front of us and the driver shouted over the rumble of the engine, "I've been watching you fellows. Could you use a little help?"

You can imagine our enthusiastic response.

The driver motioned for me to hop up in the cab with him, and in no time we had dug a section out of that hill big enough to drive a semi through! Yep! I got quite a lot accomplished that day — I, and the driver, and the bulldozer.

In the kingdom of God, the hard work gets done when you sit and ride, not when you try to sweat it out in your own strength. When the Holy Spirit comes onto the scene, our smartest move is to rely on Him to accomplish what needs to be done. When we appropriate *His* power, the tasks before us are a lot easier.[3]

■ P.S. FOR THE DISCIPLEMAKER

Don't treat this as some kind of second salvation decision, or as though if your disciple would just read the prayer written in this booklet, all his troubles would be over and he would now be a real Christian.

I'll never forget the first contact I had as a young Christian with a somewhat over-zealous brother. As soon as he heard of my decision, he ushered me off to his room, sat me down on his bed, and started reading me a tract about the Holy Spirit. I had never seen the thing before, and the lingo was unfamiliar to me, but I knew what it meant to allow the Holy Spirit to control my life. That wasn't enough for this fellow, though. Unless I prayed that prayer right then and there, I was going to be in big trouble. He kept pushing and probing, trying to find out why I wanted to keep being a carnal Christian (which I didn't — he just perceived it that way). I believe I'd still be hog-tied in his room if I hadn't gone ahead and prayed the prayer. After that, he acted like I'd been born-again again, but I didn't notice any difference.

All I'm saying here is this: Be sensitive to where your disciple is. Don't push him to do something he doesn't understand or is just not ready to do yet.

■ ENDING THE SESSION

If you go through all three Transferable Concepts with the new disciple, be sure to end each session by giving him the next booklet, and then make it clear what you'd like for him to have done by the time you get together again.

Also, be sure to let him ask any questions he might have before you separate, no matter what the subject. It's a good way to expose "potholes." You may be teaching him about the filling of the Holy Spirit, and he may be saying to himself, "Holy Spirit? Now, which of the three Gods is that? The one the Hare Krishnas worship?"

It would be appropriate to close in prayer after each session, thanking God for sending the Holy Spirit, and asking Him to help both of you experience His power and guidance more and more. By this time, your disciple should be able to do some of the praying for the two of you. Encourage him to do so, but don't push if he's still hesitant.

■ ASSIGNMENT FOR NEXT WEEK

While you're going through the Transferable Concepts (if you take that route), it's obvious what the next week's assignment will be each time. Be sure you don't pile on the homework too thick, too soon. Remember, this is only a baby Christian. The heavy work should wait until he goes to "school" (child level). For now, the key words are nourish, cherish, protect, love, and basic knowledge.

When you feel you've accomplished this training objective, the next subject I recommend covering involves his "Identity in Christ." This will be pretty crucial. You've been spending time telling him that he's a new creature and that he is indwelt by the mightiest power in the universe, yet, if he's like most of us, he doesn't see any difference. He feels like the same old creature, and wonders if being filled with Wheaties might not give him more power. He's beginning to understand how to appropriate the filling of the Spirit, but he still experiences the struggle between his old nature and his new nature. It's important that he understand that struggle early, and learns how to gain victory in the midst of it. Here are a few passages you might ask him to read that will relate to next week's subject (don't assign them all, just two or three):

Romans 6:1-14	2 Corinthians 5:14-21
Romans 7:15-25	Galatians 5:16-18,24,25
Romans 8:28-39	Ephesians 4:20-24

After he reads each passage, have him jot down these three things about it:

1. something new I learned;
2. something I want to do as a result of reading it;
3. something I have a question about.

Tell him you'll discuss them with him when you get together next time.

In each case, I said "some*thing*," but make it clear that he can list more than one thing if he wants. Do encourage at least one observation under each category. Help him out with #2, the application part. Make a few generic suggestions for him, like, "This passage makes me want to thank God for saving me"; or, "Reading this passage caused me to realize I need go ask so-and-so's forgiveness," etc.

■ EVALUATION

Here are some questions you could ask your disciple to determine if he truly understands the ministry of the Holy Spirit:

1. Where is the Holy Spirit right now in relationship with you?

2. What does it mean to be "indwelt by the Holy Spirit"?

3. At what point does a person become indwelt by the Holy Spirit?

4. What does it mean to be "filled by the Holy Spirit"?

5. If a person were to ask you, "How can I be filled by the Holy Spirit?" what would you say?

6. What is "spiritual breathing"? When does it become necessary?

7. Would you say that the filling of the Holy Spirit is a one-time occurrence, or does it happen many times?

8. (If this isn't getting too personal . . .) When was the last time you took a "spiritual breath"? Did you notice any changes?

9. Why is it important to confess our sins to God? How does one go about this?

10. What would you say is the Holy Spirit's main job here on earth right now?

When the Holy Spirit is controlling a person's life, there should be evidence of it in the form of the fruit of the Spirit talked about in Galatians 5:22,23: love, joy, peace, patience, kindness, goodness, faithfulness, gentleness, and self-control. While this fruit may not show itself full-grown immediately, if you aren't beginning to see some hints of it within a few weeks, something's not right. It may be that your disciple has head knowledge about the filling of the Holy Spirit, but isn't putting it into practice. Talk with him about it openly. The more the subject is on your lips, the more it will be on his mind. More important than anything else, however, will be your example. Be sure that you are walking in the Spirit at all times.

RECOMMENDED RESOURCES FOR DISCIPLEMAKING

THE SPIRIT-FILLED LIFE BOOKLET by Bill Bright. An easy-to-share presentation that helps lukewarm Christians discover the joy of living in dependence on the Holy Spirit.

THE TRANSFERABLE CONCEPTS by Bill Bright. Just as learning the alphabet opens up a new world to the child, so does a study of these basic principles of Christian living provide the new Christian with a framework for growth.

THE TEN BASIC STEPS TO CHRISTIAN MATURITY by Bill Bright. A comprehensive curriculum for the new Christian or anyone desiring to master the basics every believer should know and experience. These studies have been used successfully by hundreds of thousands of people worldwide, providing a solid foundation for Christian growth.

———

These resources are available at Christian bookstores,
or from Here's Life Publishers.
(Call 1-800-854-5659; in California call 714-886-7981.)

12 TRAINING OBJECTIVE #4

IDENTITY IN CHRIST

■ OBJECTIVE

The disciple has a basic understanding of his new identity in Christ and the struggle that exists between his old nature and his new nature.

■ BIBLICAL BASIS FOR THIS OBJECTIVE

When a person becomes a Christian, several fundamental changes take place regarding his basic identity. I've listed a number of these below. Look up the verses that support each point, and jot down a summary of each in your notebook.

1. He is no longer the same person he was before.

    2 Corinthians 5:17   Galatians 2:20

2. He has been given a new nature.

    Romans 6:5,6   Galatians 6:15

    Galatians 5:22,23   Colossians 3:9,10

3. His true nature as a believer is now one of righteousness, completeness, and perfection. (Notice the past or present tense in each verse listed below; it's particularly significant.)

    • Romans 8:28-30: Note especially, "justified . . . glorified."

    • Ephesians 4:20-24: Note especially, "created."

    • Hebrews 10:10,14: Note especially, "have been made holy . . . has made perfect."

    • Philemon 4-6: Note especially, "we have."

    • 2 Peter 1:3: Note especially, "has given us."

4. However, the old nature still exists in the believer. It is at war with his new nature, and can produce ungod-

182

ly behavior.

- Romans 7:15-23: Notice especially in verses 17 and 20 how Paul has distinguished clearly between his true, righteous new nature, and his old sin nature, which he disowns. We know from his writings elsewhere in Scripture that Paul in no way holds that a person is not personally responsible for his own sins (Romans 3:23; 6:23; 1 Corinthians 3:12-17; 5:9-11; 11:28-30; 2 Corinthians 2:5,6; Galatians 2:12-14; etc.). He's simply pointing out here that it's no longer part of his true nature to be sinful. It's not "like him" to sin since Christ entered his life.

- Galatians 5:16-18,24,25

■ APPLICABLE DEFINITIONS

Identity in Christ: Who we are in Jesus Christ; the distinguishing characteristics of the born-again Christian in his basic nature or essence; what is true about the basic nature of a Christian as a result of his becoming indwelt by the Holy Spirit upon conversion.

■ PEP TALK FOR THE DISCIPLEMAKER

In follow-up sessions #1, #2 and #3 you have told your disciple that he is now a new creature, indwelt by the Holy Spirit who imparts to those who belong to Him the power to live abundant and victorious lives.

Immediately upon salvation, some Christians experience a drastic, positive change of behavior. For others, the changes aren't so dramatic. They begin to wonder if there were any changes. They say to themselves, *If I'm a new creature, and the power to live a godly life is within me, why do I still lust? Why do I still covet? Why do I still fly off the handle at the slightest provocation? And look at all of these other Christians . . . so many hypocrites. I know lots of non-Christians who are so much better people than those Christians. The Bible says I have been changed on the inside, but I really don't see much evidence of it.*

What can you say to him? I'd be surprised if many of you didn't experience the same disillusionment from time to time. We've been told that we've been given a greatly improved new nature, a supernatural new power. So why don't we do the things we know are right, and stop doing the things we know are wrong? We want to change. We want to be obedient to Christ, but we just seem to lack the power.

The Holy Spirit is our power source. If He is in control of our lives, we will experience power, victory and the abundant life (Galatians 5:22,23). The trick lies in daily, even moment-by-moment, dethroning of the old self, putting the Holy Spirit back on the throne, and keeping Him there.

When you think about it, though, why should we? Before I came to Christ I had logged over eighteen years of life in Satan's shadow, and I got pretty used to it. I loved to sin, and though I hate to admit it, I still love to sin. And if the truth were known, you probably love to sin too. If we didn't love to sin, we wouldn't do it. It's the consequences we hate. We hate how it makes us feel, we hate how it grieves God, we hate the damage it does to the advancement of the kingdom of God, and we hate how Satan exults in it. So why do we tolerate this tendency in ourselves? Why can't we learn from our past mistakes?

We should be able to figure it out. Remember how sin works? First comes the temptation. It looks good, but the Spirit within warns us to steer clear of it. However, if our minds aren't set on things of the Spirit (Galatians 5:16,17), rather than obeying instantly, we begin analyzing other alternatives. We proceed to list the pros and cons of doing the suggested sin, and, being optimists, we usually list the pros first. After having such a high time listing the benefits of the act, we're in no mood to think of the liabilities. The analysis ends and we skip merrily down the road of sin, only to find we've been snookered again.

Each time we're tempted, we're given a choice: to go God's way or to go Satan's way. We're so used to going Satan's way, and (without really thinking about it) we love going Satan's way, so why should we spoil the fun by seeking the filling of the Holy Spirit?

In the midst of the temptation, the Spirit is standing there armed, ready to come to our aid, ready to do battle with our foe and rescue us. But we don't give Him the chance. He would take the throne immediately if we would let Him, but the bottom line is that, "just this once," we'd as soon He'd butt out so we could assert our own will. Of course, we always feel bad afterward. We confess our heads off, and we vow to be more stalwart in battle the next time — but why should it be any different next time?

These questions may have bothered you for many years, and your new disciple certainly will be wondering about them. The answer is not simple, nor is the process whereby one gains victory over habitual sin. And the victory usually is not complete or life-long. Temptation and sin will plague you and me for the rest of our lives here on earth. Major victory can be ours, though — with only occasional skirmishes from the resistance still residing in our flesh — if we know a few things and if we do a few things.

This training objective will deal primarily with what we need to know, while Training Objective #5 will handle what we need to do.

The main thing your disciple needs to understand is that, while he does have a new nature, he also still possesses his old sinful nature. Both are equally accessible. Actually, the old nature is probably more accessible, due to the fact that it's all we ever knew before our conversion. When we exhibit carnal behavior, it indicates that we are drawing on our old nature. Christlike behavior can be manifested only as we draw on our new nature. To get this truth across, I'm going to give you an illustration you can use. Your disciple will be able to remember the truth easily, and he can apply it, and later pass it on.

■ BROACHING THE SUBJECT

You start off your conversation something like this:

YOU: Well, Frank, you've been walking with the Lord for about a month now. Just think, one month down a road that's going to last billions of years! One month as a "new creation"! How do you feel about that?

DISCIPLE: Pretty good. There have been some ups and downs, but I'm convinced I'm doing the right thing.

YOU: That's great! How have you been doing in the "Christlike behavior" department? I mean, last week we talked about being filled with the Holy Spirit and how He would help us live more righteous lives. Has that made any difference in your life this past week?

DISCIPLE: It's helped a lot, but I've got to confess that . . . well . . . I've blown it a few times, too. I knew it was wrong, and I wanted to obey the Lord, but I just wasn't strong enough to resist temptation.

YOU: Don't let that get you down, Frank. The fact is, all Christians blow it from time to time. Our goal is to do it less and less frequently! We'll never be perfect this side of heaven, but it is possible for us to make steady progress toward perfection as we grow in the Lord.

DISCIPLE: But why does it happen? You said I have a new nature, and the Holy Spirit lives inside of me, and He will help me live a life that pleases God. Yet I still want to do a lot of the same sinful things I did before I was a Christian.

YOU: I know I said that, and it's true. The Holy Spirit is the power source in the Christian life. The problem is: He's not the only source available for us to draw on. Let me show you an illustration that should help clear it up for you.

■ SUGGESTIONS FOR GROWTH
The Two Wells Illustration

You may not be a Michelangelo when it comes to drawing, but that's OK. Stick figures will do just fine. First draw a well, with its shaft sunk into an underground stream. Also, for use later in the illustration, draw a little farmhouse next to the well. Use a full 8 1/2" x 11" sheet of paper, turned sideways, so you will have enough room. Then, you say something like this:

The way you were before you became a Christian could be represented by this well. The farmer who owned this well drew water from it all the time. The trouble was, the water that came out of it was contaminated. The underground stream that fed it ran under a toxic waste dump, and his family always felt weak and ill.

Blacken in the underground stream with your pen. If you think the toxic waste dump is too controversial a subject, just say the stream ran through a deposit of arsenic, which happens from time to time.

But since they had drunk from that well all their lives, they didn't even know they were sick. This is how the natural man is, how both you and I were before we met Christ. The farmer represents your mind, the underground stream represents your old self or your old nature, and the contamination represents your sinfulness. Jesus said in Mark 7:20-23, "What comes out of a man is what makes him 'unclean.' For from within, out of men's hearts, come evil thoughts, sexual immorality, theft, murder, adultery, greed, malice, deceit, lewdness, envy, slander, arrogance and folly. All these evils come from inside and make a man 'unclean' " (NIV).

Each time you make reference to a verse of Scripture, be sure to do two things: (1) Write the reference on the sheet, so your disciple can look it up again later if he wants to; and (2) open your Bible to the passage, and one of you read it out loud. It's also handy to jot down a one- to three-word summary of the verse.

Paul said in Ephesians 2:1-3 that we were all like this at one time, and it was our nature to be so. But just as

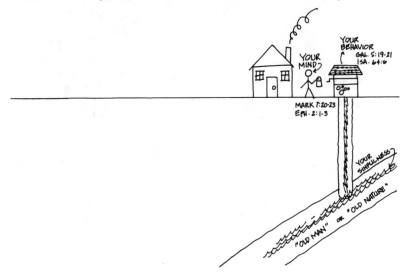

(At first, your illustration should look something like this.)

the farmer only had one well to go to, and wasn't aware of the contamination, so we had only one character to draw on, and it was contaminated. And just as the farmer and his family were headed for an early grave, so we were headed for an eternal grave. Paul tells us about the kinds of behavior that this contaminated well produces in Galatians 5:19-21 [the works of the flesh]. Isaiah tells us in Isaiah 64:6 that the best we could be in this condition was like "filthy rags" to God.

One day a man from the Environmental Protection Agency (EPA) came and tested the farmer's well, and he alerted the farmer to the contamination. Of course, the farmer immediately stopped using his well, but he still needed water. He consulted some well-drilling experts and they informed him there was a crystal-clear underground stream on the other side of his property. He sent down another well shaft and sure enough, the water there was perfectly pure.

Draw another well way over on the other side of the paper, along with its shaft and the underground stream.

This is what you did when you invited Christ into your life. This new underground stream represents your "new

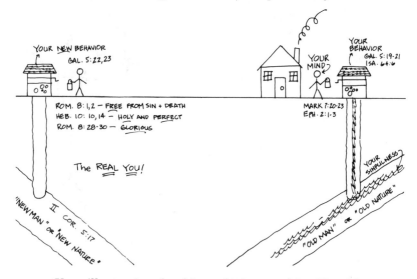

(Your illustration should now look something like this.)

man" or new nature, and it has no contaminating sin nature. Second Corinthians 5:17, which we've talked about before, says that God made you into a whole new creation, with a whole new character or nature. Galatians 5:22,23 talks about the kind of behavior that will come out of this "pure well." This new man is the opposite of the old man. Romans 8:1,2 talks about how the law of the Spirit of life has set us free from the law of sin and death, just like the pure water of this well set the farmer and his family free from the sickness and death of his contaminated well. The true nature of the new believer is now one of righteousness, completeness and perfection. Hebrews 10:10,14 talks about how we *have been made* [notice past tense] holy and perfect, and Romans 8:28-30 tells us that, in God's eyes, we are already glorious! This well represents the new you. It's the real you. From now on, you can say, "It's not like me to be selfish or lustful. It's not like me to hate this person. The real me is characterized by love and joy and peace and patience."

But almost immediately we notice a problem. Sometimes we're not loving. Sometimes we're not joyful. How is it, if we have this new nature within us, we Christians still sin? For instance, in 1 Corinthians 1:4-8, Paul addresses the Corinthian believers as "enriched in every way," "not lacking in any spiritual gift," "strong until the end," and "blameless," and yet, as we read the rest of 1 and 2 Corinthians, we see that these people were far from perfect, and sinned just about every sin in the book! The reason you and I, and all Christians, still have the ability — and even the inclination — to continue sinning is that, just as the farmer's contaminated well still sits right next to his house, our old man still exists within us.

Sometimes we decide to go back to the old well and draw from it. The farmer may, from time to time, think it's too far to walk all the way over to the new well. After all, the new well is over this hill, through these bushes across this ravine and down this hill, while the old well is right outside the door.

Draw each of those obstacles as you mention them.

Or sometimes he may doubt the EPA man's test. Or he may rationalize that "just a little of this contaminated water shouldn't hurt." In the same way, our minds may find it easier to draw from our old man. Or we may be so used to following the dictates of our old man that we don't even think about listening to our new man. We forget. For thirty years, when the farmer wanted water, he went out his front door and turned left. It may take him a while to get used to turning right.

As you say those last two sentences, draw arrows coming out of the farm house, one going toward the old well, one toward the new.

Paul talks about this in Romans 7:18-25. Just as the farmer truly wants to quit drinking the contaminated water, so Paul wants to quit following the dictates of his old nature. But it's not easy. In fact, Paul even calls it a "war" (verse 23). In the end, Paul says that the only way he'll be able to do it is with God's help (verse 25). This is where the ministry of the Holy Spirit comes in. He's like a big neon sign planted right outside the farmer's front door flashing "TURN RIGHT!"

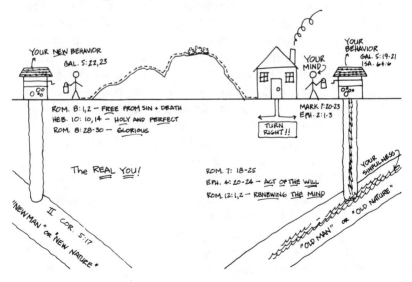

(When completed, your illustration should look similar to this.)

Draw a box underneath the two arrows coming out of the farmhouse with the words *TURN RIGHT!* in it.

However, the farmer can still choose to disregard the sign. In the same way, you can still disregard the direction of the Holy Spirit. That's why ultimately it's going to be up to you to choose which well you draw from. God will help you, but you make the decision. That's why Paul said in Ephesians 4:20-24 that we should "put off" our old self and "put on" our new self. It requires an act of our will. Every day. Every time we are tempted. And in Romans 12:1,2 Paul urges us to be "transformed by the renewing of your mind." Our minds have to be re-taught to draw upon the supernatural resources of our new man instead of the contaminated sewage of the old man. We'll learn more about that next week.

I realize that I'm asking a lot to suggest that you memorize the above illustration so you can share it clearly with other Christians. But really, am I asking any more than your sixth grade teacher did when she asked you to memorize each state's capitol? We memorize things our whole lives, whether they have any lasting application or not! If this illustration makes sense to you, and you see how it can help your disciple understand his daily struggle for victory over the sin nature, then you'll be willing to put in the time required to master it. Don't let the fact that there won't be a mid-term exam on this stop you from internalizing something you can use for yourself and in your ministry the rest of your life.

As you memorize it (not word-for-word, just the basic points and flow), feel free to use cheat sheets when you share it with a disciple the first few times. This way you'll be sure not to miss any of the points or Scripture references. You don't have to use all of the verses I suggested above, and you can supply other verses as you see fit. Adapt it any way you want! For a while I wrote out each major point and its corresponding verse on a 3 x 5 card and referred to it as I did the sketch. After sharing it a few times, it flowed along quite easily.

Often, while fellowshipping with a friend or new acquaintance, I'll sense the need to share the illustration, and there's no chance for preparation, no Bible around, no pen and no paper. It's still quite easy to get all the points across using salt and pepper shakers for wells and a hamburger for a farmhouse. We don't get to read the Scriptures together, but I've got most of the verses pretty well memorized. Despite the impromptu presentation, I see the lights go on in their minds every time!

So please, take some time to get this under your belt. Sometimes one must pay a price to be a proficient disciplemaker.

Other illustrations

1. *The Two Dogs Illustration*. Once a wise old man, who had walked with the Lord for many years, was talking with his teenage grandson who had recently become a Christian.

"Gramps, I just can't seem to get the hang of this Christian life. Sometimes I feel real close to God and have no trouble at all obeying Him, but other times I want to do and say all kinds of junk that I know would be wrong. It just doesn't seem fair to me. Why can't I be good all the time?"

"Well, Sonny, I'll tell you something I found out a long time ago. Being a Christian is a lot like having two dogs living inside of you, a good one and a bad one, and they're always fighting."

"That sure does sound like me! And the bad one wins more often than I'd like! Which one wins in you, Gramps?"

"The one I feed."

2. *The Old Ship Captain Illustration*. A ship set out on a transatlantic voyage. About three days out it was discovered that the old captain had gone insane. He began to overwork and underfeed the crew. He harassed and beat them. A few of the crew members snuck into the radio room and relayed this information back to the owner of the ship, who told them to relieve the captain of his command and to install the first mate, whom everyone knew to be reliable and honest.

This they did, but since the ship didn't have a brig, and since the old captain was really quite harmless, they allowed him to roam the ship as he pleased. He would often shout orders to the crew members, trying to get them to obey him. Some of them did from time to time, but when they did, it was for one of these three reasons:

1. They were so used to obeying his every word that they did it as an automatic response.

2. They were afraid that, despite what the new captain said, the old captain might still hold some sort of authority over them.

3. They were ignorant that he had been relieved of his command.

Many Christians still obey the demands of their old nature for very similar reasons:

1. Out of habit, because the old sinful habit patterns haven't been transformed in accordance with their new natures yet.

2. Out of fear or a resignation that, "I just can't change. I've tried and I just can't shake the old habits. They're in me too strongly."

3. Out of ignorance of who they are in Christ and of the fact that their old sin nature is "relieved of its authority" over them, and they no longer need to obey it.[1]

■ FURTHER RESOURCES

For some good, fill-in-the-blank type studies about our identity in Christ, look at the following:

"Ten Basic Steps Toward Christian Maturity" Bible Study Series by Campus Crusade for Christ:

- Step 2, Lesson 1: "What Is the Christian Life?"
  Lesson 2: "An Appraisal of Your Own Spiritual Life"
- Step 6, Lesson 1: "Obedience and the Results of Doing God's Will"

"The Discipleship Series"[2] by Campus Crusade for Christ:

- Book 2, Lesson 5: "Putting Practical Faith Into Action"
- Book 3, Lesson 1: "Living Out Our Identity With Christ."

■ ENDING THE SESSION

As usual, give your disciple the sketch to take home so he

can study it further on his own.

Encourage him to call a time-out once in a while through the coming week and analyze which well he's been drawing from the most. If he finds he's been going to the old well, he'll need to confess his sin, repent, and once again appropriate the filling of the Holy Spirit. Tell him you'll give him a call this week to see how he's doing, and to see if there's anything you can help him with. (Then be sure to do it.)

You might also encourage him to share the illustration with his family or a close friend or two. It will ingrain the concepts more deeply in his heart.

■ ASSIGNMENT FOR NEXT WEEK

As you mentioned to your disciple before (hopefully) in the introduction to the two wells illustration, we can gain consistent victory over our old nature if we *know* a few things and if we *do* a few things. Make sure your disciple understands that we've hit only the "know" part this week, and will get into the "do" part next week.

Since the next training objective I recommend is the one that involves "Basic Growth Principles," it would be a good idea to get him thinking in that direction. Consider giving him the following assignment:

> There are many activities we Christians can engage in that help us grow spiritually. Several verses are listed below. Look them up and determine what each encourages us to do and how you think it can help a person grow in his relationship with God.
> 1. John 15:5-7 – (Abiding in Christ; keeping Him on the throne)
> 2. 1 Peter 2:2 – (Reading the Bible)
> 3. Matthew 7:7,8 – (Praying)
> 4. Hebrews 10:24,25 – (Fellowshipping)
> 5. Acts 1:8 – (Witnessing)
> 6. John 14:21 – (Obedience to Christ)

■ EVALUATION

Ask yourself the following questions:

1. Does my disciple know what the Bible is talking about when it says he is a "new creation" in Christ?

2. Does he understand why he still has sinful urges, despite being born again?

3. Does he understand that it is his decision whether he follows the dictates of his old nature or his new nature?

4. Does he understand that the more he draws from his new well, the easier it becomes, and the harder it is to find his way back to the old well?

If you can answer each of those questions in the affirmative, you and your disciple have met this training objective. If you need a little more input from him to determine your answers, here are some questions to ask him:

1. Now that you are a Christian, how are you different?

2. Upon salvation, what did God give you that you didn't have before? ("A new nature.")

3. How do you explain the fact that, though you are a new creation, you still have a tendency to sin sometimes, just like the old creation? (We still have our old nature.)

4. How can we keep from acting like the old creation?

5. Let's say you've started a special relationship with a new girlfriend (or boyfriend), and she wanted to get to know you a lot better. She asks you, "What is the real you like?" How would you answer her? (Hopefully your disciple will say something here about his true, God-given new nature being that of righteousness, even though sometimes the old man slips out.)

6. What things make you forget about your new well and draw from the old well instead?

From time to time, you may see your disciple acting in an ungodly manner. If you do, you might ask him, "Simon, what well are you drawing from right now?" For a while, you will need to keep reminding him of the illustration, or at least of its concepts, until it is firmly established in his heart.

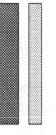

13 TRAINING OBJECTIVE #5

BASIC
GROWTH PRINCIPLES

■ OBJECTIVE

The disciple has a basic understanding of spiritual growth principles and is aware of the beneficial influences of time, adversity and the sovereignty of God.

■ BIBLICAL BASIS FOR THIS OBJECTIVE

This training objective covers a lot of ground, and you'll probably need to do a considerable amount of background study in order to master it. If you know what the Bible has to say about the basic principles of Christian growth, you will be able to help your disciple immensely in his progress toward maturity, but actually *you* will benefit even more!

So I suggest you look up the following verses and jot down a summary for each in your notebook. There is no way we can cover all existing growth principles here, nor does your disciple need to know them all this early in his life with Christ. What we're trying to do here is simply get a broad view of the major principles.

1. We grow as we give Christ top priority in our lives.

Matthew 6:33	John 15:5-7	2 Timothy 2:4
Luke 18:29,30	Galatians 2:20	Hebrews 11:26
John 12:26	Philippians 1:21	

2. We grow as we feed upon God's Word.

Joshua 1:8	Psalm 119:130	John 15:3
Psalm 37:31	Matthew 4:4	2 Timothy 3:16,17
Psalm 119:9,11	John 6:63	Hebrews 4:12
Psalm 119:105	John 8:31	1 Peter 2:2

3. We grow as we pray.

Jeremiah 33:3	Mark 11:24	Hebrews 4:16
Matthew 7:7,8	John 14:13,14	James 4:2*b*
Matthew 18:19	Philippians 4:6,7	James 5:16*b*

4. We grow as we fellowship.

1 Samuel 23:16	Matthew 18:20	Hebrews 10:24,25
Proverbs 27:17	John 17:21	1 John 4:7
Isaiah 35:3,4	Hebrews 3:13	

5. We grow as we witness.

Proverbs 11:30	Daniel 12:3	Acts 1:8
Psalm 107:2	Matthew 4:19	Romans 1:16
Psalm 126:5,6	Matthew 5:16	James 3:18
Isaiah 58:10-12	John 4:32-34*	1 Peter 3:15

*[After witnessing to the woman at the well]

6. Growth takes time.

• Luke 3:23: Jesus knew all along that He was the Savior, God the Son (Luke 2:49), yet God withheld Him from ministry until He was thirty years old, in order to properly train Him (Hebrews 5:8).

• Acts 7:23-34: God put Moses through a forty-year training program in the courts of Pharaoh, then another forty-year training program in the wilderness of Midian, and *then* decided he was ready to begin his ministry.

• Galatians 1:15 – 2:1: After Paul's dramatic conversion on the road to Damascus, God put him through a seventeen-year training program before He finally allowed him to launch his public ministry.

| 2 Corinthians 3:18 | Ephesians 4:11-13 | 1 Timothy 5:22 |
| Galatians 4:19 | Philippians 2:22 | |

7. Adversity facilitates growth.

Psalm 119:71	Hebrews 5:8	1 Peter 5:10
Romans 5:3-5	James 1:2-4	Revelation 3:19
Hebrews 12:5-11	1 Peter 1:7	

8. God sovereignly oversees our growth.

- Psalm 71:20: Even in the worst times, God is in control.
- Psalm 119:75: Sometimes the afflictions we experience are brought about by the direct action of God, but always for our good, and always prompted by His faithfulness.

Psalm 127:1   Romans 8:28   1 Corinthians 10:13

■ PEP TALK FOR THE DISCIPLEMAKER

In Training Objective #4 I said that we can gain major victory over our old, sinful natures if we *know* a few things and if we *do* a few things. We covered the "know" part in the two wells illustration. Your disciple should now know that, while he possesses a new nature, one that desires to pursue righteousness, he still has his old nature as well, and that the two of them will always be at each other's throats. But as he, through the exercise of his will, consistently draws upon his new nature instead of his old, his outward behavior will increasingly reflect his new creation status.

But we can't stop there. You've got to move on to the "do" part. Merely knowing about available resources will never give the new believer victory. A field general in a war would soon be relieved of duty if all he ever did was take inventory on his weapons, and never deployed them to the front where the fighting was going on.

There are certain specific activities that the disciple can engage in that will *without fail* help him gain victory over Satan and his old nature and help him grow in Christlikeness.

Make sure that you recognize this fact: The disciple wants to grow; he's chomping at the bit to grow; he is dying to know what things he can do that will help him become more like Jesus. If he doesn't find out soon, he'll become like most other Christians here in the United States and lose interest—and many battles. Like so many of the redeemed before him, he'll start to think, *There aren't any answers. There isn't anything I can do to help bring about my own spiritual maturity.* Soon he'll gain the attitude that infests so much of the church today: *The Christian life is sittin' in a pew on Sunday, sayin' grace before meals, and cuttin' back on the cussin'.* Many people, after being Christians for as long as twenty years, are no more mature in Christ than they were six months after receiving Him.

To my mind, there aren't many things as sad as visiting a mental institution and watching a grown man or woman acting like a baby. And yet, in the spiritual realm, people like that are as common as fleas on a dog.

That won't be the case with your disciple, though, will it? You're going to start him off right by teaching him early the principles that will help him grow and keep growing for the rest of the time he's here on earth!

However, let's get something straight right from the start. There is a fine but very deep line between "legalism" and "discipline." The activities we'll be talking about shortly do not buy us "favor" with God when practiced. God doesn't love me more when I'm faithful in my prayer life. Reading the Bible every day doesn't earn me brownie points with God. We can't have the attitude that, "I witnessed to somebody today, Lord, so now you've got to help me get that promotion I was hoping for." That's legalism, trying to buy God's favor through good works, and it can't be done. In the first place, we should obey Him no-questions-asked simply because He is our Lord (Luke 17:7-10). It's helpful to remember that He is already lavishing us with 100 percent of His favor, ever since He made us His sons and daughters! One can't expect more than 100 percent, can one?

We engage in the disciplines of Christianity as a result of *self-control,* which is the ninth component of the Fruit of the Spirit. Reading the Bible, praying, etc. won't buy us any special privileges with God, but they will help us function better and more efficiently in the spiritual realm, and in the long run, they help us become more like Jesus. If we exclude those disciplines for fear that we might slip into legalism, we can be sure, based on the Word of God, that we will not function worth beans spiritually. Putting fresh motor oil in my Chevy may not guarantee me the pole position at the Indianapolis 500, but I *will* be guaranteed a junk car if I don't.

■ BROACHING THE SUBJECT

You might start off the conversation something like this:

YOU: So which well have you been drawing on the most this week?

DISCIPLE: The new one, mainly. There were times when I could tell that I had forgotten and gone to the old well, though. Like you said, old habits are hard to break.

YOU: Believe me, I know what you mean! But today I hope to give you some ways that you can make that path out to the new well a little smoother, a little more worn down. Eventually, if you'll apply these principles faithfully, that path will be like a modern highway, ten lanes wide, and the old well will practically disintegrate from lack of use.

DISCIPLE: You mean I won't sin anymore?

YOU: I wouldn't go that far. Theoretically, I suppose it's possible, but I wouldn't get my hopes up. That sin nature will always be there, and your adversary the devil will always be thinking up new and creative ways to make you fall. But your life will be characterized by victory, power, and a much closer walk with God. And the times that you do stumble and fall will be fewer and fewer.

■ SUGGESTIONS FOR GROWTH
The Wheel Illustration[1]

The late Dawson Trotman, founder of the Navigators, originally drew this illustration and it is still a favorite of theirs. Through the years I have been in the ministry, I have never found a better way to demonstrate the basic growth principles of the Christian life, not only what they are, but also how they interact in a balanced fashion to keep a person rolling along toward spiritual maturity. I don't mean to narrow down your options regarding training your disciple, but this illustration has worked so well in so many settings that I highly recommend its use. When the lights go on in your disciple's mind about these concepts, he will be much more motivated in the holy disciplines of Christianity, not simply because you tell him to, but because he sees how they all work together to accelerate his growth and enhance his relationship with God. Plus, it will lay an excellent foundation for the following four training objectives.

First thing you do is to get out an 8 1/2" x 11" sheet of paper and draw a wheel on it that looks something like this:

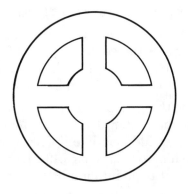

Draw the wheel so that it takes up about half of the paper, leaving room to write the verses above it and below it. Then, begin sharing the illustration by saying something like:

YOU: This wheel represents your life. A wheel gets its power or driving force from its hub. What would you say is the power source in your life, now that you're a Christian?

DISCIPLE: I don't know . . . Jesus?

YOU: Right! When you asked Jesus to come into your life, He entered in the form of the Holy Spirit, and took up residency in your heart.

Write *Christ* on the hub of the wheel. Next, share two verses with your disciple that illustrate the importance of Christ being at the center of our lives. For some ideas on what verses to share, go back to the Biblical Basis for This Objective section and pick out the two verses that mean the most to you under number 1, "We grow as we give Christ top priority in our lives." Write these references and a two- or three-word summary for each on the side of the paper next to the wheel. Point out that, just as in a car or bike wheel, if the hub is missing, the wheel will have no power, and the vehicle won't go anywhere! For the Christian, if Christ isn't at the center of his life, or if the Holy Spirit isn't on the throne (if you'd rather put it that way), the Christian will not experience God's power in his life and won't be going anywhere either!

At this point, you might want to ask him one of the following questions, depending on your bent (positive or negative):

- What are some things you can do to make sure that Christ is always at the center of your life? (You might want to do a quick review of the filling of the Holy Spirit, Training Objective #3. It fits in here nicely.)

- What are some things that might make you keep Christ from being at the center of your life? [or] What do you think your life would look like if Christ weren't at the center? (Take him to Galatians 5:19-21, the works of the flesh, if you want to go into it a little more.)

Next, move on to the spokes of the illustration.

YOU: Just as with a regular wheel, power is transferred from the hub to the rim through the spokes. There are four main activities in the spiritual realm through which power is transferred from Christ to our daily lives.

One at a time, share what each of the four spokes are, supplying two verses for each spoke (again, see the Biblical Basis section for suggested verses). The two vertical spokes represent our "vertical" relationship with God through the *Word* and *Prayer*. God speaks to us through His Word, and we speak to Him through prayer. The two horizontal spokes represent our "horizontal" relationships with other people through *Fellowship* and *Witnessing*. We fellowship with Christians and we witness to non-Christians. Share with your disciple that as we engage in these four activities, Christ's power becomes operative in our lives. To use a different analogy: We open a channel through which His power and presence can flow.

The outer rim represents *The Obedient Christian in Action*, and you should now write that around the rim.

YOU: Remember how, in the two wells illustration, the farmer had a good well and a bad one, and he could choose whichever one he wanted to draw from? It all came down to him making a decision to forsake the bad well and go only to the good well, right? It's the same

way here. These four spokes represent four ways that
Christ's power can be made available to the Christian,
but they count for nothing if the Christian doesn't
choose to obey what God has told him to do through
those spokes. Disobedience will give your wheel a flat
tire every time (John 14:21; John 15:5,6).

Notice it says here, "The Obedient Christian *in Action*." In order to experience God's power, you've got to
be in action. There is no need for God to send His power
your way if you're going nowhere. No need to gas up the
boat if it's just going to sit in the harbor all year, right?
God works in us and through us as we are in action.

When you're done, your wheel should look something like
this:

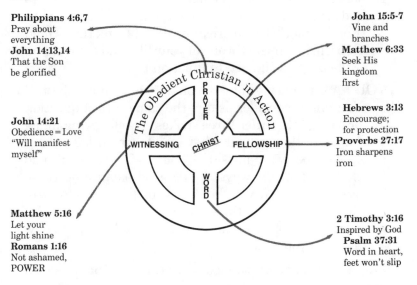

Philippians 4:6,7
Pray about
everything
John 14:13,14
That the Son
be glorified

John 14:21
Obedience = Love
"Will manifest
myself"

Matthew 5:16
Let your
light shine
Romans 1:16
Not ashamed,
POWER

John 15:5-7
Vine and
branches
Matthew 6:33
Seek His
kingdom
first

Hebrews 3:13
Encourage;
for protection
Proverbs 27:17
Iron sharpens
iron

2 Timothy 3:16
Inspired by God
Psalm 37:31
Word in heart,
feet won't slip

Now comes the key to the whole illustration. Frequently,
this is where the light comes on in the mind as to finding the
balance in the basic growth principles:

YOU: What do you think would happen if I knocked out
one of these spokes? Or what if one of the spokes was
about 2 inches shorter than all the rest?

DISCIPLE: Well, I guess it wouldn't roll as smoothly. It
would be a lot bumpier ride, and the wheel wouldn't be

balanced.

YOU: Correct, as usual! That's why serious bike riders always make sure every spoke is strong and tight. It's the same way in the Christian life. If one of our spokes is missing or short or bent, our lives will not run as smoothly. Let's say that I read my Bible every day, I'm pretty faithful about sharing my faith with others, I go to church every Sunday, but I only pray about one minute a week. How do you think my life would be rolling along?

DISCIPLE: Not too smoothly!

YOU: Why not?

DISCIPLE: Well, it seems to me that if you don't talk to God, you can't maintain much of a relationship with Him. And if there's no relationship, I think that would keep Christ off the throne of your life, and deprive you of the power you need to function properly.

YOU: A seminary graduate couldn't have put it better! (You might consider asking the same sort of question for each of the other three spokes as well, giving him a chance to think about what his life would look like if one or more were missing.) That's why we need to do what we can to always keep a good balance on these four activities. If you feel like your life is a bit out of whack from time to time, take a little inventory and inspect your spokes. It may give you a good clue as to how to regain your balance.

Time, Adversity and the Sovereignty of God

Three very important factors influence spiritual growth, and you need to share them with your disciple, even if only briefly. After you write out the wheel illustration, turn your sheet of paper over, or find an unused corner on the front, and write *Time, Adversity,* and *Sovereignty of God.* Then say something like this: "There is something else you should know, Schultz. Spiritual growth is just like physical growth in many ways. Spiritual growth takes *time,* is enhanced by *adversity,* and is *sovereignly directed by God.*"

There are many, many things you could say about each of those factors in the Christian growth, but there wouldn't be time, nor could your young Christian friend absorb it all. He just needs a basic understanding of these points, and they're really not that tough to digest. Share a verse or two on each concept (write them down for him), and perhaps a few personal thoughts. I've listed below a number of illustrations and parables that you might draw from if you need ideas about how to get the point across.

The TIME Factor

1. There are no short cuts. Both physical growth and spiritual growth take time.

2. God takes His time. Whenever God wants to do something important, time is always a big factor. Noah took 120 years to build the ark; God put Moses through 80 years of training to prepare him to lead His people; Jesus, the Son of God, was confined to the disciplines of a carpenter for 30 years before God felt He was ready to begin His ministry; nothing significant happened in Abraham's life until he was well into his 80s. It took 40 years for God to bring the Israelites to the Promised Land, a journey that should have taken no more than two weeks.

3. Quality requires time. A zealous seminary student once asked Dr. A. H. Strong if he could take an abbreviated curriculum that would enable him to get his seminary training behind him quickly and get out to the mission fields. Dr. Strong replied, "Oh yes, but then, that depends on what you want to be. It takes a hundred years to make a decent oak tree, but only three months to make a squash."

4. Complexity requires time. In the animal kingdom, the lower the life-form, the sooner it reaches maturity. A mouse is considered full-grown after only a few months; a dog requires only a couple of years; a human needs sixteen to twenty years — longer than any other animal on earth. Quality takes time, in the spiritual realm as well as in the physical.

5. Be patient; time will pass. Don't expect to become "Super Christian" in a couple of weeks. You'll need to be patient with yourself, with me, with God, and with the program He has for you. Sometimes it might seem like it's taking forever to grow up spiritually, and sometimes you'll wonder if there's been any progress at all. But you've been there before, haven't you? Remember when you were fourteen, and you wondered if you were ever going to reach sixteen, that magic driver's-license-age? Well, you finally got there, didn't you? And no amount of moaning and groaning made the time go any faster, did it? You just had to put in your time, be patient with the calendar, and the day finally came. It's the same thing with spiritual growth. It's going to take time.

The ADVERSITY Factor

1. Adversity enhances growth. Have you ever looked under a microscope at the rings of a tree? If you have, you noticed both light and dark rings. The light rings are the summer growth. Under your microscope, you'll see that the cells that were laid down then are big and fat, because they were formed when it was warm, and there were plenty of nutrients, sunlight and water available. Some trees grow more in one month during the summer than all of the other eleven months combined. Now, when you move your microscope over to the dark wood, you notice those cells are small, shriveled and tough. These cells were formed when it was winter—cold, dark, much less food and water available. Yet during the winter, when it's the toughest, a process called "solidification" goes on within that tree. If the tree didn't go through this process, it would be too weak to stand up to the storms that come its way. It's the same with our spiritual growth. God allows us to go through adversity, not because He can't help it, but because He knows it will make us stronger and it will prepare us for greater things down the road.

2. Expect both good and bad. Neither physical growth nor spiritual growth is uniform. There will always be ups and downs, and you need to expect it. There will be mountain-top experiences and valleys of despair; blasting before building; spinach as well as strawberry shortcake. There will be spurts of growth when you feel close to God, and you experience victory after victory. Other times, you will feel stale and stagnant. That's OK—we all go through dry times now and then. I guarantee you, if you'll keep Christ on the throne of your life, those dry times won't last long.

3. No pain — no gain. Look at the athletic realm. When an athlete decides he wants to compete in the Olympics, he knows he's in for a hard time — and he accepts it willingly. His coach makes him run until his body aches from fatigue. He makes him lift heavy weights. He makes him eat a variety of distasteful foods. He makes him go to bed early and get up early. And when the athlete says he's tired, the coach doesn't even listen; he just pours on more pain! The coach doesn't do all of these unkind things to the athlete because he doesn't like him — he does it because he knows that those disciplines are the very things that will help the athlete make it to the Olympics. He knows there are no short cuts. Without the adversity, there will be no victory (1 Corinthians 9:24-27). Think of God as your "Heavenly Coach" who is training you for activities of far more importance and significance than the Olympics. You need to realize that there *will be* hard times in His training program (2 Timothy 3:12; Hebrews 12:5-11).

The SOVEREIGNTY OF GOD Factor

1. God is always in control. God is more concerned about your spiritual growth than even you are! (Deuteronomy 5:29; Jeremiah 29:11) Remember a few weeks ago when we read John 10:28-30, about how you are safe and surrounded by Jesus Christ, and He, in turn, is surrounded by God, and that anything that gets to you must first get through them? It's so important that you grasp this concept as you grow in Christ. In the training program God has in mind for you, there will no doubt be some tough times. Just remember, those tough times have been thoroughly screened by God, and He has determined that you can handle them, and that they will be beneficial to you (Psalm 103:13,14; 1 Corinthians 10:13).

2. God knows, even if we don't. We might not understand everything God takes us through in order to move us down the road to maturity, but that doesn't have to bother us. I don't understand what the dentist is doing in my mouth when he's filling a cavity, but I know it's good for me, despite the discomfort. In the same way we can have confidence in God's abilities as He works on our souls. Though we can't always figure out

what He's doing, or why, we know for sure that He hasn't
flubbed up yet, and He never will.

■ FURTHER RESOURCES

If you'd like to take your disciple through a few fill-in-the-
blank type Bible studies about Basic Growth Principles (or
some of the individual components mentioned), here is a list of
good ones you can choose from:

"Ten Basic Steps Toward Christian Maturity" Bible Study
Series by Campus Crusade for Christ:

- Step 1, Lesson 4: "Principles of Growth"

- Step 2, Lesson 2: "An Appraisal of Your Own Spiritual
                        Life"

- Step 6: "The Christian and Obedience" (all 6 lessons)

"The Discipleship Series,"[2] by Campus Crusade for Christ:

- Book 1, Lesson 6: "Building a Relationship With God"

- Book 3, Lesson 8: "Obeying God's Direction"

Design for Discipleship Bible Study Series by The Navigators:

- Book 2, Chapter 1: "The Obedient Christian"

- Book 3, Chapter 1: "Maturing In Christ"
            Chapter 2: "The Lordship of Christ"
            Chapter 3: "Faith and the Promises of God"

■ ENDING THE SESSION

By the end of this session, your disciple should have a
general idea concerning what he needs to know and do to
facilitate his own spiritual growth. But it's unrealistic to expect this new babe in the Lord to launch out immediately into
a perfectly balanced application of these principles tomorrow
morning.

Let him know that for the next four (or more) weeks the two
of you will be examining each of the four spokes of the Wheel
Illustration in detail to better integrate them into his life. If
your disciple is from a fairly "religious" background, and knows
a little about prayer, Bible study, fellowship and witnessing,

the odds are good that he's tried them on his own. I assume he's already getting into the Word some, since I've recommended a number of Scripture passages for you to have him study. There's also a good chance he's been praying and maybe even talking to others about his faith. If he is, praise God! Encourage him—but let him know that you'll be covering these basics in a lot more depth during your next four sessions together.

■ ASSIGNMENT FOR NEXT TIME

Anybody got a verse that will tell us which of the four basics is the most important? Anybody know which wing of an airplane is more important? Which parent is more important? Some subject groupings are very tough to prioritize, and these four basics certainly qualify. They're all vital. So which one do we start with?

It doesn't matter which one I pick, approximately 75 percent of you will disagree. Each of you will have good, biblical, practical reasons, too. But since I'm the writer, I get to win! So "Fellowship" is Training Objective #6.

However, you remember the watch-words of this program, don't you? *You decide.* If you strongly (or even weakly) prefer to cover one of the other three spokes, feel free. More than anything else, I want you to be open to the leading of the Holy Spirit. We are sure that He knows what is the next crucial area for your disciple to receive input on, and that it will vary from person to person. So spend some time with the Lord on this matter before you make a decision. Ask His opinion. After all, your disciple is His child.

When the two of you have made your decision, choose four to six verses or passages on the chosen subject from the "Biblical Basis" section of this training objective. Once again, ask your disciple to look up the references and write down three things about each one:

1. something new I learned;
2. something I want to do as a result of reading it;
3. something I have a question about.

By having him actually write these things down, as opposed

to merely thinking about them, you accomplish several important things:

1. His thoughts and questions will become much more
   crystallized in his mind as he transfers them to paper.

2. He's more likely to do the assignment, knowing that
   you'll be asking to see the paper next week.

3. He won't forget his observations or questions between
   the time he studies and the time he sees you again.

4. It's helping him to develop important Bible study skills
   and habits early in his Christian experience, and they
   will be deeply ingrained.

If you plan to cover "Fellowship" next time, I suggest you
send him home this week with a copy of Transferable Concept
#8, "How To Love By Faith." When you talk about Christian
Fellowship, love is the foundation. This booklet will go a long
way toward opening his eyes to what Christian love is all about.

If, instead, you decide to go into "Prayer" in your next meeting, give him Transferable Concept #9, "How To Pray." It will
set up next week's discussion nicely.

If "Witnessing" is on next week's menu, give him Transferable Concept #5, "How To Witness In The Spirit." In it, Dr.
Bright lists eight ingredients of successful witnessing. Even
though no specific method is mentioned, these general principles will be helpful no matter how you like to share the good
news. Much more is said about a specific gospel presentation
in Transferable Concept #6, "How To Introduce Others To
Christ," which you could go into the following week.

■ EVALUATION

Here are some questions you can ask your disciple to help
determine if he has achieved this training objective:

1. What are some things you plan to do to help yourself
   grow spiritually?

2. If Christ is not on the throne of your life, would it still
   be helpful to stay involved in prayer, Bible study, fellowship and witnessing? (Our first tendency might be
   to answer yes to this question, but the answer we're

looking for is no. If Christ is not at the hub of our wheel, no power can be transferred through the spokes. As a result, we try to live the Christian life on our own steam, which is impossible. Staying involved with the four spokes *may* help motivate your disciple to get Christ back up on the throne, which is a tremendous benefit, but the point we want to get across here is that if Christ isn't Lord of his life *first*, it's useless for him to try to grow through Christian disciplines.)

3. If I were a brand new Christian, could you explain to me how I could grow in my relationship with God? Could you use the wheel illustration to do it?

4. If several things start going wrong in your life, and you know that you're doing your best to walk with and obey the Lord, would you say that's a good sign or a bad sign, as far as spiritual growth is concerned?

5. What should be our attitude when we encounter hard times in our life? (A good follow-up passage for this question would be Romans 5:3,4 or James 1:2-4.)

6. If we are having a tough time in several areas, does that mean that God might have lost control of our lives temporarily?

7. Why would you say Bible study (or prayer, or fellowship, or witnessing) is so important to your spiritual growth? Why is obedience so important?

8. Are there some things you can do to bring yourself to spiritual maturity within, say, six months? How long do you think it will take for you to become spiritually mature? (That's a pretty open-ended question, but that's the point. We have no idea how long the process will take. In fact, the process of maturing spiritually will go on for the rest of our lives.)

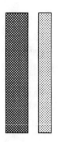

14 TRAINING OBJECTIVE #6

FELLOWSHIP

■ OBJECTIVE

The disciple has a basic understanding of the importance of Christian fellowship and is beginning to attend Christian functions.

■ BIBLICAL BASIS FOR THIS OBJECTIVE

Every believer needs to be in fellowship with other believers for mutual protection and encouragement. As you have done so many times before, look up the following verses and jot down a summary for each in your disciplemaking notebook. Add any more you can think of as well.

Ecclesiastes 4:9-12	1 Corinthians 10:24	Hebrews 3:13
Proverbs 27:17	1 Corinthians 12:12-26	Hebrews 10:24,25
Romans 1:11,12	Ephesians 4:16	
Romans 15:1-3	Philippians 2:3,4	

■ APPLICABLE DEFINITIONS

Fellowship: A building up, encouraging, and equipping of the body of Christ by the body of Christ.

■ PEP TALK FOR THE DISCIPLEMAKER

As you can see from the wording of this particular training objective, we'll be looking at two components of fellowship: (1) teaching your disciple *about* fellowship and (2) motivating him *to* fellowship. Therefore, we'll be dividing the treatment of this training objective into two sections, one addressing each of those components.

Actually, I hope you began to get your disciple involved in Christian fellowship quite some time ago. I just haven't had much of a chance to mention it until now. If you'll read this whole second section (chapters 9-20) *before* diving into your discipling relationship—as I recommended earlier—you'll know all this. You've been meeting with your disciple for six to eight weeks by this time, and if you're the only Christian he's had contact with up to now, it's high time you got that new babe into a church! You should be applying a lot of what I'll be saying about "Motivating Your Disciple TO Fellowship" long *before* you actually sit down with him to discuss the fellowship spoke of the wheel.

Section I—Motivating Your Disciple TO Fellowship

A mysterious thing has happened to your disciple: He has been grafted into the body of Christ. He is now part of his Savior's body, right along with you.

How much do you know about the human body? As an undergraduate biology major I took an astonishing course called "Cytology." In it we studied in great detail the workings of individual cells, what each of their sub-cellular components did and how they functioned in concert with neighboring cells, tissues and organs, to keep you going strong. I sat spellbound as I learned about the intricate symphony of life constantly being played within each cell in our bodies. Hundreds of microscopic sub-cellular pin-points wonderfully and obediently do their jobs in flawless rhythm twenty-four hours a day, each cell perfectly harmonizing its concert with the one being played in the cell next door. They give and receive chemicals, hormones, oxygen and nutrients in just the right quantities, and in split-second timing. All the cells together synchronize to produce a masterpiece of form and function, able to carry out whatever the brain demands in perfect coordination. Why, it's enough to thunder-strike even the most materialistic atheist.

Oh that the body of Christ could function as efficiently as our own physical bodies! Someday, in eternity, that will be reality. As we look at it now, however, we're looking through smoked glass. But that's no reason you, your disciple and I shouldn't strap on our backpacks and begin the ascent to that celestial summit. With the help of the Holy Spirit, a little knowledge, and some personal discipline and determination, we can go a long way toward helping the body of Christ around us come closer to that heavenly ideal!

What do you think your disciple will experience during his first exposure to genuine Christian fellowship? If the group you take him into is functioning as it should, probably the first thing that will strike him will be the love that he sees both from group member to group member and from group members to him. That's as it should be. Jesus said that the primary distinguishing characteristic of Christians should be love (John 13:35). Your disciple should be pleasantly surprised at the attention people pay to him, how they want to get to know him, and how they rejoice at his recent decision to trust Christ.

But if he hasn't had much church contact before, there's a good chance he'll feel a little out of place at first. Even if he HAS been a church-goer in earlier times, he may feel a little uneasy, thinking, *These people are singing songs about Jesus and praying, for cryin' out loud . . . and it looks like they're doing it because they want to, and not just because it's part of the litany.*

My first few Christian meetings were a little scary. I really did love the Lord, but did we have to do all this singing about it? I fervently hoped that none of my friends would peek in the window and see me with these fanatics. But as time went on, and I observed the camaraderie, the bonds of friendship and the unconditional love they held for each other and for me, I was caught—and I didn't care who knew it.

How warm and loving is your local body? If you bring a new believer there, will he feel welcome? Will people show genuine love and concern? Will he want to come back? Or will he feel like an outsider? Will the members of your group keep to their little cliques, give him a polite nod and then go back to their mutual-admiration societies? These ingrown fellowships are not healthy, not for the newcomer nor for the old-timers. If that's all you have to take your disciple to, you can try to help your group change, or move to another fellowship, or call a few of the more mature members of your group and ask them to put forth a special effort to make your new disciple feel more at home. In our me-centered, overly-mobile, disposable-everything society, it's already hard enough for people to establish good relationships with decent people, without fellow Christians making it even harder.

What should constitute his first Christian meeting? The obvious answer: a church service. He can meet lots of other Christians; he might be favorably impressed with the music and the big organ; he'll be fed from the Word of God during the pastor's sermon; the beauty of the building could be inspirational; etc. A lot of good things can be said about a church service.

On the other hand, it may be a little overpowering. Your disciple may feel lost in the crowd, especially if you belong to a big church. Or, since it's hard for members of big churches to keep track of who's new and who's not, he may not sense the love and warmth people ordinarily show a visitor, especially one who has just come to know the Lord. I'm not saying this will happen at every big church, but it's certainly something to take a look at.

You may prefer to invite him to a smaller group meeting, such as a home fellowship, a Bible study, a retreat, a church breakfast or dinner, or even an informal function with a bunch of close Christian friends. As I mentioned earlier, the first Christian meeting my discipler took me to was in the next town. We went with about ten other guys from his church and watched a Billy Graham movie. During that evening, I became quite impressed with the special bond among those guys, and I wanted in. I sensed that they wanted me in, too.

But let me emphasize again, "You decide." You and the Holy Spirit know the facts surrounding your particular church, and you can figure out what would meet your disciple's needs.

■ BROACHING THE SUBJECT

Not only is it tough for me to advise you specifically as to *what* should be your disciple's first Christian meeting, it's equally tough to say *when.* You may invite him to join you immediately after he accepts Christ, or you may want to wait a week or two. I can't think of any reason you would want to wait any longer than three weeks, however. It's up to you and the Holy Spirit to determine the proper timing.

If you've got a dynamite group, with brothers and sisters who really walk with the Lord and would immediately welcome your disciple into the warmth of their fellowship, invite him soon. If you're a little hesitant about your group, and think he might have a negative experience if he went right away, put it off a while. Take a little time to develop a strong relationship with him yourself, and look for an opportunity to divulge to him the startling fact that Christians are sinners, too.

■ SUGGESTIONS FOR GROWTH

The Actual Invitation

Most Americans already understand that churchgoing is part and parcel of being "religious." For that reason, a new believer rarely would be reluctant to begin getting involved in fellowship with other believers. They already *expect* to be asked. Generally speaking, all that you will need to say is something like, "Hey, Jodi, how'd you like to come to church with me next Sunday?" Or, "Hank, a bunch of us get together every Thursday night to study the Bible. How about coming along this week?"

On the other hand, you may choose to be a little more creative, and say something like:

YOU: Hmmmm. I wonder what you are.

DISCIPLE: Beg pardon?

YOU: Do you think that you're more the "hand" type or the "foot" type? Or maybe the "eye" type?

DISCIPLE: I don't know what you're talking about.

YOU: Maybe you're a heart . . . or a liver . . . or a gall bladder . . .

DISCIPLE: Would you please tell me what you're babbling about?

YOU: Well, all through the New Testament, Christians are spoken of as being part of the body of Christ, and I just wonder where you fit in. Ankle?

DISCIPLE: I think I know where you fit in—the pits. What do you mean, "part of the body of Christ"?

YOU: Take a look here at 1 Corinthians 12:12-27 (or whatever passage you want to use; read it or have him read it). So you see, all Christians are like one big, supernatural body, with Christ as the head. Just like the different parts of our bodies have different functions, each of us has an different function within the body of Christ, and each is important. Plus, whenever one part of the body is hurt, the entire body stops to help it out. That's the way it's supposed to be in a local group or church, too. Ear—maybe you're an ear. How would you like to meet your elbow, big toe and left eyebrow?

DISCIPLE: What?

YOU: You know what I mean. How would you like to come with me to church next week and meet some other members of the body of Christ? It's never too soon to start learning just where you fit in.

What if he says no?

There are several reasons a new Christian might not want to get involved in a local fellowship:

- a bad experience at a younger age;
- too shy to go to public meetings;
- hesitant about being branded a "holy roller" by his friends;
- jealous about his time and not willing to take on any more time-consuming activities;
- has a problem with the hypocrisy he's seen in other Christians;
- and, no doubt, many others.

The main thing you need to do is figure out what misconception he may be operating under regarding fellowship, and then try to help him accurately assess the situation. A simple and relatively nonthreatening way of going about that is to say, "All right, McGill. Suit yourself. But I'd really be interested in knowing why not."

Depending on the situation, you may want to have it out

with him then and there, gently but firmly sharing with him from Scripture how vital it is that he be involved with a local body of believers. With other people, it may be appropriate to drop it for now, and try again in a week or so. Of course, during that week, you should spend much time in prayer on the matter. You also can slip in a plug for fellowship whenever you get the chance.

In any case, don't give up. You may have to work on him for months before he finally relents, but work you must. If the person you are working with is indeed a Christian, and he is showing reluctance to attend Christian activities, don't forget your "fifth front," the Holy Spirit. He will be working within that new Christian to help him overcome preconceived notions or prejudices about fellowship. It's not totally up to you to be the big "convincer" here. Just keep loving him, praying for him, and gently nudging him in the right direction.

The person's aversion toward Christian fellowship may be because he himself actually is not a Christian, in which case being around other Christians makes him sick (2 Corinthians 2:15,16). If your overtures continue to fail, you might explore this possibility. Maybe you should ask him point blank, "Ralph, I hope you don't take this the wrong way, but ever since you asked Christ into your life you seem unwilling to get involved in fellowship with other believers. Now, the Bible says this is a trait of someone who is not saved (2 Corinthians 2:15,16), and to tell the truth, I'm beginning to wonder about you. Are you convinced that you do belong to Jesus Christ, that you really meant it when you asked Him to come into your life?"

By laying all the cards on the table like that, you may be able to come to the source of the problem. I recommend this recourse only as an *extreme* resort. We don't want to induce our disciples to start doubting their salvation left and right, but if you think there is a legitimate concern that he has misunderstood salvation and is not a Christian, better give it a whirl.

Section II — Teaching Your Disciple ABOUT Fellowship

Now we're back to the present again. Your disciple has been

going with you to church or small group Bible studies for
several weeks now, you've shared the wheel illustration with
him, and now you want to give him a little deeper education on
what Christian fellowship is all about.

■ BROACHING THE SUBJECT

Your disciple needs to understand that, contrary to what he
may observe in most churches in the U.S. today, Christian fellowship is a lot more than saying, "Hi! Hawayah?" to a bunch
of casual acquaintances on Sunday morning, or having lunch
with a Christian friend and knitting or talking baseball the
whole time. At the core of fellowship is *love*. Not shallow, casual
or inconsistent love, but unselfish, willful, accepting, dynamic,
constant, accountable, provocative (in the biblical sense) love.
The kind of sacrificial love that Jesus had for us. The kind of
love that would cause outsiders to take one look and say,
"THAT is from GOD!" (John 17:23).

For this reason, I think it's a good idea to help your disciple
warm up to this subject by having him read Transferable Concept #8, "How To Love By Faith"[1] before you meet. You could
have him complete the thought questions or Bible study prior
to your meeting, or do some of them together during the first
part of your meeting. If your disciple doesn't have a firm grasp
on what true Christian love is, all the rest of what you say about
fellowship will be meaningless.

Another potentially interesting way to get your conversation revved up is to ask him if he could make up, or has ever
heard, a good definition of *love*. Or look it up in the dictionary,
and see if the two of you agree with its definition, or think you
can improve on it.

■ SUGGESTIONS FOR GROWTH

Remembering that your disciple is still a very young Christian, and that you'll be going into much more detail later in his
development, you will be wise to focus now on just three concepts, which I've listed below. Each is accompanied by several
verses, with a brief summary of each verse (so you will see the
same point I did in each). You still need to look them all up,
however, and decide which ones you want to use with your dis-

ciple. I suggest you simply sit down with him, using your Bible and a sheet of paper, and look up each reference. Ask him questions like, "What does this verse say about love as a priority in the Christian life?" Or, "Why should we fellowship, according to this verse?" Then, lead him to more in-depth thinking about his answers by asking guiding questions such as, "What do you think it means to 'speak the truth in love?' Do you think it's possible to speak the truth 'not in love'?" Don't put words in his mouth, but guide his thoughts if he has trouble answering.

1. The priority of love in Christian fellowship

If he has already read Transferable Concept #8, simply discuss it. If not, read and discuss some of the following passages:

Matthew 22:37-40 — Loving God and loving man are the two greatest commandments.

John 13:34,35 — Commanded to love by Jesus; mark of a true disciple.

Romans 13:8-10 — Love is the fulfillment of the law.

1 Corinthians 13 — The great love chapter.

1 Corinthians 16:14 — Do everything in love.

Galatians 5:22 — Love is the first component of the fruit of the Spirit.

1 Peter 4:8 — Love covers a multitude of sins.

1 John 3:16-18 — Love prompts us to sacrifice for others. If not, love of God isn't in us. Need to love in deed, not just word.

1 John 4:7,8 — Love is a characteristic of all those born of God.

1 John 4:16-21 — Abiding in love = abiding in God. We love because He first loved us; you can't love God and hate your brother.

2. Why we should fellowship

Proverbs 27:17 — We "sharpen" each other.

Ecclesiastes 4:9-12 — Better return for labor, and protection, warmth and strength in numbers.

Matthew 18:20—Christ has promised to be there in a special way.

John 17:21—To unify ourselves, to become better witnesses.

Romans 1:11,12—We all strengthen, benefit and encourage each other.

1 Corinthians 12:12-26—We are all part of Christ's "body," and need each other; we help each other by supplying each others' needs.

Hebrews 3:13—Keeps us from being hardened by sin.

3. What we do in fellowship

Acts 2:42—Study the Word together, have communion, pray together.

1 Corinthians 10:24—Seek each other's benefit, not our own.

Galatians 6:2—Carry each other's burdens.

Ephesians 4:15,16—Speak the truth in love; build each other up.

Ephesians 5:19,20; Colossians 3:16—Worship God together.

Philippians 2:1,2—Seek unity and like-mindedness.

Hebrews 3:13—Exhort each other to maintain a lifestyle.

Hebrews 10:24,25—Get together often with other Christians; provoke each other to love and good works.

1 Peter 5:5,6—Serve each other in humility.

■ FURTHER RESOURCES

For some good, basic, fill-in-the-blank type studies on the subjects of fellowship and love, investigate the following Bible study booklets:

"Ten Basic Steps Toward Christian Maturity"[2] Bible Study Series by Campus Crusade for Christ:

- Introduction, Lesson 6: "The Church of Jesus Christ"
- Step 1, Lesson 6: "The Church"

Design For Discipleship[3] Bible Study Series by The Navigators:

- Book 2, Chapter 4: "Fellowship With Christians"
- Book 4, Chapter 2: "Genuine Love In Action"

■ ENDING THE SESSION

An important concept to stress — not just at the end, but throughout this session — is that fellowship doesn't have to take place only in a formal setting, such as at Sunday services at church, during a Christian retreat or at a Bible study. The principles of fellowship govern our relationships with other Christians at all times. We should take the initiative to "do good to . . . the household of faith" not only in the midst of a church service, but also throughout the week.

■ ASSIGNMENT FOR NEXT TIME

With the above in mind, have your disciple consider for a minute or two (and you do the same) how he could stimulate a particular Christian friend toward having love and doing good deeds (Hebrews 10:24,25) sometime this week. Each of you write your plans down. Then spend time in prayer together about it and check with each other next week to see what success crowned your intentions.

Also, anticipate what training objective you are going to go over next week and give your disciple an appropriate assignment. For ideas on that, go back to chapter 13 (Basic Growth Principles — Training Objective #5) under the "Assignments for Next Week."

■ EVALUATION

The main signpost you're looking for on this trip is, obviously, regular church attendance. What's regular? In the long run, you're not done until he's going weekly. I can't presume to lecture anyone about how *often* each week. Some feel that once on Sunday is enough, others would vote for "every time the church doors are open." So again, you and the Holy Spirit need to confer on the subject and come up with a decision. My personal conviction is that an active, growing Christian should be involved a minimum of once a week in all three group dynamics:

one to one, small group, large group.

If you're interested in a little more evaluation on whether or not your disciple has grasped the concept of Christian fellowship, here are a few questions you could ask:

1. Of all of the components of the fruit of the Spirit, which would you say should be the most evident in our relationships with other believers?

2. How is Christian fellowship like being part of a physical body?

3. Does it make you uncomfortable being around other Christians? (If so . . .) Why do you think that is?

4. What do you think you should do if you know a Christian friend has a grudge against you about something?

5. Can you think of anyone you're at odds with right now? (If so . . .) What do you think you should do about it?

6. Do you think it's possible to love God and to not love our brother at the same time?

7. Why do you think Christ was so concerned that His disciples be unified and so like-minded?

8. How can fellowshipping with other Christians keep us from getting "hardened by the deceitfulness of sin?"

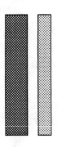

15 TRAINING OBJECTIVE #7

THE WORD

■ OBJECTIVE

The disciple has a basic understanding of the importance of biblical input, is familiar with the physical layout of the Bible, and has begun to read the Bible on his own.

■ BIBLICAL BASIS FOR THIS OBJECTIVE

Just as a newborn baby has an almost immediate, instinctive craving for its mother's milk, so a newborn spiritual baby craves spiritual food. He may not know that's what he wants, but then, neither does a physical baby when he's only ten minutes out of his mother's womb. Go ahead and ask him. All he'll do is cry and holler; he won't give you anything close to a civil answer (the real baby, that is). The reason both types of babies crave this food is that their Creator put that desire in them. He knows that, in order for them to stay healthy and grow, their little bodies need nourishment. Physical babies grow through the intake of food; spiritual babies grow through the intake of the Word.

The following references depict the Bible as equivalent to food in the spiritual realm, and without it a new Christian (or an old Christian, for that matter) cannot grow. Look up each reference and write a short summary of the verse in your disciplemaker's notebook.

Deuteronomy 8:3	Acts 20:32	2 Timothy 3:16,17
Job 23:12	1 Timothy 4:6[1]	1 Peter 2:2,3
Matthew 4:4		

■ PEP TALK FOR THE DISCIPLEMAKER

A physical newborn can do almost nothing for himself. Oh,

he can nurse, breathe, pump blood, cry, sweat, support diaper company executives, but that's about it. He's dependent on his parents for almost everything else. But can you blame him? All he knows of life was either part of the package deal he got when God gave him a brain or what he learned in the womb—and there weren't a lot of instructional materials there. Not only that, he had no previous contact with the outer world that would give him an idea of what it was like, no "womb with a view" (hoo-boy!). So it was scary when he suddenly found himself in a room filled with light and noise and people wearing masks. It's the same way, to a certain degree, with a spiritual newborn. They've been born into an entirely different realm, and they are a little bewildered, and somewhat dependent on you to show them the ropes.

However, we shouldn't carry this too far. Your primary objective in all of this disciplemaking activity is to bring your disciple to the point where he can "dig his own well," and lose his dependence on you.

Now, we know that it takes most humans sixteen to twenty years to reach physical maturity, so we don't get too uptight when our kid is two years old and still hasn't figured out Euclidean geometry. He's got plenty of time. He needs to master the art of drool prevention first. But a spiritual baby's growth rate should be much faster, so, while we recognize that he will be dependent on us for a while in many areas, we need to start moving him toward independent functioning as soon as possible.

I'm not saying that a mature Christian should be independent of everybody and everything; no one can be a Lone Ranger in the spiritual realm. It's our nature as the body of Christ to need our brothers and sisters around us for us to function properly. But just like a physical baby needs to learn to walk, communicate, feed himself, go to the bathroom and pay taxes on his own, so a spiritual baby must gain the ability to stand on his own. In the kingdom of God, no man is an island, nor is he totally land-locked. I guess he's more like a peninsula than anything else.

When our daughter Jessica was just a little snip, we administered all of her meals via spoon. Much of it reached its intended destination, while the rest met with a tragic fate, crashing on her high-chair table. The perplexing outgrowth of this was that Jessica seemed to get more satisfaction from scooping up the wreckage and finishing it off, rather than taking what we had for her on the nice, neat spoon. So we let her pursue her own designs. She was not an instant expert, and often confused her mouth with her nostrils, eyes, ears, and chest. I could have fed her with a much higher degree of efficiency. My major was biological sciences in college, and I can distinguish all cranial orifices with almost no difficulty at all. Was she impressed? No way. She was determined to continue in her folly, despite her low percentage of direct hits. But as time went on, her marksmanship improved to the point where she now feeds herself completely.

I hope you get the picture. Our disciple needs to learn how to feed himself early. He needs to get into the Bible and discover truths in there for himself. He may not be real good at it at first, but he'll get a lot more satisfaction and excitement out of experiencing for himself what it's like when the Holy Spirit illumines Scripture than he would experiencing it second-hand from you. What he discovers will stick with him longer, too. For a while, he'll still be getting the bulk of his nourishment from your spoon-feeding, but encourage his urge to feed himself.

As you prompt your disciple to get into the Word on his own, remember that the things God will teach him, the things he'll excitedly report back to you on, will be kid stuff. Plan ahead as to how you will react. One bright morning, your disciple may come to you and say:

"Hey, Frank! Listen to this! I was reading the Bible this morning, and WHAM! It hit me like a bolt out of the blue! It says right here in John 1:12 that we actually have the right—now get this—the *right* to be called children of God! Can you believe it? Children of GOD! Doesn't that just blow you right out of the tub? CHILDREN OF GOD!"

"Yeah, Ron. Everybody knows that. I already told you that myself over a month ago. You mean to tell me it's taken this long for it to finally sink in?"

The sound you just heard was that of a rather large bubble bursting. Can you remember when you finally grasped some basic truth of the Christian life? Didn't you feel like doing a triple back-flip right out your bedroom window? Well, let's show a little excitement and enthusiasm when our disciples reach that same spot. Frank could have responded more like this:

"Ron, I think you've hit upon one of the most incredible truths in the whole Bible. It kinda gives me goose-bumps just thinking about it. Children of GOD! There we are, in rebellion against God, and yet He pursues us, redeems us, and decides to make us His sons! Whew! Makes you wonder about the vastness of God's love for us, doesn't it?"

The people who have put together most of the tracts and booklets have drawn on many years of experience, wisdom and knowledge, and they know just what a new Christian needs. But the tracts and booklets are not enough. Don't disregard them, but don't rely on them totally, either. Get your disciple into the Word of God – that's where the most nourishing food of all can be found.

■ BROACHING THE SUBJECT

Once again in this training objective, we really have two objectives: (1) We want our disciple to gain a basic understanding of what the Bible is and why it's so important for him to study it; and (2) we want to see our disciples *in* the Book, gaining nourishment from it. Just as in the fellowship objective (Training Objective #6, chapter 14), the idea is to get him into the Word on his own within the first week or so of conversion, and later, as we expand on the Wheel Illustration, fill in the details about how vital the Word is to him. If you've been following the training objectives in sequence and following my suggestions as to homework for your disciple, by now he has already spent quite a bit of time wandering through the Scriptures. I'm assuming, therefore, that you've passed on some of the concepts covered in this training objective in the early days of your disciple's walk with God. Others you've saved until you could cover them in greater depth, which would be about now.

I'm not dogmatic about when you should first prompt your

disciple to read the Bible on his own. Some disciplers might feel
convictions about getting a new Christian into the Word immediately after conversion (many new Christians will do this
whether you come up with the idea or not). Others will want
to spoon-feed for a few days or weeks before urging their disciple to read on their own. They want to make sure the disciple
understands a few of the ground rules of Bible study before
they dive in. Once again, I'll have to say that it's up to you.
When do you think is the best time?

Here's an idea about introducing Bible reading to your disciple:

> YOU: Sharon, if you wanted to learn all about Prince
> Charles, how would you go about it?

> DISCIPLE: Well, I guess the best thing to do would be to
> go to England, and try to get in to see him, and ask a
> lot of questions.

> YOU: But wait a minute. You're hardly making your tui-
> tion payments here at college. How are you going to
> afford a trip to Great Britain?

> DISCIPLE: Hmmm. Guess you're right. I suppose I could
> read some books about him.

> YOU: That sounds a lot easier—and less expensive. But
> how will you know which books to buy? Some might be
> giving you an accurate description, while others could
> have been written by charlatans who don't really know
> anything about him.

> DISCIPLE: I'd look at the author's references; I'd try to
> find one that was written by someone who had spent a
> lot of time studying the Prince, or, better yet, someone
> who knew him personally.

> YOU: I'll buy that. Well, what if you wanted to learn
> about God? How would you find out more about Him?

> DISCIPLE: I guess I'd get some books about God.

> YOU: I'll ask the same question again: Which ones? How
> will you know which ones are right, and which ones
> might be trying to pull a fast one on you?

DISCIPLE: We-e-e-ell . . .

YOU: I've got a suggestion. One book is the source book of all books written about God, and that's the Bible. It was written by people who were very close to God, and in fact, 2 Timothy 3:16 says that each of the writers of the Bible wrote down things that were actually directed by God Himself. If you want to find out about God, you should go to the one book that claims to be the direct revelation of God to man. Have you started reading the Bible on your own yet?

DISCIPLE: I haven't known where to start. A few years ago I tried to read it, but got kinda bogged down in all these "thou shalt's" and "thou shalt not's" in the book of Levictopus, or whatever it's called.

YOU: I know what you mean. The Old Testament has a lot of laws that were meant for the nation of Israel, and though pages and pages of important passages that pertain to us today are in there, they're sometimes hard to find among all the heavy-duty theology. As you learn more about God and the Bible, those passages will be a lot easier to find and will start to become more interesting. You'll be able to understand them better. But when you're just starting out, it's a good idea to begin in the New Testament. Would you mind if I gave you some suggestions about where to start reading?

DISCIPLE: Well, OK. But why do I need to start reading the Bible? I'm learning about all I can handle right now just from meeting with you.

YOU: I'm glad you're learning a lot—that's what I'm here for. But the Bible is kind of like "food" for your spirit. Look here at Matthew 4:4: "Jesus answered, 'It is written: Man does not live on bread alone, but on every word that comes from the mouth of God.' " From now on, as a Christian, you'll need to keep feeding yourself continuously with this spiritual food in order to stay healthy and to grow. And just like a baby needs to learn to feed herself, so do we, as spiritual beings, need to learn to feed ourselves.

Besides, this way, you'll be going straight to the source, the Bible. I study hard to be sure that the things I pass on to you are accurate, but there's always a chance I could make a mistake. If you get into the habit of depending on the Bible as your ultimate source, rather than on me or some other person, it's a lot less likely that you'll ever be led astray.

Here are the major points covered in that interchange:

1. The knowledge you receive (on any subject) is only as good as your sources, so check your sources first.

2. The ultimate source for knowledge about God and Christ is the Bible.

3. While books about God are useful, they are no substitute for the Bible itself.

4. The sources of the Bible are unimpeachable, men who knew God well — and ultimately, God Himself, since He superintended the writing of the Bible.

5. Parts of the Bible are difficult to understand and are somewhat uninteresting to a new believer. Other parts will be very interesting and helpful. He should concentrate on these passages first.

6. Bible intake is essential for growth.

7. Every Christian should be able to study the Bible on his own, and not have to rely totally on others for spiritual feeding.

■ SUGGESTIONS FOR GROWTH

I. First, Introduce Your Disciple to the Bible

Following are a few concepts that you should cover with your disciple. I've included a little narrative with each one to give you an idea how I might address them. Adapt or adopt as you see fit.

A. What the Bible is.

If you look at the Bible in its broadest sense, it's simply a history book, a record of the times God has interjected Himself into human history. People are always saying, "Oh, if God would only show Himself, then we'd have no trouble believing in Him." Well, that's what this book is — God showing Himself to man, telling us what He's like, what's in store for us, what pleases Him, what displeases Him, where we came from, where we're going, etc. God has said and done some pretty incredible things through the years, and the Bible is where people have written those things down so we'll never forget them.

B. Old Testament/New Testament.

The Old Testament was written before Jesus Christ was born (B.C. = "before Christ"), while the New Testament was written after He died and rose again (A.D. = *"anno Domini"* or "year of our Lord"). They are called the Old and New *Testaments* because they refer to the agreements existing between God and man before and after the sacrifice of Christ. During Old Testament days, people who wanted to follow God had to obey hundreds of laws that had been set down by God through Moses. Another word for *Testament* is *covenant* or *agreement*. The people agreed to follow these laws and God agreed, if the people kept their part of the bargain, to protect them, bless them and make them a great nation. It was like a "deal" they had between them. During those days, if a person sinned, there was an elaborate system of animal sacrifices that would "cover" the sin of that person with the blood of an innocent animal.

But when Jesus was sacrificed on the cross, He ushered in the period of the New Testament or "New Agreement." He was the perfect, innocent sacrifice, and while the blood of the animal sacrifices was capable of only covering the peoples' sin from God's eyes, Jesus' blood actually took it away — *paid* for our sin. Under this New Agreement, we no longer are subject to all of those nit-pickin' laws. Instead, we have God Himself, in the form of the Holy Spirit, living right inside of us helping us do right instead of wrong. And it's our faith in Christ, not how well we can follow all of the laws, that makes us righteous in God's eyes.

We are no longer under the Old Agreement, but a lot of important things in the Old Testament still apply to us, and we will spend some time on some of them.

C. Who wrote the Bible.

The Bible is not just one book; it's actually sixty-six books written by over forty different authors over a period of 1500 years. These authors include a spectrum of people, from common laborers to the most powerful world leaders ever to walk the face of the earth: kings, statesmen, the heir to the throne of pharaoh, prophets, rabbis, a physician, a tax collector, a farmer, fishermen and others. Yet the bond of the Holy Spirit ties all of these writings together. Through the centuries, God Himself told each of these writers exactly what to write down. In 2 Timothy 3:16 we read that all Scripture is "God-breathed," meaning that, though humans wrote it on paper, its ultimate source was God. The prophecies of the Bible never had their origins in the minds of mere men, but "men spoke from God as they were carried along by the Holy Spirit" (2 Peter 1:21).

We won't have time to get into it right now, but I'm convinced that these authors wrote the very words of God. Here are some of the reasons I believe this:

1. All of the prophecies have come true exactly as they were prophesied.

2. The general structure of today's world governments, including details concerning which nations would be allied and which would be enemies, was foretold thousands of years ago in the Bible.

3. It is historically accurate. The Bible supplies details of history which for hundreds of years were scoffed at by historians because they seemed so inaccurate. Yet as more and more archaeological evidence continues to be unearthed, we continually find more confirmation of the Bible's historical accuracy, and the scoffers are strangely silent.

4. The dietary and health laws in the Old Testament closely approximate what modern science has only just recently found out concerning beneficial and harmful practices. How could Moses have simply figured all of that out by himself in 1350 B.C.?

5. The Bible has been transmitted with incredible ac-

curacy through the centuries. We know for a fact that the Bible we have in our hands today is the same as it was during the time of Christ, thanks to the discovery of the Dead Sea Scrolls.

D. The structure of the Bible.

Take your disciple to the Bible's table of contents and show him how it is set up. You might even want to draw lines and squares right there in his Bible, so he'll remember. Better ask first, though.

Old Testament

1. The Law:
    Genesis; Exodus; Leviticus; Numbers; Deuteronomy

2. The Histories:
    Joshua; Judges; Ruth; 1 and 2 Samuel; 1 and 2 Kings; 1 and 2 Chronicles; Ezra; Nehemiah; Esther

3. The Poets:
    Job; Psalms; Proverbs; Ecclesiastes; Song of Solomon

4. The Prophets:
    a. (Major Prophets) Isaiah; Jeremiah; Lamentations; Ezekiel; Daniel
    b. (Minor Prophets) Hosea; Joel; Amos; Obadiah; Jonah; Micah; Nahum; Habakkuk; Zephaniah; Haggai; Zechariah; Malachi

New Testament

1. The Histories:
    a. The Gospels—accounts of the life of Jesus—Matthew; Mark; Luke; John
    b. The Acts of the Apostles—accounts of the early church after Jesus' resurrection

2. The Epistles—"letters" written by various apostles to churches, groups of people or individuals:
    Romans; 1 and 2 Corinthians; Galatians; Ephesians; Philippians; Colossians; 1 and 2 Thessalonians; 1 and 2 Timothy; Titus; Philemon; Hebrews; James; 1 and 2 Peter; 1, 2 and 3 John; Jude

3. The Apocalypse—prophesy concerning the end of the

world — Revelation

II. Next, Tell Your Disciple Where to Start Reading

Here are some suggestions.

A. The Gospel of John. This Gospel presents Jesus in His deity, and we find more proof texts for Jesus as the unique Son of God in this book than in any other Gospel. Plus, Jesus is presented very personally here. We see considerable detail concerning His personal life, His relationships with His disciples and His relationship with His Father. The word *believe* (and its different forms) is found ninety-seven times in this book, and will give the reader a good sense of the centrality of faith in the Christian life.

B. The Gospel of Mark. This Gospel is the shortest of the four Gospels and definitely the fastest-moving and most action-packed of them all. It's like listening to the six o'clock news on TV. It focuses more on what Jesus did than on what He said. Descriptions of Jesus' miracles abound in this book. As J. Sidlow Baxter said, "Mark is the camera-man of the four Gospel writers, giving us shot after shot of unforgettable scenes."

C. The Gospel of Matthew. The longest Gospel, is recommended only for those who seem to be the studious sort, the type who think nothing of spending an hour at a time reading. It starts with great descriptions of the birth of Christ, John the Baptist, the temptation of Jesus and the calling of the first disciples, all narratives that should easily catch the attention of your disciple. Then comes the Sermon on the Mount, an excellent introduction for the new Christian regarding how radical the Christian lifestyle is meant to be. If your disciple is of Jewish descent, this is the one for him, as it is written by a Jew, for Jewish readers, and strongly presents Jesus as the Messiah. There are 130 quotes from the Old Testament in this book.

D. The Gospel of Luke. Another long Gospel, but it starts out with the most extensive narrative of Jesus' birth and childhood days, great for young people and those who are already somewhat familiar with Christianity. The Christmas narrative will probably bring back many pleasant memories for them. It could be compared to watching a motion picture documentary, with a heavy emphasis on factual reporting of historical events. Originally intended to be read by the intellectual, logical Greeks.

E. The Psalms. I wouldn't recommend a strong dose of these yet. To us who have walked with Christ for a while, they are among the most precious passages in all of God's Word. For a new believer, though, they could be a bit tiresome, and he could be confused by some—they could even prompt thoughts like, *Why is David praying for God to smash his enemies to smithereens? That doesn't seem like the Christian thing to do.*

You might suggest that your disciple read one a day, in addition to his reading of the Gospels. Consider assigning specific psalms that you know he can grasp with a minimum of confusion and a maximum of inspiration, such as Psalms 1, 2, 8, 18, 19, 23, 24, 25, 32, 34, 37, 42, 46, 47, 49, 51, 52, 53, 56, 62, 63, 66, 67, 71, 84, 86, 91, 92, 96, 100, 101, 103, 107, 111–118, 119, 122, 123, 126, 130, 138, 139, 145-150. (If your favorite isn't listed above, add it!)

F. The Proverbs. The same approach applies to Proverbs as to Psalms. Perhaps your disciple could read the chapter in Proverbs that corresponds with the current day of the month (i.e., on May 12, read Proverbs 12).

G. The Acts. After he has read a Gospel or two, the next logical book would be the Acts. It describes the growth of the early church, and heavily emphasizes the role of the Holy Spirit in the lives of Christians. It's easy in this book to see the results of living a life of faith, and Paul sets an excellent example of how to live victoriously in the midst of personal trial and affliction, a concept all Christians need to grab early.

H. The Epistles. After your disciple has read a couple of the Gospels and Acts, you could encourage him to begin reading an epistle. They are a lot more heady, so you should recommend that he limit his intake to a chapter a day.

Start him off with one of the short ones. Ephesians would be excellent, because it covers a lot of the major themes of the Christian walk. Galatians would be good as well, especially since it contains the section contrasting the works of the flesh to the fruit of the Spirit.

Next, a couple of the personal epistles; 1 and 2 Timothy would be good because of the personableness, intimacy and challenging nature of Paul's writing to his own young disciple.

Follow that up with 1 John. The great "Apostle of Love" can't help but be a loving influence on your disciple. He should be able to grasp important concepts about the love that exists in the heart of God for us, as well as the love that ought to exist in our hearts for Him and for our brothers and sisters.

Bible Study Notebook. You may want to just say, "Read this; it'll do you good"; or you may want to go one step further and suggest he begin his own Bible study notebook. His notebook could be a spiral notebook or three-ring binder, and he should allow at least half a page for each day's entries.

As he begins to read the Gospels, help him keep his notebook simple. Give him three or four things to think about and make notes on after each chapter, such as:

1. The thing that amazes me the most in this chapter:

2. The verse I liked the most:

3. Something I need to do in response to reading this chapter:

4. Questions that came to my mind as I read it:

You might even consider making him a notebook yourself. Type those four questions out, leaving writing space after each one, then duplicate them, put them in a notebook and give it to him. He'll be much more likely to carry out the suggestions you made if you do this.

III. Provide More Detail About the Importance of the Word

Here we are in the present again. Now it's time, as you're expanding on the Wheel Illustration, to wade a little deeper into the central importance of the Word in the life of a growing Christian. You may have already covered much of what I mentioned above on the run — perhaps tacked on to the end of an earlier training objective, as you were talking informally, in response to questions your disciple had, etc. But now you need to set aside a specific time to make sure your disciple has a strangle-hold on how vital it is that he be in the Word. Following are some concepts I suggest you explore with your disciple, with some Scriptures you can study together.

A. Characteristics of God's Word.

1. Joshua 23:14 — Reliable
2. Psalm 12:6; Proverbs 30:5 — Pure
3. Psalm 18:30 — Tried and proven
4. Psalm 19:7-10 — Perfect, sure, right, pure, true, more desirable than gold, sweeter than honey
5. Psalm 119:105,130 — Enlightening
6. Psalm 119:160 — True
7. Isaiah 40:8; Matthew 5:17-19; Mark 13:31 — Eternal
8. Isaiah 55:10,11 — Accomplishes God's purposes
9. 2 Timothy 3:16 — God-breathed
10. Hebrews 4:12 — Alive
11. 1 Peter 1:23-25 — Incorruptible, eternal
12. 2 Peter 1:20,21 — Initiated by God, not man

B. Benefits of Reading God's Word.

1. Joshua 1:8 — Makes us prosper; gives us success
2. Psalm 19:7 — Restores our soul; makes wise the simple
3. Psalm 19:8 — Rejoices the heart
4. Psalm 19:11 — Provides warnings; provides rewards
5. Psalm 37:31 — Keeps us from "slipping"
6. Psalm 119:9,11 — Keeps our way pure; keeps us from sin
7. Psalm 119:24 — Provides delight; provides counsel
8. Psalm 119:50 — Gives comfort in affliction
9. Psalm 119:98; 2 Timothy 3:15 — Makes us wise
10. Proverbs 6:22 — Guides us; watches over us in unguarded moments
11. Matthew 4:4 — Provides spiritual nourishment
12. John 15:3; 17:17 — Sanctifies us

13. John 20:30,31 – Helps our faith

14. Romans 15:4 – Gives us hope for the future

15. 2 Timothy 3:16,17 – Teaches, rebukes, corrects, trains in righteousness, thoroughly equips

16. 1 Peter 2:2 – Makes us grow to spiritual maturity

C. What we do with God's Word.

1. Joshua 1:8 – Meditate on it

2. Psalm 119:11 – Hide it in our hearts

3. Proverbs 6:20-22 – Stay in constant contact with it

4. Mark 4:3-20 – Sow it

5. Luke 24:25 – Believe it

6. John 8:31 – Continue in it

7. John 14:21 – Obey it

8. Acts 17:11 – Study it diligently

9. Colossians 3:16 – Let it "dwell" within us

10. 2 Timothy 3:15 – Handle it correctly

D. How we can get a "firm grasp" on God's Word.

The Navigators have an illustration that has been helpful to thousands in giving them a clear picture of how they go about assimilating the Word of God into their lives. It's known as the "Word Hand."[2]

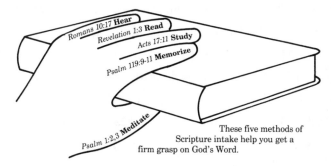

These five methods of Scripture intake help you get a firm grasp on God's Word.

As you can see from the above illustration, there are five ways we can go about getting a firm grasp on God's Word: hearing, reading, studying, memorizing and meditating. A good way to demonstrate this graphically is to trace the outline of your hand on a sheet of paper, and label each finger appropriately. Be sure to label each finger just as they are above—there is a reason for it, as you will soon see.

Next, take the fingers one by one and look at a Scripture that backs up each method, writing the reference next to its corresponding finger. Choose from the following:

Hear: Romans 10:17; Luke 6:45-49; Luke 11:28

Read: Deuteronomy 17:19; Revelation 1:3

Study: Acts 17:11; 2 Timothy 2:15

Memorize: Psalm 37:31; Psalm 119:9-11

Meditate: Joshua 1:8; Psalm 1:2-3

Finally, explain that, if we want to get a strong grip on an object, we use all our fingers. If we try to hold on with only two or three fingers, the object is easily grabbed away (demonstrate this as you talk about it). In the same way, we should use each of these methods of biblical intake if we want to get a firm grasp on the Word of God. We need to hear, read, study and memorize it. Then, just as our thumb opposes (can easily touch) each of our fingers, meditation should touch each of the other activities: We should meditate on what we hear, meditate on what we read, meditate on what we study, and meditate on what we memorize. It does no good at all if God's Word goes in one ear and out the other. We need to let it sink down into our hearts through meditation.

You'll notice that, in the illustration, the bigger the finger, the harder its corresponding activity is. It's easier to listen than to read, easier to read than to study, etc. However, it's also true that the bigger the finger, the more effective the activity is. Experts tell us that after a 24-hour period, we can recall only about 5 percent of what we hear, 15 percent of what we read, 35 percent of what we study, and 100 percent of what we memorize. Since this is true, we would be wise to give special attention to the more effective activities.

■ FURTHER RESOURCES

For some good, basic, fill-in-the-blank type studies on the

Word, consider using a couple of the studies contained in the following Bible study series:

"Ten Basic Steps Toward Christian Maturity"[3] by Campus Crusade for Christ:

- Step 1, Lesson 5: "The Christian's Authority"
- Step 5: "The Christian and The Bible" (all seven lessons apply)
- Step 7, Lesson 4: "Witnessing and the Word of God"
- Step 9: "Old Testament Highlights"
- Step 10: "New Testament Highlights"

"The Discipleship Series"[4] by Campus Crusade for Christ:

- Book 2, Lesson 1: "Using the Bible in Daily Life"

Design for Discipleship[5] Bible Study Series by The Navigators:

- Book 2, Chapter 2: "God's Word In Your Life"
- Book 5, Chapter 2: "The Authority of God's Word"
- Book 7: "Chapter Analysis Study of 1 Thessalonians"

■ ENDING THE SESSION

This may be a lot of material to cover in one session, especially if you decide you want to look up all of the verses I supplied. If it would be helpful, take two sessions to cover it all.

When you're done, however, the prime objective is that your disciple begin to get into the Word on his own. This is when you should begin talking to him about the importance of having a daily quiet time, or devotions, a time he sets aside each day to communicate with God through prayer and Bible study. At this point, you may want to introduce the topic formally by saying something like, "Let me tell you about having a quiet time"; or you may want to keep it informal, "Why don't you, starting tomorrow, begin a habit of reading one chapter in the Bible each morning?" Whatever you think best. Personally, I prefer waiting until after I've had a chance to talk with my disciple more extensively about prayer before I broach the subject of a formal quiet time, but it's up to you. I'll be going into more detail about how to get your disciple started in quiet time toward the end of Training Objective #8 on prayer (chapter 16), if you'd like some input.

■ ASSIGNMENT FOR NEXT TIME

Browse through the "Tell Your Disciple Where to Start Reading" section a few pages back and decide which book of the Bible would be most appropriate for him to begin with. Consider whether or not he would be able to begin keeping a Bible study notebook. If you think he can handle it, get him started.

Do you think he's up to memorizing Scripture yet? You might be surprised. If he's been watching you quote the Bible, he may be itching to give it a shot himself. The Navigators have an excellent Scripture memory program called the "Topical Memory System" (TMS). You can pick one up at just about any Christian bookstore. The TMS has sixty of the most basic and useful verses in the Bible printed on handy little cards in their own carrying case. Each verse is connected to a topic, to make it easier to call to mind after you've memorized it. There are three secrets to being successful in Scripture memory: (1) Review; (2) Review; and (3) Review. Consider memorizing Scripture *together*. It helps a lot if you can encourage each other and hold each other accountable.

Also, anticipate what training objective you are going to go over next week and give him an appropriate assignment. For ideas on that, go back to chapter 13 (Basic Growth Principles, Training Objective #5) and look under Assignments for Next Week, or look ahead to next week's training objective and consider some of the selections under Further Resources.

■ EVALUATION

Ask yourself these questions:

1. Does my disciple understand how important it is that he be involved in regular Bible input?

2. Does he see the Scriptures as spiritual nourishment, indispensable for growth?

3. Does he have a basic understanding of the layout of the Bible? Does he know the significance of each major section?

4. Has he begun to read the Bible on his own?

If you can answer each of those questions in the affirmative, then this training objective has been met. If you need a little more input from him to determine your answers, here are some questions you can ask him:

1. If a Buddhist were to ask you, "Who wrote the Bible?", how would you answer him?

2. Do you think the Bible is true? All of it?

3. Do you think it's important to read the Bible? Why or why not?

4. How much time do you think a Christian should spend reading the Bible? Every day? How long each day? Why so long (or so short)?

5. What are some of the main benefits you receive from reading the Bible? Are there some benefits you've heard about that you're not experiencing yet?

6. Have you been reading your Bible lately? (If so) What have you been reading? What have you been learning? What's the greatest or the most exciting thing you've learned from the Bible recently?

7. If you had held a personal opinion about something for a long time, and then discovered something in the Bible contradicting that opinion, how would you respond?

8. If you read something by the leader of some great world religion, say a Buddhist, and it seemed to contradict what you know is in the Bible, how would you respond?

9. How do you know that what's in the Bible is really true?

10. Why is there an "Old" Testament and a "New" Testament?

11. What are some things you can do to assimilate the Word of God?

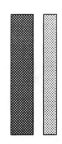

16 TRAINING OBJECTIVE #8

PRAYER

■ OBJECTIVE

The disciple has a basic understanding of the importance of prayer, knows the fundamentals of prayer, and is beginning to pray on his own.

■ BIBLICAL BASIS FOR THIS OBJECTIVE

At the vortex of the tornado called "The Christian Life," there is a fact that should affect everything we do as Christians: Christianity is a *relationship* with God through the auspices of the risen, glorified Savior. It's not really a "religion," though some choose to define it as such; it's not merely a code of ethics, though that is involved; it's not a certain collection of behaviors, though as a result of our relationship with God, certain behaviors will come to the fore. At its very foundation it's a two-way, vital, dynamic *friendship* between the Creator and His creature.

We all know that, if you want to carry on a relationship with someone, it is necessary to communicate with that person. No communication—no relationship. It's that simple. Since we desire to carry on a relationship with God, we must talk to Him. We call this "prayer."

Jesus commanded us in the Great Commission recorded in Matthew 28:19,20 to "make disciples . . . teaching them to observe all that I commanded you." He gave us a lot of instructions concerning prayer, and a number of them are listed at the top of the following page. As usual, look up each reference, and jot down a short summary for each in your disciplemaker's notebook.

243

Matthew 5:44	Matthew 26:41	Luke 18:1
Matthew 6:5-9	Mark 11:22-25	Luke 21:36
Matthew 7:7,8	Mark 13:33	John 14:13,14
Matthew 9:38	Luke 6:28	John 15:7,16
Matthew 24:20	Luke 11:2	John 16:24-27

■ APPLICABLE DEFINITIONS

Following are a few definitions of prayer by people who know what they're talking about. I thought you might find them interesting:

Rosalind Rinker: "Prayer is a dialogue between two persons who love each other."[1]

William R. Bright: "Prayer is simply talking to God."[2]

S. D. Gordon: "Prayer is the word commonly used for all intercourse with God."[3]

Dick Eastman: "Prayer is to verbalize our total dependence on God concerning all our efforts."[4]

Andrew Murray: "Prayer is fellowship with the Unseen and Most Holy One. The powers of the eternal world have been placed at its disposal. It is the very essence of true religion, the channel of all blessings, the secret of power and life."[5]

Robert A. Cook: "Prayer is a cry. The physician expects the newborn babe to cry out, as first evidence of life. If it does not cry, he shakes or spanks it to produce a cry. If it continues silent, it will soon be dead."[6]

Dr. Jack Taylor: "Prayer is weakness plugged into strength. Prayer is saying, 'I can't, but You can,' and plugging into God's 'I will.' "[7]

■ PEP TALK FOR THE DISCIPLEMAKER

Your disciple is a brand new spiritual baby, and his needs are simple—so far. What we want to do at this point is to make sure he understands the most basic facts of prayer; we want to give him the equivalent of a first-grade education. The heavy-duty industrial-strength concepts will come when he's older and more able to absorb them. They'll come through specific instruction from you, or through Bible studies you have him complete, or through others who will be ministering to him. Yes, it is possible for your disciple to learn something from a source other than you or this program! In fact, you should encourage it.

Think about the Navigator's Wheel Illustration for a minute (chapter 13). Remember the four spokes? Two of them, the Word and fellowship, usually aren't difficult to engage in. The Bible is a rather interesting and popular piece of literature. And since we humans are by and large gregarious creatures, fellowship is practically a natural tendency, a pursuit filled with exciting possibilities.

But when you begin the businesses of prayer and witnessing, you discover some spokes of a different color. It's harder to pray and to witness—you and I both know that. This is because our adversary, the devil, recognizes the immense holes these two activities bore into the foundation of his infernal kingdom. Prayer short-circuits his power and authority, while witnessing—which causes conversion—depletes the ranks of his prisoners. This is not to say that the Word and fellowship are by any means less important, just less of a hassle. For this reason, you can be sure of two things: (1) Satan plans to resist your efforts as you teach your disciple to pray; and (2) the sooner your disciple learns about prayer, the better off he'll be.

You've probably heard that "there are no atheists in foxholes." Though men everywhere have an innate knowledge that they can and should call out to their Creator, our new natures are quite unfamiliar with *true* prayer which is intimate communion with our Father. Much instruction, practice, discipline and perseverance is required to learn this new and vital art. Few Christians have spent as much time learning how to communicate with God as the average ham radio operator has spent learning Morse Code. This could be the reason so few Christians know how to send out an SOS to the Captain of their souls. So keep in mind that this training objective is merely the beginning of your disciple's education about prayer.

If your disciple has any kind of religious upbringing, he may think that his prayer life is perfectly acceptable. After all, he figures he's been praying most of his life—and to some rudimentary degree, perhaps he has. In a way that's good, because talking with God will come easier for him than for someone who's never tried it. But in another way, it could be a problem—it could open the door to spiritual pride.

At this writing, my five-year-old daughter is going through the "I-can-do-it-I-can-do-it-I-can-do-it" stage. It matters not what feat is being contemplated; she, in all of her preschool pomposity, is convinced it's a piece of cake. I'm faced with a dilemma: On the one hand I want to shout, "You have no knowledge of the skills of which you boast!" On the other hand, I want to encourage her ambitious voyage toward maturity, and keep her from ripping off her mainsail in the process.

So my wife and I have become expert diplomats in this area. As much as possible, we avoid saying, "You can't do that." As long as her request doesn't involve lethal weapons or potentially destructive and catastrophic consequences, we respond with a hearty, "Go for it!" Sometimes we grant permission with full knowledge that she'll fail, but we see that as part of the learning process.

Apply the same principles to the new Christian who is an "expert-in-his-own-eyes" pray-er. Don't squash his fragile ego by saying things like, "Forget everything you think you know about prayer. I will show you how to do it the right way"; or "The way you're praying is just plain silly." If the man is talking to God, encourage him! Portray the "Go for it!" attitude.

I'll never forget the first prayer I heard Eloy pray a few days after his conversion back in college. There were several of us sitting around my dorm room having a prayer meeting. Eloy piped up, "God? This is Eloy. I'm here in Ingersol Hall . . . " Should I have taken time at that moment to explain to him that there was no need to clue in an omniscient, omnipresent God as to his identity and location? I don't think so, at least not right then. It was one of the most priceless, honest, innocent prayers I've ever heard, and if he could retain that innocence and reverence for the rest of his life on earth, he would do far better than most. The theology could wait.

If your disciple's praying requires some adjusting, he'll pick it up by and by with your gentle, sensitive guidance. Let him progress toward maturity in this area a step at a time. Allow him the freedom to stumble and fall. Stand back and let him grope around in the dark a little. Discovering the light switch after grabbing around for it is such a sweet and memorable occasion.

One of the best educations he can receive is through listening to *you* pray. That's the way Jesus began teaching the disciples about prayer (Luke 11). Since He had a knack for providing rather capable instructional techniques, we would do well to imitate Him. Every time you pray with your disciple, whether you know it or not, you teach him something about prayer. For this reason, it would be advisable for you to examine your own prayer life.

- Do your prayers reflect a personal, intimate relationship with a loving Father, or are they stiff, strained and formal?

- When your disciple listens to you pray, can he tell that you are engaging in an activity you are very familiar with because you do it a lot, or do your prayers seem curiously rusty, hesitant, unseasoned?

- Are you addressing your heavenly Father, or are you delivering a speech for the benefit of the human hearers in the room?

- Are you being specific in your requests?

- Are you believing God for big things? Are you stretching your faith as you pray?

- Is worship an integral part of your prayers? Are your prayers God-centered and God-honoring, or do your prayers amount to little more than a celestial shopping list — a "gimme-gimme-gimme" session?

■ BROACHING THE SUBJECT

How you get into the subject of prayer will depend somewhat on how much "pre-Christian" experience your disciple has had with it, as was mentioned in the Pep Talk. You might get into the subject by asking some intriguing questions about prayer to pique his interest, as well as to discover where he is in his prayer life. Here are a few suggestions (you wouldn't ask all of these questions, however):

- What has been your background as far as prayer goes? Do you do much of it?

- Have you ever seen God answer a prayer you prayed? How about a prayer someone else prayed?

- Do you think God really does hear and answer our prayers?

- What sort of things do you pray about? Just the big things, or do you pray about anything that comes to your mind?

- Why do you think Christians pray? Why do you think God wants us to pray?

- Do you think it matters to God if we sit or stand or kneel when we pray? Is it necessary to close our eyes?

- Have you ever prayed out loud with a group of people? Were you nervous?

Based on his responses to questions like these, you can figure out how much detail you need to go into with this very basic training objective.

■ SUGGESTIONS FOR GROWTH

In this section, we will answer the disciple's most basic question about prayer: "How do I do it?" I'll assume we're talking about someone who has just stepped off a boat from Antarctica, and who knows virtually nothing about communicating with his Creator. You can weed out the material that is too basic for your disciple.

Go through the list of statements and corresponding verses enumerated below and pick out the ones you think your disciple is unaware of or needs a refresher course on. Write the statement and verses on a sheet of paper you can refer to during your meeting with him. You'll probably want to use only one or two verses for each point, but I put a whole truckload of them down for you to choose from. Looking up each verse will be a great study on prayer for you. Just before the verses, I've written a few thoughts I might share with a new believer regarding the subject. You might want to pass them along, or perhaps they'll trigger some other ideas in your own mind.

Facts the New Christian Should Know About Prayer

1. Prayer is simply talking with God.

Though God is far more than a mere person, He is more like a person than anything else our minds can conceive of. For this reason, He asks us to converse with Him just as we would with another person.

Since the essence of the Christian life is maintaining a vital relationship with God, and since communication between two people is the only way to build a relationship, you've got to *talk* together in order to have that relationship.

Genesis 18:22-33 (example: Abraham)

Isaiah 1:18

Psalm 139:23,24 (example: David)

Matthew 6:9-13 (example: Jesus)

Matthew 11:25,26 (example: Jesus)

2. You can pray about anything you want to, any time, any place.

Many people think God doesn't want to be bothered with "insignificant" matters. They think He's too busy with such big, important pursuits as stopping wars, ending droughts and trying to tell presidents and kings how to run their countries. Nothing could be further from the truth. Proverbs 15:8 says that the "prayer of the upright is His delight." That means that He loves to hear from us, no matter what it is we've got on our minds. God is everywhere-present and all-powerful, so He doesn't have to stop what He's doing to listen to us.

Do you remember when John F. Kennedy was the President of the United States? Did you ever visit him personally? Probably not. He was a very busy man! It would almost take an act of congress, or maybe even an act of God, for people like you or me to get an audience with him. But his two children, John Jr. and Caroline, seemed to wander in and out of the Oval Office as they pleased, and he was always glad to see them. It was reported that he would never reprimand them for their lack of decorum in barging in on his meetings; instead he often would take them up on his lap, give them a big hug and talk with them for a couple of minutes.

It's the same way now between us and our heavenly Father. We can enter His throne room anytime we want to, for any reason at all, and He'll always welcome us with an open lap.

- Anything:
  1 Chronicles 4:10 (for blessings)
  2 Chronicles 7:14 (for national peace)
  2 Chronicles 14:11 (for help in trouble)
  Psalm 18:1 (to express love to God)
  Psalm 22:1,2 (when in anguish)
  Psalm 52:9 (to express thanks to God)
  Psalm 143:8 (for direction)
  Psalm 143:9 (for protection)
  Psalm 143:10 (for instruction)
  Psalm 145:1,2 (in praise and worship)
  Proverbs 3:5,6 (for guidance)
  Matthew 5:44 (for your enemies)
  Matthew 6:11 (for daily needs)
  Mark 11:22,23 (for the impossible)
  Mark 11:24 (for your desires)
  Luke 18:13 (for God's mercy)
  Luke 22:31,32 (for your friends)
  John 15:16 (for your ministry)
  Romans 10:1 (for another's salvation)
  Philippians 4:6,7 (for EVERYTHING)
  James 1:5 (for wisdom)
  James 5:16 (for physical healing)
  1 John 1:9 (for forgiveness)
  1 John 5:14 (for ANYTHING)

- Any time:
  Exodus 15:11,2 (when you're "up")
  2 Samuel 12:15 (when you're "down")
  1 Kings 18:36 (in spiritual battle)
  Psalm 5:3 (morning)
  Psalm 51:3,4 (when you've sinned)
  Psalm 55:17 (evening, morning, noon)
  Psalm 88:1 (day and night)
  Mark 1:35 (before dawn)
  Luke 10:21 (spontaneously)
  Acts 16:25 (when in trials)
  2 Timothy 1:3 (night and day)

- Any place:
    1 Samuel 1:9,10 (in the house of God)

    Matthew 6:6 (in your room)

    Matthew 14:23 (out in the hills)

    Matthew 18:19,20 (with others)

    Mark 1:35 (alone)

3. God does hear our prayers.

Praying is not merely some psychological exercise or discipline. It's not like a form of meditation where we engage in it strictly for our own benefit and edification. It's a genuine conversation. You speak, and God listens. He'll speak back to you through His Word (the Bible), or through circumstances, or even through direct impressions to your spirit.

| Psalm 10:17 | Psalm 40:1 | 1 Peter 3:12 |
| Psalm 34:15,17 | Psalm 65:21 | John 5:14,15 |

4. God answers our prayers one of three ways: yes, no, or wait.

Just asking God for something in prayer doesn't guarantee that we will receive it. God is all wise. He knows us inside and out. He knows that some requests we make will be good for us, so to those requests He answers yes. Some requests would be bad for us—to those He answers no. Some requests would be good for us in the future, but not right now. That's when He says, "Wait." Our attitude should be one of quiet acceptance. If my toddler asked me to let her play with the pretty butcher knife, I'd be a terrible father if I said yes. She might not understand my decision—even if I tried hard to explain it to her—and she might cry and moan trying to convince me to give it to her, but I would remain firm in my negative resolve, because I love her. Eventually, I will let her use the butcher knife, but not now.

- God answers, "Yes":
    Psalm 32:5—David's prayer for forgiveness
    1 Samuel 1:11,19,20—Hannah's prayer for a son (Samuel)
    2 Kings 20:1-6—Hezekiah's prayer that God would spare his life
    Genesis 24:12-27—Abraham's servant's prayer for Jacob's wife

Genesis 25:21 — Isaac's prayer that barren Rebekah would have children

1 Chronicles 4:9,10 — Jabez's prayer

2 Kings 6:15-18 — Elisha's prayer that his enemies be blinded

Matthew 9:27-31 — Blind men asking Jesus to restore their sight

Luke 17:11-14 — Ten lepers asking Jesus to heal them

Luke 18:35-43 — Blind beggar asking Jesus to restore his sight

- God answers, "No":

    2 Samuel 12:15-18 — David's prayer that his son, the result of his sin with Bathsheba, would live. Request denied.

    Matthew 26:37-42 — Jesus's prayer that He would not have to undergo the crucifixion. Request denied.

    2 Corinthians 12:7-10 — Paul's prayer (three times) that God would heal his "thorn in the flesh." Request denied.

- God answers, "Wait":

    Genesis 15:2-5 — Abraham's prayer for a son. God said yes, but it was many years before Isaac was born.

    Genesis 50:24,25 — God's promise to Joseph that He would take him and his family from Egypt back to Canaan. He did, 440 years later.

    Exodus 5:22,23; 6:6-8 — Moses asking God to rescue the nation of Israel. God said He would, but only *after* He demonstrated His power and presence to the world through the Ten Plagues.

5. There are four types of prayer: Adoration, Confession, Thanksgiving and Supplication (A.C.T.S.).

Prayer does not consist entirely of asking God for things we want. Imagine having a relationship with someone in which all the other person ever did was ask you for things! This condition does not exist in real life (except between college students and their parents). So it should not exist in our relationship with God, either. Following are some verses that either talk about or give examples of each of the four types of prayer:

- Adoration:

Exodus 15:1-21	Matthew 11:25,26	1 Timothy 1:17
2 Samuel 22	Luke 1:46-55	1 Peter 1:3-5
Psalm 63:1-8	Luke 4:8	
Daniel 2:19-23	Ephesians 3:20,21	

- Confession:

Psalm 32	Psalm 139:23,24	Luke 15:17-21
Psalm 51	Proverbs 28:13	Luke 18:9-14
Psalm 66:18	Mark 11:25	1 John 1:8-10

- Thanksgiving:

Daniel 6:10	Romans 1:21	Colossians 2:7
Psalm 105:1	Ephesians 1:15,16	Colossians 3:17
Luke 17:11-19	Philippians 4:6	1 Thessalonians 5:18

- Supplication:

Genesis 18:23-32	Proverbs 30:7-9	Philippians 1:9-11
1 Chronicles 4:10	Luke 11:5-13	Philippians 4:6,7
2 Chronicles 14:11	Luke 18:1-8	James 4:2,3
Psalm 34:15	John 16:24	1 John 5:14,15
Psalm 143:8-10	Ephesians 6:18,19	

6. God will hear your prayers regardless of your physical posture.

It doesn't matter to God what's going on with your physical body as you pray—He's much more interested in what's going on in your heart. It's important to come to God with a humble and reverent heart, and if getting down on your knees or prostrating yourself helps you express those qualities, then by all means do it. In today's America, most people bow their heads and close their eyes, for two reasons: (1) out of reverence and respect to God; and (2) to keep the things and people around us from distracting us as we pray.

Here are biblical examples of variety in prayer posture:

Genesis 18:22,23 (Abraham stood)	2 Kings 20:1,2 (Hezekiah on his bed)
Exodus 34:8 (Moses bowed)	Daniel 6:10 (Daniel kneeled)
Joshua 7:6 (Joshua was prostrate)	Matthew 26:39 (Jesus was prostrate)
1 Samuel 1:26 (Hannah stood)	Mark 11:25 ("When you stand . . . ")
1 Kings 8:54,55 (Solomon kneeled)	Luke 22:41 (Jesus kneeled)

7. Faith is vital in prayer.

Let's say I asked you to do me a favor. Then, at the end of my request I said, "But I don't know why in the world I'm talking to you about this, anyway. I know I can't trust you any farther than I can throw you. Never mind, I'll take care of it myself." Do you think you'd eagerly and graciously set out to fulfill my request? Not likely.

Many Christians come to God with the same attitude. Is it any wonder God remains unmoved by their requests, and they give up on prayer after a while? Throughout the Bible God says, "If you want Me to work in and through you, you've got to have faith that I can and will do it." Faith is one of the primary character qualities God wants to develop in you, and He'll do everything He can to help you grow in trusting in Him.

Psalm 37:5	Mark 11:24	Hebrews 11:6
Proverbs 3:5,6	Romans 4:20,21	James 1:6,7
Matthew 17:19-21		

8. We can't expect God to grant our requests if we are unwilling to grant His (importance of obedience).

A father spoke with his son at breakfast one Saturday morning:

"Ted, today's the day you promised to mow the lawn. I'd like to see it done before noon, because we're having the Bakers over for lunch."

"No way, Dad. That's just too much work for a guy like me. You'll have to go find someone else to do it. Now, not to change the subject, but Bill and I want to go to the beach this afternoon. The surf's really up today! Would you drive us over there so we don't have to walk all that way with our surfboards?"

What do you think Dad's answer is going to be? Obviously, if Ted's unwilling to obey his father, dear old Dad is not going to be exactly thrilled about doing favors for Ted. Ted's dad would probably love to see Ted out there enjoying himself in the sun and the surf, but if he's a good father, he knows that learning responsibility and respect for authority is much more important than a good tan and great waves.

Our heavenly Father has the same sentiments. How can we expect God to look favorably upon our requests when He is saying to us through the Bible and His Holy Spirit, "My child, here is what I want you to do," and we respond with, "No. Now, here's what I want *You* to do"? So one thing to keep in mind: Our willingness to obey God will greatly influence the effectiveness of our prayer life.

| Psalm 37:4 | Proverbs 28:9 | 1 John 3:22 |
| Proverbs 15:8 | Matthew 6:14,15 | |

9. We must deal with any known sin in our lives before we can expect God to hear and act upon our prayers.

It's foolish to think that you and I will never disobey God. We're human; therefore, we will blow it from time to time. Our goal is that, as we grow more mature in the Lord, we'll blow it less and less. In the meantime, when we become conscious of disobeying God, we need to get things right with Him as soon as possible. If we don't, our conversations with God will be a lot like this one between two friends:

"Hi, Mike! How's it going? Hey, I've been meaning to ask you, do you think you could let me borrow your truck next week? I've got to help a friend move and . . . "

"Uh, Dennis, did you know that you're bleeding?"

"What? Where? Oh, that? That's nothing. Just a little nick. As I was saying, you've got about the greatest truck in town for moving, and I was really hoping . . . "

"Dennis, that thing is really bleeding! In fact, I think you may have sliced an artery there. Don't you think you should get it taken care of?"

"Nah! It's no big deal. I'm pretty sure it'll stop bleeding in a while. Now, about that truck. I love how it handles the big loads and . . . "

"Look, old buddy, I really don't think we should be standing here talking about trucks when your arm is about to fall off! You've lost about a pint of blood just standing here! Look at the sidewalk!"

"I'm sure it's nothing to be concerned about! If you really cared about me, you'd let me borrow your truck!"

"Nothing doing! I'll not listen to another word until you let me take you to a hospital and get that gash taken care of."

The thing that was heaviest on Dennis's heart was borrowing a truck so he could help a friend move. A noble cause, but Mike knew that if Dennis didn't take care of his wound soon, he wouldn't be alive to help with the move. We have a lot of important things on our hearts, too, as we come to God in prayer, but our Father isn't going to take the time to listen to them if he sees sin in our lives, cutting us to ribbons.

Psalm 32:3-5	Psalm 139:23,24	Isaiah 59:2
Psalm 66:18	Proverbs 28:13	1 John 1:9

10. Prayer is hard work, and, as in all work, a very important factor is patient perseverance.

Let's say you wanted to become a champion ice skater. Probably one of the first things you'd do is to go out and buy a pair of skates. Next, you'd find a rink where you could get lessons and practice what you learn. If you're really serious, you might even dip into your savings account and hire a professional coach. Now your lessons start, and after a while, you begin to lose heart. The ice skates hurt your ankles. The rink is cold, and each fall reminds you of how hard it is, and how tender your poor body is. The coach yells at you a lot, and the money's not there for you to do the things you used to. This is all rather discouraging! As you watched the skaters on Wide World of Sports, it looked like so much fun! So carefree! So easy! But now that you're into it, you see there's a lot more to it than first met the eye.

But because you are determined to become a great skater, you stick with it. Even when it's inconvenient, when it's boring, when it hurts, when it's expensive, when you'd rather be doing something else—you persevere. And you're patient. Patient with yourself, your coach, the program; patient when it doesn't seem like you're making much progress; patient when others seem to be doing better than you are; patient when things don't turn out as you'd hoped. And after many years, the patient perseverance pays off, and you become one of the best skaters in the world.

While the ice skater may be pursuing a perishable wreath (1 Corinthians 9:25), what you and I are doing when we are involved in prayer will have eternal consequences. In order to become good at prayer, you must understand that it is not only an activity that looks like fun—carefree and easy—but that it is also a discipline that requires perseverance and patience to master. Yet if we keep in mind that this activity will reap eternal, positive results, our motivation should be even stronger. At times you will be exhilarated and joyful, but you must anticipate a person's natural inclination to grow weary, and meet it with the same sort of stick-to-it-iveness that the aspiring ice skater does. The Bible says that this attitude will not go unrewarded.

Psalm 40:1	Luke 18:1-8
Luke 11:5-9	1 Corinthians 15:58

11. We must approach God in humility, remembering who we are talking to.

Have you heard people refer to God as the "man upstairs," or the "big guy," or the "boss"? This could indicate that the speaker does not have a genuine relationship with the Lord. Though the Lord deeply loves us, and desires an intimate relationship with us, He's not our "good buddy." It's very important that we remember He is the all-powerful, sovereign, ruler of the universe, and He is eminently worthy of our utmost respect and reverence. As you read the Bible, you'll find that it greatly pleases God when we come to Him in humility, and it has the opposite effect when we exhibit pride.

2 Kings 22:19	Psalm 10:17	James 4:10
2 Chronicles 7:14	Psalm 51:16,17	1 Peter 5:5,6
2 Chronicles 34:27	Luke 18:9-14	

12. Yet we can feel bold and confident about approaching Him in prayer, because He fully accepts us as His children.

It may seem difficult to balance this concept (approaching

God confidently) with the previous one (approaching Him with humility), but when you think about it, it's not so hard. It's like the orphan servant boy who was adopted by the benevolent king. As long as he could remember, the boy had been in awe of the king. He had seen the king as the epitome of wisdom, power, courage and love. After the astonishing day the king adopted the boy, the boy's feelings in no way depreciated concerning the king. In fact, his opinions of the king soared higher than ever. Only now he didn't have to wait by the door outside the king's chambers, fearing for his life if he should anger the king. Now he could approach the king any time he wanted to, because now the wise, powerful, courageous, loving king was also "Daddy." He wouldn't come bounding in like a uncontrolled schoolboy on the last day of school, hooting, hollering and swinging from the chandeliers, because of the respect he held for the king and his office. On the other hand, he wouldn't come cowering and flinching, either, afraid of losing his head, because he knew this man loved him enough to make him his son.

The analogy holds true between us and our heavenly Father. We approach Him in prayer with a humble heart, because of His position as our Creator, Savior, King of kings and Lord of the universe, but we also approach Him with boldness and confidence because He loved us enough to die for us, to adopt us, to exalt us. And besides — He said we could!

Ephesians 3:12   Hebrews 4:15,16   Hebrews 10:19-22

13. When you pray out loud, don't try to impress other people who might be listening in; just concentrate on talking to God.

It's a shame, but some people, when they are praying out loud in public, are really just making a speech for the benefit of the other people listening in. They aren't talking to God at all. They're interested in having people exclaim when they're done, "My, wasn't that a lovely prayer. How eloquent he is. Someone as silver-tongued as he is *must* be a righteous man." Prayer is meant to be an exercise where you talk to God, and God listens. If you're interested in talking to people, that's OK, but that's not prayer. That's a sermon.

Now this doesn't mean public prayer is to be avoided. On the contrary, Jesus *encouraged* us to pray out loud with other believers. There is something special and powerful about group prayer. It's just that we need to be careful about our motives during public prayer. If we're trying to get people to be impressed with our prayers, they may be, but God won't be. And we have lost our primary target audience!

    Matthew 6:6   Luke 20:46,47

14. Use your brain when you pray; don't just repeat phrases.

When we pray to God, we are supposed to be communicating with Him from our heart. If we just repeat memorized phrases, it's easy to let our minds wander, and our prayers can become meaningless chatter, rather than deep expressions of our inner being. I don't think God appreciates that. What would your feelings be if you were conversing with a friend and he started stammering, "John, I really like the way you pitch. John, I really like the way you pitch. John I really like the way you pitch . . . "

You'd probably wonder if your friend hadn't gone off the deep end. "Lights are on, but nobody's home," as they say. Remember, God is an intelligent being, and our prayers to Him should be intelligent as well.

Matthew 6:7

15. Pray expectantly, being specific in your requests.

This is only logical, right? If you expect a specific answer, make a specific request. We do this in every other area of our lives. When you drive up to the gas pump, you don't ask for "some liquid." You specify gasoline, and you specify the grade of gas, and you specify how much you want. You don't tell the waitress, "Just bring me some food." The surgeon doesn't tell the nurse, "Hand me something pointy." In those situations, if you were the askee, you'd probably say to the asker, "Please be more specific. I don't want to start acting upon your request until I've got a better idea of what you want."

God is our benevolent, loving Father, and He loves to give us good gifts (James 1:17). Not that He'll lavish you with your every whim and urge, but He gets great satisfaction out of "making your joy complete" (John 16:24). Often He will take the initiative and bestow terrific things upon us without us even asking, but frequently He wants to know what *we* want! He *asks* us to *ask* Him! But when we ask, we need to ask in such a way that He is able to answer, and not have to say, "Could you be a little more specific? What do you mean, 'Bless Pastor Dave'? Do you want me to let him die so he can come to heaven and be with Me? That would be a great blessing. Do you want me to make him a millionaire? Do you want me to run him through some terrible trials, in order to spur him on to greater spiritual maturity? Do you want me to lead him out of his current occupation? *He* might consider *that* a blessing. What is it you want?"

Genesis 18:23-32	2 Kings 6:15-18	John 16:24
Judges 6:36-40	Matthew 7:7-11	Philippians 4:6,7

16. Wait expectantly; take time to listen.

Communication is a two-way street. You talk to your Father, and He talks to you. You can expect God to speak to you in many ways: through the Bible, through the wise and inspired words of other people, through nature, through the different circumstances you encounter — but also, from time-to-time, through direct impressions to your mind. This is quite a dramatic occurrence, and you shouldn't expect to experience these types of communiqués too frequently (remember the fact-faith-feeling train diagram?) but they do happen, and you should be prepared for them.

During your times of prayer, you don't have to be talking all of the time. Take an occasional break and just listen. You might even first ask God if there is anything in particular He'd like to say to you, and then sit silently, expectantly, head bowed and eyes closed, straining to be aware of any impression He might want to send your way. This is also a discipline — sometimes you will have to fight to keep your mind from wandering. Many times He *will* have something to say, and it would behoove you to listen. He may communicate His message through an image that appears in your mind, a memory, a song, perhaps even a "spoken" sentence or two. Sometimes His message might be so vivid that you think He has spoken audibly! Perhaps He has! We talk to Him, why is it unthinkable that He should talk to us? If you take the time to listen, you may be amazed at what He's got to say!

1 Kings 19:11,12	Psalm 62:5	Isaiah 55:1-4
Psalm 27:14	Psalm 85:8	Hebrews 3:15

■ Further Resources

As I mentioned at the end of chapter 13, Transferable Concept #9, "How To Pray," would be an excellent booklet for your disciple to read prior to your meeting, or you could send it home with him to read as a homework assignment. If nothing else, you should read it for your own education and edification.

For some good fill-in-the-blank type Bible studies on the subject of prayer, check out the following lessons:

"Ten Basic Steps Toward Christian Maturity" by Campus Crusade for Christ:

- Step 4: "The Christian and Prayer" (all six lessons)
- Step 7, Lesson 5: "Witnessing and Prayer"

"The Discipleship Series"[8] by Campus Crusade for Christ:

- Book 2, Lesson 2: "Developing Confidence in Biblical Prayer"

Design For Discipleship by The Navigators:

- Book 2, Chapter 3: "Conversing With God"
- Book 3, Chapter 3: "Faith and the Promises of God"

■ P.S. FOR THE DISCIPLEMAKER

Some of the verses listed in the foregoing sixteen statements can fit several categories, so you might want to pick out key verses and present the material backwards. In other words, instead of sharing the principle and then its corresponding verse, share the verse first, and then glean from it the two or three basic principles of prayer found in it.

Once again, this is a lot of material to try to go through in one session. If you only need to skim over these concepts with your disciple, you might make it in one session, but I doubt it would be possible to adequately cover the ground if you're working with a new Christian. Take as many sessions as necessary to cover the subject, and don't be concerned if it takes longer than you had first anticipated. The objective is not to "get him through the material," but to get the material into him. Time is not of the essence, here—absorption is!

If your disciple already has had some input about prayer and you are planning to skim over these concepts just to be sure he understands them, you might want to write out each of the sixteen statements, along with a verse or two for each, and just ask him, "What do you think of this? Do you agree with it?"

Or, to put a little spice in it, reword some of the statements, making them false, and use it as an "Agree/Disagree" test. For instance, you could make statement #6 read: "The physical posture we assume as we pray plays a crucial role in whether or not God will hear our prayers." Then ask your disciple, "Do you agree or disagree with that? Why or why not? Let's look up some verses that might shed some light on that question." Or statement #8 could be changed to read: "As long as we have enough faith that God will answer our prayers, disobeying Him will have no effect on the outcome of our requests. Agree or disagree? Why?"

■ ENDING THE SESSION

Quiet Time. Since you've spent a lot of time during this training objective talking with your disciple about how important communication is to his relationship with God, now would be a great time to introduce him to the notion of a daily quiet time, if he doesn't already know about it.

There are two very important aspects to a quiet time: (1) *education* and (2) *communication.* They each have several facets. You could look at them as the development of the head and of the heart; as an act of self discipline and an act of love; as growth-focusing and God-focusing; as Bible study and prayer. Both are needed. If a person's daily devotions are all just education, with no communication, he ends up theologically sound but without heart or fire, no real relationship. If it's all communication and no education, the result is a compassionate, on-fire "baby," no substance or depth to his walk with

Christ. As with so many things in the Christian life, it's *balance* we're after. Share this concept with your disciple.

Here are a few other vital aspects to discuss with your disciple:

What Content? In keeping with the education/communication idea, suggest he spend about half of his time reading the Bible and the other half praying.

Bible reading. Go back to chapter 15 (Training Objective #7) on the Word and read over the section titled "Next, Tell Him Where to Start Reading" in the Suggestions for Growth. You could decide on a book of the Bible for him to begin reading, or you could rely on the weekly assignments you keep giving him, or you could combine the two. If he's going to start reading a book, recommend that he read only a chapter at a time so he can absorb it properly.

Prayer. Help him to start a prayer list. His list could contain not only supplications, but also things to thank God about, and things to worship and praise God about. In fact, you could encourage him to begin a prayer diary, where he actually writes out the things that come to his mind that he wants to praise and thank God for. Teach him how to "pray through" a psalm. On the supplications part of it, help him brainstorm about things he would like to see God do in his life, in the lives of his friends and family, and in the world.

How Long? Whenever you're trying to establish a new habit—whether it be jogging, painting, piano lessons, brain surgery—it's best to start out easy. A good first goal for most Christians is ten minutes. Most people can go along with the notion of setting aside 1/144th of their day to communicate with their Lord and Master. For some, that might not be nearly enough time. Great. Make it twenty minutes. But it's much better to start out short and have to lengthen the time than to do it the other way around. Ten minutes will give them five minutes to read the Word and five minutes to pray. They'll be amazed at how fast the time goes, and will be motivated to set aside more and more time.

How Often? From the very outset, you need to instill in your disciple that his quiet time is vital to his growth. We do vital things every day. We breathe every day, we eat every day, we sleep every day, we brush our teeth every day, we read the comics every day (wait a minute . . .) Spending time with God regularly is just as important to our spiritual health and development, and consequently to our whole lives. Therefore, help your disciple to understand that if he is serious about his new life in Christ, his quiet time should become a daily habit.

He needs to know there will be days when he just won't feel like spending time with God. That's OK; it happens to us all. But urge him to do it anyway. What would happen to his teeth if he decided not to brush them every time he didn't feel like it, or whenever it wasn't convenient?

Tell him that, when it comes down to it, our private times alone with the Lord will do us the most good when we are consistent with them. Long quiet times are great; spine-tingling, earth-moving quiet times are also quite memorable; but if we have to choose between consistency, quantity or quality as we shoot for effective quiet times, choose consistency every time. A sumptuous, well balanced, twelve-course dinner once a week, with no other nourishment, will not a healthy body make. However, three humble but adequate meals a day will see you through a lifetime.

Behaviorists tell us that if a person desires to introduce a new habit into his life, if he will perform that habit without fail every day for twenty-one days, in most cases the new behavior will be established. Challenge your disciple with this fact. Ask him if he would be willing to commit himself to this discipline just for twenty-one days, and then he can reconsider it at the end of the test period. Nine times out of ten, it will be the beginning of a lifetime of successful quiet times.

"Even Sunday? But I'll be going to church anyway . . . " If your disciple asks that question, he still hasn't grasped the function of a quiet time. It's supposed to be a time of intimate, one-to-one communion between him and his Father. He can get lots of other very important things in church, but not that close, private, distraction-free communion. We eat on Sunday;

we sleep on Sunday; where's the precedent for not spending personal time with the Vine on Sunday?

Though you have challenged him to have a quiet time every day, don't be surprised if it takes a few weeks for him to actually be seven for seven. When you get together next week, if he's only had two or three, don't be negative in the least! Let him know that it's a great start! It took most of us a while, too.

All this coming week, be sure you are diligent in praying for your disciple's success in quiet times. Your prayers could be your most strategic contribution to this whole matter.

When? Recommend to your disciple that he have his quiet time first thing in the morning if at all possible. At that time of the day the mind is the most receptive to new input. Things are usually quieter. He's not carrying around a day's load of hassles like he might at the end of the day. His Q.T. won't have a chance to get squeezed out of the schedule. He can prepare himself spiritually for any significant events coming up that day. It's a way of "checking in with our Commander-in-Chief" for our daily marching orders. Having it first, giving the Lord the best part of his day, will set the tone for the rest of his day. A good time to tune up an instrument is before the concert.

Some people say, "But I'm not a morning person. I think much clearer at night." Fine. Do your lengthy Bible studies and significant praying in the evening. But it's still important to start the day spending a little time with your Father. Can you find five minutes to simply read a psalm or a short selection from a devotional book, and have a short conversation with your Master? Let the Lord know that, sleepy or not, you want Him to hold top priority in your day. If a person would start every day with even that little dab, he would be amazed at the results that occur over a long period of time.

The whole secret to a successful morning quiet time is *going to bed on time* the night before. Satan will try to keep us up watching TV, reading magazines, doing cross-word puzzles — any number of things. But if we lay down an unalterable time each evening when the lights must go out, our bodies will fall into a wake/sleep rhythm that will make us fall asleep within five minutes of hitting the pillow, and wake us up at the same time each morning, refreshed and ready for the day. Varying the time you go to bed each night keeps your body confused, makes for a lot less efficient sleep, and makes it tough to get a blanket victory the next morning. You'll become sack-religious. Quiet times will be too quiet.

Where? Someplace quiet and secluded, if at all possible. Freedom from distraction is important. Satan will be working already to make it hard to concentrate, without additional factors coming to play. Someone might say, "Impossible! You have no idea the pandemonium around my house in the morning!" C'mon, now. Think of some creative alternatives! How about out in the car? The back yard? The attic? The bathroom? The basement? The garage? How about getting up before the pandemonium begins? How about telling the pandemonium to leave you alone for ten minutes? How about teaching the pandemonium to have their own quiet times?

■ ASSIGNMENT FOR NEXT TIME

Obviously, assign him to have seven quiet times before you see him next week. Tell him you'll call him up a few times during the week to see how he's doing. Help him "trouble-shoot" if he needs it.

Be sure that, before the end of today's session, you've spent some time helping him brainstorm about specific things he can pray about. Consider a two-person conspiracy to pray about a certain request.

Also, anticipate what training objective you are going to go over next week and give him an appropriate assignment. For ideas on that, go back to chapter 13 ("Basic Growth Principles," Training Objective #5) and look under the Assignment for Next Time section, or look ahead to next week's training objective and consider some selections under Further Resources.

■ EVALUATION

Ask yourself these questions:

1. Does my disciple really understand how important prayer is to his growth?

2. Does he see prayer as a ritual? Is he delivering a speech

for the benefit of others listening in, or is he really communicating with God?

3. Does he have a firm grasp on the fundamentals of prayer?

4. Is he praying on his own?

5. Do his prayers reflect a good balance between Adoration, Confession, Thanksgiving and Supplication?

6. Is he praying for significant matters, or are his prayers shallow and unsubstantial?

7. Is he moving toward having a daily quiet time?

If you can answer each of those questions in the affirmative, then your disciple has met this training objective. If you need more input from him to determine your answers, here are some questions you can ask him:

1. Why do you pray?

2. Why do you think God invented prayer?

3. Do you think you pray differently when in a group than you do when you're alone with God? (If so . . .) Why do you think that is?

4. Have you been having personal times of prayer lately?

5. What are some of the things you're praying about?

6. What are some things I can pray for, for you?

7. Are you hesitant to pray about certain things? (If so . . .) Would you mind sharing them with me? Why do you hesitate?

8. When God doesn't answer one of your prayers, what do you think happened?

9. What role do you believe faith may play in prayer? Obedience? Confession?

10. Is prayer fun for you, or is it more like work? (If work . . .) Does that keep you from praying as much as you'd like?

17 TRAINING OBJECTIVE #9

WITNESSING

■ OBJECTIVE

The disciple has a basic understanding of the importance of witnessing, knows the primary elements of the gospel, and can tell another person how to become a Christian.

■ BIBLICAL BASIS FOR THIS OBJECTIVE

We've already seen (chapter 3) that when Jesus gave His disciples the Great Commission (Matthew 28:19,20), one of the three primary activities He told us to practice to fulfill that commission was witnessing. This is even more clear in the Mark version: "Go into all the world and preach the gospel to all creation" (Mark 16:15). And in Acts 1:8: "But you shall receive power when the Holy Spirit has come upon you; and you shall be My witnesses both in Jerusalem, and in all Judea and Samaria, and even to the remotest part of the earth."

Throughout the Bible it's obvious that God intended witnessing to be a normal part of our lives as "called-out ones." Here are a few verses that underscore that fact. Look them up and jot down summaries in your disciplemaker's notebook.

Psalm 107:2	Mark 5:18-20	Romans 1:16
Proverbs 11:30	Luke 24:46-48	Romans 10:13-15
Proverbs 24:11,12	John 4:4-26	1 Corinthians 9:19-22
Ezekiel 3:18,19	John 20:21	2 Corinthians 5:11
Matthew 4:19	Acts 4:12	2 Corinthians 5:18-20
Matthew 5:13-16	Acts 4:20	2 Corinthians 6:1,2
Matthew 9:37,38	Acts 17:1-3	Ephesians 3:8
Matthew 24:14	Acts 18:28	

■ APPLICABLE DEFINITIONS

Witnessing: "Sharing the gospel of Jesus Christ in the power of the Holy Spirit and leaving the results to God."[1]

Gospel: All men are guilty of sin before God. The penalty for sin is death—eternal separation from God. But because of His great love for us, God sent His Son, Jesus Christ, to take the penalty of our sin on Himself when He died on the cross. Three days later He was resurrected from the dead and is alive today and forever. If a person will repent of his sinful way of life, and have faith that Jesus Christ is the Son of God and able to save him from eternal death, he will be saved.

Scriptural "nutshells" of the gospel:

John 3:16	Acts 20:21	1 Corinthians 15:3,4
Luke 24:46-48	Romans 6:23	
Acts 16:30,31	1 Corinthians 2:1,2	

■ PEP TALK FOR THE DISCIPLEMAKER

Oh, how we love to fellowship! Also Bible study is quite interesting, and praying is OK, though it has its ups and downs. But witnessing . . . that's a real toughie. For many of us, some of the most exhilarating moments we've had as Christians were while witnessing, especially when God grants us the privilege of being there when someone receives Christ. On the other hand, a lot of us are pretty squeamish about putting our egos out there on the chopping block alongside the Four Spiritual Laws booklet, risking the axe of rejection. When you sweep away all the rationalizations and excuses—and we can manufacture them by the gross—the primary reason Christians don't share their faith is that they are afraid people will react negatively. And that fear is not groundless. Some people *will* reject the gospel—if it happened to Jesus and Paul, it's bound to happen to us.

Two things must be said about that. First: *Nobody said Christians were supposed to win popularity contests.* In fact, Paul said in 2 Timothy 3:12, "And indeed, all who desire to live godly in Christ Jesus *will* be persecuted" [my emphasis]. We are guaranteed it won't always be moonlight and roses, especially when we share Christ.

So how do we respond? That's the second point: *We need to decide whom we want to please.* When we share our faith, we may not please men, but we definitely please God. When we are silent about our faith, we may avoid the taunts of men, but we do not please God. Which would you prefer? Paul put it like this: "For am I now seeking the favor of men, or of God? Or am I striving to please men? If I were still trying to please men, I would not be a bond-servant of Christ" (Galatians 1:10). John described the spineless rulers of Jerusalem who would not openly confess Christ because of the Pharisees this way: "They loved the approval of men rather than the approval of God" (John 12:43). The approval of man fades rapidly – the approval of God, never.

Disciplemaker, it wasn't really pleasant for me, but I just emptied both barrels at you on this matter – and for good reason. If you are like the vast majority of Christians in the U.S. today, you hardly ever share your faith. You have led between zero and two people to the Lord. And your opinion regarding any future witnessing is that you'd prefer being flogged with a bullwhip – you figure it may hurt more, but it's over quicker.

If this is a description of you, you need to be shaken out of your sleep. Dr. Walter Martin of Christian Research Institute has said, "As far as Satan is concerned, the next best thing to a damned soul is a silent Christian." The devil is working overtime to keep Christians quiet about the Good News. He blew it at Golgotha, but there is some semblance of victory he can glom onto if he can just keep the whole thing under his hat. How I hope you are not cooperating with him. If you are one of the silent ones, I implore you to wake up, and speak up – don't let your malady infect yet another generation of disciples.

If Christians would open their mouths a little more, they would discover that many people are eager to experience a close relationship with God if only they knew how. Bill Bright has written, "One of the greatest misconceptions of the centuries, in my opinion, is the idea so prevalent among Christians that men do not want God. Wherever I go – in this country or in other countries – I find ample proof that just the opposite is true. The Holy Spirit has created a hunger for God in the hearts of multitudes."[2]

We want our disciples to be fruitful witnesses for two reasons: (1) so they can experience the joy of the Lord as they obediently and whole-heartedly share their faith; and (2) so they will be active soldiers in the army of Christ, tearing down the strongholds of Satan and working with Christ to set the captives free, thus advancing the kingdom of God.

You can help your disciple get started on the right foot toward that goal. Most brand new Christians are still trying to figure out what the Christian life is. Before he has a chance to sample the abnormal standard most of Christendom has adopted in witnessing, you can serve him the normal standard that is presented in the Bible!

What will motivate him in the proper direction? Two things: First, above all else, if his relationship with Jesus is one of vital intimacy, love and obedience, his witnessing will flow naturally from a Spirit-controlled lifestyle. That's what we're looking for — over*flow,* not over*work.* The effectiveness of his "horizontal" relationships depend upon the vitality of his "vertical" relationship.

Second, when he sees you openly identify with Christ and share your faith, and then share with him the thrills and the agonies associated with witnessing, this will motivate him as well. He really does want to be like you; the things you do he is likely to do, and the things you don't do he's likely to skip.

■ BROACHING THE SUBJECT

A good way to get into the subject of witnessing is to ask your disciple two simple questions. One, "What is the greatest, most significant thing that has ever happened to you?"

If he's been listening for the past several weeks, and has truly understood the consequences of his salvation, he'll answer something like, "Receiving Jesus Christ as my Savior."

At that point you ask question number two: "What, then, is the greatest, most significant thing that a Christian can do for another person?"

Logically, his answer would be, "To help him come to know Christ too."

Then you can say, "That's what we're going to talk about today—helping others enter into a personal relationship with Christ. What are your thoughts concerning the subject of witnessing for Christ?" I always like to ask that question first just to see what his sentiments and concepts are before we dive in. I want to find out if he's looking at it with tremendous fear and trepidation, scared that I'm going to take him out to sell lapel flowers and beat people over the head with a ten-pound Bible, or if he's open and interested and as yet unspoiled by most Christians' aversion to witnessing. It will make a difference in the presentation.

In the first case, you'll need to do some blasting before you can build—getting rid of wrong notions of what it means to witness for Christ. It's important that you allay your disciple's fears as quickly as possible. Let him know that you have no intention of asking him to do something he isn't ready to do.

In the second case we can dispense with the demolition and proceed right to the superstructure.

■ SUGGESTIONS FOR GROWTH

For helping a new Christian gain the proper concepts early about this matter of witnessing, I don't know of a better way than by using Bill Bright's award-winning book, *Witnessing Without Fear*. Easy to read and highly anecdotal, this book takes a Christian by the hand and guides him step by step through a process that will give him both the desire and the ability to share the gospel. Each chapter includes a summary and questions for discussion and reflection. You can use these to help your disciple personalize the training presented in each chapter.

It is important for you to get the following major points regarding witnessing across to your disciple. Some of them are contained in *Witnessing Without Fear* and some are supplementary. Read through them and consider how you can best use them. I'll be supplying a few thoughts on how I'd share each point with a generic Christian along with a few Scripture references you could go over together.

One thing to remember: It is not yet time to communicate

a lot of theology about witnessing. You might be able to write an entire book on the subject, but it would be of little use to your disciple at his current stage of development. You can get into greater detail later, but for now it's basic, first-grade-education time.

I. What Is Witnessing?

Witnessing, in its broadest sense, is simply telling what you know. As Peter and John said to the Sanhedrin (who were trying to make them stop witnessing), "We cannot stop speaking what we have seen and heard" (Acts 4:20). What have you seen and heard about Christ? As you relate those things to others, you are witnessing.

Think of it in terms of being a witness in a court of law. If you're a witness, you don't have to try to be the prosecuting attorney, the defense attorney, the judge, the jury, or the bailiff. All you have to do is tell what you have "seen and heard." As you step up to the witness stand, you would be instructed to "tell the truth, the whole truth, and nothing but the truth." It would be dishonest, as a witness for Christ, to falsely represent yourself by exaggerating or minimizing what has taken place in your life. To hold back the truth wouldn't do either. You must be prepared to let your life be an open book to be read by anyone who wants to. It's not your job to convince anyone of anything. All you do is tell what you know.

II. Why Should I Witness?

A. *Because it's the only way people will come to know Christ.* Jesus said in John 14:6, "I am the way, and the truth, and the life; no one comes to the Father, but through Me." He also said in John 8:24, "Unless you believe that I am He, you shall die in your sins." Acts 4:12 says that "there is no other name under heaven that has been given among men, by which we must be saved."

I think you get the idea that this is a very important message. What method did God use to get the message out? Write it across the skies? Use angels equipped with portable P.A. systems to broadcast it around the world? Look at 1 Corinthians 1:21: "For since in the wisdom of God the world through wisdom did not come to know God, God was well pleased through the foolishness of the message preached to save those who believe." For reasons known only to Him, God has limited Himself to getting this vital message out through mere human instrumentality — one person passing it on to another. Romans 10:13,14 says: "For whoever will call upon the name of the Lord will be saved. How then shall they call upon Him in whom they have not believed? And how shall they believe in Him whom they have not heard? And how shall they hear without a preacher?"

B. *Because we want to see the benefits of a life with Christ passed on to others.* God is deeply in love with every individual on the face of the earth and He desperately desires to have a relationship with each one. He is eager to pass on to others the same benefits He gave us. Our desire should be the same. Unless someone tells them, non-Christians will never know how to experience the following (and much, much more!):

John 4:14	John 8:14	John 11:25,26
John 6:35	John 8:32,36	John 14:2,3
John 6:40	John 10:9,10	John 14:12-14
	John 10:27,28	

(For a good way to go through the above verses quickly, giving your disciple a panoramic view of the tremendous blessings tied to salvation, chain-reference them in your Bible. In the margin next to John 4:14, write "John 6:35," to show you where to go next. Flip forward to John 6:35, and beside it write "John 6:40," etc.)

C. *Because by sharing our faith we grow and mature.* Read John 4:1-34, the story of Jesus witnessing to the Samaritan woman at the well. Notice verse 32 especially. What do you think this "food to eat that you do not know about" is? Jesus gives us the answer in verse 34: "My food is to do the will of Him who sent Me, and to accomplish His work." There was something about witnessing to this woman that nourished and strengthened Jesus. When we share our faith, we are nourished and strengthened in the same way.

D. *Because it's the natural result of being honest.* When you came to know Jesus Christ, you became an entirely new creature. Yet so many Christians go back to the closet of their old life, rummage around, find the disguises they used to wear, and put them on again. After a while, they are so much like non-Christians that it's difficult to tell them apart. They have put on their worldly clothes to hide their true natures as glorified, sanctified sons and daughters of the Living God.

When a Christian walks with God and lives honestly, when his day-to-day lifestyle accurately reflects the changes that occurred on the inside, his whole life will be a witness to the world. Our Christlikeness will seem peculiar to the world, and it would be only natural to explain the difference to them.

Proverbs 4:18	Romans 13:11-14	1 Timothy 5:24,25
Isaiah 60:1-3	Ephesians 5:8	1 Peter 2:9
Matthew 5:16	Philippians 2:15	

E. Because God has commanded us to. A big part of the Christian life involves letting Jesus Christ be our Lord — giving Him the same place in our lives that He already holds in the universe. If someone is your "lord," that means he gets to call the shots. As Christians, our attitude should be that of Saul just after he had met the risen Christ on the way to Damascus: "What shall I do, Lord?" (Acts 22:10). Jesus has told us in the Scripture what He wants us to do. If we love Him, we will keep His commandments (John 14:15).

Matthew 28:19,20	John 15:16
Mark 16:15	Acts 1:8

III. Who Do I Witness To?

The thing that weighs heaviest on the great heart of God is the need for the humans He created to cease their rebellion and return to Him (2 Peter 3:9). From before the day they were born God has been working to draw them back to Himself (Jeremiah 31:3). He cannot compromise their free will, but He can patiently arrange circumstances around them that eventually (hopefully) will convince them of their need for the Savior.

The primary tools He uses to win people back to Himself are

people that have been won previously. Therefore, He will use anyone who is handy. If you are alone with a non-Christian for more than a few minutes, you can assume that God may want to use you to move that person a little closer to making a decision for Christ, through your words or your actions, or both. That's called a "divine appointment." It may be in God's strategy that you give a complete gospel presentation, or He may not want you to share verbally at all right then. The important thing is to be open to whatever the Spirit leads you to do.

God will set up divine appointments for you with members of your family, friends, coworkers, barber or hairdresser, the washing machine repairman, even complete strangers. If you are willing and obedient, God will use you. You don't have to lob a gospel grenade at everything that moves, nor should you make yourself obnoxious to your friends. The key is simply asking God, day by day, to fill you with His Spirit and make you aware of the divine appointments He has for you. When His Spirit nudges you, respond in loving obedience, and leave the results to Him.

IV. How Do I Witness?

Some people say we should witness by our *lives*. Jesus said in Matthew 5:16, "Let your light shine before men in such a way that they may see your good works, and glorify your Father who is in heaven." As Joe Aldrich, president of Multnomah School of the Bible says, "We must be Good News before we can share Good News."

Others say that witnessing is to be done by our *words*. After all, the non-Christian needs to make a decision. How can he know what the decision is unless someone tells him specifically?

The fact is, witnessing involves both of these components. If we try to make do with only one of them, our witness will be hollow. The words form the content of the message, but our lives serve to validate the message in the mind of the unbeliever.

A. Your life. When given a choice, most people opt for what

they see over what they hear. Picture yourself walking down a
dark alley late one night. You see, barely visible under a fire
escape, a big, burly, unkempt character standing there holding
a knife in one hand and a half-empty whiskey bottle in the
other. He stares at you with a lean, hungry look. What do you
think? Now, would you change your mind if he were to say,
"Pardon me, buddy. Would you mind coming over here a sec' –
I can't seem to find my contact lens"? What he says seems
pleasant enough, but what you're looking at looks decidedly
*un*pleasant, and if you are smart, you'll either call for Superman on your secret de-coder ring or do a back flip with a
half-twist and start sprinting. You would consider what you see
as valid, rather than what you hear.[3]

Non-Christians are no different from you. If Christians act
one way and talk another, people always will assume that the
actions portray the truth about that person. Talk is cheap.

For this reason, our actions form a large part of our Christian witness. When we forget this fact, we hurt the advance of
the kingdom of God. Paul blasted the Corinthian believers for
their lackadaisical attitude toward sinning because of the effect it was having on the unbelievers around them: "Become
sober-minded as you ought, and stop sinning; for some have no
knowledge of God. I speak this to your shame" (1 Corinthians
15:34).

You are the only Bible that some people will ever read. They
will look at you and say to themselves "So that's Christianity."
One way or the other, you *will* be a witness – good or bad. Your
actions will cause people either to be favorably impressed and
drawn closer to Christ, or to be repulsed.

Most non-Christians will never come close to the majority
of the church's methods of evangelism. They'll never go to a
Billy Graham crusade; they'll never go to any church that
preaches the gospel; they'll never look at the tracts they find
in phone booths; they'll never listen to a Christian radio or TV
program. Some will, but most won't. But they'll talk with you.
They'll rub shoulders with you at work. They'll watch you over
the back fence to see how you treat your family. They'll watch
how you live in the dormitory. Your job is to let them see as

much of Christ in you as possible.

B. Your words. But don't stop there. Unfortunately, most Christians do. They focus on the first part of Matthew 5:16 and say, "Yep, I'm gonna let my little light shine, shine, shine," and take it no further. They forget about the purpose of the shining, that men may "glorify your Father who is in heaven." What ultimate good is accomplished by them watching you shine, if that's as far as it goes? Can that save them? Our job isn't done until we can add some "content" to our witness. Unless they hear the gospel, all the shining in the world will be of no benefit to them.

Paul instructed his disciple Timothy: "Preach the word; be ready in season and out of season; reprove, rebuke, exhort, with great patience and instruction" (2 Timothy 4:2). That's a lot of content. The same Jesus who told us to let our light shine also told us, "Go into all the world and preach the gospel" (Mark 16:15). Peter made clear what our marching orders are in Acts 10:42: "And He ordered us to preach to the people, and solemnly to testify that this is the one who has been appointed by God as judge of the living and the dead."

V. What Do I Say?

There is so much to say about Jesus that we could talk for hours on end. But usually, in a witnessing situation, the person we are talking to doesn't have that kind of time. So the best thing to do is to have the basics of the gospel firmly in mind, and then expand on it as the opportunity provides. In addition, it's helpful to share your own personal story, your "testimony," about how you came to know Jesus Christ.

A. The basics of the gospel. In its most basic essence, the gospel can be boiled down to four very simple points.[4] They are:

1. God loves every individual and created each one to have eternal fellowship with Him.

Jeremiah 29:11	John 3:16	John 10:10
Jeremiah 31:3	John 4:13,14	

2. Every individual has sinned, severing this fellowship with God, ultimately resulting in eternal separation.

| Psalm 14:2,3 | Romans 3:10-12 | Romans 6:23 |
| Isaiah 53:6 | Romans 3:23 | Hebrews 9:27 |

3. God sent His Son, Jesus Christ, to take the penalty of our sin on Himself, making reunion with God possible.

| John 3:17 | Ephesians 1:6,7 | 1 Peter 3:18 |
| Romans 5:8 | Titus 2:14 | 1 John 4:9,10 |

4. The sacrifice of Jesus is applied to us individually as we, in an act of our will, receive Christ through faith.

John 1:12	Acts 16:31	Ephesians 2:8,9
John 3:1-8	Romans 10:9,10	1 John 5:11-13
John 5:24	Galatians 2:16	Revelation 3:20

Note to the disciplemaker: I realize this could be a sticky wicket for some people. "How does one 'receive Christ'?" "Have faith in exactly what?" "Where does grace come in?" "Where does repentance come in?" "Where does 'born again' come in?" "Where does public confession come in?" You can go into the details about these things later, but the one thing your disciple must understand now is that salvation comes by grace, *through faith* (Ephesians 2:8,9). If a person embraces a personal faith that Jesus Christ is the Son of God, was sacrificed on the cross in our place, was raised from the dead, and is able to bring us back to God, he's on safe ground. The evidence (or result) of this faith is the decision to repent from sin (Acts 3:19; Romans 2:4) and begin to pursue a lifestyle of good works (Ephesians 2:10; 1 John 2:4-6). If a person "asks Christ to come into his life," or "receives Christ," and a corresponding change in his behavior is seen, it's a strong indication that he has bought into "saving faith."

There are two roads you can take with the four basic points of the gospel listed above: (1) Use them as a lead-in to teaching your disciple a specific method of sharing his faith ("Now, let me show you how we can use these four points in an interesting and easy method of sharing the gospel . . . "); or (2) leave them out altogether and just go right into sharing your favorite method. Help your disciple understand that different people will need to be spoken to in different ways about different things when it comes down to an actual gospel presentation, but if one knows a basic presentation, he can adapt and personalize it as needed.

If you don't know a specific method of presenting the gospel yourself, I'd suggest getting hold of *Witnessing Without Fear* by Bill Bright, or asking your pastor or someone else who has been trained to show you.

B. Your testimony. It may be easy for a non-Christian to argue with our theology or opinions, but he can't argue with our personal experience. It's a lot like the blind man Jesus healed in John 9. The Pharisees questioned his conversion theologically up one side and down the other, but all their arguments fell flat when the man finally said, "Whether He is a sinner, I do not know; one thing I do know, that, whereas I was blind, now I see."

Note to the disciplemaker: The best way to help someone work out his testimony involves three steps. First, share your testimony with him. As he listens to yours, he'll get a good idea what one is supposed to sound like. Second, talk him through his own testimony. Use an interview format, asking him the three divisional questions:

1. What was your life like before you met Christ?

2. What were the circumstances surrounding your conversion?

3. What changes have you seen in your life since you met Christ?

Guide him to expand on his answers as necessary, so that you and he can perceive the flow of his conversion experience. As he shares his answers, you might want to jot down a few notes to remember what he says, or better yet, record your conversation on tape.

Third, have him go home and write it out. The discipline of thought required for him to actually put it on paper will give him a chance to really think through what went on the day he was saved, and how best to relate it to another person. Have him write out the above three divisional questions, one on each of three sheets of paper, and then write his answer to each one below it. Tell him that it should take him from three to five minutes to read his testimony.

Here are a few things he should *avoid* as he writes:

1. Exaggeration.

2. Glittering generalities ("My life is wonderful now, totally full of joy and peace, and all my problems are gone").

3. Talking negatively about any particular church or denomination.

4. Religious lingo ("I was immediately born again and transformed into a new creation by exercising faith in the substitutionary atonement of Christ").

5. Too much detail.

6. Irrelevant material.

Here are a few things he should *include:*

1. The three divisions: Before, How, After.

2. Exactly how he received Christ, so that when he finishes sharing, the listener will have a good idea how he, too, can receive Christ.

3. A Bible verse or two.

After your disciple has written out his testimony, critique it and determine if it needs some beefing up, changing or toning down. When all the rewrites are done, have him become very familiar with it, either by writing an outline of it and sharing it orally with you or a small group, or by actually memorizing it.

If you'd like to study a good, biblical example of someone sharing his testimony, turn to Paul's in Acts 22:3-21 or 26:4-23.

VI. What If a Person Rejects What I Say?

From time to time, that will happen, but there are two facts you need to get firmly implanted in your frontal lobe.

First, realize they are not rejecting you as a person. In their minds they are merely disagreeing with an opinion you hold. They do that all the time. So do you. The only one they are really rejecting is Jesus Christ, for He said in Luke 10:16: "The one who listens to you listens to Me, and the one who rejects you rejects Me; and he who rejects Me rejects the one who sent Me." So try not to take it personally.

Second, realize that evangelism is a process, not an event, or more accurately, a process that leads to an event. The last step of the process is the event of conversion, but it is a rare thing for a person to receive Christ the first time he hears the gospel. A non-Christian needs to go through a process of supernatural education that will gradually dispel his doubts and dissipate the smoke screens Satan has been setting up for years. The non-Christian may hear the Good News from five or ten people, moving a little closer to faith in Christ each time, until finally he is ready to "take the plunge." Paul said in 1 Corinthians 3:5-10 that one man may "plant the seed," others may "water" it, but in the end, God causes the growth. As you share your faith with others, I'm sure you will have the tremendous privilege of reaping from time to time, but even when there doesn't seem to be any positive response at all, you can be sure that your witness has helped in some way to move that person closer to the Lord. God's Word "shall not return to Me empty, without accomplishing what I desire" (Isaiah 55:10,11).

VII. Some Important Points to Remember While Witnessing

Here are a few attitudes and actions your disciple should try to employ while sharing the gospel.

1. Remember, it's your job to witness. It's God's job to convert people.

   John 6:44   John 16:7-11

2. Depend on the Holy Spirit to work supernaturally. Before you talk to men about God, talk to God about men.

   2 Corinthians 10:4,5   1 Thessalonians 1:5

3. Don't look at people as "projects." Don't look at witnessing as "zapping them with the gospel" or "going after scalps." These are precious individuals whom Jesus Christ loves and died for, and sharing the gospel

is a high and holy calling. Those you witness to can detect your attitude toward them. As Joe Aldrich says, "People don't care how much we know until they know how much we care."

4. As you witness, be pleasant, friendly and positive.

   Proverbs 12:18   Colossians 4:5,6   Ephesians 4:29

5. Avoid getting into arguments.

   2 Timothy 2:16,23-26

6. Avoid "rabbit trails." Stay on the subject of the gospel. If the person gets off track with questions, even legitimate ones, for example, "What about the heathen in Africa?" say, "That's a good question, and worth an answer, but I'm not sure I can give you one right now. Let me do some studying on that and I'll get back to you." Or, "Why don't we carry on through this presentation for now; if it's not answered by the time we're done, ask it again."

7. Be sensitive. Don't try to cram the gospel down a person's throat. As Paul said in Colossians 4:3, "Praying . . . that God may open up to us a door for the Word, so that we may speak forth the mystery of Christ," God needs to open the door — we don't need to bash it open ourselves.

8. Use Scripture. God's Word has a supernatural effect on the listener. No need to defend a lion — just unleash it!

   Isaiah 55:10-12   Hebrews 4:12

9. If he asks a question that stumps you, be honest and say, "I don't know the answer to that, but I'll find out for you." Then find out. Dawson Trotman, founder of the Navigators, made it a personal policy never to be stumped on the same question twice.

10. Don't preach. Have a conversation; ask questions; let the person talk; listen to what he says and respond appropriately.

11. Be yourself. Don't put on any phoney airs of bubbliness,

religiousness, or superiority. Remember, you're just one beggar telling another beggar where to find the soup kitchen.

12. If at all possible, bring the witnessing situation to a point of decision by saying something like, "Would you like to ask Christ to come into your life right now?"

VIII. Long-Term, Behind-the-Scenes Preparation

Following are a few attitudes and actions a Christian should give attention to over the long-haul in order to be a fruitful witness.

1. Pray daily for "divine appointments."

    Ephesians 6:19   Colossians 4:3   2 Thessalonians 3:1

2. Maintain a lifestyle that is above reproach.

    1 Timothy 1:7   1 Peter 2:12   1 Peter 2:15

3. Don't isolate yourself from non-Christians.

    Matthew 5:16   1 Corinthians 5:9,10

4. Make long-term, ongoing, advance preparation by studying Scripture so you will be increasingly effective in sharing your faith.

    2 Timothy 2:15   1 Peter 3:15

■ FURTHER RESOURCES

For some good, fill-in-the-blank type studies on witnessing, consider using one or more of the following selections:

"Ten Basic Steps Toward Christian Maturity" Bible Study Series by Campus Crusade for Christ:

- Step 7: "The Christian and Witnessing" (all lessons)

"The Discipleship Series"[5] by Campus Crusade for Christ:

- Book 1, Lesson 5: "How to Witness in the Spirit"
- Book 2, Lesson 3: "Understanding the Ministry of Reconciliation"
    Lesson 4: "Communicating the Message of Reconciliation"
- Book 3, Lesson 4: "Understanding Initiative Evangelism"

Design for Discipleship Bible Study Series by The Navigators:

- Book 2, Chapter 5: "Witnessing For Christ"
- Book 6, Chapter 3: "Helping Others Find Christ"
  Chapter 4: "Follow-up"

■ ENDING THE SESSION

Role playing. After you've spent two or three weeks on this subject, do a little role playing. You be the non-Christian and let your disciple practice going through the actual gospel presentation with you. Ask appropriate questions and throw up a few smoke-screens, but don't be too hard on him. Let him use the time to build up his familiarity with the material — and his confidence.

Transition statements. Another helpful bit of information you can pass on to your disciple would include some of the "transitional statements" which can be used to steer a conversation toward the gospel. Here are a few ideas:

1. Take a non-Christian friend to a Christian function such as a Christian concert, a church service, or to hear a special speaker. When it's over, weave these four questions into your conversation:

   a. What did you think of [the function, the message]?

   b. Did what they have to say make sense to you?

   c. Have you ever made the discovery of knowing Christ personally?

   d. Would you like to?

If your friend reacts negatively, remember Proverbs 15:1: "A soft answer turns away wrath." You might respond in a gentle manner with something like this, "It seems like you've had an unfortunate experience with Christianity at some time. I'd be interested to know why you feel this way."[6]

2. Start by asking one of the following questions from the *Evangelism Explosion* presentation by Dr. James Kennedy[7]:

a. Have you come to the place in your spiritual life where you know that you have eternal life; that is, do you know for certain that if you died today you would go to heaven?

b. If you were to die today and stand before God, and He were to say to you, "Why should I let you into My heaven?" what would you say?

After the person gives an answer (and if he's a non-Christian, there may be evidence of misinformation in his answer), say something like, "That's interesting. Many people feel the same way about the qualifications for heaven. Can I share with you what I've learned from the Bible about eternal life?"

3. If you meet someone you think is a non-Christian, but he's wearing some kind of religious symbol, try this transition: "I noticed your cross [or whatever]. Does that mean you're a Christian?" If he answers no, or isn't sure, you might respond with something like, "It's interesting to me that such an obvious Christian symbol could come to lose its Christian significance. Do you know what that originally symbolized?" Then, a little later in the conversation, "Has anyone ever taken the time to explain to you what real Christianity is?"

4. Whenever you have the opportunity to go out of your way to do something especially kind or helpful for someone, it's a great opportunity to "let your light shine." As that person thanks you, you could say something like, "A few years ago I probably wouldn't have done that. But something happened to me a while back that changed my life. It gave me a desire to want to help people whenever I could. Maybe you could identify with me . . . " Then share your testimony. When you're done with your testimony, ask, "Have you ever done anything like that, asking Christ into your life?"

5. "If someone were to ask you what a real Christian was, what would you say? Can I share a few verses from the Bible that really cleared that up for me?"

6. "Tell me, Joe. Do you know Christ personally, or would

you say you're still 'on the way'?"

7. If you have a gospel tract with you: "Has anyone ever taken the time to share this little booklet with you?"

8. If you have a copy of The Four Spiritual Laws with you, "Have you ever heard of the Four Spiritual Laws?"

9. "I've been real interested in spiritual things the last several years, and I'm curious about people's spiritual [or religious] convictions. Do you have any? Would you mind sharing them with me?"

Prayer project. Help your disciple brainstorm a list of about eight or ten non-Christian family members or friends that he could begin praying for, kind of a "Ten Most Wanted" list. Be sure he writes their names down on his prayer list, and you should write them on yours as well. Check back with him every few weeks to be sure he's still praying for them and to see if the Lord has given him any opportunities to share the gospel with them. Remind him frequently to keep his eyes peeled for those "divine appointments."

Get him involved. If anything will stimulate your disciple's desire to witness it will be actually getting involved in real-life witnessing situations. Take it in two steps. Step one, take him out witnessing with you, with the understanding that you'll do all the talking, and he should simply observe and pray. Step two, after you've done this a few times, let him take the lead — he'll share and you watch and pray. Some great places to do this: college campuses, shopping malls, parks and beaches.

■ ASSIGNMENT FOR NEXT TIME

Assuming you are moving on to Training Objective #10 regarding spiritual warfare, have your disciple look up the following verses and ask himself the corresponding questions:

1. Isaiah 14:12-17 (the fall of Lucifer)

   • What did Satan do to warrant being rejected from heaven and consigned to Sheol?

   • How do we mimic him in this sometimes in our lives?

2. Matthew 4:1-11 (Jesus' temptation in the wilderness)

- What was the main thing Satan was trying to get Jesus to do?

- In each of the three temptations, how did Jesus defend Himself?

If you are taking the training objectives out of order, and haven't yet done 6, 7 or 8, anticipate which of those you'll do next and give your disciple an appropriate assignment. For ideas on that, go back to chapter 13 ("Basic Growth Principles," Training Objective #5) and look under Assignments for Next Time, or look ahead to the next week's training objective and consider some of the selections under Further Resources.

■ EVALUATION

Ask yourself the following questions:

1. Does my disciple understand why witnessing is so important?

2. Can my disciple tell me what the basic elements of the gospel are?

3. Can my disciple tell another person how to be saved?

If you can answer each of these questions in the affirmative, your disciple has met this training objective. If you need more input from him to determine your answers, here are some questions you can ask him:

1. Why is it important for Christians to witness?

2. Why do you share your faith with others? What is it that motivates you?

3. How would you define "witnessing"?

4. What are some of the things that tend to make you hesitant to witness?

5. What goes through your mind when, after you have shared the gospel with someone, he rejects it?

6. What would you say are the basic components of the gospel?

7. Which would you prefer, sharing your faith or being bullwhipped?

8. (If he prefers the whip) What is it about witnessing that bothers you the most?

9. What are some of the things that make a Christian a good witness-er?

10. Do you think you could do a good job of telling another person how to become a Christian? Let's see.

11. How are you benefited when you witness?

12. In what ways is witnessing just the natural result of being honest?

13. Who should Christians witness to?

14. What is the difference between witnessing through your life and witnessing with your words? Why are both important?

15. What is the Holy Spirit's job in the witnessing process?

16. What part does prayer play in witnessing?

**RECOMMENDED RESOURCES
FOR EVANGELISM TRAINING**

WITNESSING WITHOUT FEAR by Bill Bright. A reader-friendly, step-by-step guide that will help your disciples learn to share their faith with confidence. This helpful book was awarded the Evangelical Christian Publishers Association's "Gold Medallion" as 1988's best book in evangelism and missions. It is suited for both individual and group use, and is endorsed by national Christian leaders including Billy Graham and James Kennedy.

TELL IT OFTEN, TELL IT WELL by Mark McCloskey. A well-reasoned, biblically based, and philosophically sound case for initiative evangelism. The author is Campus Crusade's director of training for the Campus Ministry, and his book has become the text for evangelism and outreach classes in several seminaries.

Both books are available at Christian bookstores,
or from Here's Life Publishers.
(Call 1-800-854-5659; in California call 714-886-7981.)

18 TRAINING OBJECTIVE #10

SPIRITUAL WARFARE

■ OBJECTIVE

The disciple has a basic understanding of the fundamental facts concerning adversity, Satan, temptation and sin.

■ BIBLICAL BASIS FOR THIS OBJECTIVE

God wants us to know the facts regarding the working of Satan, the consequences of following Satan, how to escape his influences, and how to pick ourselves up when we fall spiritually. As if it's never been said before, why don't you look at the following passages of Scripture and jot down a brief summary for each in your disciplemaker's notebook?

Psalm 37:23,24	Luke 22:31,32	1 Peter 5:8-10
Psalm 119:9-11	2 Corinthians 2:11	1 John 2:1,2
Psalm 145:14	Ephesians 4:27	1 John 2:12-14
Proverbs 24:16	Ephesians 6:10-18	1 John 4:4
Micah 7:8	James 4:7,8	1 John 5:3-5

■ PEP TALK FOR THE DISCIPLEMAKER

Now we come to one of the most strategic topics you'll cover with your new disciple. Everything we've gone over so far is important, but this subject could almost be called pivotal. Satan has been, and will continue to be, working overtime to scuttle the new Christian's ship. Your disciple will be in the most vulnerable position of his spiritual life these first few months, so you need to do whatever you can to help his defenses. It's hard to defend yourself against an attacker if you don't know what he looks like, where he's coming from, or even if you're really under fire. During the "Jesus Movement" of the early 1970s David Wilkerson wrote:

Jesus Christ is not a trip. He is not another high in a series of highs. Enough of this frivolous joy-pop feeling for Jesus. Never again will I tell a young person to "trip out on Jesus; He'll make you high." An acid freak attended a recent crusade and confessed to me, "I'm back on acid. I used to be tripped out on Jesus. I was really zapped by the Spirit. I was really up on Christ. But it was a bummer. Nobody told me about forsaking the crowd—nothing about temptations, about the devil trying to bring me down. Somebody wasn't honest with me, man. Be sure you always tell kids to quit tripping with their heads and start learning how to die." That's it exactly; Jesus has to be a way of dying before He can be a way of living.[1]

You want to be honest with your disciple, right? He needs to know that, far from joining a religion-of-the-month club, he's joined a *war*—and *he's* the disputed territory.

Someone might be thinking, *Why all the scare tactics? We don't want to frighten the poor guy to death.* This is true—we don't want to frighten him to death. Good disciples are hard enough to come by without us bumping them off right and left. However, if there's one thing our disciples should be scared of, it's what Satan can do to a person who doesn't know how to defend himself. We are informed in 1 Peter 5:8 that Satan's objective is not to bother, bug or bum us out, his desire is to devour us. This is not a friendly game of Trivial Pursuit here. Satan is playing for keeps. You and your disciple need to keep that fact in mind at all times.

In this session, you want to pass on to him a few fundamental facts regarding adversity, Satan, temptation and sin. A rather negative line-up, but as Thoreau wrote in 1849, real life is not "a stroll upon the beach." What he wrote five years later is a more accurate assessment: "The mass of men lead lives of quiet desperation."[2] If we don't deal with this ragged edge in our discipling relationships, we will not meet the needs of those God has entrusted to us. This session is designed to help the disciple understand that the Christian life isn't Disneyland, but that he can experience an abundant and fruitful life despite that fact.

Two words of caution as you approach this particular meeting: *Watch out.* Whenever I have to prepare a study or to speak on this subject, the battle heats up. Satan doesn't like the spotlight, and whenever I shine it on him, I experience his resistance. My word processor has already broken down once and both my wife and I have gotten quite ill just in the course of the few days it's taken to type this training objective into my computer. Some will say it's coincidence, but I've seen it far too many times to agree with that. You can expect the same treatment, my friend. Don't be surprised if your disciple doesn't show up for this appointment. He may have forgotten, or his roommate may have persuaded him to go with him down to the ol' fishing hole, or out-of-town visitors may have dropped in unexpectedly, or a UFO may have crashed into his house. Whatever it may be, just keep rescheduling. Then, don't *you* forget, or let your car run out of gas, or lose your Bible, or have a fight with your wife. The devil will work his game from both sides. Bathe this one in prayer.

■ BROACHING THE SUBJECT

Your disciple has already had some input from you on this topic, so he's probably somewhat familiar. He knows that Satan exists, that adversity is a normal part of the Christian life (see Training Objective #5), and that when he sins, confession and repentance will restore fellowship between him and God (see Training Objective #3). You might start like this:

"I know we've already talked a little about trials and Satan, but I thought we'd spend some time today getting down to a little more of the nitty-gritty on those subjects. I'd be interested to know what your pre-Christian concept of Satan was."

It doesn't really matter how he answers; this is just a good way to break the ice and get into the subject.

Your response: "That's interesting. The Bible talks a lot about Satan and how he works to oppose the work of God. There's no way we'll be able to exhaust the topic completely here today, but I wanted to pass on to you seven Fundamental Facts about adversity, Satan, temptation and sin."

The best way for you to proceed from here is to read through the Suggestions For Growth section below, choose a few key verses from each of the seven Fundamental Facts, and then write down the "F.F.'s" and their corresponding verses on a piece of paper. The paper can be a focal point as you two talk, and also will be a nice take-home piece for your disciple to study later. Share experiences you have gone through and insights you may have about the various F.F.'s or verses, but be careful about monopolizing the conversation. Your disciple can wait until Sunday to get his sermon, just like the rest of us. Keep the tone as conversational as you can.

■ SUGGESTIONS FOR GROWTH

Fundamental Fact #1:

Becoming a Christian doesn't mean you will no longer have problems; but you now have the supreme problem-solver of the universe living within you.

Deuteronomy 31:8	John 16:33	2 Timothy 3:12
Psalm 34:7	John 17:14,15	1 Peter 5:7,8
Isaiah 41:10	Acts 14:21,22	2 Peter 2:9
John 15:18-21	Romans 8:36-39	
John 16:1-4	1 Corinthians 10:13	

Fundamental Fact #2:

The difficulties you will experience as a Christian will come from one of four sources:

A. The natural consequences of foolish (but amoral) actions.

　　　　　Hosea 8:7a　　　　　　　Galatians 6:7

What I'm referring to here are things like hitting your finger with a hammer, stubbing your toe, catching a cold because you didn't dress warmly enough for the football game, having your car repossessed because you cosigned a loan for a bum with no money, etc. This is not to say that God never causes these kinds of things to happen for one reason or another, nor am I saying that God won't use them to accomplish His purposes. But usually they are simply due to the natural laws of the universe faithfully performing their duties.

B. The temptations of Satan.

Satan's number one activity all day every day is to try to induce you to disobey God. First John 2:15,16 tells us that these inducements will come from one of three directions:

(1) The lust of the flesh — the misuse of your natural appetites for food, sex, comfort, pleasure, etc.

         2 Samuel 11:2-4   Matthew 4:2,3

(2) The lust of the eyes — the compulsive desire to possess things; materialism; wanting whatever one sees.

         Matthew 4:8   2 Timothy 4:10

(3) The pride of life — the compulsive pursuit of fame, power, recognition, exaltation in the eyes of others; anything that might possibly supplant God's position of priority in your life; pursuits that could take God off the throne and put you on it.

         Matthew 4:5,6   Obadiah 3,4

Look at Genesis 3 and see if you and your disciple can pick out these three elements in the serpent's temptation of Eve. You can see it also in his temptation of Jesus in Matthew 4.

C. The discipline of God as a consequence of sin.

God loves His children, and no loving father allows his kids to stray into forbidden territory without administering discipline. Just as our earthly children need to know that there are negative consequences to undesirable behavior, so we, as children of our heavenly Father, need to expect His loving — albeit not always completely enjoyable — correction when we err. It's for our own good.

         Deuteronomy 8:5   Hebrews 12:5-11

         Proverbs 3:11,12   Revelation 3:19

D. The testing of God designed to cause spiritual growth.

We often experience adversity because God is working on us. Like a coach putting his athletes through rigorous workouts to produce top contenders, God puts us through some pretty tough training, with a view to making us mature, useful to the Master, and prepared for service.

         Psalm 119:71,75   John 12:27   Hebrews 5:8

         Isaiah 30:20,21   2 Corinthians 12:7

Fundamental Fact #3:

Adversity caused by any one of these four sources is allowed by God through a perfect blending of two biblical principles:

- Galatians 6:7,8 – One reaps what one sows, good or bad.
- Romans 8:28 – God can turn even the bad into good.

While it is true that "God loves you and has a wonderful plan for your life," it is not true that every step and every facet of His plan is what we would term "wonderful." A foundational law of the universe is that you will reap what you sow. Every cause has an effect, and God has instituted these laws, both physical and spiritual, in order to keep His creation running smoothly. These laws are entirely impersonal. If you break them, they'll break you, no matter who you are. If you jump off a five-story building, you are going to break some bones and experience a lot of pain, child of God or not. That's cause and effect, action and reaction. But God can then take this tragic, painful experience, and work it out for the very best for those who allow Him to. You never can tell if God is the primary cause of a particular trial or mishap. Sometimes He is, and sometimes He isn't, as mentioned in F.F. #2 earlier. But one thing you can be sure of, He will react to that trial, come to your aid, make sure it isn't more than you can bear (1 Corinthians 10:13), mix it with a little grace, and use it to work out His absolutely perfect plans.

Biblical examples:

Joseph, Genesis 37, 39 – 50. It certainly wasn't wonderful when Joseph's brothers attempted to murder him (Genesis 37:18-24), when he was forced into slavery in Egypt (37:28), when he was falsely accused by Potiphar's wife and imprisoned (39:11-20), or when he was double-crossed by Pharaoh's cupbearer and left to rot in jail (40:20-23). It was all part of God's plan, though, to exalt Joseph to the position of the second most powerful man in the world, and to save the seed of Abraham from extinction in a famine (45:4-8; 50:19,20).

Moses, Exodus 2:11 – 3:10. It wasn't wonderful when Moses had to flee Egypt to escape the wrath of Pharaoh. Yet as a result of his flight to Midian, he not only met the girl God had prepared to be his wife (2:21), but he also received some of the best training in the world for the ministry God had for him. Forty years of tending a bunch of headstrong, self-centered sheep turned out to have a high degree of transfer value when it came time to spend forty years tending a bunch of head-strong, self-centered Israelites.

Noah, Genesis 6:9 – 7:16. It wasn't high on Noah's list of fun things to do to spend 120 years as the town laughingstock, while he and his sons built a huge boat in his back yard, miles from any large body of water. Still, because of his patience and obedience to the Lord in the midst of incredibly trying circumstances, God rescued him and his family from the Great Flood and used him to accomplish the cleansing of the world.

Jesus. Hanging on the cross, enduring the unimaginable pain of separation from His beloved Father, accepting the shame, beatings and humiliation, and experiencing the horror of our sinfulness laid upon His holy body – I'm sure that Jesus considered none of these things wonderful. But He knew that it was all part of the Father's perfect plan to purchase our salvation, and He gladly submitted to it. Hebrews 12:2: "Who for the joy set before him endured the cross, scorning its shame, and sat down at the right hand of the throne of God."

Fundamental Fact #4:

Christians are to flee temptation and resist the devil.

From time to time, people talk about "resisting temptation" and "fleeing from the devil." Those actions are exactly opposite from what the Bible tells us to do!

Temptation is not to be resisted, it is to be *fled* from. If you know that you have a hard time with alcohol, don't spend your time in bars. If sexual sin is a problem for you, don't go downtown where the prostitutes hang out. If overeating is something you can't seem to get victory over, don't go out and buy a bunch of chocolate eclairs, put them in your refrigerator, and then pray for God to keep you from eating them.[3]

Proverbs 4:14,15   Romans 13:14   2 Timothy 2:22

Matthew 26:41   1 Timothy 6:10,11

Satan, on the other hand, is not to be fled from, but to be actively *resisted.* Though Satan is our number-one enemy, and a very powerful one at that, the Bible tells us clearly that the only way to deal with him is to stay and fight.

Matthew 4:1-11   Ephesians 6:10-18   1 Peter 5:8,9

2 Corinthians 10:3-5 James 4:7,8   Revelation 12:11

Note to the disciplemaker: Go over James 4:7,8 with your disciple—it's a great format for resisting Satan. Think of dealing with Satan in terms of dealing with a burglar in your house[4]:

	Burglar	Satan
Step One: Detect	"I think there's a burglar in the house!"	"I think Satan is trying to make me sin!" (2 Corinthians 2:11)
Step Two: Empower	Grab an "equalizer," like a shotgun!	"Submit therefore to God." Ask God to help you fight Satan. By yourself, you couldn't stand up to him—you must have God's help. (Psalm 59:9)
Step Three: Trap	"Gotcha covered! Reach for the sky, or I'll shoot!"	"Resist the devil, and he will flee from you." Address him directly, just as Jesus did. Your weapon: the Word. (Ephesians 6:13-17)
Step Four: Reinforce	Call the police!	"Draw near to God, and He will draw near to you." After the fight, spend a short time in prayer or Bible reading, to seal the victory and strengthen yourself.

Be sure to get across to your disciple that the Bible doesn't say we have to thrash Satan to within an inch of his life. It's a good thing, too, because we don't, by ourselves, have the knowledge, skill or strength to do battle with one as magnificent in war as Lucifer. He'd pulverize us! All we have to do is resist Satan, and he will flee as a vanquished foe. That's all it takes — a little resistance.

For Step Three, "Trap": Turn to Matthew 4 and see how Jesus addressed Satan during His temptation. You'll notice three principles Jesus applied (verse 10) that we should utilize too:

1. Address him directly.

2. Command him to leave (or to cease his activities in your area).

3. Remind him of the authority by which you command him: God's Word.

The way Jesus did the third part of this format was to quote Scripture. In essence, Jesus was saying, "You can't make me do what you have suggested, because God has already spoken on that subject in His Word, and He says not to, so I don't have to. You are working contrary to God's will. You are in the wrong; I am in the right. Therefore, I have the authority of God Himself to command you to leave. Begone!"

Most new Christians are not familiar enough with the Bible to quote Scripture verbatim, as Jesus did, but I don't think they need to. The truth is still the truth whether it's in New American Standard, King James, French, Watusi or in your own words. (This is not to say that there is not immense value in memorizing Scripture word-perfect; we all know there is.) If a person will simply inform Satan that he no longer belongs to his kingdom, that he has been bought with the shed blood of Jesus Christ and no longer has to follow Satan's dictates, and that he is sure that God's Word commands that he obey Him alone, Satan must flee. I believe this is what Revelation 12:11 talks about when it says: "They overcame him by the blood of the Lamb and *by the word of their testimony*" (emphasis mine).

Fundamental Fact #5:

Salvation does not give us a license to sin; sin interrupts fellowship with God and short-circuits the power that God has made available to us.

Isaiah 59:2	1 Corinthians 6:12	1 Peter 4:1,2
John 15:6	Galatians 5:13	1 John 2:3-6
Romans 6:1-6	Titus 1:16	1 John 4:20
Romans 6:16	James 2:19,20	Jude 4

Fundamental Fact #6:

When you do sin, confession, humble repentance and reappropriating the filling of the Holy Spirit will restore you to a right relationship with God.

Note to the disciplemaker: You probably already have covered the filling of the Holy Spirit when you went over Training Objective #3 in chapter 11, but this would be a great time for a quick review. Following are a few points you might want to touch on. You probably won't want to take the time to examine each verse with your disciple, but *you* should take a look at each one, jot that often-recommended summary in your notebook, and choose one or two for each point.

1. We're all going to slip up and sin from time to time.

Psalm 14:3	Romans 3:23
Isaiah 53:6a	1 John 1:8

2. Jesus has already paid for our sins.

Isaiah 53:6b	Colossians 1:13,14	1 Peter 3:18

3. God is in the business of forgiving and forgetting sin.

Psalm 103:12	Isaiah 1:18
Psalm 130:3,4	Isaiah 43:25

4. To experience cleansing and thereby restore fellowship with God, confess your sins to Him, that is, agree with God that what you did was wrong, and reappropriate the filling of the Holy Spirit.

Psalm 66:18	Proverbs 28:13	1 John 1:9

5. Mouthing the words is not enough; there must be genuine humility and repentance (to "repent" means "to turn around and go the other way").

2 Chronicles 7:14	Psalm 34:14,17,18	James 4:9,10
Job 11:13-15	Psalm 51:17	

Fundamental Fact #7:

Above all else, no matter how badly you may blow it, you can know that God still loves you, you are still "fully accepted in the Beloved," and God still wants to help you overcome your problems and become more like Christ.

1. God still loves you.
   Romans 5:8   Romans 8:38,39
2. You are still acceptable in His eyes.
   Ephesians 1:6,7   1 John 2:1,2
3. God still wants to help you to overcome your problems and become more like Christ.
   Romans 8:28,29   2 Corinthians 3:18

■ FURTHER RESOURCES

For some good, fill-in-the-blank type Bible studies on the subject of spiritual warfare, choose some selections from the following:

"Ten Basic Steps Toward Christian Maturity" Bible Study Series by Campus Crusade for Christ:

- Step 2, Lesson 6: "The Christian Armor and Warfare"
         Lesson 7: "Attitude"

"The Discipleship Series"[5] also by Campus Crusade for Christ:

- Book 1, Lesson 2: "How to Experience God's Love and Forgiveness"

- Book 3, Lesson 2: "Dealing With Life's Trials"

Design for Discipleship Bible Study Series by The Navigators:

- Book 2, Chapter 1: "The Obedient Christian"

- Book 4, Chapter 3: "Purity of Life"
         Chapter 4: "Integrity in Living"
         Chapter 5: "Character in Action"
- Book 5, Chapter 4: "Spiritual Warfare"

■ P.S. FOR THE DISCIPLEMAKER

Once again, this may be too much material to cover with your disciple in one session, so you have the same options to cut the amount of material, talk fast, or break it into two sessions. If it were me, I'd go for the last option, due to the importance of a Christian's gaining a good, early grasp of these concepts. Spending two sessions on it, therefore dwelling on it twice as long, will imbed the truths of this subject more firmly in his mind.

■ ENDING THE SESSION

Practice some "war games" with each other. Drawing on the four-step format for resisting Satan under Fundamental Fact #4 (detect, empower, trap, reinforce), develop scenarios of temptation and formulate plans about how you would conduct yourselves. One person could set the scene, while the other decides how he would flee the temptation, what Scripture he would use to resist Satan, what he would say to him, etc.

If the two of you are close enough, and you can do so comfortably, you each could share one or two areas of temptation that you have a hard time getting consistent victory over. Spend some time in prayer over them, and continue to pray for each other during the next several weeks.

■ ASSIGNMENT FOR NEXT TIME

Both of you should agree to apply the four-step format for resisting Satan at least once in the coming week. Tell your disciple that when you get together next week, you'll both share what happened.

Since the next training objective is "Time Management," ask your disciple to write out a schedule of one of his typical weeks. You'll go over it with him next week. In addition, give him Charles Hummel's classic little booklet, "Tyranny of the Urgent," published by InterVarsity Press, and tell him it's urgent that he read it.

■ EVALUATION

Ask yourself these questions:

1. *Adversity.* Does your disciple understand that adversity is a normal part of the Christian life, and that God will use the trials he encounters to help him to grow spiritually?

2. *Satan.* Does he understand that Satan is a personal being, who, with his demons, is constantly seeking to use the world and our old fleshly nature to cause us to rebel against the authority of God?

3. *Temptation.* Does he understand that he is to *flee* temptation and to *resist* Satan? Has he shared a few personal experiences with you that represent this understanding?

4. *Sin.* Is he convinced that, even though sin interrupts his fellowship with God and God is grieved about his sin, God still loves and accepts him fully as His child? Does he know how to restore fellowship with God through confession, humble repentance and the reappropriation of the filling of the Holy Spirit? Has he shared a few personal experiences with you that represent this understanding?

If you can answer each of these questions in the affirmative, then your disciple has met this training objective. If you need a little more input from him to determine your answers, here are a few questions you can ask him:

1. When you became a Christian, did it seem like all of your problems just dried up and blew away? (He'll probably say no.) Well, if you're now one of God's children, why do you think He allows you to keep having troubles?

2. What is usually your first reaction when something goes wrong? What do you think is the proper attitude for a Christian to have?

3. Do you think we'll ever come to the point where we'll no longer experience adversity in our lives?

4. Where do you think difficulties in our lives come from? Do we cause them ourselves, does the devil cause them, are they a consequence of our sin, or does God cause them? (Correct answer, of course: "all of the above.")

5. What would you say is the objective of every temptation of Satan? (He's trying to get us to rebel against the authority of God, and put ourselves under his authority

once again.)

6. Can you think of any time in your life when God turned a bad situation into a good one?

7. What is our best plan of action when we meet temptation? (Flee it.)

8. What is our best plan of action when we meet Satan? (Resist him.)

9. How would you go about resisting the devil in a particular situation? (Make up a scenario for him.)

10. What role does the Word of God play in spiritual warfare?

11. Since Jesus has already paid the penalty for our sin, and since we already have been given eternal life, wouldn't it be OK to go out and sin our heads off now? Why not? What harm would come of it?

12. What effect does your sin have on God? What does it do to your relationship with Him? Does it cause Him to hate you?

13. When you sin, what do you do to restore your relationship with God?

14. How important is "repentance" to restoring your relationship with God?

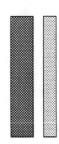

19 TRAINING OBJECTIVE #11

TIME MANAGEMENT

■ OBJECTIVE

The disciple has a basic understanding of the principles of time management and has begun to utilize his time better.

■ BIBLICAL BASIS FOR THIS OBJECTIVE

In Scripture, time is seen as a precious commodity which God commands us to invest wisely. We each have been given time to accomplish everything God wants us to do. Eventually, we will all stand before the judgment seat of Christ and account for how we used the time He entrusted to us. The following passages underscore these facts. Why not look them up and jot down a brief summary of each in your disciplemaker's notebook? Or had you already thought of that?

Ecclesiastes 3:1-8	Mark 13:33-37	2 Corinthians 5:10
Ecclesiastes 9:12	Romans 13:11,12	Ephesians 5:15,16
Psalm 90:12	Romans 14:12	

■ PEP TALK FOR THE DISCIPLEMAKER

"Time management? Right up there with prayer and the filling of the Holy Spirit? With the *holy* stuff? I thought these training objectives were to help our disciples grow in Christlikeness. How could you bring up a subject so mundane as time management?"

My defense of the inclusion of this topic is very simple.

Life on earth is short—and it gets shorter all the time. And we want to have a positive impact for Christ on our world in the few hand-breadths of time we have remaining, right? But for most of us, making it through each day is a lot like wrestling a gorilla. You can't stop when *you* get tired; you stop when

304

the *gorilla* gets tired. How in the world can we take on any more? How can our disciples?

You are asking a lot of your disciple—to make an additional two to five hours a week available to you and to the Lord. Eventually, as he matures and develops a ministry, that may go up to around twenty to thirty hours a week. Where will he find the time? Where can *you* find the time to keep ahead of him? It doesn't matter how high and holy our world-changing intentions are if we don't have the time to carry them out.

As David Dawson, founder of Equipping the Saints Ministry wrote, "The real difficulty is not the lack of time but *what we do with the time we have.* Since we can never accumulate, stockpile, replace or turn back time, we must learn to control it as it passes. If we fail to manage our time, nothing else in our lives can or will be managed."[1]

Life is one big exchange. We give our time to an employer in exchange for money. We give our money to a store in exchange for food. We give our food to our bodies in exchange for energy. We give our energy to our wives in exchange for a checked-off "Honey-Do" list. Through it all, the main coinage is time. It's what starts the transaction and it's charged to our account all along the way. Time is our number one resource. We may want a million other things—money, love, a motor home, maturity—but what we've got is time. You can't stipulate how much time you start with, but it's completely up to you what you'll exchange it for.

Some exchange it for nothing. At this writing the average American spends more than one-fifth of his waking hours in front of a TV set. So each year, he has spent every sentient moment from January 1 to March 13 doing nothing but stare at a cathode-ray tube. Some exchange it for junk. Maybe you've seen the slogan on a bumper sticker or T-shirt, shouting in puzzling triumph, "The one who dies with the most toys wins!" That really is the motivating credo of millions of people today, whether they realize it or not. But in the end, all the toys are worthless. They break down, are stolen, get worn out, or are left behind on this world when their owner goes to the next.

Some, on the other hand, exchange their time for gold, sil-

ver and precious jewels, the kind talked about in 1 Corinthians
3:11-14 . . . the eternal kind.

We want to throw our lot in with that last group, and we
hope our disciples will too. But we can't tell a busy housewife
how important it is to set aside an hour a week for Bible study,
and not tell her where to find that hour. We can't suggest to a
harried account executive that he find twenty minutes a day to
pray when he's already sprinting from dawn to dusk. We've got
to help them organize the *secular* so there will be enough room
for the *sacred*.

Actually, disciplemaker, this training objective is as much
for you as for your disciple. If you struggle in this area, inadequate time management is hindering your ministry, and I urge
you to assimilate these principles along with your disciple.

■ BROACHING THE SUBJECT

First, see where your disciple is on the matter of time. He
may be more squared away on it than you are! Ask him a few
of the following questions:

1. Have you ever thought about your specific purpose or
   mission in life? I don't mean "as a Christian" or "as a
   human," but "as YOU." What do *you* want to accomplish in the seventy-five or so years you've been
   given on earth? (If he can answer . . .) Do you feel
   you are accomplishing your purpose?

2. What are some of your major goals in life? Do you think
   those goals line up with goals that God has in mind for
   you? (Or, How does God fit into those goals?) What
   specific steps are you taking toward reaching those
   goals?

3. What are your top five priorities in life? How do you
   rank them in order of importance? Now, how would
   you rank them according to the amount of time you
   spend on each one each day? How do those priorities
   line up with your life's purpose and major goals?

4. Do you often feel that there are not enough hours in
   the day to do everything you'd like to do?

5. Are there some activities eating away at your time that

you wish you could get rid of? (If so . . .) What are they?

6. Have you got a system of time management that you're pretty satisfied with? (If so . . .) Would you mind sharing it with me?

7. Do you conduct your affairs with the aid of a personal calendar and "to-do" lists?

■ SUGGESTIONS FOR GROWTH

When it comes right down to it, the battle for effective time management is won or lost in our ability to make intelligent, consequential decisions regarding day-to-day activities. Most of our time is frittered away, not on bad things, but on needless things. We make tons of decisions every week about the use of our time, often the wrong ones. But one cannot make those decisions intelligently unless he has some overriding frame of reference with which to evaluate the pros and cons of each decision.

Major companies each have a "Mission Statement," a succinct way of expressing why they exist and what they're trying to accomplish. General Motors might say, "We exist to produce the best cars and trucks in the world." When someone comes to the company executives and proposes building the world's best lawn mower, they confer. "Does this fit in with our mission statement? Well, it says here that we exist to make cars and trucks. A lawn mower doesn't fit either of those categories. Thumbs down." Someone else comes along with a proposal to make car engines less expensively, but sub-standard. "It's good to save money, but we're committed to making the *best*. Give him the boot." Another fellow proposes a state-of-the-art, computerized, fuel-injection system. "Let's see — it goes in a car or a truck, it will make GM fuel-injection systems the best in the world. This looks like a winner! Let's start production!" Their mission statement has helped them say no to activities that would hinder their function, and yes to the ones that would help.

We individuals should learn from those conglomerations. The principle that is vital to their existence ought to prove beneficial to us.

But before we can come up with a mission statement, we have to figure out what's important to us — our priorities. If we don't have a clear idea of what we value, we aren't going to know the first thing about using our time wisely in going after it. You rarely hit what you can't see.

Christians, particularly, need to set their priorities. "What's on God's heart? What's important to Him? In light of eternity, what is of utmost value to me?" When a person has answered those questions, he's ready to decide how best to utilize his time now in going after his priorities.

So the construction of an effective time management system should proceed according to this sequence:

1. Determine *life priorities*

2. Determine life *mission statement* that reflects priorities

3. Determine *major goals* that will combine to make the mission statement functional

4. Determine *intermediate goals* that will help in reaching major goals

5. Determine *short-term goals* that will help in reaching intermediate goals

6. Determine a *schedule* that will allow for the reaching of short-term goals and will screen out unnecessary activities.

To help your disciple get established in the area of time management, we'll follow that order. One of the first things you should do with your disciple is share the above sequence with him so he'll know where you're taking him.

I. Determine Life Priorities

A. Priorities from God's perspective.

To construct a criteria by which you can make day-to-day decisions regarding your use of time, you have to start at the top of the list: life priorities. As Christians, we want to subordinate our priorities to God's priorities, so we need to find out what those are.

Start by reading Matthew 22:37-40 together. Here Jesus describes what man's two greatest concerns should be: (1) loving God; and (2) loving his fellow man. Write those two commands at the top of a piece of paper. These priorities are listed in other passages also: Leviticus 19:18; Deuteronomy 6:4,5; Micah 6:8; Acts 24:16; 2 Corinthians 4:5.

Next, let your disciple brainstorm a little about what might be entailed in those two priorities. Ask him something like, "What are some ways you and I could do those two things? How do we go about loving God?" You're looking for general activities such as:

Loving God	**Loving Fellow Man**
Obey Him	Help the poor and needy
Trust Him	Encourage the downhearted
Learn about Him	Fellowship with them
Communicate with Him	Tell them about Christ
Do things for Him	Help them grow spiritually
Put Him first	Take care of my family
Don't be ashamed of Him	Don't hurt anyone in any way
Worship Him	Serve them

If he has a hard time getting started, help him by suggesting a few yourself. List at least six things in each column.

Now, using the bottom half of the paper, go into more detail about each one. Encourage your disciple with, "Say that starting tomorrow, you wanted to begin making some of these activities a habitual part of your life. Taking them one at a time, and keeping in mind your unique gifts and circumstances, what could you do to start?" You're looking for "specific activities" here, things like:

Loving God

- Obey Him
    - Study the Bible to learn His general commands
    - Take steps to comply with them
    - Forsake the sinful things I know of that I'm doing

— Spend time in prayer asking God to help me obey
- Trust Him
    — Study the Bible to find what it says about trust and faith
    — Talk to somebody about the doubts I feel
    — Pray and ask God to give me more faith
    — Think of something to do that will require me to rely on God for its outcome
- Etc.

B. Assessment of present personal priorities.

The next step is to see how your disciple's present priorities stack up against God's priorities listed above. At the end of last week's assignment (Training Objective #10), you asked your disciple to write out a schedule of one of his typical weeks. Hopefully, he has brought that with him. Have him take the schedule and run through the "Priority Assessment Exercise" here.

We each are given 168 hours a week. How do we spend them? In the blanks provided (or on a separate sheet of paper with its own blanks), have your disciple examine his personal schedule and write in how much time he spends each week on each listed activity.

Priority Assessment Exercise

____ Sleeping	____ Housework
____ Eating	____ Commuting
____ Family time	____ Class and homework
____ Visiting with others	____ Bible study (preparation and meetings)
____ Relaxing; personal time	
____ Exercise program	____ Prayer
____ Employment	____ Fellowship
____ Home and car main-tenance	____ Ministry
	____ Dressing, shaving, shower, make-up, etc.
_____	_____
_____	_____

Realizing that we find time to do the things we feel are important, this exercise will help your disciple see where his current priorities lie. A person may *say* church attendance is important to him, but if he rarely goes, he has cause to wonder.

Have your disciple total his hours. The difference between the total and the 168 given hours should be considered "lost time." With some people it doesn't amount to much, while with others it's quite significant. The latter will be appalled, and will immediately begin keeping a lookout for unexplained "time leaks."

Now go back and look at the lists of general and specific activities you've already written. How does his current use of time fit his idealized, Christ-centered list of activities? How much of what he's currently doing wouldn't fit anywhere on the first two lists? More important, how much of the specific activities list fits into his current activities list? Should some activities be added to the first two lists?

Unless he's already exceptionally mature spiritually, he'll see quite a distance between the first two lists and the third. This should motivate him to begin changing. Make sure he understands that all Christians start with flawed priorities. One of the primary reasons God gave us the Holy Spirit is to help us make list 3 line up with lists 1 and 2. It doesn't happen overnight, and it's not necessarily easy, but if we'll cooperate with God, He'll bring it to pass.

II. Determine Life Mission Statement That Reflects Priorities

A personal mission statement simply expresses what one is accomplishing or hopes to accomplish. It probably will include answering needs he feels uniquely qualified and deeply burdened to meet. Bobb Biehl asks on his Masterplanning Arrow,[2] "What needs make us weep or pound the table?"

Above all else, the mission statement should reflect the disciple's personal priorities talked about above. Biehl defines this statement as being made up of three important characteristics: "directional" (taking you somewhere; accomplishing something), "umbrella" (taking in everything you do), and "lifetime" (on-going; never completely accomplished; never needing to change).

Here are a few examples of personal mission statements:

Mine: "To cooperate with God in His program to conform me to the image of Jesus Christ, using all my available resources to serve Him, my family and my fellow man mainly through a fruitful ministry of disciplemaking, writing and speaking."

David Dawson, founder and director of Equipping the Saints Ministry: "To walk in daily fellowship with God and to order my life and family in accordance with the Word of God so that we are daily exchanging our lives for the fulfilling of Christ's Great Commission."[3]

John Klein, associate national director of Athletes in Action: "To love the Lord with all my heart, soul and mind and my neighbor as myself, and to be a good steward of the resources God has given me, glorifying Him in all that I do."

Bobb Biehl, founder and director of Masterplanning Group International: "To love God and my fellow man and to show this love by helping people see life with increasing clarity and know how to cope with life's pressures and challenges."

Terry Valentine, associate director of admissions, Spring Arbor College: "To make disciples in all areas and among all peoples toward the fulfillment of the Great Commission, providing vision, strategy and training in prayer, evangelism and discipleship, working through the church where viable and directed toward society in general."

This might be a good note on which to end this session with your disciple, giving him the assignment to spend the coming week formulating his own personal mission statement. You might need to call him once or twice during the week to remind him, primarily so that he won't throw it together during the five minutes before next week's meeting. Encourage him to spend a good, solid hour working on it — he'll need that kind of concentration.

III. Determine Major Goals That Will Combine to Make the Mission Statement Functional

The next three steps, the setting of major goals, intermediate goals and short-term goals, are pretty well known and widely used strategies of time management. I like the way Richard Furman, M.D., talks about them in *Reaching Your Full Potential.*[4] His succinct, down-to-earth capsulization of weighty principles stands out to me. About a major goal, he says, "Set it and never change it." These are the big, long-term dreams that we might spend months, years or decades pursuing. All of your major goals balled up and stirred together will accomplish your mission statement. The mission statement is the car; the major goals are the wheels that enable the car to roll along.

Dr. Furman's first major goal was to become a surgeon. That's no small feat. One of my major goals is to become a writer. The more specific a goal is, the better, but at the major goal level being specific is not crucial. The day Dr. Furman completed his surgical residency, he could say, "Today I have reached my goal."

Some goals are like that, quite specific. Mine, however, isn't. When I was a college athlete, I could say, "I'd like to be a writer," and the goal was made very clear by its contrast to what I was doing at the time. The road to "writer" was very distinct from the road to "professional athlete," "car mechanic" or "insurance salesman." As time passed and I became an administrator for Athletes in Action, the goal started to get fuzzy — the contrasts weren't as sharp. I did some writing, true, but it was utilitarian, things like slide shows, memos, reports, proposals. It didn't really represent my earliest visions of "a writer." For that reason, I needed some more specific intermediate goals. But we'll talk about them in a minute. The first step is to just get some major goals down on paper — specific or not.

Have your disciple come up with some of his goals. These could deal with some or all of the following areas of his life:

1. Spiritual   5. Financial

2. Physical   6. Family

3. Personal   7. Social

4. Vocational   8. Political

What would he like to see happen within the next twenty or thirty years? What would he like to look back upon when he's seventy? What would it take for him to be able to say at the end of his life, "I have no regrets"? Raise a family? Become a commercial pilot? Move to France? Earn a million dollars? Compete in the Olympics? There must be *some* specificity—it wouldn't do to have as a goal, "To be happy," for instance. One must then ask, "What is it that would make me happy?"

After he lists his major goals, (there might be anywhere from two to ten) see if they fit in with his mission statement. If they don't, either the goals or the statement needs to change. It's OK for him to change the mission statement, by the way, especially during these early days when he's still trying to figure out what's important in his life. Frequently, when one starts thinking in terms of specific goals, the picture of the life goals clears up considerably. Also, he may want to revise it as he matures in Christ and gets a clearer picture of God's mission for him.

IV. Determine Intermediate Goals That Will Help Reach the Major Goals

Intermediate goals are stepping stones to the major goals. All of the intermediate goals stacked up equal one major goal. Remember Dr. Furman? The first intermediate goal he set for himself was to get accepted to medical school. That gave him something pretty specific to shoot at—and rather imperative. It was his first stepping stone. If he couldn't accomplish that, he could forget about becoming a surgeon.

My first intermediate goal in becoming a writer was, "Find out if you have any talent." If I had none, I should either forget the major goal, or take measures to *get* some talent. The next intermediate goal was, "Publish an article or book." Then, "Publish five articles or books." And finally, "Publish a bestseller." My desire was to serve Christ by having a fruitful ministry through writing, as mentioned in my mission statement. I figured that if there were quantity (five books and articles) and quality (a bestseller), those would be strong indications that I had indeed achieved a "fruitful ministry through writing." I have not yet accomplished all of those goals—but I'm working on them!

Have your disciple look at each of his major goals and, in the light of wise use of time, formulate the intermediate goals necessary to reach them. If he wants to become a commercial pilot, he'll first need to get his private pilot's license, then his commercial pilot's license, then get a job. If he wants to earn a million dollars, maybe he first needs to get out of debt. Then perhaps he needs to get a degree in finance. If she wants to raise a family, her first goal had better be to get married. Then she should have a baby. Very important.

V. Determine Short-Term Goals That Will Help Reach the Intermediate Goals

The next question the goal-setter needs to ask himself is, What can I do right now to get the ball rolling toward that first intermediate goal? His answer will be a list of short-term goals. During his second night in college chemistry, Dr. Furman realized that his entire goal structure depended on what he did *that night*. If he did poorly that night, he could fail a test. If he failed a test, he could get a low grade for the course. If his grades were low, no medical school. No medical school, no surgeon. Conversely, if he did well that night, the doors would continue to swing wider and wider along the way to that surgeon shingle. It all depended on how he used his immediate time, and that was: "Study now." He had to say no to friends who wanted him to join them for football and pizza. Nothing wrong with pizza or football, but he had determined that his mission, his major goal, his intermediate goal, the whole operation hinged on what he did, not next week, not in the morning, not later today, but right now. His first short-term goal: "Set study time each day and never depart from it."

In order to find out if I have any talent as a writer, I set short-term goals to talk with specific people I knew would be honest with me. They had read a lot of what I had already come up with, and without putting them on the spot, I was able to get their candid opinion. I don't know what *you* think, but they thought I had potential. Next I set a short-term goal to submit an idea to a publisher, along with a brief selection of the piece, in order to see what the pros thought. I accomplished that and they also gave me the green light, in the form of a signed contract! This signified to me that I did indeed have some talent as a writer. Not that it didn't need a major tune-up, but there was talent, nonetheless. The coast was clear to move on to my next intermediate goal: Publish an article or book. You hold in your hands the fulfillment of that goal! So now it's two down, two to go!

Have your disciple examine his intermediate goals one at a time and write out the stepping stones required to reach each one. These should describe specific activities in clear, concise terms *hooked to a time frame.* He may come up with twenty to thirty of them, so he should wade through the list and underline the ones he can handle within the near future. Those become his short-term goals.

This list may look suspiciously like a to-do list, but it has a grand purpose—to move him toward the goals God has set before him. It's a list of specific activities that have their roots sunk deep into his life's mission.

VI. Determine a Schedule That Will Reach Short-Term Goals and Screen Out Unnecessary Activities

The second-to-last mile in this journey is traversed when the short-term goals are placed on the disciple's schedule. The last is when they are completed. "Desire accomplished is sweet to the soul!" (Proverbs 13:19) It's not likely he'll ever taste that sweetness if he doesn't get those desires onto a timetable!

Make sure your disciple has a personal calendar. It could be a month-at-a-glance type, week-at-a-glance or day-by-day. It all depends on how much writing per square inch needs to go on it. It can be a "Day Timer," or a "Snoopy and Friends," or even a bunch of lined paper in a notebook. If one has a calendar, one can schedule things. If one can schedule things, when someone calls one to do something one doesn't really have time for, one can truthfully say, "One is busy at that time. How about some other time?" That's an important key to mastering your time—knowing when and how to say no. If your disciple schedules the activities that reflect his priority structure, people will not be able to come along and fill up his days and nights with pursuits he doesn't really value. Like the saying goes, "If you don't schedule your days, someone else will do it for you—and you probably won't like it."

Here are a few practical hints you could pass on to your disciple (and to yourself) about this matter of managing your time effectively:

A. *Make sure you are filled with the Spirit, asking God to control your days.* If you're not, you may be adding things to your schedule that He really doesn't want in there, and leaving things out that He wants in. As Gordon MacDonald wrote, "To bring order into one's personal life is to invite His control over every segment of one's life."[5]

B. *Re-evaluate your mission statement, major goals and intermediate goals periodically.* People change. They grow up. They get smarter. They figure out things they didn't know before. For these reasons, we can't assume that the goals we work out today will remain static the rest of our lives. It's a good idea to get away for a half-day all by yourself to ask God for whatever input He'd like to have as you think through your goals. You will probably find it necessary to change them from time to time. Set aside a time for this about every six months—that means put it on your schedule *today!*

C. *Schedule your days, weeks, months, years.* As I said before, if you don't, someone else will. Another tired but very true cliché is: If you fail to plan, plan to fail. The important things get scheduled, the unimportant things don't happen at all. Which category do these things belong in?

Personal Bible study time	Call Mom on her birthday
Personal prayer time	Family vacation
Son's football game	Have neighbors to dinner (yum)
Daughter's dance recital	Pay bills
Date with wife	Correspondence

If you don't get them on your calendar, they'll buzz right by you and you'll miss out on some of the most meaningful things in your life.

A couple of other activities you should include in your schedule are relaxation and family time.

By relaxation, I don't mean playing softball or fishing or sleeping at night. I'm talking about a little time each day, and a longer period once a week, when you can *just do nothing*. Total rest, physical and mental. Daydream. Look at the trees outside. Decompress. This will keep burn-out and mental and physical exhaustion at bay. If you don't schedule relaxation, it'll get crowded out — and you need it. If someone wants you to do something of low priority to you during your relaxation time, you can honestly say you're booked.

As for family time, I work all day, and often at night, too, but each evening from 6 to 8, at least three evenings a week (but usually five), I hold jealously for my wife and daughter. They also get Sunday afternoon, and it's a rare day when I let . someone else have it. People who have accomplished much in the world's eyes at the expense of their families die just like the rest of us. You rarely hear them lament from their death beds, "If only I'd spent more time at the office!" We can learn from them.

D. Use to-do lists. Prioritize them daily. What's the most important short-term goal you have today? Write it at the top of a piece of paper and put a big #1 next to it. What's next most important? Write it down and put a #2 next to it. List these goals as far as you need to go. Then, set about doing #1. Don't stop until it's done, no matter how long it takes. When it's finished, go on to #2 and hammer away at it 'til it's flat. Then move to #3. You may not check off your entire list, but you've gotten the most important things done, and they're the ones that really count. The rest can wait until tomorrow.

E. Just say no. When someone tries to get you to commit some of your hard-won time to something that does not lead you toward your goal, kindly, graciously, patiently, and with utmost decorum say, "WHAT?!! ARE YOU CRAZY? FORGET IT!!" Or something to that effect. If you don't have the guts to say no right then and there (or if you're not real sure what to say), just tell them you'd like to think and pray about it a while. After that, if you're still convinced it just isn't the best use of your time, get back in touch with them and say, "I just don't think I would be able to give it the time and attention it deserves. But I really appreciate your asking me!"

F. Don't fritter away your time on non-essentials. Do the insides of the trash cans *really* have to be spotless? Does the tree house *need* four coats of paint? Do I have to wash the car *every* Saturday? Can I leave *a little* dust on the garage floor? I know this will sound heretical to some, but I believe that we have to do some things in a mediocre fashion in order to have the time to do important things well. In Mark 7:31-37 Jesus took the time to do an excellent job of healing the deaf and dumb, but less important tasks, such as paying a non-essential tax or setting up a room for the Passover meal, He delegated (Matthew 17:24-27; Luke 22:7-13).

G. Get rid of "time-eaters." Assuming you did the Priority Assessment, were you amazed at how much time you spent watching television? reading the newspaper? browsing through magazines? These enterprises will eat up your time before you know what's happening. You might be better off making the ruthless decision to cancel your Mad Magazine subscription, or cut off your cable TV, or not take the paper.

H. Multiply your time. If you look, you'll find that many times during the day you could be doing two things at once. Driving, standing in line, waiting for a bus, waiting for an appointment, cooking, and walking are all prime time for doing double duty with Scripture memory, meditation, reading the Bible, listening to teaching tapes, writing letters, prioritizing your to-do list, etc. If it's not too redundant to say it, kill "dead time" wherever you find it!

I. Pray Godly perspectives and priorities into your life. Look up the following passages and add the appropriate ones to your daily prayer list:

1. This world is not my home; I'm just a-passin' through.

Matthew 6:19-21	2 Timothy 2:3,4
Matthew 6:33	James 4:14
1 Corinthians 3:11-15	1 Peter 1:17
Colossians 3:1-3	1 John 2:15,16

2. What time I have here should be invested for God's kingdom through the spiritual gifts, natural talents and acquired skills God has given me.

| 1 Corinthians 12:7 | 2 Timothy 1:6 |
| Colossians 3:17 | 1 Peter 4:10,11 |

3. God is the Master, I am the slave. He owns me and my time.

| John 6:38 | 1 Corinthians 6:19 |
| John 12:24 | 2 Corinthians 5:15 |

4. Time is running out.

| Psalm 39:4 | Luke 12:16-20 | John 9:4 |
| Mark 13:33-37 | Luke 12:35-40 | |

■ FURTHER RESOURCES

If you would like your disciple to complete some Bible studies on time management, consider the following:

"Ten Basic Steps Toward Christian Maturity" Bible Study Series by Campus Crusade for Christ:

- Step 8,   Lesson 1: "The Ownership Of God Our Father"
             Lesson 2: "Stewardship Of Our Time"

"The Discipleship Series"[6] also by Campus Crusade for Christ:

- Book 3, Lesson 7: "Planning for Leadership Development"

Design for Discipleship Bible Study Series by The Navigators:

- Book 6, Chapter 2: "The Responsible Steward"

■ ENDING THE SESSION

Write an appointment with your disciple on both of your calendars to get together and re-evaluate his mission statement and his major and intermediate goals in about three months. It will take him about that long to find out if his current inventory is valid.

Enter into a mutual accountability pact. Vow to pray for each other every day regarding your use of time. Check up and encourage each other to keep the bulk of your day-to-day activities in line with your goals. Make sure he writes down his mission statement and his major and intermediate goals and puts them in a place where he can see them frequently. On the wall across from the toilet is a good one . . .

■ ASSIGNMENT FOR NEXT TIME

The next topic to cover with your disciple, and the last in this group of "Newborn Care" objectives, is "Vision" — helping your disciple to see his individual significance to the kingdom of God and motivating him to continue in his spiritual development toward achieving that significance. By having him think through such heady things as his priorities, life's mission, major goals, etc., you already have him thinking much about where he fits into God's long-term plans. Next week you'll be tying everything together and, hopefully, he'll be eager to go on with the Lord and with you in your discipling relationship.

Dawson Trotman wrote a very inspiring booklet (not much bigger than a tract) called "Born To Reproduce."[7] It would be an excellent instrument for you to send home with your disciple to read during the week. As the booklet's name suggests, it demonstrates that the ultimate purpose for which humans are created is to reproduce spiritually, and it will set up next week's discussion nicely.

Another excellent booklet with the same effect is Campus Crusade's "Transferable Concept #7: How To Help Fulfill The Great Commission."[8] It explores vision and commitment from the standpoint of Christians working together world-wide to advance the kingdom of God. Both booklets stress the importance of individual commitment and corporate cooperation. The Transferable Concept is more team and evangelism oriented; "Born to Reproduce" is more disciplemaking oriented.

■ EVALUATION

Ask yourself these questions:

1. Does my disciple have a God-centered perspective on his personal priorities?

2. Does my disciple have a mission statement that reflects the Lordship of Christ? Does it fit the criteria of a good mission statement?

3. Does he have major and intermediate goals that fit in with his mission statement and priorities?

4. Does he formulate valid short-term goals that will help him achieve his larger goals?

5. Is he using a to-do list and a personal calendar?

6. Is he aware of the practical hints mentioned under subsection VI of the Suggestions for Growth section?

If you can answer each of those questions in the affirmative, then your disciple has met this training objective. If you need a little more input from him to determine your answers, you can ask him these questions:

1. As far as God is concerned, what should be our two highest priorities?

2. What is your idea now of your mission in life?

3. Do you feel that God maintains a central position in your mission statement?

4. What are some of your major goals? What do you want to see happening in your life twenty-five years from now? Describe a day in your life in the year 2013.

5. Do you still have a hard time saying no to requests for your time that will conflict with your priorities? (If so . . .) What do you plan to do about it?

6. How would you respond if someone were to ask you to serve on a prestigious committee at your church when you had the time for it but knew it didn't fit in with your priority structure?

7. Are some activities needlessly eating away your time? (If so . . .) What are they? What do you plan to do about them?

8. Are you maintaining a personal calendar and a daily prioritized to-do list?

9. How are you doing with your daily schedule? Are you able to stick to it?

10. How important is it to ask God daily to be in control of our schedules?

11. How are you doing at multiplying your time and utilizing dead time?

20 TRAINING OBJECTIVE #12

VISION

■ OBJECTIVE

The disciple understands how significant he is to the advance of the Kingdom of God, has a clear picture of some of the broad plans God has in mind for him, and is motivated to actively pursue his spiritual development and his relationship with God.

■ BIBLICAL BASIS FOR THIS OBJECTIVE

It's clear from Scripture that two things weighed heavily on the hearts of the writers of the New Testament, and therefore on the heart of God: (1) that God's children would mature; and (2) that they would spread His gospel to the ends of the earth. Here's a novel idea: Look up the following passages of Scripture and jot down a summary of each in your disciplemaker's notebook.

1. God wants His children to mature:

John 15:16	2 Corinthians 3:18	1 Thessalonians 2:19,20
John 21:15-17	2 Corinthians 13:9	1 Thessalonians 3:9,10
Romans 8:29	Ephesians 2:19-22	Hebrews 12:1,2
1 Corinthians 3:1,2	Ephesians 3:14-19	Hebrews 5:14
1 Corinthians 13:11	Ephesians 4:11-16	Hebrews 6:1
1 Corinthians 14:20	Colossians 1:28,29	1 Peter 2:2

323

2. God wants His gospel to be spread to the ends of the
   earth:

Matthew 4:19	John 3:16-18	2 Corinthians 5:18-20
Matthew 13:37,38	John 6:33	1 Timothy 1:15
Matthew 24:14	John 8:12	2 Peter 3:9
Matthew 26:13	John 12:32	Revelation 1:7
Matthew 28:19,20	John 17:18,21,23	Revelation 5:9
Mark 13:27	John 20:21	Revelation 11:15
Mark 16:15,16	Acts 1:8	Revelation 14:6
Luke 4:5-8	Acts 13:47	
Luke 24:46-48	Romans 9:17	

■ PEP TALK FOR THE DISCIPLEMAKER

When a certain fellow first started selling real estate, he took a listing for the worst-looking, most run-down, dilapidated house you ever saw, and the seller wanted $250,000 for it. The man's boss was beside himself. "How could you be so dumb?! You're *never* going to sell that place, especially at that price!"

The eager novice said, "Oh, yes I will! You just wait! I'll get it sold before the end of the week!"

Three days later, the salesman came dragging into the office, scratched, cut and bleeding, but triumphantly proclaimed, "I sold it!"

His boss said, "That's incredible! But what happened to you? Did you have to fight the customer to sell it?"

The realtor said, "No, but I had a rough time with his seeing-eye dog."

Without physical vision, people sometimes get swindled. And without spiritual vision, people get worse than swindled. Solomon said in Proverbs 29:18, "Where there is no vision, the people *perish*" (KJV). Solomon was referring to "revelations from God" about the present and the future. Back in those days, before most of the Bible had been written, God spoke to mankind primarily through prophets who had visions. Without them, people could not have known what God had on His mind, or what was in store for them down the pike. Without this knowledge, they would neglect or eventually forget about Him altogether. But now that we have both the Old and New Testaments, God speaks to us primarily through His Word. We can read God's thoughts any time we want.

God has plans for your disciple. *Big* plans. But if your disciple has no inkling as to what these plans might be, there is a good chance he'll lose his motivation and bail out. He'll "perish"—like a seed that falls on concrete, unable to grow or reproduce. Obviously, we're not talking about eternal perishing, but as far as living a victorious life and having an impact on this world, he'll be as good as dead.

If your disciple has vision he'll be much more motivated to strap himself in for the entire trip. He needs to grasp the fact that he himself, personally, has the potential of being used significantly by God to advance His Kingdom here on earth. He needs to see long-term value and personal benefit in that. He needs to focus on the things above, to value the eternal over the temporal. He needs to, as Dawson Trotman said, "Get on your heart what is on God's heart—the world."[1]

Besides, we're really not interested in investing our lives in people who will walk with the Lord for four months and then slip into neutral for the rest of their years on earth. That practice has gotten the body of Christ into an overweight and undernourished condition. Never before has the gospel made such astounding inroads into the world's population with such minimal effect. The land that most of today's church seems to have been sown on is the second type described in Matthew 13:

> And others fell upon the rocky places, where they did not have much soil; and immediately they sprang up, because they had no depth of soil. But when the sun had risen, they were scorched; and because they had no root, they withered away.

We *are* interested in investing our hard-won time in seed that falls on good ground—the kind that will produce thirty, sixty or a hundredfold. The kind that germinates and keeps on growing. As Paul said in 2 Corinthians 8:11, "But now finish doing it also; that just as there was the readiness to desire it, so there may be also the completion of it by your ability." Or as Solomon wrote in Ecclesiastes 7:8: "The end of a matter is better than its beginning." It's not that we don't love, care for and pray for those who turn back, but as far as our target activities, we'd all probably just as soon put our time in on those who will be going on with the Lord. It's normal to want to see some return for our labor.

There are things that we as disciplemakers can do to help "prepare the soil" to receive the seed. That's what disciplemaking is all about, isn't it? The planting, watering, fertilizing, weeding—to facilitate maximum growth. We can't *make* them grow—that's God's job—but we can help create the environment that encourages growth. Actually, we've been doing that all along. But we could add one last squirt of high-potency fertilizer: vision.

There is no sure-fire way of instilling long-term commitment in a person, but vision can lead to commitment. We impart vision by *teaching* about it, *modeling* it, and *praying* it into our disciples, as we learned back in Chapter 4 with the Three Pillars of Disciplemaking: *Content, Relationship* and *Prayer*. You'll have to hold yourself accountable on the modeling and praying parts, but I can give you a few ideas concerning what to teach.

■ BROACHING THE SUBJECT

Assuming you asked your disciple to read either *Born to Reproduce* or *How to Help Fulfill the Great Commission,* as was suggested in Training Objective #11's Assignment For Next Week section, use it to get your discussion off the ground. Here are a few launching questions if he read *Born to Reproduce:*

1. What did you think of it?

2. What impressed you the most about it?

3. Would you say you're ready to become a "spiritual reproducer" yet? (If no, go to question 4; if yes, go to question 5.)

4. What do you think it will take to get you there? What do you think is involved in being a spiritual reproducer?

5. Do you *want* to be a spiritual reproducer?

6. (If so . . .) Why? (If not . . .) Why not?

If he read "How to Help Fulfill the Great Commission," use some of these questions:

1. What did you think of it?
2. What impressed you the most about it?
3. Can you remember what the "Great Commission" is?
4. To whom was the Great Commission given?
5. What do you think we need to do in order to help fulfill the Great Commission?
6. Helping to fulfill the Great Commission — is that something you are personally interested in?
7. (If so . . .) Why? (If not . . .) Why not?

After discussing his answers a little, I'd move into the material by saying something like the following:

We've covered a lot of territory over the last few months, Sam. You've learned how to be filled with the Spirit, the importance of "drawing from the new well instead of the old"; you've learned some practical things you can do to help yourself mature in your walk with Christ, such as praying, studying the Bible, fellowshipping and witnessing, how to defend yourself in spiritual warfare and how to get the most out of your days through efficient time management.

I was really impressed with some of the major goals you came up with last week, too, especially the one about . . . [Hopefully he has a goal or two in there about long-term commitment to Christ and/or having a ministry for Christ. Highlight those.] I don't know if you have any idea how reachable those goals are for you. I think God is more interested in helping you reach your goals than even *you* are!

In God's eyes, you are an extremely significant person, and you have the potential of being greatly used by Him to further His kingdom here on earth. I'm not talking about becoming another Billy Graham or anything, but wherever you are, God wants to use you to extend His kingdom, through whatever gifts and talents He's given you.

Let's take the rest of this time today looking at what might be in store for you around the bend.

■ SUGGESTIONS FOR GROWTH

In order to move the disciple to the point of seeing his own significance in God's broad scheme, and of being motivated to deepen his commitment, I like to progress through three major concepts:

    I. What is important to God?

    II. What are some of His important plans for you?

    III. What do you need to do to fit in with His plans?

We'll be wading through a lot of Scripture here, for which there is no need for apology. It's God's Word that will cut your disciple's heart to the quick, so we should use it. I'd suggest you spend an extra amount of time in prayer before this one, asking the Holy Spirit to use His Word mightily in your disciple's life during this session. As usual, you need to look up the references first, decide on which ones will mean the most to your disciple and share them with him. Allow him to read the verse and comment on what it means to him.

I. What Is Important to God?

There are lots of things important to God, and if you've got a spare decade, we could go into them right now. If you don't, let's just look at three things. If we know what is important to God, it's a good first-step toward making them important to us.

A. The Eternal Over the Temporal. We humans tend to put so much emphasis on the here-and-now. We often hear slogans like, "Live for today," and "You go around only once in life, so grab all the gusto you can." God, on the other hand, while not dismissing the temporal as totally irrelevant (after all, we *live* there!), places a much greater emphasis on the eternal.

Matthew 18:8,9   John 12:24,25   2 Corinthians 4:16-18

How can we as Christians involve ourselves in the eternal? In the Bible, three things are listed as being eternal. To the extent that we are involved in those things, we are involved in the eternal. Those three things are:

- God: Psalms 90:2; 93:2; 102:24-27

- The Word of God: Psalm 138:2; Mark 13:31; 1 Peter 1:25

- People: 1 Thessalonians 4:16,17 (Christians); 2 Thessalonians 1:7-10 (non-Christians)

Eventually, we Christians all will stand before the judgment seat of Christ, not to be judged as to our eternal destiny — that has already been settled — but according to our works, what we did while here on earth. Activities that fall outside the range of eternal will be burned up, gone, as if they had never happened. But those that are of eternal quality will remain, and they will be rewarded (1 Corinthians 3:10-15).

B. The Spiritual Over the Material. This goes along with **A** above, but hits a little closer home for most of us. It gives us something to sink our teeth into.

Many Americans have gone absolutely bananas with their materialism. As a recent "Cathy"[2] comic pointed out, we buy safari clothes that will never be near a jungle; aerobic footgear that will never set foot in an aerobics class; deep-sea dive watches that will never get damp; four-wheel-drive vehicles that will never experience a hill; 27-time-zone international clocks in indestructible molded alloy cases that will never leave our zip code. We have entered the age of abstract materialism: moving past the things we want and need, and craving the things that have nothing to do with our lives!

God, on the other hand, is much more interested in the spiritual than the material. Again, it's not that He advocates all His children becoming Essene monks, eschewing all material possessions — He just wants us to put our affections in the right place.

Matthew 6:19-21	Matthew 22:37-40	Colossians 3:1-3
Matthew 6:24-34	Luke 9:24,25	
Matthew 19:16-30	Luke 12:16-21	

C. Availability Over Ability. God isn't looking for a bunch of high-powered, well-traveled, over-educated wiz-kids to come up with and execute their big ideas. He's looking for faithful, available servants who will carry out *His* big ideas. First Peter 5:6 says: "God is opposed to the proud, but gives grace to the humble." Throughout the Bible God resists the activities of the proud and joins the team of the underdog, a sentiment reflected in the people He chooses to be His ambassadors.

Matthew 11:25	1 Corinthians 1:26-29
1 Corinthians 1:18-21	James 2:5

God doesn't need men and women of great ability. All He needs are people with availability, people who are willing and able to do what He wants them to do, say what He wants them to say, go where He wants them to go, and be what He wants them to be. He doesn't care what your background has been, what challenges you are facing, what handicaps you have. All He wants is for you to give Him your five loaves and two fishes, and then stand back!

Think about some of the great men and women of the Bible — how little they had going for them and yet how mightily God used them.

Abraham: Idolater (Genesis 11:26-31; Joshua 24:2); Abram and his relatives were Chaldeans, known to have worshipped Nanna, the moon goddess, who required strict obedience); nothing of significance done in his life until he was well up in years (Genesis 17:1-8). Became the father of the Jews, ancestor of the Savior (Genesis 12:1-3; 15:1-7).

Jacob: Liar, cheater (Genesis 27:1-40); chased from his homeland by his brother (Genesis 27:40-45). Became the progenitor of the twelve tribes of Israel (Genesis 35:22b-26) and heir to the blessings of Abraham (Genesis 28:1-4).

Joseph: Papa's pet; tattletale; hated by his brothers (Genesis 37:1-4); kidnap victim (Genesis 37:18-28); sold into slavery (Genesis 39:1); falsely accused of rape (Genesis 39:7-19); jailbird (Genesis 39:20; 41:1). Became the prime minister of Egypt and saved the embryonic nation of Israel (Genesis 41:37-45; 45:4-13; 50:19-21).

Moses: Murderer (Exodus 2:11,12); fugitive (Exodus 2:13-15); sheepherder in exile (Exodus 2:22; 3:1); a man of great reluctance and little faith (Exodus 3:11,13; 4:1, 10,13). Became God's primary ambassador to earth, the one with whom God spoke "face to face" (Genesis 33:11) and whom God spoke of as "My servant" (Joshua 1:2).

Jephthah: Illegitimate child (Judges 11:1); cast out (Judges 11:2,7); rabble-rouser (Judges 11:3). Became a judge in Israel and was greatly used by God to free the nation (Judges 11:32,33; 12:7).

Ruth: A Moabitess in exile, widowed, childless, destitute (Ruth 1:1-18). God set her up with Boaz, a wealthy land-owner, and they became the great-grandparents of King David (Ruth 4:21,22).

David: Shepherd boy, youngest child of an insignificant family (1 Samuel 16:1-12); weird-looking because of his red hair and pale skin (1 Samuel 16:12). Used by God to slay Goliath, embolden Israel (1 Samuel 17:26-53), and later to bring Israel to the pinnacle of world power (2 Samuel 7:1,18-29).

Jonah: Originally rebelled against God's orders to preach (Jonah 1:1-3), and got real down-in-the-mouth about it (Jonah 1:15-17). Used by God to save the city of Nineveh (Jonah 3:1-10).

Esther: An orphan, raised by her elder cousin, an exile in a pagan country (Esther 2:5-7). Became queen to King Ahasuerus (Esther 2:17) and kept Israel from annihilation (Esther 4:13-16; 7:2-10; 8:5-12).

Peter: All mouth (Matthew 26:33-35); impetuous (Matthew 17:4); puffed-up (Matthew 16:21-23); openly denied Christ in His hour of need (Matthew 26:69-75). Became one of the all-time pillars of the Christian movement (Acts 2:14-41; 3:1-26; 10:1-48; wrote 1 and 2 Peter).

Paul: Vicious, zealous persecutor of Christians, sent

many of God's children to prison and death (Acts 8:3; 9:1,2; 22:4,5; 26:9-11; 1 Corinthians 15:9). He turned out to be the most influential Christian ever to have lived. (He was inspired to write *half* of the books of the New Testament.)

Jesus: Carpenter's son from a backwater town in Galilee. Made salvation available to the whole world.

To go over the *available servants* mentioned above, you could name them one by one and ask your disciple if he can think of what hardship he or she might have been up against, and how God used them in spite of it (or maybe *because of* it). For the ones he isn't familiar with, either you supply the information or the two of you look up the references supplied. Now, back to your discussion with your disciple . . .

God has done some pretty significant things through some seemingly insignificant people! All that was required was that they be *available,* willing to be used by God however He wanted. Did you know that it is possible for you *personally* to reach the world for Christ? You don't need to be a pope or a Billy Graham or have a billion dollars or anything. All you have to do is faithfully apply a biblical principle. It's found in 2 Timothy 2:2. Paul wrote this to his disciple Timothy: "And the things which you have heard from me in the presence of many witnesses, these entrust to faithful men, who will be able to teach others also."

Notice the "things" were to be passed through four generations: from Paul to Timothy to "faithful men" to "others also." This is called "spiritual multiplication."

Here's how it works: First you win one person to the Lord each year and train that person to live a victorious, reproductive Christian life. Then the two of you do the same thing with two more people the next year, thus doubling your numbers each year thereafter. After 5 years there would be 32 of you. Big deal. After 10 years, your numbers would be up to 1024. Still not too impressive for 10 years' labor. But at 15 years you're up to 32,768. By the end of the 20th year, your ranks have grown to

1,048,576! Sometime during the 28th year, you have reached the entire population of the earth for Christ!

Sam, you're my "faithful man." And it's been my prayer for the last several months that you would eventually come to the point of being able to "teach others also." As long as we can keep the chain going, we have a chance to win the whole world to Jesus Christ!

II. What Are Some of His Important Plans for You?

One more thing is very important to God, and that's *YOU!* You are *eternal,* you are *spiritual,* and you are becoming more *available* all the time. When God redeemed you from the hand of the enemy, He did not intend for you to come in from the battle, get cleaned up and go sit in a chair for the rest of the war. He redeemed you for many important reasons, not the least of which was to help Him in His plans to redeem others. There is no way I can tell what *specific* plans God has for you, but the Bible can give us some good ideas of His *general* plans. The specific plans will flow from the general ones. Let's look up a few passages and see if we can spot some of those plans.

A. His Plans for You in This Life

1. To lead you to a positive future:
   Jeremiah 29:11   Psalm 16:11   1 Corinthians 2:9
2. To enlighten you:
   John 8:12   John 8:32
3. To increase the intimacy of your walk with Christ:
   Isaiah 40:11   Philippians 3:10 (especially see Amplified Bible)
4. To supply all your needs:
   2 Corinthians 9:8   Philippians 4:19
5. To strengthen you:
   Isaiah 41:10   Philippians 4:13
6. To help you have a significant, positive impact on the world:
   Matthew 5:13-16   John 15:16   Ephesians 4:11-13

7. To help you develop and use the unique gift(s) He has given you for the good of the Body:
    1 Corinthians 12:4-30   1 Peter 4:10,11
8. To formulate a training program designed to meet your specific needs:
    Deuteronomy 8:3   Psalm 32:8,9
9. To discipline you when you need it:
    Proverbs 3:11,12   Hebrews 12:6-8
10. To help you grow in Christlikeness:
    2 Corinthians 3:18   2 Peter 1:3,4

B. His Plans for You for Eternity:

1. To let you see, know, and experience first-hand the presence of God and Christ:
    John 17:3,24   1 Corinthians 13:9-12
2. To install you in an eternal mansion:
                 John 14:2,3
3. To give you a new, supernatural body like Christ's:
    1 Corinthians 15:35-53   2 Corinthians 5:1-4
4. To give you authority so you may reign with Christ in eternity:
    1 Corinthians 6:2 2 Timothy 2:12 Revelation 5:9,10
5. To give you the fortunes you have amassed through your good works on earth:
    Matthew 6:19-21   1 Corinthians 3:11-14
6. To abolish your hunger, thirst and sadness forever: Revelation 7:16,17
7. To have you eat from the Tree of Life; drink from the Water of Life; see the curse lifted from earth; reign with Christ forever:
                 Revelation 22:1-5

III. What Do You Need to Do to Fit in With His Plans?

Many of the plans that God has for you are "unconditional," meaning they'll happen no matter what. But quite a number of His plans and blessings for you are "conditional." Let's take a look at several verses of Scripture to see what we are responsible for in order to see

God's plans accomplished in our lives.

Following is a short list of some of the many conditional promises God has made to His children in His Word. It's by no means an exhaustive list. All we want to do here is help our disciples see that God is not some celestial Good Humor Man, distributing eternal goodies to whoever happens to be around. We want them to understand that there are *both* benefits *and* responsibilities for those who would experience the abundant life. We're hoping to answer the questions our disciple may be silently asking: Why *should* I go on? What's in it for me?

Take a sheet of paper and divide it into three columns. At the top of the left-hand column print "Verse." At the top of the middle, print "If I . . . " At the top of the right-hand column, print "God will . . . " something like this:

VERSE	IF I . . .	GOD WILL . . .
Ezra 8:22		
Job 36:11		
Psalm 34:10		
. . . etc.		

Together, look up as many of the above and following verses as you want, and write in the corresponding requirements and benefits. If you don't see your favorite promises here, by all means add them!

Psalm 37:3-5	Daniel 11:32	2 Corinthians 5:10
Psalm 37:23,24	Matthew 5:3-12	Philippians 4:6,7
Psalm 55:22	Matthew 6:33	2 Timothy 2:20,21
Psalm 81:10	Matthew 10:28-30	2 Timothy 4:8
Psalm 84:11	Matthew 10:32	James 1:12
Psalm 91:14-16	Luke 6:22,23	1 Peter 5:2-4
Proverbs 3:5,6	Luke 6:38	1 Peter 5:6
Proverbs 16:7	John 12:24-26	1 John 1:9
Isaiah 1:19,20	John 14:21	Revelation 2:10
Isaiah 40:31	Romans 8:28	
Isaiah 58:10-12	1 Corinthians 9:24-27	

■ FURTHER RESOURCES

If you'd like some additional fill-in-the-blank type studies on topics that could help your disciple gain vision, select a few from the following:

"The Discipleship Series"[3] by Campus Crusade for Christ:

- Book 2, Lesson 6: "Practicing Spiritual Multiplication"
   Lesson 7: "Living in Light of Eternity"
- Book 3, Lesson 9: "Fulfilling the Great Commission"

Design for Discipleship Bible Study Series by The Navigators:

- Book 3, Chapter 1: "Maturing in Christ"
- Book 4, Chapter 1: "The Call to Fruitful Living"
- Book 5, Chapter 5: "The Return of Christ"
- Book 6, Chapter 1: "What Is a Disciple?"
   Chapter 5: "World Vision"

Also, you could share the little booklet by Dawson Trotman called *The Need of the Hour.*[4] In it, Trotman exposes this need as being an army of men and women "who want what Jesus Christ wants and believe He wants to give them the power to do what He has asked."

Of course, if you haven't done so yet, you should now pass on to your disciple either *Born To Reproduce,*[5] also by Trotman, or Transferable Concept #7: "How to Help Fulfill the Great Commission,"[6] by Bill Bright. Or pass on both — they address long-term commitment from two different perspectives.

■ ENDING THE SESSION

The main idea behind this session is that your disciple would come out of it motivated to maintain or deepen his commitment to the Lord and to the ministry He has for him to fulfill. The primary way he would demonstrate this commitment is by his eagerness to continue to meet with you for further discipling.

You may recall that in chapter 8, when we were talking about enticing a person into this discipling process, I recommended you ask him to commit to a five-month block of time in which you would go over twelve subjects that would be vital to his future spiritual health and growth. I also recommended you tell him that at the end of that period he would have the option of going on with the program or shelving it indefinitely. Today is the day of reckoning. You might approach it something like this:

YOU: Well, Sam, we've done it! We've completed the twelve subjects that I told you a few months ago would help you get established and grow in your new walk with God. Do you think it has helped you?

DISCIPLE: Yes! Of course! Tremendously! Wonderfully! Fantastically! Incredibly! To the max. (I'm trying to be a little optimistic about his response, here. Did you notice?)

YOU: I'm glad to hear that! You've come a long way through the past few months, no doubt about that! But I'm wondering—do you think you've still got a ways to go yet? Especially after today's session and all we've seen about the things God has in store for you, do you think there is still more for you to learn?

DISCIPLE: Unquestionably. No doubt about it. I can't begin to tell you . . . (Still optimistic.)

YOU: I don't suppose *any* of us will ever come to the point of saying, "I know it all now. No need to learn anything else." There is always more that the Lord wants us to learn. That's the *definition* of a disciple, anyway, "a learner." When we stop being a learner, we stop being a disciple. Remember that, at the beginning of this series, I told you I would give you the option of continuing your training when we finished the twelve subjects? Well, now's the time to decide. Have you given any thought as to whether you want to keep meeting as we have been?

DISCIPLE: I've given it some thought, but I have a few questions. If we continued to meet together, would it be for another five months or what?

YOU: If we continued on, I think we are talking about a one-year commitment. Obviously, we can flex some on that. One or the other of us is bound to have to miss once in a while, with business trips, vacations, etc. But overall, I think we're looking at a year.

DISCIPLE: Will I be done at the end of that year?

YOU: Actually, no one's ever "done." But you'll be a lot further along than you are now. At the end of a year, if we are able to be pretty consistent in our times together and if your commitment level remains high, I could see you being firmly established in your walk with the Lord, with Bible study, prayer and fellowship being fixed habits in your life. I see you taking advantage of many opportunities God gives you to share your faith, and doing so with ease and confidence. I see you having discovered what your spiritual gifts are and beginning to use them for the good of the Body. I see you personally helping other people mature just like I'm helping you. And I have no doubt that, if things keep going as they are, you'll be helping and encouraging *me* in *my* walk with the Lord! However, even then, there will be more to learn. But at the end of that year, we would do again what we're doing today, re-evaluating whether or not you want to continue meeting with me. If you do go on, eventually we'll be spending less and less time with each other, and more time with younger Christians who need training. It's not like you'd be stuck meeting with me for an hour and a half each week for the rest of your life! But that bond and relationship will always be there.

DISCIPLE: This coming year, would it involve about the same amount of my time each week?

YOU: To be honest with you, the time commitment will be going up. My objective is to help you not only mature in your walk and faith, but also to help you develop your own ministry, and begin to do with others what I've done with you. This will involve not only the time it takes for *you* to learn, but also the time it takes for you to teach others. This won't happen all at once, but over the next year, the time you put in on your dis-

cipleship could gradually double—or even triple. It
depends on you, and how much time you are able to put
into it.

DISCIPLE: Well, I can't imagine anything I'd rather do!
Where do I sign? When do we start? (There's that op-
timism again . . .)

What if he says no?

There is one fact we must all face, however. Some will not
want to go on meeting with you. They'll come up with very
plausible excuses—some fairly legitimate, some not. If that
happens to you, *don't* do two things. First, *don't push it.* If he's
not ready, he's not ready. It's better that you let him bail out
now instead of after you've invested a year of your life in him.
You can pray for him, do fellowshippy things together, encourage him as you have the opportunity, and stimulate him
to love and good deeds. Perhaps he'll reconsider down the road
a piece. But you can't squeeze a commitment out of him that
he's unwilling to make.

When I was in college, I challenged a young Christian in my
dorm to a discipling relationship. He was a freshman on the
basketball team and showed excellent leadership potential. He
thought about it, but declined, saying that he didn't think he
would have the time. I said fine, backed off, and just prayed for
and stayed in casual contact with him. A year later he regretted
his decision, and wanted to be trained. I was already over-com-
mitted to several other guys, but was able to have some input
while others did the lion's share of work with him. Tim Hall
went on to have a great impact for Christ at Colorado State as
one of their top hoopsters ever, joined the Athletes in Action
Basketball Team where he influenced thousands of people to
faith in Christ over a seven-year period, graduated from Denver Seminary, and he and his wife are now missionaries in Italy.
You see, you never know what God's going to do in a person's
life. He might do it right now, or He might wait awhile!

Second, if he says no, *don't let it get to you!* Don't allow Satan
to discourage you over it. Your job was to plant, water and fer-
tilize. God is in control of the growing *and* the timetable of

maturation. Don't start second-guessing, trying to figure out where you went wrong. In all probability, you didn't go wrong anywhere. You did your job, now leave the results to God. Move on to the next assignment He has for you, and be assured of this: God's Word does not return void (Isaiah 55:10,11). Your faithfulness *will* bear fruit eventually, one way or another.

Jim Gibson was a fellow-member of the Colorado State Track Team while I was there. After helping this half-miler begin his walk with Christ, I started to disciple him. I couldn't get Jim nailed down to an actual week-by-week meeting, but we spent a lot of time together on track trips, and had occasional bursts of consistent discipling encounters on campus. When we went our separate ways after graduation, however, I didn't feel that I had done a very good job with him. He hadn't responded the way I had hoped, and I felt primarily at fault.

Years later, out of the blue, here comes a letter from Jim! He'd deepened his commitment to Christ and was enrolled in Southern Baptist Seminary in Louisville! He eventually graduated, is on fire for Jesus and is now a pastor in Canada. My glum thoughts about Jim were totally unfounded, and they demonstrated my lack of faith in God's ability "to will and to work for His good pleasure" (Philippians 2:13). Don't let Satan drag you into the same useless trap.

■ ASSIGNMENT FOR NEXT TIME

Assuming he has decided to go on with the program, you now have some big decisions ahead of *you*! The question you need to ask is, "Where should he go from here?" You'll need to figure out where his strengths and weaknesses are, and you'll need to know what his next, most crucial step of growth is. The Holy Spirit is the one who knows what those are, and you can get the information from Him.

The last section of this book will give you a strategy of discerning where your disciple's greatest needs lie and how you might map out a long-term plan to meet those needs with the help of the Holy Spirit. What you do next time will depend on that plan, so I suggest you read chapter 21 for some insight.

If he has decided not to go on with you, your assignment is

to pray for him daily, to ask God to cause your love for him to increase, to encourage him in his growth "off the cuff" as you have opportunities, and to expect great things for him from God. You're not allowed to harass him or make him feel guilty, like a failure or a spiritual "second-class citizen." You have not been called to judge, you've been called to love. But keep your eyes open — God may be doing something in his heart yet!

■ EVALUATION

Ask yourself these questions:

1. Does my disciple understand that he is personally very significant to God?

2. Does he understand that it is within the plan of God to use him in a significant way to further His kingdom?

3. Does he understand some of the broad plans that God has determined for all of His children?

4. Does he understand that some of God's promises are "unconditional" while some are "conditional"?

5. Does he understand that if we desire to experience all the privileges God has in mind for us, we also have certain personal responsibilities to carry out?

6. Does he seem motivated to pursue his spiritual development and his relationship with God?

7. Does he seem motivated to eventually develop a ministry of his own?

If you can answer yes to each of those questions, your disciple has met this training objective. If you need more input from him to determine your answers, here are some questions:

1. When you think of how God looks at you, do you see yourself as just another face in the crowd, or do you see yourself with Him one to one, friend to friend?

2. What do you think your ministry potential is? I mean, if everything went perfectly for you, how much of an impact do you think you might be able to have on this world for Christ?

3. If you could name it, what one thing would you like

God to use you for in this world?

4. Of all the general plans that you know God has in mind for you, which one excites you the most?

5. What do you think some of God's *specific* plans for you might be?

6. On a scale of one to ten, with one being a brand new convert and ten being a fully mature Christian, how close would you say you now are to having "arrived" spiritually?

7. On a scale of one to ten, how motivated are you to carry on your spiritual development?

8. Where does your relationship with God fit on your list of life priorities?

9. The Bible says that "God causes the growth" (1 Corinthians 3:7), but do we have any responsibilities in that process? Or does God accomplish what He wants to regardless of our participation?

10. How does the idea of you someday having a ministry of your own affect you? Do you feel nervous about it? Confident? Eager to get on with it?

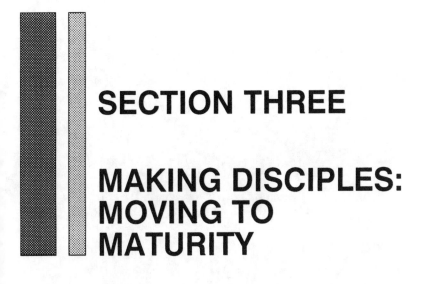

SECTION THREE

MAKING DISCIPLES: MOVING TO MATURITY

21
LONG-TERM DISCIPLEMAKING

Now you've done it. You've *really* put your foot in it. You've helped someone get established in the basics of his faith, and, with the Holy Spirit, you have motivat :d him to go on with the Lord. Now he's looking to *you* for direction. Isn't that great?

So where do we go from here? Well, I'm afraid this is my stop—time for me to get off the bus. But I will not leave you without a plan.

You can carry on the "disciple-sensitive, training-objective-oriented" strategy we looked at in chapter 7 indefinitely. To do this, you:

1. Determine your disciple's current level of spiritual growth (note strengths, weaknesses, previous training, etc.).

2. Determine his next crucial step of growth.

3. Formulate a training objective relating to that step.

4. Design curriculum that will help him reach that training objective.

5. Develop an evaluation so you will know when he has reached the training objective.

This procedure looks fairly simple, but when we actually try it on a live, human subject, it becomes quite complicated, because people are complicated! If we can put a man on the moon, though, we can work out a procedure to launch a person toward spiritual maturity. The first thing to do is find the starting point. If you were the one who led your disciple to the Lord, and if you've just taken him through the twelve Newborn Care Training Objectives, you already have a pretty good handle on where he is. But if you've picked up a disciple who has been a

Christian for some time, you may need a period of assessment to determine his current spiritual status.

To evaluate somebody, you need something to measure him against. I'm 6' 5" — most people would say that's tall. They say that because when they measure 6' 5" on a wall and make a mark, they usually have to tilt their heads back a little. They have an efficient system for evaluating height. Is there a system for evaluating spiritual maturity?

The only one I know of is the Bible. In it you will find hundreds of specific examples. God says time and again, "This is what I want you to become. This is what I want you to do. These are the things that please Me." At the same time He also says, "If you're doing *this,* you need to change, to grow, to mature. It's not acceptable behavior. Grow out of it."

The trouble is, these statements are all jumbled up together. They're not set forth in any organized fashion. The Bible was written as historical narratives, poetry, prophetic messages from God, and letters to individuals or groups. It was not written in sequence as to motivation or behavior from spiritual infancy to spiritual maturity. The spiritual "rulers" are hard to find. To some extent the Bible is arranged according to chronological events. Genesis is about what God did first, and Revelation is about what He will do last — everything else is what God's doing in the middle. As His servants, we need to become aware of what God's doing here in the middle and *fit in* with His program. We've got to dive into the Word with both feet and rummage around until we come out with growth principles in an order we can use.

This could take a while. So to save time, I've tried to do it for you. As you already know, the Bible is quite clear about four stages of growth: *baby* (Hebrews 5:12,13); *child* (Ephesians 4:14,15); *adolescent* (1 John 2:14*b*); and *adult* (Ephesians 4:13).

I wrote those four "Levels of Growth," along with their key verses listed above, across the top of a very large piece of paper.

Then I wanted to see if Christian growth could be categorized. It could — into these seven separate areas:

1. *Prayer* — The act of communing or conversing with God

(Luke 11:1).

2. *The Word* — Activities undertaken to absorb and apply the Bible to one's daily life (John 8:31).

3. *Witnessing* — Attitudes and actions that influence non-Christians toward salvation (John 15:8).

4. *Fellowship* — Attitudes and actions that enhance one's relationships with other Christians and build up the Body of Christ (John 13:35).

5. *Personal Growth* — Attitudes and actions that help one develop a closer relationship with God and a more Christlike lifestyle (Matthew 10:25). (Includes character development; devotional life; ability to deal with adversity, Satan, temptation and sin; discernment of the will of God; and exercise and diet.)

6. *Ministry* — Specialized, concentrated activities in specific groups or by individuals utilizing God-given gifts, natural talents and acquired skills to:
   a. serve those who are in need;
   b. influence non-Christians toward salvation;
   c. encourage Christians toward spiritual maturity (Matthew 28:19,20).

7. *Family* — Attitudes and actions that enhance one's relationship with his family and make him better able to fulfill his unique role and responsibilities within his family (Joshua 24:15).

I wrote each of these "Areas of Growth," along with their key verses, down the left side of my very large sheet of paper. With the growth levels forming a horizontal axis across the top, and the growth areas forming a vertical axis along the side, my paper looked a lot like a "scope and sequence chart." I drew lines vertically separating each level, and horizontally separating each area. Thus was born the "Disciplemaking Growth Grid." Only one problem — except for the axes, the grid was blank.

Now came the fun. I wanted to find out if the Bible could tell us what a growing disciple would look like in each area, at each level. This information would put some content into the grid's boxes. So I took on the grid, one area at a time.

First, I did an exhaustive study of prayer, looking up every verse on that subject that I could find in the Bible. I found more than 160 passages that had something to say about prayer (not counting parallel Gospel passages and scores of similar praise and thanksgiving passages in the psalms, which I lumped together). I examined each verse and tried to discern what it said ought to characterize someone who is mature in the area of prayer, ending up with about seventy characteristics.

Next, I combined near-duplicate characteristics, then summarized them and grouped them together. When the smoke cleared, I had squeezed them all into these five "profile statements":

1. Is becoming increasingly knowledgeable about and sensitive to God's priorities and concerns, which form the backbone of his prayer life.

2. Sees God as the primary agent to affect the outcome of any situation or concern, and firmly believes that God *will* consider and *will* act on his requests.

3. Prays regularly, frequently, often for long periods of time, sometimes accompanied by fasting.

4. Regularly takes an active role in group prayer sessions.

5. Regularly observes times of prayer that are steeped in worship.

These statements went into the box under "Adult," across from "Prayer." Then I worked my way back through adolescent, child and baby, figuring out the logical steps one would need to take to reach that adult level. I constantly referred back to the 160 Bible passages and the 70 characteristics, and took into account what characterizes a growing Christian at each level along with the importance of hitting all three elements of growth: head knowledge (information), heart knowledge (convictions and motivation), and hand knowledge (actions).

When I had completed the prayer band on the grid, I moved on to the Word band and followed the same procedure. I continued on through all seven areas of growth. After about eight months, I emerged from my office with a completed Disciplemaking Growth Grid, with each box containing from three to ten profile statements. This provided me with an extensive, fairly detailed profile of what a growing disciple should look like in each area, at each level.

In the following pages I will share with you the fruit of that study. But first a word about the numbering system. Each profile statement (which later you will turn into training objectives, by the way) is indexed by a three-digit number. The first digit (the hundreds place) indicates the growth level. Thus, all baby profile statements will be in the 100s. Child profile statements will be in the 200s, adolescent in the 300s and adult in the 400s, just like the numbering of your freshman, sophomore, junior and senior classes in high school or college. The second digit (the tens place) refers to the growth area. Prayer = 10s, the Word = 20s, witnessing = 30s, fellowship = 40s, personal growth = 50s, ministry = 60s and family = 70s. The third digit (the ones place) refers to the number of a profile statement within a specific area/level box. For instance, there are nine profile statements for a disciple at the child level (200s) in the area of witnessing (30s), and they are numbered 230, 231, 232, 233 . . . 238.

OK! Time to move on to the actual profile statements. All told there are 211 of them. (Some numbered profile statements may have several sub-statements, which could actually stand alone, so I'm counting them as full-fledged profile statements.) Browse through them on the next several pages, and I'll pick you up on the other side.

GROWTH AREA	**LEVEL 1 – BABY** Profile Statements	**LEVEL 2 – CHILD** Profile Statements
PRAYER	110. Understands the basics of prayer, including: a. types of prayer (Adoration, Confession, Thanksgiving, Supplication – ACTS) b. proper motivation c. praying with others d. how and why God answers prayer 111. Is convinced that God is personal, and that He derives great pleasure from our communication with Him 112. Has a time of personal prayer three or four times a week, each session lasting 4 to 8 minutes	210. Understands the principles involved in getting yes answers to prayer 211. Has a good grasp of the sub-types of prayer, including: intercession, petition, prayer without words, waiting on God, self-examination before God, fellowshipping with God, praying prepared prayers, praying Scripture 212. Is convinced that prayer IS the ministry, and that his prayer life will greatly affect his fruitfulness in all other areas of growth 213. Has a daily prayer time of 7 to 10 minutes 214. Is able to pray out loud in a small group situation 215. Prays spontaneously throughout the day 216. Is beginning to pray for more than physical needs and shows an increasing concern for the things on God's heart 217. Is growing in the art of worshiping God

LEVEL 3 – ADOLESCENT Profile Statements	**LEVEL 4 – ADULT** Profile Statements
310. Is increasingly challenged to deepen his prayer life through exposure to the lives of some of the great "prayer warriors" of history (biographies) and through reading some of the great classics on prayer	410. Is becoming increasingly knowledgeable about, and sensitive to, God's priorities and concerns, which form the backbone of his prayer life
311. His convictions regarding the efficacy of prayer are deepening as he breaks increasingly substantial faith barriers	411. Sees God as the primary agent to affect the outcome of any situation of concern, and firmly believes that God will consider and will act on his requests
312. Knows that God earnestly desires communion with him and is eager to comply	412. Prays regularly, frequently, often for long periods of time, sometimes accompanied by fasting
313. Is increasing length of daily prayer time to 20 or 30 minutes	413. Regularly takes an active role in group prayer sessions
314. Is able to pray for one hour straight	414. Times of prayer are steeped in worship
315. Is able to fast for 24 hours	
316. Praises and thanks God naturally and frequently, both in formal times of prayer and spontaneously	

GROWTH AREA	**LEVEL 1 – BABY** Profile Statements	**LEVEL 2 – CHILD** Profile Statements
THE WORD	120. Understands all the five means of assimilating God's Word (hearing, reading, studying, memorizing and meditating) and has a basic understanding of how to go about each one 121. Is convinced that the Bible is the Word of God and, therefore, is absolutely true and authoritative 122. Sees the Word of God as spiritual food that will help him grow, and expresses a desire to learn more about it 123. Is beginning to receive a balanced intake of the Bible by: a. hearing the Word weekly at a local church service b. reading the Word by himself three or four times a week c. completing a few simple Bible studies assigned by you, and becoming familiar with the basic structure of the Bible d. memorizing a few key verses of Scripture e beginning to apply basic concepts of Scripture meditation	220. Is growing in his ability to assimilate God's Word by: a. becoming familiar with various bible study aids b making a filing system for conserving the fruit of his study 221. Believes that the Bible is inerrant, infallible, authoritative, plenary and verbally inspired, and that God has superintended in its transmission over the centuries 222. Is convinced that a thorough grasp of the Word is vital for effective witnessing, ministering and personal growth 223. Talks openly about the Word and is gaining skill in using the Word when: a. encountering trials b. battling Satan and sin c. seeking direction 224. Is gaining depth in the Word by: a. listening to Christian teaching tapes at various times each week b. reading the Word by himself daily c. completing a prepared Bible study series covering the major doctrines of the Bible d. memorizing Scripture at a rate of one or two verses (or verse cards) per week e. regularly meditating on God's Word

LEVEL 3 – ADOLESCENT Profile Statements	LEVEL 4 – ADULT Profile Statements
320. Continues to grow in his ability to assimilate God's Word by: a. learning to study the Bible through various methods (verse-by-verse analysis, chapter, book, topical, and character studies) b. learning the basic principles of hermeneutics c. becoming familiar with more advanced types of Bible study aids d. memorizing the order of the books of the Bible 321. His convictions regarding the Word are deepening due to personally experiencing its reliability in the events of daily life 322. Is teaching the Word to others by means of discipling, leading a Bible study, teaching a Sunday school class, or through spontaneous exhortation and counseling 323. Is gaining skill in using the Word when witnessing and ministering to others 324. Is gaining depth in the Word by: a. listening to God's Word through various means and taking notes when possible b. reading through the Bible once per year c. broadening his Bible study methods to include verse-by-verse analysis, chapter, book, topical, and character studies d. memorizing two verses (or verse cards) per week and/or longer portions of Scripture such as chapters or books	420. Has developed a consistent, lifetime habit of assimilating the Word of God through all five means, resulting in an ever-strengthening grasp of the Bible's themes and doctrines. 421. Holds the Word in highest regard as the standard and authority for all that he does 422. Demonstrates the personal conviction that the Word of God is living, active, powerful and efficacious in his life, resulting in regular personal application and complete obedience

GROWTH AREA	**LEVEL 1 – BABY** Profile Statements	**LEVEL 2 – CHILD** Profile Statements
WITNESSING	130. Has a basic understanding of God's role in evangelism and knows that, while he has a responsibility to witness, it is not his responsibility to "convert people" 131. Is convinced that non-Christians are lost, and expresses a desire to help them toward salvation 132. Has made a public confession of his faith in Christ	230. Has learned two methods for sharing the gospel one-to-one; one with the aid of a tract, and one without 231. Can recount his personal testimony in three to five minutes 232. Knows the basic how to's, do's and don'ts of a gospel presentation 233. Can answer the five most frequently made objections of non-Christians to Christianity* 234. Is convinced that his attempts at witnessing would be useless without God's full involvement in the process 235. Knows that people sometimes react negatively or not at all to a gospel presentation, but does not let that dissuade him from his commitment to witnessing 236. Has openly identified himself as a Christian where he lives and works 237. Is praying for opportunities to share Christ with specific acquaintances 238. Has taken advantage of a few opportunities to share his faith

*See page 365

LEVEL 3 – ADOLESCENT Profile Statements	LEVEL 4 – ADULT Profile Statements
330. Has a good understanding of the doctrine of salvation (soteriology) 331. Has a broad familiarity with Christian apologetics 332. Knows the major non-Christian cults, religions and occultic belief systems, and is well-versed in how to witness to their adherents 333. Has growing convictions regarding the importance of witnessing, the privilege of witnessing and his responsibility in witnessing, but at the same time is growing in his reliance upon God to accomplish the work of conversion 334. Is taking advantage of more and more opportunities to share his faith, and is increasingly taking the initiative to start conversations about Christ 335. Is growing in his ability to relate to and minister to non-Christians "where they live," being sensitive to their physical, social and emotional needs	430. Is continually gaining knowledge in the apologetics of the Christian faith 431. Has an ever-increasing burden for the lost 432. Is committed to lifelong witnessing despite hardships and negative reactions 433. Actively seeks opportunities to share the gospel in increasingly creative ways, and does so with boldness and clarity, yet in a gracious and winsome manner

GROWTH AREA	LEVEL 1 – BABY Profile Statements	LEVEL 2 – CHILD Profile Statements
FELLOWSHIP	140. Understands Christ's analogies about being part of a body or a building, and recognizes his advantages and responsibilities in that context 141. Feels it is important to be in regular fellowship with other believers for the sake of his own growth and protection 142. Is attending church regularly 143. Has been baptized 144. Is taking part in communion services 145. Is spending less time with old non-Christian friends and more time with Christian friends	240. Has done a study on appropriate selections of the 26 Attributes of the Mature Fellowshipper* and exhibits a desire to see them incorporated into his life 241. Is aware of the various spiritual gifts** and is beginning the process of discovering his 242. Is convinced that he is valuable to the Body of Christ and really can be used by God to minister to the needs of other Christians 243. Has formally joined a church and is beginning to get involved in church-related activities and responsibilities in addition to those offered on Sunday mornings 244. Is increasingly going out of his way to serve, encourage and build up other believers

*See page 365
**See page 366

LEVEL 3 – ADOLESCENT Profile Statements	**LEVEL 4 – ADULT** Profile Statements
340. Is beginning to broaden and deepen his knowledge of various aspects of biblical fellowship through studying books and articles, by applying what he learns, and by acting upon constructive feedback	440. Is continually gaining insight, sensitivity and skills in the areas of counseling, encouragement, communication, interpersonal relationships, family relationships and the use of his spiritual gift(s)*
341. Has gained a humble, accurate assessment of his own fellowshipping strengths and weaknesses and is determined to develop them for the good of the Body	441. Holds the conviction that close association, frequent interaction in harmony with other believers is indispensable for the growth, protection and proper functioning of each Christian and the Body as a whole
342. Recognizes, respects and seeks to augment the gifts, talents and ministries of others within the Body	442. Exercises his spiritual gift(s)* faithfully and skillfully
343. Has discovered his spiritual gift(s)* and is taking steps to develop and exercise it (them)	443. His life is characterized by a consistent, ever-deepening demonstration of the 26 Attributes of the Mature Fellowshipper**
344. The 26 Attributes of the Mature Fellowshipper** are becoming increasingly evident in his life	
345. Is committed to a small group of believers that have covenanted together to encourage, build up and hold each other accountable	

*See page 365
**See page 366

GROWTH AREA	**LEVEL 1 – BABY** Profile Statements	**LEVEL 2 – CHILD** Profile Statements
PERSONAL GROWTH	150. Knows that God wants to develop Christ-like characteristics in him through a combination of personal discipline, consistent obedience to God and the direct action of the Holy Spirit 151. Understands the two main functions of a quiet time to be those of relationship building and maturity building, through prayer, worship, the Word and meditation 152. Has gone through a more in-depth study on how to deal with adversity, Satan, temptation, and sin, expanding on what he learned under "Newborn Care" 153. Has grasped the concept that Christianity is not merely a code of behavior or a social club, but an active, personal relationship with a living Being that requires development through concentrated attention 154. Is having a personal quiet time of 8 to 10 minutes three or four times a week, preferably in the morning, in a secluded place 155. Is seeking to obey the "moral will of God" by taking steps to separate from sins as God reveals them in his life	250. Has done a study on appropriate selections of the Areas of Character Development* and exhibits a desire to see them incorporated into his life 251. Understands the fundamental facts regarding the will of God and how to discern His will on specific matters 252. Understands that his body is the temple of God, and is seeking help in curtailing any habits that are harmful to his body or his witness 253. Realizes that his lifestyle and his walk with the Lord will greatly affect his fruitfulness in the areas of prayer, witnessing, fellowship, and ministry, and in other areas of his personal growth 254. Has a personal quiet time of at least 15 minutes almost every day 255. Is gaining effectiveness at resisting Satan and sin and is taking steps to "separate from the world" 256. Has been faced with at least one dilemma that he has solved by actively seeking and discovering the will of God on the matter 257. Has completed all high priority applications with regard to character development 258. Has begun a regular program of physical exercise and healthy diet

*See page 366

LEVEL 3 – ADOLESCENT Profile Statements	LEVEL 4 – ADULT Profile Statements
350. Has learned how to vary the content of his quiet time in order to keep it fresh and challenging	450. Is continually gaining insight through personal study regarding the factors involved in personal growth, paying close attention to the elements that would enhance his own journey toward maturity
351. Has done an in-depth study on the question: If God is loving, why is there suffering in the world?	451. Holds the conviction that he will never "arrive" regarding spiritual maturity, and is committed to a lifetime of active progress in personal growth
352. Holds the conviction that his quiet time should be a first priority activity of each day, approaching it not as a duty, but as the meeting of two friends	452. Actively pursues his relationship with God by making quiet time a top priority each day, but also seeks brief (or not-so-brief) periods of communing with God spontaneously throughout the day and night
353. Is gaining a positive attitude toward trials, seeing them as beneficial opportunities for growth	453. Gains victory over adversity and effectively resists Satan and sin with great consistency, but when he does stumble, quickly restores fellowship with God through confession and repentance
354. Knows that God's will is not always pleasant or easy, but is nonetheless willing to subordinate his own will to the will of God	454. Actively seeks the will of God in all major decisions, while constantly maintaining an attitude of deference and submission to the will of God in minor, day-to-day decisions
355. Has increased his quiet time to a minimum of 30 minutes and rarely misses one, regardless of work schedule, leadership responsibilities or personal trials	455. Demonstrates a life characterized by consistent exhibition of all of the Areas of Character Development*
356. Is showing more and more inclination toward, and effectiveness in resisting Satan and sin	
357. Shows no major deficiency in any of the Areas of Character Development*	
358. Has curtailed all harmful personal habits	
359. Has established long-term consistency in the areas of exercise and diet, setting and attaining appropriate goals	

*See page 366

GROWTH AREA	LEVEL 1 – BABY Profile Statements	LEVEL 2 – CHILD Profile Statements
MINISTRY	160. Knows that, as a child of God, he has been uniquely gifted to minister to others, and that God will hold him responsible to develop and use those gifts 161. Has the desire to discover and use his spiritual gifts, natural talents and acquired skills for the good of the Body of Christ and the expansion of the Kingdom of God 162. Is beginning to use his natural talents and/or acquired skills in the service of others	260. Is aware of the various spiritual gifts* and is beginning to discover his own 261. Is aware of the different types of ministries available and is beginning to evaluate which ones he would be best suited for 262. Knows what it means to be a "world Christian" 263. Knows what is involved in the initial follow-up of a new Christian ("Newborn Care")** 264. Is gaining an increased respect and desire for a servant's heart 265. Is properly related to his job (whether secular or sacred) and sees it as one of his primary ministry contexts 266. Is convinced that his ministry would be fruitless without God's full involvement in it, but also recognizes his own responsibilities 267. Is becoming increasingly involved in a wide variety of ministries and service projects in order to gain a servant's heart and to more accurately assess his own areas of giftedness 268. Is showing growth in the areas of humility, diligence, faithfulness, obedience, joyfulness, honesty, kindness, compassion and impartiality as they relate to ministry

*See page 366
**See page 102

LEVEL 3 – ADOLESCENT Profile Statements	**LEVEL 4 – ADULT** Profile Statements
360. Is narrowing down the options as to which ministries he would be best suited for based on his gifts, talents and skills, and on where the greatest needs exist (locally and world-wide) 361. Knows the basic principles of disciplemaking and has been shown how to use this disciplemaking program 362. Is developing understanding about basic leadership principles 363. Is becoming increasingly self-less and more willing to endure hardship for the sake of his ministry 364. Has taken a new Christian through initial follow-up (New-born Care*) and has begun to disciple him 365. Is taking steps to develop himself in the areas of ministry where he feels God may have equipped him 366. Is effectively ministering where he works through example and word	460. Has a clear understanding of how the Lord has uniquely gifted him for the ministry, and is continually gaining insight on how to further develop and perform his ministry 461. Recognizes that ministry often involves hard work, and is willing to sacrifice, endure hardship and face danger for the sake of his ministry 462. His primary motivation in ministering is love 463. His ultimate objective in ministering is to influence others toward Christlikeness 464. Sets an example of Christlike behavior that others are inclined to emulate 465. Is actively involved and is developing leadership abilities in the ministry(s) he feels God has equipped him for 466. Consistently exhibits humility, diligence, faithfulness, obedience to God, joyfulness, honesty, kindness, compassion and impartiality as he performs his ministry to others 467. Is actively involved in the process of making disciples and disciplemakers

*See page 102

GROWTH AREA	**LEVEL 1 – BABY** Profile Statements	**LEVEL 2 – CHILD** Profile Statements
FAMILY	170. Has a basic understanding of what the Bible says is his unique role as a family member and what his responsibilities to his family are 171. *Married:* Recognizes the differences between the world's plan for marriage and God's plan for marriage 172. Sees his family as God's primary mechanism for providing him with love, comfort, support, companionship and accountability, and desires to commit himself more fully to it 173. Is taking appropriate and effective steps to assume his unique role and responsibilities within his family 174. Is praying daily for the other members of his immediate family and for his own family responsibilities 175. *Parent and child:* Is involved in at least one "family only" activity per month 176. *Parent:* a. sees to it that the family is beginning to receive effective spiritual input through regular attendance at a local church b. has established regular family devotions	270. Knows basics of relating with other family members in a Christ-like manner 271. *Married:* a. has attended one weekend marriage conference with his spouse b. has completed a more thorough examination of his unique role and responsibilities to his family by completing a study (with you) of a recommended book or tape series on marriage and, if a parent (or soon to be), an additional one on parenting c. if married to an unbeliever, understands the basic principles involved in living at peace with his spouse and potentially influencing her toward faith in Christ 272. *Single:* Knows how to relate with the opposite sex in purity, discretion and brotherly love 273. *Divorced:* a. understands how to relate with his children and former spouse in a responsible, Christ-like manner b. understands what the Bible teaches about divorce and remarriage 274. *Married:* a. unconditionally accepts his spouse as God's primary provision for his interpersonal and sexual needs, has made a recommitment to remain faithful to her, and has (Continued on page 364)

LEVEL 3 – ADOLESCENT Profile Statements	**LEVEL 4 – ADULT** Profile Statements

370. *Married:* Has completed study of a second recommended book or tape series on marriage
 	
371. *Parent:* Has completed study of a second recommended book or tape series on parenting
 	
372. *Single:* Knows the basic characteristics of a good marriage partner, and knows how to discover whether it would be within God's will to marry a certain individual
 	
373. Has gained strong convictions regarding extra-marital sex, divorce, homosexuality and abortion, and can defend his position intelligently and biblically
 	
374. *Married:* Sees his ministry to his family as one of his highest priorities
 	
375. *Single:*
  a. has made up his mind to shun notions of dating or marriage to a non-Christian
  b. sees his singleness as an advantage and a (temporary or permanent) gift from God
 	
376. Is praying daily for most (or all) members of his extended family
 	
377. *Parent:* Co-discipling children, with an emphasis on training them for and integrating them into the family's unique ministry team
 	
378. *Child:* Takes part enthusiastically in family ministry activities
 	
379. *Single:*
  a. depending on age and employment situation, is becoming increasingly independent of parents
  b. takes full advantage of his singleness to maximize his ministry
	470. *Married:* Has become a "student" of his spouse and children – the world's greatest authority on "what makes them tick"
	
	471. Committed to maintain long-term unity with his family, even when both he and they have reached adulthood
	
	472. *Married:* Sees his spouse as God's primary provision for his interpersonal and sexual needs, and looks nowhere else
	
	473. *Parent and child:* Sees his household as his top priority, second only to his relationship with God
	
	474. *Single and child:* Has made up his mind to obey his parents in all things (to the degree dictated by his age and dependence upon them)
	
	475. *Parent:*
	  a. co-discipling children in a consistent, conscientious, long-term discipling program, involving them in regular times of family worship, prayer and ministry
	  b. continually seeks harmony, unity and understanding with spouse and children through honest, sensitive communication
	
	476. *Husband:*
	  a. effectively manages his household socially, behaviorally, and financially
	  b. is the spiritual leader and pace-setter of his household
	  c. loves, honors, respects, understands, encourages and cares for his wife as Christ does the Church
	
	(Continued on page 364)

(Continued from page 362)

gained a profound, holy fear of the consequences of sexual sin

b. recognizes that marriage forms an unbreakable unity and that divorce is not an option

275. *Parent and child:*

a. makes his relationship with — and ministry to — his household an increasingly higher priority

b. is beginning to see his family's potential as a ministering team

c. sees his children as unique gifts from God, assets, and a godly heritage through whom the next generation can be affected for Christ

d. sees his parents as God's primary provision for his growth needs intellectually, physically, spiritually and socially; seeks to learn from them, obey them and please them

276. *Single:* Is convinced that marriage to a non-Christian would be a big mistake, and demonstrates this conviction in his dating life

277. *Married:*

a. sets aside specific times (daily, weekly, monthly, yearly) to spend quality time with his family (individually and as a group) with an emphasis on intra-family communication

b. has established a workable family budget and is making a strong effort to adhere to it

278. *Parent:*

a. is beginning a specific program to co-disciple his children

b. has established household responsibilities and allowances for each child and holds each one accountable

279. *Child:* Pitches in enthusiastically to perform his household chores

(Continued from page 363)

477. *Wife:*

a. is effective and industrious in her role as helper/companion to her husband and servant/leader to her children

b. loves, honors, respects, understands, encourages, obeys and submits to her husband

REFERENCE

Some of the profile statements make reference to lists of subjects. They are listed below:

Five most-frequent objections to Christianity (#233):

1. I don't believe God exists.
2. I don't believe Jesus is the only way.
3. What about those who die never hearing the gospel?
4. I don't believe the Bible is the Word of God.
5. If God is good, why is there so much evil in the world?

Attributes of the Mature Fellowshipper (#240, #344, #443):

1. Loving
2. Patient
3. Kind
4. Faithful
5. Gentle
6. Self-controlled
7. Humble
8. Servant attitude
9. Accepts correction and reproof
10. Willing to endure hardship for others
11. Gracious in speech
12. Merciful
13. Compassionate
14. Forgiving
15. Willing to suffer wrong
16. Returns good for evil
17. Honest
18. Hospitable
19. Peacemaker
20. Generous with time, talent, treasure
21. Sensitive and aware of needs of others
22. Seeks to build up others
23. Willing to identify, confront and help correct error in the Body
24. Recognizes, respects and appreciates spiritual leaders
25. Recognizes, respects and appreciates gifts, talents, and ministries of others
26. Desires company of other Christians

Areas of Character Development
(#250, #357, #455):

1. Fruit of the Spirit
   a. Love
   b. Joy
   c. Peace
   d. Patience
   e. Kindness
   f. Goodness
   g. Faithfulness
   h. Gentleness
   i. Self-Control
2. Faith
3. Humility
4. Servant's Heart
5. Obedience to God
6. Social Activism
7. Wisdom
8. Diligence
9. Courage
10. Teachable Attitude
11. Honesty
12. Purity
13. Thankfulness
14. Endurance
15. Forgiving Others
16. Submission To Authority
17. Faithful Stewardship
18. Orderliness
19. Heartiness
20. Correct Social Graces
21. Contentment

Spiritual Gifts
(#241, #260, #343, #360, #440, #442, #460):

1. Speaking gifts:
   To explain God's truth
   a. Prophecy
   b. Teaching
   c. Exhortation
   d. Word of Wisdom
   e. Word of Knowledge
2. Serving gifts:
   To enable God's work
   a. Serving
   b. Giving
   c. Leadership
   d. Administration
   e. Mercy
   f. Faith
   g. Discerning of Spirits
   h. Helps
   i. Hospitality
3. Sign gifts:
   To establish God's authority
   a. Tongues
   b. Interpretation of Tongues
   c. Miracles
   d. Healing
4. Special gifts:
   To equip God's people
   a. Apostles
   b. Prophets
   c. Evangelists
   d. Pastor-teachers

Welcome back! A few comments on the preceding profile statements:

(1) Though thoroughness was my objective, I'm a far holler from omniscient, so I must present this material — not as a set of absolutes, not as complete and entire, lacking nothing, not as flawless, and not closed to further refinement — but as a good start. As you and I learn more about the process of disciplemaking, I'm sure we'll want to modify the contents of the grid. If nothing else, it will give us a good blueprint to look at and say, "That doesn't look quite right. What if we adjusted this over here a little?" If you have suggestions, I would welcome your feedback. My address is in the reference note for this chapter.[1] If your observation seems valid, we'll include it in subsequent printings of this book. We got a deal?

(2) Not all of the profile statements are precisely biblical. For instance, nowhere in the Bible does it say that a baby Christian should eventually get to the point of having "a time of personal prayer three or four times a week, each session lasting 4 to 8 minutes" (#112). However, those who were presented as *mature* in the area of prayer prayed "regularly, frequently, often for long periods of time, sometimes accompanied by fasting" (#412). Profile Statement #112 is merely a measurable, arbitrary but logical, stepping stone designed to move the new disciple toward the maturity depicted in Profile Statement #412. We know that if he doesn't make it to #112 (which is a fairly subjective, open-to-debate goal), he'll *never* make it to #412 (which is an objective, manifestly biblical goal). So on the logically, culturally, or pragmatically generated goals, if you care to alter them somewhat, feel free.

(3) There are several very similar profile statements when you compare different areas of growth. That's because each area is so intertwined with the others. One's prayer life will greatly affect his time in the Word and vice versa. Time in the Word will greatly affect his fellowship and witnessing. His abilities in those areas will affect his ministry, which will affect his prayer life again, which will affect his personal growth and family, which will . . . and the beat goes on. It's impossible to isolate a certain character quality, conviction or activity and say, "This relates exclusively to fellowship." Therefore, it may show up in several areas.

(4) Within each area/level set of profile statements, there will always be at least one statement for each of the three growth elements of head, heart and hand knowledge. For instance, in the prayer area at the baby level, the setup is:

110. head knowledge

111. heart knowledge

112. hand knowledge

At the child level, this is the distribution:

210, 211. head knowledge

212. heart knowledge

213, 214, 215, 216. hand knowledge

As you wade through the profile statements, you should be able to recognize which is which in most cases.

(5) Since I formulated the profile statements and assembled the growth grid on my "very large piece of paper," I have had it typeset and printed as a poster. You would be amazed at how illuminating it is to be able to see the entire flow of Christian growth on one sheet of paper! If you are interested in obtaining your own very large piece of paper (a little less than a yard square) with the growth grid on it, you can obtain it through Here's Life Publishers. The Growth Grid is a major part of a "Personal Disciplemaking Kit" which you can order directly from the publisher. See the bottom of page 374 for more information.

Step 1. Determine Your Disciple's Current Level of Spiritual Growth

Now that you have some kind of standard by which to measure your disciple's previous spiritual input and growth, how do you actually go about it? There are two ways: one is for you to formulate a "Self-Evaluation Questionnaire" for each area of growth just like the one I cooked up back in chapter 8 relating to Newborn Care. Simply formulate a question or two that would stimulate your disciple's thinking about each profile statement and help him to rate himself. Use the questionnaire in chapter 8 as a guide. All you're trying to do is to foster dialogue between you and your disciple about his current spiritual status, so the questions don't have to be right out of *Psychology Today*. I recommend that you set aside seven weeks for this assessment period. *Don't* . . . I repeat, *DON'T* . . . ask your disciple to evaluate himself in more than two growth areas per session. One would be even better. I have found that it is pretty depressing for *anyone,* whether he is a spiritual babe or a spiritual old man, to think deeply about and evaluate several areas of his spiritual growth in one sitting. It's incredibly convicting! We can handle one or two per week, though.

The other way is to obtain printed self-evaluation questionnaires for each area of growth, another part of the "Personal Disciplemaking Kit" available through the publisher.

Next, you need a way to keep track of what you learn about your disciple's spiritual condition through the Self-Evaluation Questionnaires. Write out or type the profile statement numbers of each area of growth on a piece of paper, just as if you were making a blank growth grid. Get them all on one sheet of paper, even if it's larger than standard size. This will help you to get an at-a-glance profile. Your disciple's Growth Profile Chart will look something like this:

Area: PRAYER	BABY	CHILD	ADOLESCENT	ADULT
	110	210	310	410
	111	211	311	411
	112	212	312	412
		213	313	413
			314	414
Area: THE WORD	BABY	CHILD	ADOLESCENT	ADULT
	120	220	320	420
	121	221	321	421
	122	222	322	422
	123	223	323	
		224	324	

Etc. . . .

If you're interested, ready-made Growth Profile Charts are also included in the kits mentioned above.

After you and your disciple discuss his self-evaluation of each area, spend some time alone with God and put a check mark next to any profile statements that you feel are already true of him.

When you've done this with all seven areas of growth, you will be able to see major trends of strengths and weaknesses on the chart. No one will have a straight-line profile. A person may be primarily a child in the area of prayer, a baby in witnessing, and an adolescent in the Word. Even within a single area, he may conceivably have check marks and blanks at all four levels. Everybody's profile is unique, with assorted holes in previous training.

Step 2: Determine Your Disciple's Next Crucial Step of Growth

Look closely at the profile statements at the baby level on your disciple's Growth Profile Chart that are not fulfilled yet. Those are the ones to go for first. But there may be eight, ten, maybe even thirty of them! Where do you start? That will have to be decided upon between you and the Holy Spirit. Spend time in prayer, asking the Lord for insight into which of the 100-level profile statements reflects your disciple's next, most crucial step of growth. If you're still stumped, try asking your disciple what he thinks. He probably has some very good ideas about where his greatest needs lie!

You'll want to focus on the baby level as a priority. Work to fulfill all of these profile statements in every area before moving on to the upper-level ones. This will promote balanced growth. However, don't fixate only on his areas of weakness. Look for his hot spots, too, from time to time, and help him to excel there as well.

Step 3. Formulate a Training Objective Relating to That Step

After you and the Lord decide on one particular profile statement, it is magically turned into a *training objective*! For the next week, several weeks, or several months, the fulfillment of that training objective becomes the focus of your discipling relationship. Eventually, you may find yourselves working on several training objectives at a time, because they might be interrelated, or one may be leading naturally into another. That's fine! Beware, however, of getting overloaded and spread too thin. Better to do a few things well than a raft of things at a mediocre level.

Step 4. Design Curriculum That Will Help Him Reach the Training Objective

Once you have settled on a specific training objective, you can ask the manager of your local Christian bookstore for good Bible studies or books on that subject. (Refer to the resources I've recommended throughout the book.) Ask your pastor for ideas. Ask the person who is discipling you (if there is one) or somebody in your fellowship whom you know to be knowledgeable about the things of the Lord. Look up related verses in your concordance (you should do this *with* your disciple). Rummage around in your sermon notes file and see what you can find. Pick your brain to remember how that issue was settled in your own experience. Think of illustrations or parables you could use. Think of object lessons. Think of activities the two of you could share. Utilize role-playing. Be creative. Above all, *pray*! Ask the Lord for help. You'll be amazed at the ideas He can bring to mind if you listen hard enough!

Step 5. Develop an Evaluation Procedure

Before you launch out on a specific training objective, you need to have clearly in mind what you're trying to accomplish in your disciple's life. How will you know when he's arrived at the objective? Follow the pattern in the Evaluation section at the end of each of the Newborn Care Training Objectives. What questions do you need to ask yourself? What questions do you need to ask your disciple?

What's so good about it? I think what I like best about this method of discipling is its overriding directionality, yet its complete flexibility. That is, it's *going* somewhere, but you, the Holy Spirit, and your disciple can decide where, when, how, and how fast. Say you know you've only got six months to spend with a person. By using this procedure, you can take a few weeks to assess his current growth profile, zero in on his next crucial step of growth, and accomplish some significant things in a short period of time. You may only get around to covering one or two training objectives, but they were the most critical ones of all for him. On the other hand, perhaps you're discipling your next door neighbor, and you know that you're going to have several *years* together. With this method, you've got plenty of ground to cover. It's not likely you'll *ever* run out of areas to work on, and the whole time both you and he know that you are *taking* him somewhere. He's not getting bogged down in a bunch of time-filling busy work; you aren't just trying to entertain him for a few hours each week. Instead, he's making step-by-step, long-term, measurable progress toward spiritual maturity. That's what the Christian life is all about!

When do I let my disciple in on all of these training objectives? It will depend on the disciple. If he's a graduate of M.I.T. and likes charts and grids and extensive long-range strategies, show him the list of profile statements or the growth grid early. If he is acquainted with the grid, he could give you some valuable input as the two of you decide together what path he should take through the objectives.

But for the average person, it would be a bit overwhelming for him to see the vast scope of the Christian maturing process right off the bat, and could be quite disheartening for him to see how far he has to go. Plus, some might resent the classifications of "baby" and "child" if they didn't understand them in context. Others might resent the whole idea of boxes and check marks, not understanding that it is merely a means to help us organize our thinking. We're not trying to label or cubby-hole people.

For that reason, I think it's best to hold off showing him the entire program until he is pretty far into the level of child in the area of ministry. Profile Statement #263 says that at this level he "knows what is involved in the initial follow-up of a new Christian ('Newborn Care')." In the pursuit of this training objective, it might be a good time to explain the long-range plan with him. Show him the twelve Newborn Care Training

Objectives (if he hasn't already seen them). Then show him the whole growth grid, and explain that this is what you have been using to think through how to disciple him.

What about legalism? I suppose one of the few criticisms I hear about this method of discipling is the claim that it's legalistic. "Hey! I'm free in Christ! I don't have to measure up to any so-called standards of performance. I'll not allow myself to be put under the Law!" Unfortunately, the accusations of legalism come from those who don't have a firm grasp on what legalism really is. A legalist thinks that if he performs certain actions he will gain favor with God, and if he fails to perform certain actions, he will lose the favor of God and be penalized. But we Christians know that we already have 100 percent of God's favor. That's grace! We'll never have less and it's impossible to have more.

However, the Bible points out specific things we can do to *enhance our relationship with God*. We spent a good deal of our lives turning our backs on our relationship with Him. There had been very little communication between Him and us. We kicked in the picture tube, smashed the phone, tore up all the wires, crumpled up the writing paper, broke all the pencils and stomped on all the pens. It's going to take some effort to make the necessary repairs.

God has a plan for us. He plans for us to grow up. And the Christian has an active role in this growing-up process, a role requiring discipline, sacrifice, effort, patience, perseverance. The apostle Paul knew this well, and did not hesitate to exhort his charges to include self-discipline in their repertoire of character qualities (1 Corinthians 9:24-27; Philippians 3:13,14; 2 Timothy 2:3-6; 4:7; 6:11,12; Titus 1:8; Hebrews 12:1) as did Peter (2 Peter 1:6). We must never lose sight of the fact that God causes the growth; the working of the Spirit in our lives brings us to maturity (1 Corinthians 3:7; Galatians 3:2,3). But this must not give us the idea that we are like some Studebaker sitting passively up on the mechanic's rack while He soups us up. We are free in Christ, but we are not free to become non-volitional blobs with no responsibilities, no accountability, no role in the process of our own maturation (1 Corinthians 6:12;

Galatians 5:13). Far from being a doctrine from the pits of hell, as the rabidly anti-legalists would depict it, self-control is the ninth component of the fruit of the Spirit (Galatians 5:22,23).

"Go ye therefore . . . " I think I just heard the final bell. School is out. Now the time has come for you to go out into the real world and begin to apply what you have learned. My greatest prayer during the preparation of this material has been that it would not accumulate and calcify as mere head knowledge, but that it would seep down to the depths of your soul to become energized as heart knowledge and actualized as hand knowledge. The time you have spent reading these principles will have been in vain if you don't get up off that chair, break out of your comfort zone, take a little risk, believe God, and begin to disciple a real, live, human being.

If you will be faithful to the charge that has been passed down to you through untold generations, if you will cultivate that precious ability God has entrusted to you — availability — and invest it in the life of another, I guarantee you will know what John was talking about in 3 John 4: "I have *no greater joy* than this, to hear of my children walking in the truth." And I further guarantee that your heart will blaze in ecstasy when you stand before your Master on that final day, and He says to you, **"Well done, good and faithful servant . . . enter thou into the joy of thy Lord!"**

NOTES

Introduction

1. 1 Peter 1:3
2. Ephesians 4:12,13

Chapter 2

1. Dietrich Muller, *The New International Dictionary of New Testament Theology*, 3 vols., ed. Colin Brown (Grand Rapids: Zondervan, 1975), Vol. I, p. 486.

2. James Strong, appendix: "Greek Dictionary of the New Testament," *Strong's Exhaustive Concordance* (Grand Rapids: Associated Publishers and Authors, Inc.), p. 45.

3. Joseph Henry Thayer, *Greek-English Lexicon of the New Testament* (New York: Harper Brothers Publishers, 1899), p. 389.

4. William F. Arndt and F. Wilbur Gingrich, *A Greek-English Lexicon of the New Testament* (Chicago: University of Chicago Press, 1957), p. 491.

5. Harold K. Moulton, ed., *The Analytical Greek Lexicon Revised* (Grand Rapids: Zondervan, 1981), p. 257.

6. W. E. Vine, *An Expository Dictionary of New Testament Words* (Old Tappan, NJ: Fleming H. Revell Co., 1966), p. 316.

7. C. S. Lewis, *Letters to Malcolm: Chiefly on Prayer* (Glasgow: Fount Paperbacks, 1979), p. 34.

Chapter 3

1. Dr. G. R. Beasley-Murray in *Dictionary of New Testament Theology*, 3 vols., ed. Colin Brown (Grand Rapids: Zondervan, 1975), Vol. I, p. 144.

2. Dr. Klaus Wegenast in ibid., Vol. III, pp. 759-60.

Chapter 4

1. Mark Twain, [Samuel Langhorne Clemens], *Letter to an Unidentified Person [1908]*, quoted in John Bartlett, *Familiar Quotations*, chief ed., Emily Morison Beck (Boston: Little, Brown and Co., 1980), p. 626.

2. Stephen A. Bly, *Radical Discipleship* (Chicago: Moody Press, 1981), p. 45.

3. Dr. Ron Jenson, *Dynamics of Church Growth* (Grand Rapids: Baker Book House, 1981), p. 23.

4. Dr. E. M. Bounds, *Power Through Prayer* (Grand Rapids: Baker Book House, 1984), pp. 17-18.

5. Campus Crusade for Christ, *How to Make Your Mark* (San Bernardino: Campus Crusade for Christ, 1983), p. 366.

6. An illustration from a sermon by Herb Evans, Teaching Pastor of Grace Community Fellowship, Eugene, Oregon.

7. Quoted by Dr. Gordon Kirk, Senior Pastor, Rolling Hills Covenant Church, Rolling Hills Estates, California, in a talk on "The Sovereignty of God."

Chapter 5

1. *teknia*: a diminutive form of *teknon* (a child, with respect to descent or posterity), derived from *tikto* (to bear or bring forth children). [Harold K. Moulton, ed., *The Analytical Greek Lexicon Revised* (Grand Rapids: Zondervan, 1981), pp. 399-400, 404.] Its primary meaning is "an infant." [James Strong, *Strong's Exhaustive Concordance* (Grand Rapids: Associated Publishers and Authors, Inc.), p. 71 of "Greek Dictionary of the New Testament."]. *Teknon*, in some contexts would also denote "infant" [Acts 21:21; 1 Thessalonians 2:7; Revelation 12:4,5].

2. *brephos*: a child; whether unborn . . . or just born, an infant [Moulton, *Lexicon*, p. 73].

3. *nepios*: not speaking, infant [Moulton, *Lexicon*, p. 277].

4. Nourish = *anatrepho* which means "to nurse, as an infant (Acts 7:20); to bring up, educate (Acts 7:21; 22:3)." From Moulton, *Lexicon*, p. 26.

5. Cherish = *thalpo* which means "primarily to heat, to soften by heat; then, to keep warm, as of birds covering their young with their feathers. Metaphorically, to cherish with tender love, to foster with tender care" [W. E. Vine, *An Expository Dictionary of New Testament Words*, 4 vols. bound in one (Old Tappan, NJ: Fleming H. Revell Co., 1966), Vol. 1: p. 184]. "Cherich" (*thalpo*) is also used to describe how we care for our own bodies, and how Christ cares for His Church (Ephesians 5:29).

6. *teknon*: "a child, with respect to descent or posterity." [Moulton, *Lexicon*, pp. 399-400, 404.] This means that the technical definition doesn't necessarily specify a child age-wise. For instance, I am a *teknon* (descendant) of my father, even though I'm an adult. Often, though, the context will make it obvious that the *teknon* being talked about *is* a child age-wise.

7. *pais*: "a child between 7 and 14 years old" [G. Braumann in *The New International Dictionary of New Testament Theology*, 3 vols., ed. Colin Brown (Grand Rapids: Zondervan, 1975), Vol. 1: p. 282-83].

8. *paidion*: "a neuter diminutive of *pais*; a childling . . . a half-grown boy or girl" [Strong, *Concordance*, p. 54 of Greek Dictionary.] In certain contexts, *paidion* can mean anyone from an infant to a child and *pais*

can denote a child, teen, or full-grown man. As in all interpretation of Scripture, look at the context.

9. Braumann in Brown's *N. T. Dictionary*, Vol. 1: p. 281. See also Matthew 8:6; 12:18; 14:2; Luke 1:69; 12:45; 15:26.

10. Ibid. See 1 Corinthians 3:1-3; Hebrews 5:11-14.

11. See especially Ephesians 6:4; 2 Timothy 3:16.

12. Style and grammar "observations" inspired by Frank L. Visco, "How To Write Good," *Writer's Digest* (June 1986), p. 48.

13. *paidion* as both child and servant is inextricably woven; for example, see Acts 4:27,30 referring to Jesus as God's Child and Servant. In NAS and NIV the word is translated "servant." In KJV it's "child."

14. H. Haarbeck in *N. T. Dictionary*, Vol. 2: p. 674.

15. Ibid. The most frequently used forms of *neos* pertaining to adolescents are these [all from Moulton, *Lexicon*, p. 276]:

neanias: a young man, youth, used of one who is in the prime and vigor of life

neaniskos: a young man, youth, used of one in the prime of life

neoteros: (comparable of *neos*) younger, more youthful

neotes: youth [figuratively; "youth" as opposed to "adulthood."]

As mentioned earlier, there are instances where *teknon* (a child with respect to descent) and *pais* (child/servant), used in certain contexts, can refer to an adolescent as well.

16. Here are a few of the words used to describe adult characteristics:

pater: a father . . . an elder, father in age, a spiritual father . . . [Moulton, *Lexicon*, p. 312].

meter: a mother [Moulton, *Lexicon*, p. 269].

gonus: a father; pl. parents [Moulton, *Lexicon*, p. 79].

ab: [Hebrew for] father [O. Hofius in Brown's *N. T. Dictionary*, Vol. 1: p. 617].

em: [Hebrew for] mother [E. Berreuther in Brown's *N. T. Dictionary*, Vol. 1: p. 198].

presbyteros: an elder, senior; older, more advanced in years [Moulton, *Lexicon*, p. 340]. "In the central portion of Acts, the Pastoral Epistles, James 5:14, and the salutations in 2 and 3 John, the Christian elder is meant" [L. Coenen in Brown's *N. T. Dictionary*, Vol. 1: p. 198]. In other words, it doesn't *only* refer to the holder of the office of presbyter or bishop.

17. Vine, *Expository Dictionary*, p. 81.

18. William Shakespeare, *Sonnets [1609]*, 15, l.1, quoted in John Bartlett, *Familiar Quotations*, chief ed. Emily Morrison Beck (Boston: Little, Brown and Co., 1980), p. 244.4.

19. *The Amplified Bible* (Grand Rapids: Zondervan, 1971), p. 351 of New Testament.

Chapter 6

1. Marcus Aurelius [Antoninus], *Meditations, II, 2*, quoted in John Bartlett, *Familiar Quotations*, chief ed. Emily Morrison Beck (Boston: Little, Brown and Co., 1980), p. 124:24.

2. Harold K. Moulton, ed., *The Analytical Greek Lexicon Revised* (Grand Rapids: Zondervan, 1981), p. 263.

3. "Don't let the world around you squeeze you into its own mould, but let God re-make you so that your whole attitude of mind is changed" [J. B. Phillips, *The New Testament in Modern English* (New York: MacMillan Publishing Co., 1972), p. 332].

4. E. M. Bounds, *Power Through Prayer* (Grand Rapids: Baker Book House, 1984), p. 7.

5. Dr. and Mrs. Howard Taylor, *Hudson Taylor's Spiritual Secret* (Chicago: Moody Press, n.d.), p. 32.

6. George Harris, quoted in *The Little, Brown Book of Anecdotes*, gen. ed. Clifton Fadiman (Boston: Little, Brown and Co., 1985), p. 266.

Chapter 7

1. Leroy Eims, *The Lost Art of Disciple Making* (Grand Rapids: Zondervan and Colorado Springs: NavPress, 1978), p. 73.

2. A. W. Tozer, *The Knowledge of the Holy* (New York, Evanston, and London: Harper & Row, c. 1961), p. 9.

3. William R. Bright, "Ten Basic Steps Toward Christian Maturity" (San Bernardino, CA: Campus Crusade For Christ, 1968, revised 1983). Order from Here's Life Publishers, P.O. Box 1576, San Bernardino, CA 92402. Also available in most local Christian bookstores.

4. *Design for Discipleship* (Colorado Springs, CO: NavPress, 1973, revised 1980). Order from NavPress, P.O. Box 6000, Colorado Springs, CO 80934. Also available in most local Christian bookstores.

5. William R. Bright, "The Transferable Concepts" (San Bernardino, CA: Campus Crusade for Christ, 1972). Order from Here's Life Publishers, P.O. Box 1576, San Bernardino, CA 92402. Also available in most local Christian bookstores.

Chapter 9

1. William R. Bright, "Have You Heard of the Four Spiritual Laws?" (San Bernardino: Campus Crusade for Christ, 1965).

2. Harold K. Moulton, *The Analytical Greek Lexicon Revised* (Grand Rapids: Zondervan Publishing House, 1978), p. 11.

3. Joachim Guhrt in *The New International Dictionary of New Testament Theology*, 3 vols., ed. Colin Brown (Grand Rapids: Zondervan Publishing House, 1975), Vol. III, p. 832.

4. Campus Crusade for Christ, "Discipleship Series" Bible Study Series (San Bernardino, CA: Here's Life Publishers, 1983).

Chapter 10

1. Albert Barnes, *Barnes' Notes on the New Testament* (Grand Rapids: Kregel Publications, 1970), p. 1014.
2. See Ezekiel 28:11-19; Isaiah 14:12-17; Revelation 12:3-9.
3. William R. Bright, "Ten Basic Steps Toward Christian Maturity" Bible Study Series (San Bernardino, CA: Campus Crusade for Christ, 1968, revised 1983).
4. Campus Crusade for Christ, "Discipleship Series" Bible Study Series (San Bernardino, CA: Here's Life Publishers, 1983).
5. *Design for Discipleship* Bible Study Series (Colorado Springs, CO: NavPress, 1973, revised, 1980).

Chapter 11

1. Campus Crusade for Christ, "Discipleship Series" Bible Study Series (San Bernardino, CA: Here's Life Publishers, 1983).
2. Illustration from Jay Wheeler, Navigator Community Ministry Representative in Phoenix, Arizona.
3. Illustration from Bill Bright's "How to Be Filled With the Spirit," Transferable Concept #3 (San Bernardino: Campus Crusade for Christ, 1972), pp. 21-22.
4. Illustration from Dr. Robert Frederich, pastor of Galilee Baptist Church in Denver, Colorado.

Chapter 12

1. Illustration by Robert T. Price, founder of the Athletes in Action Track Team, currently a computer wiz in Southern California.
2. Campus Crusade for Christ, "Discipleship Series" Bible Study Series (San Bernardino, CA: Here's Life Publishers, 1983).

Chapter 13

1. "The Wheel Illustration," © 1976 by The Navigators. Used by permission of NavPress. All rights reserved.
2. Campus Crusade for Christ, "Discipleship Series" Bible Study Series (San Bernardino, CA: Here's Life Publishers, 1983).

Chapter 14

1. William R. Bright, "The Transferable Concepts" Bible Study Series (San Bernardino, CA: Campus Crusade for Christ, 1972).
2. William R. Bright, "Ten Basic Steps Toward Christian Maturity" Bible Study Series (San Bernardino, CA: Campus Crusade for Christ, 1968, revised 1983).
3. *Design for Discipleship* Bible Study Series (Colorado Springs, CO: Navpress, 1973, revised 1980).

Chapter 15

1. KJV "Brought up" = "nourished up." George V. Wigram, *The Englishman's Concordance of the New Testament* (Grand Rapids: Zondervan, 1980), p. 264.
2. WORD HAND ILLUSTRATION, © 1976, The Navigators. Used by permission of NavPress, Colorado Springs, CO. All rights reserved.
3. William R. Bright, "Ten Basic Steps Toward Christian Maturity" Bible Study Series (San Bernardino, CA: Campus Crusade for Christ, 1968, revised 1983).
4. Campus Crusade for Christ, "Discipleship Series" Bible Study Series (San Bernardino, CA: Here's Life Publishers, 1983).
5. *Design for Discipleship* Bible Study Series (Colorado Springs, CO: Navpress, 1973, revised 1980).

Chapter 16

1. Rosilind Rinker, *Prayer: Conversing With God* (Grand Rapids: Zondervan, 1959), p. 23.
2. William R. Bright, "Have You Heard of the Four Spiritual Laws?" (San Bernardino: Campus Crusade for Christ, 1965), p. 10.
3. S. D. Gordon, *Quiet Talks on Prayer* (Grand Rapids: Baker Book House, 1980), p. 37.
4. Dick Eastman, *Change the World School of Prayer Seminary Notebook* (Studio City, CA: World Literature Crusade, 1976), p. A-15.
5. Andrew Murray, *With Christ in the School of Prayer* (Old Tappan, NJ: Fleming H. Revell Co., 1977), p. 14.
6. Robert A. Cook, *Now That I Believe* (Chicago: Moody Press, 1947, 1985 edition), p. 81.
7. Jack Taylor, address to staff of Campus Crusade for Christ during 1983 Summer Senior Staff Conference.
8. Campus Crusade for Christ, "Discipleship Series" Bible Study Series (San Bernardino, CA: Here's Life Publishers, 1983).

Chapter 17

1. Definition adapted from William R. Bright's "How To Witness in the Spirit," Transferable Concept #5 (San Bernardino, CA: Campus Crusade for Christ, 1972), p. 31.
2. William R. Bright, "How To Introduce Others To Christ," Transferable Concept #6 (San Bernardino, CA: Campus Crusade for Christ, 1972), p. 6.
3. Illustration from Pastor Erhardt G. von Trutzschler, Pastor-at-Large of Clairemont Emmanuel Baptist Church in San Diego. Also Director of "Spectrum Ministries."
4. The four points are adapted from William R. Bright's tract "Have You Heard of the Four Spiritual Laws?" (San Bernardino, CA: Campus Crusade for Christ, 1965).
5. Campus Crusade for Christ, "Discipleship Series" Bible Study Series (San Bernardino, CA: Here's Life Publishers, 1983).

6. From Mark McCloskey, *Tell It Often, Tell It Well* (San Bernardino, CA: Here's Life Publishers, 1985), p. 248.

7. Dr. James Kennedy, *Evangelism Explosion* (Wheaton, IL: Tyndale House Publishers, 1977), appendix A.

Chapter 18

1. David Wilkerson, *Jesus Person Maturity Manual* (Glendale, CA: Regal Books Division, G/L Publications, 1971), p. v.

2. Henry David Thoreau, *Walden*, I, Economy, quoted in Bartlett, John, *Familiar Quotations*, chief ed. Emily Morrison Beck (Boston: Little, Brown and Co., 1980), p. 559.4.

3. Illustration from Jay Carty, founder, director and, in my opinion, the best speaker of "YES! Ministries," Corvallis, Oregon.

4. The idea for this illustration is adapted from C. S. Lovett's excellent little book, *Dealing With The Devil* (Baldwin Park, CA: Personal Christianity Chapel, 1981) p. 92ff, and is used by permission. I have changed a few of the words and the structure somewhat, not to improve it necessarily, but to make it more my style.

5. Campus Crusade for Christ, "Discipleship Series" Bible Study Series (San Bernardino, CA: Here's Life Publishers, 1983).

Chapter 19

1. David Dawson, *Equipping The Saints Notebook*, 4 vols. (Greenville, TX: ETS Ministry, 1982), Volume 1, Lesson 4: "A Biblical Perspective On Time," p. 1.

2. Information about The Masterplanning Arrow is available from Masterplanning Group International, Box 61281, Laguna Niguel, CA 92677-6128.

3. Dawson, *Equipping The Saints*, Volume 2, Lesson 2: "How To Write Good Objectives," p. 8.

4. Richard Furman, M.D., *Reaching Your Full Potential* (Eugene, OR: Harvest House Publishers, 1984).

5. Gordon MacDonald, *Ordering Your Private World* (1st Printing, Moody Press, 1984; 2nd Printing, Nashville: Thomas Nelson, Inc., 1985), p. 9.

6. Campus Crusade for Christ, "Discipleship Series" Bible Study Series (San Bernardino, CA: Here's Life Publishers, 1983).

7. Dawson Trotman, *Born To Reproduce* (Colorado Springs: NavPress, n.d.).

8. William R. Bright, "How To Help Fulfill The Great Commission," Transferable Concept #7 (San Bernardino, CA: Campus Crusade for Christ, 1972).

Chapter 20

1. *Design for Discipleship* Bible Study Series, 7 Books. (Colorado Springs: NavPress, 1973, revised, 1980), Book 6, Chapter 5, p. 39.

2. Cathy Guisewite in her daily comic strip "Cathy," copyrighted by Universal Press Syndicate, appearing August 30, 1987.

3. Campus Crusade for Christ, "Discipleship Series" Bible Study Series (San Bernardino, CA: Here's Life Publishers, 1983).

4. Dawson Trotman, *The Need Of The Hour* (Colorado Springs: NavPress, n.d.).

5. Dawson Trotman, *Born To Reproduce* (Colorado Springs: NavPress, n.d.).

6. William R. Bright, "How To Help Fulfill The Great Commission," Transferable Concept #7 (San Bernardino, CA: Campus Crusade For Christ, 1972).

Chapter 21

1. Christopher B. Adsit, c/o Here's Life Publishers, P.O. Box 1576, San Bernardino, CA 92402-1576.

INDEX